红庵牡丹，花开世界

HONG'ANLI PEONY BLOSSOMING FORTH
INTO A BEAUTIFUL WORLD

牡丹对中国传统服饰和雅莹而言都是具有重要意义的元素。在 30 多年的发展历程中，雅莹已从最初的那株红庵里牡丹，长成为繁花簇锦的雅莹花园，高雅华贵，仪态万千。这一簇簇盛放的牡丹，述说着雅莹一路一世的芳华。

我们邀请艺术家特别创作了封面上这幅牡丹艺术作品，以此盛放之美，纪念雅莹 30 多年来对"平衡·爱·幸福"价值主张的坚持。同时致敬当代女性，宛如牡丹内在从容，外在优雅的自信、独立、活力与智慧之精神。雅莹视牡丹为潜心创造"中国美"与"女性美"的核心基因与典雅象征，并将持续照鉴未来的美丽世界。

The Peony possesses significant meaning in Chinese traditional costumes and EP YAYING's heritage. In its 30 over years of growth, EP YAYING has grown from a "budding Peony" that originated in the village of Hong'anli into a "full bloom garden" today — fully embodying the national flower's grace, nobility and elegance. The cover illustration of a blossoming Hong'anli Peony is a dedication to EP YAYING's commitment to the values of "Balance", "Love" and "Happiness", which now serves as the Group's philosophy.

We worked with an artist to specially create this Peony artwork, outrageously beautiful in bloom, as an homage to all the beautiful people at EP YAYING, to all our partners who joined us on this beautiful journey, and most importantly, to all women — confident, chic and inspiring! The Peony has become EP YAYING's symbol and icon, an endearing inspiration to our interpretation of Chinese fashion and feminine beauty, and this beautiful world we call our home.

"雅，《诗经》中大雅之雅，雅代表了正，美丽美好；

莹，象征一种向上的生命力，清莹透澈，自然纯真。"

世间美好之意，都在这两字之中……

"Ya, (Chinese: 雅), used in the *Classic of Poetry*, means righteousness and grace;

while Ying, (Chinese: 莹), represents an upward vitality, pure and natural."

All that is fine and good in the world is contained in these two Chinese characters.

谨以此书献给所有亲爱的雅莹伙伴

To all dear friends of EP YAYING, with gratitude

EP YAYING

雅莹·美述史

FASHION & CULTURE

EP YAYING 雅瑩集團
EP YAYING FASHION GROUP

DAYA+ DOUBLOVE Npaia LITTLE SPACE

30

优雅而立30年

Years
in ELEGANCE

卷首

为美而生，优雅而立

中国服饰，源远流长，雅莹之美，生生不息。

三十多年前，改革开放的春风吹拂中，雅莹的创业者们以18台家用缝纫机，在借来的车间作坊，为美而生，向美而行。经过三十余年、两代人的持续努力，今天的雅莹已经是中国时尚产业积极的一分子，在中国服饰的美丽卷轴，持续书写着新的美篇。

三十多年来，雅莹人秉承"想要做好事，先要做好人"的信念，从"做一件好衣服"的朴素理念出发，以真诚的心、专注的心、感恩的心，百折不挠、永不放弃，跟随中国经济发展步步向前，走出一条自己的美丽道路，也一步步实现着自己的梦想。

三十多年的风雨兼程，感受文化与时尚、美学与科技、艺术与匠心的互汇碰撞，述说雅莹潜心创造"中国美"与"女性美"的历程。有鉴于此，特出版此册《雅莹·美述史》，承托起两代雅莹人亲手所绘的时代之美：三十年的道路告诉我们，只要坚守心中的美好信念，困难总能被一一克服，美好的理想终将一一实现。

未来三十年，是中华民族继续伟大复兴的三十年，也是中国时尚产业大有作为的三十年。雅莹人坚定地走中国时尚品牌之路，以志为本、以顾客为本、以产品为本、以文化为本，以坚定步伐朝向"世界级的品牌，国际化的公司"砥砺前行，为更广世界的消费者贡献中国时尚之美。

雅莹的"雅"是优雅，是高雅；雅莹的"莹"，是晶莹，是宝玉一样的纯洁与精粹。感恩信任、支持雅莹的每一位员工、顾客、伙伴，感恩时代给予雅莹人追求自我、奉献自我的机遇：

是你们让雅莹的美述之旅更加美好。
此心庄严，优雅而立！
未来三十年，雅莹大有可为！

INTRODUCTION

A STORY OF CHINESE FASHION: TIME-HONOURED ELEGANCE

Chinese fashion has a long and storied tradition. Today, EP YAYING continues this exciting and beautiful legacy...

Over 30 years ago, when China's reforms and opening-up continued to deepen across the country, a group of craftspeople began working on fine garments for their village with 18 household sewing machines in a makeshift workshop. Through dedication continued over two generations, EP YAYING has gone from strength to strength. Today, it is an active player in developing China's fashion industry.

For these three decades, we at EP YAYING Fashion Group believe in "being a virtuous person if we want to succeed in life". Hence, our starting point is simple — make good clothes — which motivates us to work devotedly and relentlessly for evermore beautiful creations, growing together with China and realising our dream for a beautiful society.

These past 30 years of ups and downs, days and nights have paved the way for EP YAYING's stirring success today. A passionate entrepreneurial journey lies beneath the fusion of fashion and culture, aesthetics and technology, arts and craftsmanship. Now documented in this unprecedented publication, this journey showcases EP YAYING's heritage and its enduring influence on Chinese fashion and feminine beauty.

As we look ahead to the next 30 years, we are absolutely proud and excited about China's blooming beauty. As we author a new chapter in this era, the EP YAYING Group believes that fashion rooted in the cultural strengths of the nation will continue to flourish. Our aspiration, our customers, our fashion, our culture and our united hearts are our key pillars in becoming a world-class Chinese fashion brand, sharing exquisite contemporary fashion from China with consumers all around the world.

Ya, (Chinese: 雅), means elegance; while Ying, (Chinese: 莹), represents the purity of jade. Just as our mission: "Dignified Hearts, Steadfast in Elegance" continues to drive us in our endeavours, the brand serves as an emotional connection between all of us. We are deeply grateful to every single employee, customer and partner for the trust and support given to us over the years. Each passing generation has been kind to us, providing us with opportunities for self-growth and breakthroughs.

EP YAYING has come a long way and the next 30 years hold greater promise for us all!

目录
CONTENTS

序章
PROLOGUE

梦想发端，
美的起源

1979

THE BIRTH OF A BEAUTIFUL DREAM

1979年3月19日，法国知名品牌皮尔·卡丹来到中国，以一场凭邀请函方可入场的时装秀引起轰动，也将多姿多彩的时装概念带入当时普遍还是蓝衣蓝裤的中国。也是这一年，35岁的张宝荣怀抱发展实业、成就自我、造福乡里的创业热情，投身到完全陌生的服装行业开始了新的奋斗。历经挑战，张宝荣从乡办企业家一步步走向自主创业者，也开启了对雅莹美丽事业的播种。

The 19th of March 1979 saw Pierre Cardin, a well-known French fashion brand, come to China for their debut show on an invite-only basis. The show was an immediate sensation as it introduced colourful fashion to the then "blue workwear" era of the Chinese community. It was also the same year that our Group's late founder, the then 35-year-old Zhang Baorong, decided to embark on a new journey in the garment industry. It was a completely new and foreign trade to him, but he maintained faith in hard work, self-growth and the pursuit of a better life for his village. He would overcome challenge after challenge on a tough entrepreneurial journey, beginning from a collectively-owned township garment enterprise that would grow to become EP YAYING and occupy a special place in today's Chinese fashion world.

"

江南水乡，蕴藏了丰富的文化内涵，
在这一片白墙瓦黛的天地间，还拥有织造锦衣罗衫的天然条件，
江南的开放包容是雅莹人追求美的缘起……

江南，长江下游南岸，东南丘陵北部的长三角地区。
狭义上指代宋朝时的江南东路即江东和两浙路，
广义上还包括江苏和安徽两省的长江北岸、江西、福建、广东及湖北、
湖南、广西部分地区。古代又称吴越、江东、江左。

"

发展实业，肩负使命
AN UNSHAKABLE ENTREPRENEURSHIP SPIRIT

服装这个陌生的领域，让张宝荣只争朝夕。这给他建功立业的新机会，也给他前所未有的挑战。秉承"想要做好事，先要做好人"的精神，他一步步筑梦踏实，从行业的陌生人成为行业创新开拓队伍的一员。

Zhang Baorong seized every minute to familiarise himself with a garment industry that was foreign, but in his eyes, he only saw opportunities outweighing the challenges. He stuck to his down-to-earth ethos — being a virtuous person to succeed in life — and step by step, Baorong grew from an interested layman to an industry trailblazer.

起于行业萌芽之端
AN EARLY MOVER IN AN EMERGING INDUSTRY

1978 年召开的中国共产党第十一届三中全会，决定将国家的工作重心转移到社会主义经济建设上来，深刻改变中国和中国人命运的改革开放由此开端。

第二年，被改革开放春风吹拂的京杭大运河畔——浙江省嘉兴市洛东乡，继缫丝厂、水泥预制厂之后，筹资设立了第三家乡镇企业——洛东服装厂。

雅莹美丽事业的奠基人、时年 35 岁的丝厂厂医张宝荣，被组织安排为洛东服装厂筹备人员，并在两年后被委任为厂长。

参与筹备时的张宝荣并没有服装业的经验，但已在其他岗位拥有突出的工作表现并深得民心。张宝荣先生出生于 1944 年嘉兴新塍镇洛东乡的一户农家。他务过农，靠自学成长，在生产队当过会计，1965 年加入了农村的医疗队伍，成为走在中国农村田埂上的第一代"赤脚医生"，后来成为洛东丝厂厂医。任何岗位上，他都吃苦耐劳、勤奋好学、业绩突出，富有奉献精神，被大家爱戴。

The 3rd Plenary Session of the 11th Central Committee of the Chinese Communist Party held in 1978 set China on the course for nationwide economic development. This marked the beginning of the "Reform and Opening Up" policy which has profoundly altered the face of China and the Chinese people.

In the second year of China's economic reform, the Luodong Town of Jiaxing, Zhejiang Province, began preparing the setup of its third township and village enterprise (TVE) — Luodong Garment Factory — following the successful establishment of the town's silk mill and precast concrete production plant. TVE was one of the key reform mechanisms used early on by the government to activate the rural area's labour forces to more efficiently engage in industrial outputs that spark new growth in the economy.

The young Zhang Baorong had been working as a physician at the silk mill for 3 years, and was selected by the town to join the setup of the Luodong Garment Factory. Within just two years, he was appointed director of the factory.

洛东公社 赤脚医生留念 1973. 3. 5.

加头县洛东公社赤脚医生复训班 74. 6. 1日

洛东公社防痨学习班

"

张宝荣务过农，靠自学成长，在生产队当过会计，
1965 年加入了农村的医疗队伍，
成为走在中国农村田埂上的第一代'赤脚医生'，
后来成为洛东丝厂厂医。
在任何岗位上，他都吃苦耐劳、勤奋好学、业绩突出，
富有奉献精神，被大家爱戴。

"

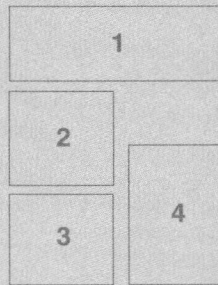

左页：

1. 1973 年 3 月，洛东公社赤脚医生留念合影（后排左二：张宝荣）

2. 1973 年 3 月，洛东公社赤脚医生培训合影（第二排左二：张宝荣）

3. 1970 年代，洛东公社赤脚医生防病学习班培训场景

4. 1974 年 6 月，洛东公社赤脚医生复训班合影（后排左三：张宝荣）

OPPOSITE

1. Zhang Baorong (back row, second from left) and Luodong's commune barefoot doctors, March 1973

2. Zhang Baorong (second row, second from left) and Luodong's commune barefoot doctors, March 1973

3. A training session for barefoot doctors organised by Luodong's commune, 1970s

4. Zhang Baorong (back row, third from left) and Luodong's commune barefoot doctors during a refresher course, June 1974

张宝荣非常务实，又很有创新精神，总能不断想出新方法解决实际问题。

成为医生之前，他是医学零基础，但他通过不断自学，成为乡村常见疾病的治疗能手。在张宝荣十数年的从医生涯中，他努力克服乡村医疗基础薄弱的情形，带头耕种药材，解决当时药物奇缺的问题，降低乡民的医疗成本。他还带头打井，从健康饮水的源头防治血吸虫病，并因为突出的成绩被评为先进个人。

作为医者的张宝荣，一直被与生俱来的仁心驱动着，救治了很多人于生命危难之间。有关他的善良和品德的故事，至今还被很多乡邻传颂……其中一个故事是，在他当乡村医生时，一位村民被毒蛇咬伤，没有排毒医疗设备的他，竟然直接用嘴吸毒。

Although Baorong did not have any experience with the garment industry, he did have an outstanding track record for excelling in each job he undertook, and was a people person. Zhang Baorong was born in 1944 as the son of farmers in Luodong Town. He both worked on the farm and was an accountant at a production brigade before he joined the rural healthcare team, becoming part of China's first generation of "barefoot doctors", and subsequently joined the town's silk mill as an in-house physician. His relentless endeavor, studiousness and dedication won the hearts of many.

Baorong was a pragmatic yet innovative man, who could always lend a fresh perspective to solve problems. Although he had never received formal medical training, he became a barefoot doctor through self-study and observation. For over 10 years, he worked hard to address the challenges facing rural healthcare, such as growing medicinal plants to address the scarcity of medicines at the time and reduce medical costs for the villagers. He vigorously advocated the excavation of water wells to eliminate the spread of schistosomiasis from poor drinking water sources. Having helped many people and saved many lives, Baorong was highly regarded and respected by his fellow villagers, and they would tell many fond memories of him. There was a time when he encountered a villager who accidentally got bitten by a snake, and with a lack of nearby medical equipment, Baorong proceeded without hesitation to suck the venom out.

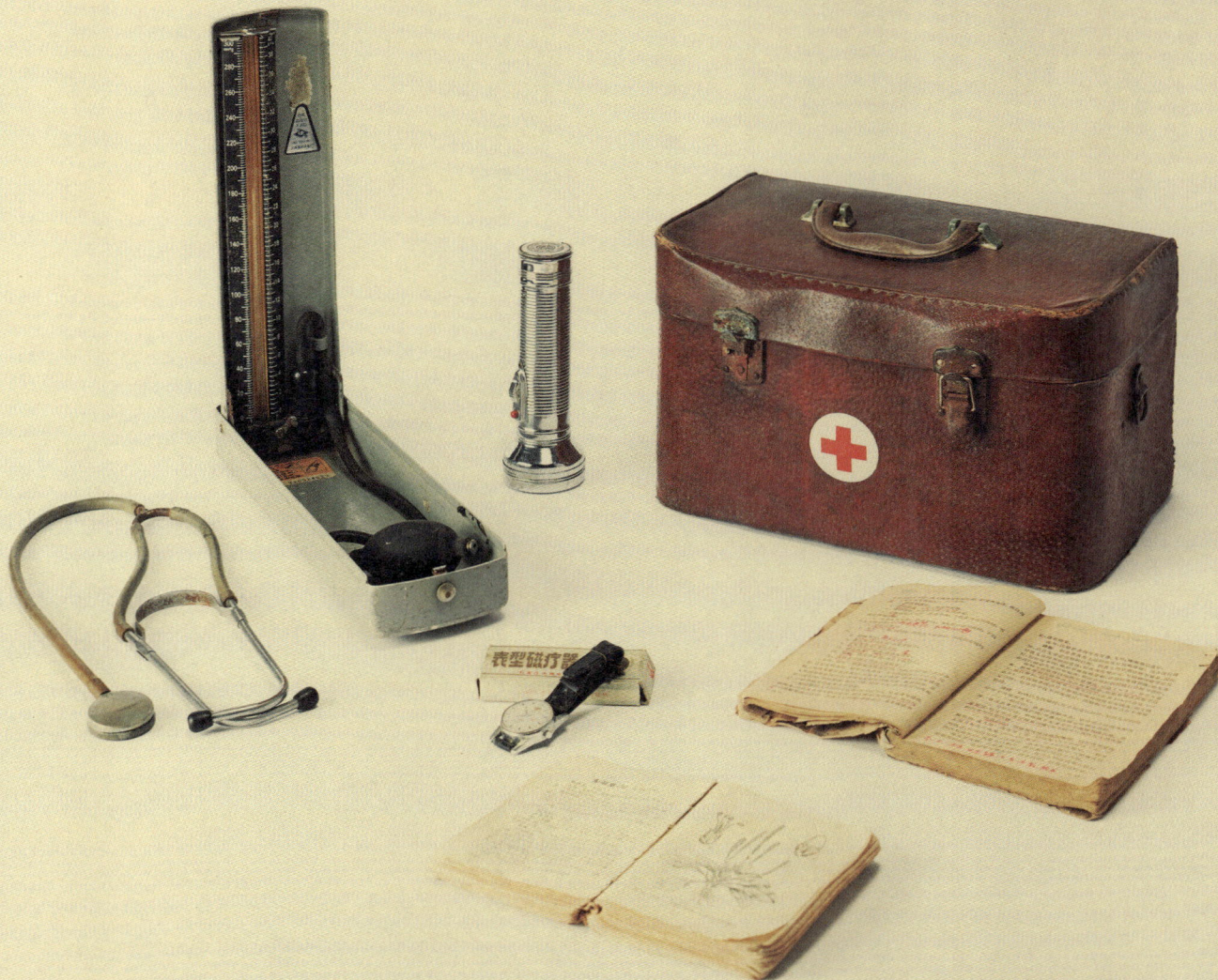

上图：
张宝荣自 1965 年从医后，所使用过的
医疗器械及医学典籍

ABOVE

The medical equipments and medical
reference books used by Zhang Baorong when
he became a barefoot doctor from 1965

左图：
1978 年 12 月，法国知名时尚设计师皮尔·卡丹首次来访中国北京

LEFT
Famous French fashion designer Pierre Cardin visits China for the first time in 1978, and strolls along a street in Beijing in December

因为这些，当服装厂筹备时，大家相信没有工厂管理的经验，他也能办厂成功。

当时，正值中国服装产业萌芽发展的开端。法国知名品牌皮尔·卡丹就是在那一年来到中国，并在北京民族文化宫以一场特别的时装秀引起轰动，刷新了国人对服装的认知。此后，美和时尚的意识渐渐星火燎原：

1980 年，中国大陆地区最早的时尚刊物——《时装》诞生；

1981 年，中国大陆第一支时装模特队成立。3 年后，这支表演队出访欧洲引起轰动。

1982 年，中央工艺美术学院（现清华大学美术学院）设立了全国首个与服装相关的本科专业……市场上，越来越多的人开始在裁缝店之外购置成衣，服装款式、花色也越来越丰富。

时代在破旧立新。服装，这个陌生的领域，让张宝荣只争朝夕，这是他建功立业的新机会，也给他前所未有的挑战。

As a result, the villagers had no doubt that Baorong could succeed in the garment industry, even if he had not worked in the field before.

The year 1979 marked the beginning of the growth of China's garment industry. It is no coincidence that famous French fashion designer Pierre Cardin chose the same year to come to Beijing to stage China's first fashion show from a Western couturier at the Beijing National Culture Palace, creating an instant sensation. Since then, the concept of fashion began to influence Chinese society:

In 1980, the earliest fashion magazine in the Chinese mainland *Fashion* was published.

In 1981, the country's first modeling agency was formed. Three years later, their visit to Europe for a show caused a sensation.

In 1982, the Central Academy of Arts and Crafts (now known as the Tsinghua University Academy of Fine Arts) opened the country's first undergraduate course related to fashion. Meanwhile, consumers were beginning to shop for increasingly available styles and colours.

Gradually, Chinese people began to break from the local tradition of going to the tailor to get clothes made, and started shopping for ready-to-wear garments that were increasingly available in more exciting styles. In an era of reform, Baorong lived every day to the fullest, breaking into the garment industry and starting a new chapter in his life.

nger, right, enjoying one of the delights of
a walk along the Bund, now called the Zhong-
which separates the city into two worlds. On
s side in a park along the river... people strol
h the boats. On the western side ... officer
ple rushing ... all the liveliness of a crowded
ity.... At the Great Wall, above, left to right.
dame Ge Yiyun who accompanied our group in
king), and Madame Zhao Jia who was with us
China. Both women are from the Ministry of
airs. Nancy's wearing Calvin Klein's easy suede
jacket over a cashmere sweater and flannel
warmth, for ease in moving around.

Everywhere
in Shanghai, masses
of people descend...
always in
great friendliness

IN **china now**

上图：
1979 年 8 月，美国版 *VOGUE* 首次
来到中国拍摄，记录了当时美国国
务卿基辛格的夫人南希·基辛格随
访中国上海的画面

ABOVE
Nancy Kissinger, wife of then US
Secretary of State Henry Kissinger, in
Shanghai, China, for American *VOGUE*'s
first feature of China, August 1979

25

时装
FASHION
1980 Summer

对外贸易出版社

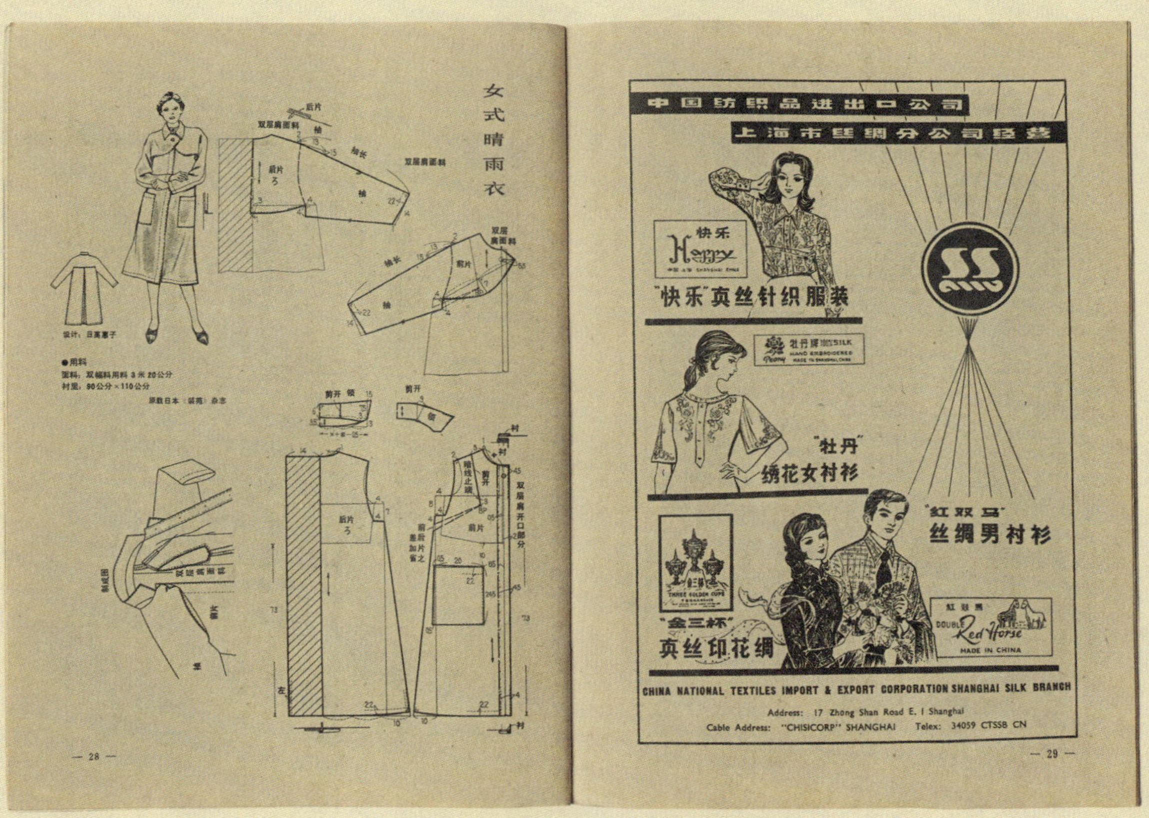

左页：
1980 年 4 月，中国大陆地区最早发行的
时尚杂志《时装》的夏季创刊号

右图：
《时装》杂志 1980 年夏季创刊号内页

OPPOSITE

Fashion magazine, Summer 1980. The inaugural
issue of the earliest local fashion magazine to
be published in China, April 1980

RIGHT

Inside pages of the inaugural issue of China's
Fashion magazine, Summer 1980

超前的品牌意识
A FORWARD THINKER

领导众人办好一家厂，比自学成才当好医生要难。

初创时的洛东服装厂，只是在当地一家灯泡厂租借了一个车间试着生产服装，设备简陋，业务有限，技术不成熟，运营管理等也都缺乏经验。

做会计、医生，虽然都是从头学起，但只要精于业务，做好自己的事就行。现在，人员、技术、生产、销售……作为厂长，张宝荣需要对一切负责。各种挑战下，他先从让自己懂行、让同仁们懂行开始。他买了所有能买到的关于裁剪、服装生产管理与时装专业的各种刊物，刻苦自学；聘请了当地最专业的裁剪师傅来把关技术，还不断向周边地区的同行请教，让自己不断专业，也让工厂持续向专业靠近。

市场拓展方面，学习能力强的张宝荣也是一马当先，不断创新、尝试。

洛东服装厂主要是加工生产男式中山装和女士上衣，而且是给当地大企业嘉兴服装公司做配套。张宝荣认为，工厂要长远发展，必须建立自己的销售渠道，自己掌握命运。

Running a factory was much more difficult than learning the ropes of a doctor on one's own.

As the first local collectively-owned township garment enterprise, Luodong Garment Factory started humbly in a makeshift workshop originally used for light bulb manufacturing. Soon, it was facing many stumbling blocks, from lack of proper equipment, paltry orders and poor know-how to inexperienced management.

However, Baorong would learn to apply his past experiences as an accountant and doctor. In starting from scratch, he needed to remain focused on the task at hand and stay the course. As director of the factory, he was now in charge of a multitude of operational responses, including people, technical skills, production and sales. He soon realised that the top priority was improving both his and his team's knowledge on the industry. He bought all publications available on clothing, tailoring and production management, and also invited the most experienced local tailors and dressmakers to teach them, tirelessly consulting his peers and experts in the industry from near and far. He strongly believed in being professional if the factory was to have a future.

At that time, Luodong Garment Factory's primary business was the processing and manufacturing of men's tunic suits and women's tops, contracted by local large garment companies. Baorong sensed that in the long run, the factory must take its future into its own hands and develop its own distribution channels.

于是，他带着徒弟扛着装满样衣的蛇皮袋，奔波在全国各地。太原、阳泉、大同、石家庄、呼和浩特、郑州……他们一座城市接着一座城市地拜访，一家公司接着一家公司地谈判，一个柜台接着一个柜台地出样和签约，最终以一笔又一笔的订单打开了洛东服装厂的市场空间。

真正让张宝荣与众不同的，还是他的前瞻意识和商业敏感。虽然当时的他还只是企业经营的新手，服装厂规模也很小，但在外跑市场期间，他已超前地意识到商标和品牌的重要性："有自己的商标和牌子，商品就会跟人不同，就会更有价值。"

于是，洛东服装厂成立不久，张宝荣就向当地工商局申请注册了"洛丰"商标，并于 1980 年 4 月 8 日获得了国家工商行政管理总局核发的"商标核准通知书"。

通知书显示，这是我国第 5339 号商标。

当时，全国的商标、品牌意识都还非常淡薄。直到 1982 年，中国第一部商标法《中华人民共和国商标法》出台，尚处于初级阶段的服装纺织行业，也基本以贴牌加工生产（OEM）模式为主，商标问题普遍不受重视。张宝荣的这个意识可谓走在了整个时代的前面。

时任嘉兴丝绸厂（现浙江嘉欣丝绸股份有限公司）质检员、现任雅莹集团党委书记的仇瑛也曾感叹："当时连我们国营企业都没有商标注册这个意识，他一个乡镇企业（家）却已经有了。很有（品牌）意识！"

To this end, Baorong and his apprentice carried large PVC bags full of garment samples and travelled across China. From Taiyuan, Yangquan and Datong to Shijiazhuang, Hohhot and Zhengzhou, they visited one city after another, one company after another, one store counter after another. Their hard work paid off, as the factory finally had orders coming in.

What made a real difference was Baorong's forward-looking vision and business acumen. Although he was only a novice in the business and his factory was small, he was already aware of the importance of trademarks and branding. He would say, "Once you have your own trademark and brand, your products will stand out from the crowd and become more valuable." Soon after Luodong Garment Factory was setup, Baorong successfully registered the "Luofeng" trademark (China's No.5339 trademark) on April 8, 1980. At that time, China's clothing and textile industry was still in its infancy, and most of the companies were OEMs (Original Equipment Manufacturer), hence intellectual property awareness and owning trademarks were generally lacking in China. It was not until 1982 that China's first trademark law, *Trademark Law of the People's Republic of China*, was adopted. Baorong was ahead of his time.

Qiu Ying, the then quality inspector of Jiaxing's Silk Mill (now Zhejiang Jiaxing Silk Co., Ltd.) who serves as the Party secretary of EP YAYING Fashion Group today, also admired Baorong's innovation, saying, "Few state-owned enterprises had the awareness to register one's trademark, whilst a township-village enterprise entrepreneur already had. He was a visionary leader indeed!"

011

注 册 商 标 栏	注册商标名称	洛丰		
	商标注册证号	审吕53		
	注 册 人	张兆昌		
	核准日期	80.4.8号		
	核 准 使用商品	中山装		
	实 际 使用商品	中山装		
	何年、何月获过何种名称奖	无		
	商标标识的主要印制单位名 称	苏州印册厂 海安红星牌美术印刷厂		
	有否允许他人使用你单位注册商标？有否签订许可合同	否		
	有否使用他人注册商标？有否签订许可合同？	否		
	出口商品名称、在哪些国家已注册？哪些使用未注册商标？	无		

在上报此表的同时、附商标注册证复印件壹份

012

未注册商标栏	商标名称			
	启用日期			
	实际使用商品			
	商标未注册原因			

实际使用商标标识
样张或照片粘贴处

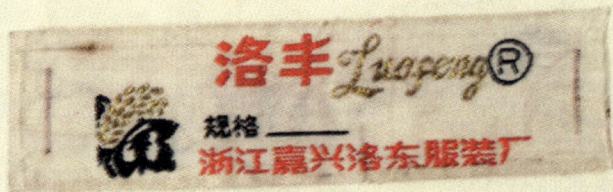

左图：
1980 年 4 月，由张宝荣注册的"洛丰"商标核准通知书

LEFT
"Notice of Trademark Approval" issued by the State Administration for Industry and Commerce for the "Luofeng" trademark registered by Zhang Baorong, April 1980

左页：

1980 年代，洛东服装厂生产的不同
纹样的 "洛丰" 牌女士上衣

上图：

经典的盘扣设计，成为当时 "洛丰"
牌女士立领上衣的一大特色

OPPOSITE

Women's shirts in different patterns
with Luofeng's brand label produced by
Luodong Garment Factory, 1980s

ABOVE

The classic Chinese button knot is a
signature feature of Luofeng women's
mandarin collar shirts

上图：
1980 年代，"洛丰"红色提花女士上衣

ABOVE
Red floral jacquard shirt, Luofeng 1980s

右页：
1980 年代，"洛丰"男士中山装及女士上衣

OPPOSITE
Blue men's tunic suit and red floral
jacquard women's shirt, Luofeng 1980s

想要做好事，先要做好人
BEING A VIRTUOUS PERSON ABOVE ALL

"想要做好事，先要做好人"是张宝荣做人做事的信念，他在过往岗位的突出表现有赖于这一信念，进入陌生的服装业后，他也秉持这一信念面对和处理纷繁挑战。

如何做好人？首先是以身作则。

初创的企业条件艰苦，张宝荣就带头吃苦。每次出差跑业务，他都带着一个黑色的公文包，除了很简单的工作和生活用品，包里必不可少的就是白煮蛋，那是家人心疼他，给他补充的营养。有时出差长达一个多月，他会带着40多个鸡蛋上路，行程中饿了，就从包里摸出两个鸡蛋，配着在当地水果摊上买的苹果吃。

爱吃苦的张宝荣，对吃也是最不讲究的，也不舍得为吃多花一分钱。苹果，他往往是买最便宜的夹带着坏果子的那一种。即便家人和同事都心疼他，要求他不如此刻薄自己，转身他还是烂苹果照买，能多节约一分钱就多节约一分钱。

当时的交通极为不便，张宝荣也是带头克难。一次赶着到呼和浩特出差，没有座票，他就从嘉兴一路站到天津站，近20个小时下来，腿脚都站肿了。天津到北京小坐一段之后，又马不停蹄转车再站到呼和浩特。

晚上，则常常在便宜的地下旅社将就过夜。

Baorong always emphasised "being a virtuous person if we want to succeed in life." It is with this belief that he continued to succeed in the many roles he took up and the slew of challenges he was thrown into. And his definition of being a virtuous person? Walk the talk.

Starting a business from scratch was no easy job and Baorong once again took the lead. He carried a simple black document bag wherever he went for business. In addition to the essentials, it would always hold boiled eggs that his family prepared for him as a form of nutrition, because they knew he did not pay attention to his meals. Some business trip could last more than a month, and he would bring along more than 40 eggs as his main source of food when travelling — 2 eggs plus an apple was his typical meal. He often bought the cheapest, and sometimes unknowingly rotten apples in order to save money. His family and colleagues would always implore him not to skimp on himself, but he would carry on in his frugal way of life and thought that whenever he could save a penny, he should.

He was a persevering man who did not back down from any hardship. Once, there was an urgent business trip to Hohhot and Baorong was not able to book a train seat. So he stood all the way from Jiaxing to Tianjin station for nearly 20 hours, his legs and feet became swollen but he did not have any thought to stop and rest. He would carry on transferring trains, from Tianjin to Beijing, and then to Hohhot. On business trips like these, he would also stay in the most inexpensive hostel, most of the time in basements.

In addition to running the factory, Baorong still had another responsibility — as the preferred local doctor, he was often requested by the villagers for home visits. As a result, he hardly had time for his own family. His two sons were taken care of by their grandparents, whilst all the farm work rested squarely on the shoulders of his wife, Shi Yueying.

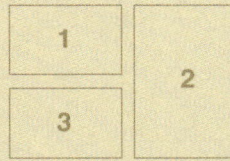

下图：

1. 1967 年，张宝荣与妻子史月英的结婚证件照

2. 1990 年代早期，张宝荣与妻子在嘉兴南湖之畔合影

3. 1990 年代早期，张宝荣与妻子在北京人民大会堂前合影

BELOW

1. Zhang Baorong and Shi Yueying's marriage registration photo, 1967

2. Zhang Baorong and Shi Yueying by the South Lake in Jiaxing, early 1990s

3. Zhang Baorong and Shi Yueying in front of the Great Hall of the People in Beijing, early 1990s

"

'想要做好事，先要做好人'
是张宝荣做人做事的信念，
他在过往岗位的突出表现有赖于这一信念，
进入陌生的服装业后，他也秉持这一信念面对和处理纷繁挑战。

"

右页：
1985 年 10 月，跑供销至洛阳的张宝荣

OPPOSITE
Zhang Baorong on a business trip to Luoyang
City, October 1985

洛阳喷水池留影
85.10.7

那个时期，除了服装厂忙个不停，张宝荣还有一个责任在身：村民依然常常请他出诊。为了照顾大家的需求，他几乎彻底放弃了自己的小家：将两个儿子一个交由爷爷管，一个送到外婆家，家里种的地，收、割、种、养全托付给了妻子月英。

后来，厂里忙不过来，他干脆把刚刚初中毕业的大儿子张建明喊进厂，同样也是严格要求。他让建明从学徒开始，跟着嘉兴服装公司的郭师傅学技术。郭师傅当时已经 70 多岁，张建明是他的关门弟子。师傅对弟子要求严格，而张宝荣对儿子的要求更是严格，要他必须比其他员工更努力、更无私。

严格要求自己、刻薄自己的张宝荣，对员工非常宽厚。员工家里的农事和家事，他都非常关心和重视，工作、生活上有什么困难，都千方百计帮忙解决。

对工厂利益，张宝荣也是看得比家里的利益还重。即便工厂的效益已经不错了，在工厂给小儿子张华明做套西服，张宝荣也是要分文不少地自己上交材料费和人工费。

张宝荣的这种以身作则和无私奉献，让工厂格外团结，上下同心。众志成城之下，洛东服装厂不但在艰难的环境发展起来了，还获得乡党委颁发的"企业贡献突出奖"，张宝荣本人也被授予"优秀企业家"荣誉称号。

With the factory's business continuing to grow, Baorong requested Zhang Jianming, his eldest son, who had just graduated from junior high school, to help in the factory. He sent Jianming to apprentice with Master Guo from Jiaxing Apparel Company to first master tailoring. Master Guo was in his 70s at the time and Jianming was his last disciple. Guo was very strict with this young man, so was Baorong, who encouraged him to work hard and selflessly.

Where Baorong was tough on himself, he was generous to his employees. He cared for them and did everything possible to help them solve any difficulties in work and life. He always placed the interest of the factory and his employees as the first priority, personally seeing to all accounts and their wages. He never abused power for his personal gain, and even once, when he had made a suit for his younger son from the factory, he insisted on paying out of his own pocket.

Baorong set an excellent example of a man of the highest integrity and principle. Everyone at the factory, young or old, new or experienced, were united and loyal to him. Luodong Garment Factory continued to make strong headway and even won the "Outstanding Enterprise Award" issued by the township's Party committee. Baorong himself was also awarded the honorary title of "Outstanding Entrepreneur".

另起炉灶从头越
BREAKING NEW GROUND

张宝荣全情发展洛东之时，同属嘉兴的海盐县，出了位著名人物——步鑫生。步鑫生创立的海盐衬衫总厂是海盐县首家产值超千万元的企业，也是当时浙江省最大的专业衬衫厂。他的一系列改革发展举措更是闻名全国，上过新闻联播，得到中央政府的肯定。主张多向同行学习的张宝荣曾登门拜访过步鑫生，向他讨教企业管理经验，但步鑫生的改革之路并非一帆风顺。

张宝荣也很快遇到类似的挑战，不过，他比步鑫生要幸运。相比个性刚烈的步鑫生，张宝荣更温和一些，他处理矛盾的方式是退步与妥协，这最终让他以退为进地走向了更好。

改革开放初期，在一个对姓资还是姓社争论不休的大背景下，办企业面临着市场之外的诸多挑战。这给一心一意想要发展好洛东服装厂的张宝荣制造了很多障碍。最突出的表现就是，工厂越是往前发展，越面临来自上级和周围环境的理念、措施，让张宝荣难以适从。工厂管理、财务管理和销售制度执行上的矛盾、冲突，也时有发生。

1985 年，张宝荣还被从厂长降为供销科长。

被降职后，张宝荣依然对工厂热情不改，尽心尽力地做好本职工作——跑销售、催货款，成绩也得到上下一致认可。1986 年，他还被嘉兴市郊区政府评为"优秀供销员"。

当时的《郊区优秀供销员推荐表》评价张宝荣："热心于企业

When Baorong's first venture into the garment industry began in Luodong, Jiaxing was seeing the rise of a famous figure in Haiyan County's garment industry, Bu Xinsheng, who started Haiyan Shirt Factory. The factory was the first enterprise in the country with an output value of over 10 million CNY, and at the time was the largest professional shirt factory in Zhejiang Province. Xinsheng's series of reforms were well-known throughout China, hitting the headlines of CCTV news and affirmed by the central government. Baorong, a strong advocate of learning from his peers, personally visited Xinsheng to consult his business management experience. However, Xinsheng's entrepreneurial journey was not smooth sailing, and he was eventually demoted by the government. Baorong would soon encounter a similar setback but he was relatively more fortunate. Compared with Xinsheng, who had a strong personality, Baorong was more gentle in his communication and handling of conflicts, taking one step back to take two steps forward.

At the early stage of China's economic reform, constant debates over capitalism and socialism raised many challenges beyond the market itself. This macro context created many obstacles for Baorong, most prominently, the more the factory developed, the more resistance would come from the top and peers, making it more and more difficult to manage. There were frequent disputes and conflicts about production, account management and sales. In 1985, Baorong was demoted from factory director to a sales manager.

In spite of his demotion, Baorong maintained his passion for the factory and gave his all in his new position. His efforts and performance were soon recognised. In 1986, he was awarded "Outstanding Salesperson" in the district by the local government office. His recommendation application wrote, "Baorong is an enthusiastic worker who wholeheartedly commits to the company,

右图 / 下图：
1986 年 8 月，嘉兴市郊区人民政府专门表彰了全区一批"优秀供销员"，张宝荣名列其中

RIGHT / BELOW
Zhang Baorong is awarded "Outstanding Salesperson" in the district by the local government office in Jiaxing, August 1986

工作，积极为企业发展和生存做贡献。一心一意为企业，千方百计提高经济效益。不为名不为利，积极做好供销员的本职工作。完成和超额完成厂里的销售业务，对厂里销售业务非常关心，积极回笼工厂的销售资金。"

因为工作业绩实在突出，被降职之后依然任劳任怨，一如既往地开展工作，大家也是有目共睹，1987 年 2 月 28 日，张宝荣东山再起了：被升级为工厂副厂长。

被降职，张宝荣没有什么抱怨；被升职，张宝荣也没有什么惊喜。他像过去一样，千方百计开展工作，希望让工厂发展得更好。但他越是想做些开创性的事，越是感到无奈：之前束缚和制约他专心经营的问题并没有得到解决，矛盾继续存在。

这让他身心俱疲，壮志难酬，有力使不出。

一次次对现实失望之后，张宝荣开始思考自己的未来。与其在不遂心，也不能真正施展自己的环境委曲求全，甚至与人不愉快，不如走出去自己办企业，这渐渐成为他越来越坚定的想法。

时代也鼓舞着张宝荣走出这一步。1986 年，国家出台的第七个五年规划（1986~1990）将纺织服装行业列为重点发展行业之一。1987 年，党的十三大胜利召开。

服装业的春天就要来了，私营企业的春天就要来了。受到鼓舞的张宝荣于是找到时任洛东乡红政村村支书的朱和生，与他推心置腹地交流了自己希望开办新厂的想法。朱和生与张宝荣是发小，他很清楚张宝荣的才干和人品，非常支持张宝荣更自主

ensuring its survival and growth, and doing everything possible to improve its financial performance. He does not work for fame or money, and remains steadfast in his role as a sales manager, not only meeting sales targets but exceeding them. He cares deeply for the factory and is very proactive in ensuring the factory's cash flow."

Baorong's outstanding performance and selfless attitude in spite of all that he faced did not go unnoticed. He was promoted to associate director of the factory on February 28, 1987, making a successful comeback.

However, Baorong was neither beat down by the demotion nor surprised by the promotion. He threw himself into work and always focused on further progress. Unfortunately, the more he was hoping for a breakthrough, the more he ended up feeling helpless — he found himself constrained by that same resistance that had previously thwarted his efforts and remained unsolved. This exhausted him physically and mentally, and he found his aspirations nearly impossible to achieve under these circumstances. He began to seriously consider a new future. Instead of compromising his beliefs for the sake of being accepted or getting trapped by the office politics, he became more and more certain in stepping out and starting his own business.

In 1986, the 7th Five-Year Plan (1986-1990) issued by the State Council of China identified the textile and garment industry as one of the key industries for development. A year later, the 13th National Congress of the Party was successfully held. With change comes opportunity, for garment enterprises, for private enterprises, and in this case, for Zhang Baorong.

His spirit was greatly lifted with the forthcoming development. He reached out to Zhu Hesheng, the then Party secretary of Hongzheng Village of Luodong Town, and had a heartfelt conversation about

『张宝荣生平』连环画

Zhang Baorong,
A Comic Strip
Memoir

（1）1951年，七岁的张宝荣在洛东红庵里小学求学。

7-year-old Zhang Baorong studies at Luodong Hong'anli Primary School in 1951.

（2）1961年，少年张宝荣经过田间地头几年磨砺，在17岁那年经大队长章绶华举荐开始担任生产队会计，自此年轻的张宝荣成为山家浜集体经济的管账人。

After years of hard work on the farm, 17-year-old Baorong becomes an accountant of the collective economy of Shanjiabang in Luodong Town at the recommendation of Zhang Shouhua, the leader of the production brigade in 1961.

（3）二十出头的张宝荣在江苏震泽新虹义务帮助犁田打草时，初识了日后的妻子史月英。

Baorong, in his early twenties, volunteers to help with ploughing and weeding on the farm in the Xinhong Village of Zhenze Town, Jiangsu Province, and meets his future wife, Shi Yueying.

（4）1967年2月14日（农历正月初六），张宝荣与史月英喜结良缘。

On the 14th of February 1967 (the sixth day of the first lunar month), Zhang Baorong and Shi Yueying tie the knot.

（5）担任赤脚医生期间，为降低农村就医成本，张宝荣收集民间土方，组织种植中草药植物。通过"自种、自采、自制、自用"的办法，制作成各味中草药剂。

Facing resource scarcity, Baorong compiles folk remedies, and leads the growing and harvesting of Chinese medicinal plants for producing herbal medicines.

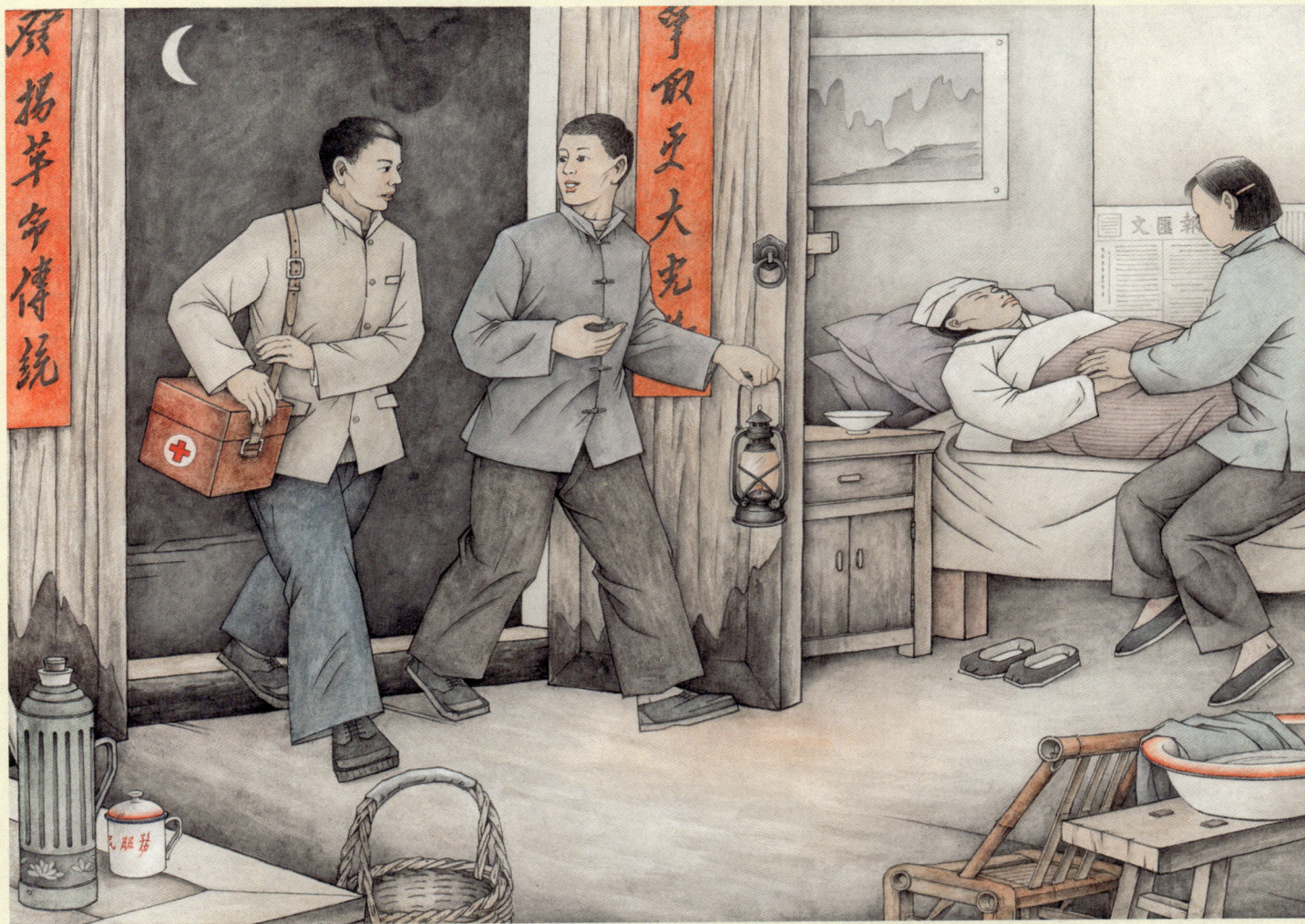

（6）某个初冬深夜，洛东丝厂缫丝工郭阿菊病毒性心肌炎发作，张宝荣凭借临床经验诊断后亲自护送郭阿菊到洛东卫生院，由于送医及时，郭阿菊终于转危为安。

Late one night in the early winter, Guo Aju, a worker at Luodong Silk Reeling Mill, has a sudden heart attack caused by viral myocarditis. After receiving an initial diagnosis from Baorong, she is escorted to the Luodong Health Clinic immediately. Thanks to the timely treatment, Aju's life is saved.

（7）农村夏天多蛇，年轻的16岁姑娘山金鑫不幸遭遇毒蛇，经张宝荣紧急救治，他将蛇毒一口口吸出再涂上草药半边莲，最终山金鑫脱离了危险。

During the summer, snake bites become rampant in the countryside. A young 16-year-old girl, Shan Jinxin, unfortunately gets bitten by a venomous snake. Baorong sucks out the snake venom as emergency treatment and smears medicinal plants over her wound, helping her out of danger.

（8）邻家孩子在玩耍时不慎将一颗黄豆塞入鼻孔，情急之下孩子哇哇大哭，为避免黄豆倒吸进入呼吸道，张宝荣立刻让孩子平躺并镇定引导孩子采取轻吸重呼的方法，令黄豆逐步从鼻腔移出。

A neighbour's child accidentally inhales a soybean into his nostril when he was playing. In order to prevent him from crying and causing the soy bean to further enter the respiratory tract, Baorong quickly lies him down, and calmly guides the boy to inhale lightly and exhale heavily, pushing the soybean gradually out of the nasal cavity.

（9）张宝荣深知自己获得的知识、职业、荣誉都离不开党组织的教育和培养，他在1971年11月9日，郑重向党组织递交入党申请书，并于1973年5月15日光荣加入中国共产党。

Baorong is grateful to the Communist Party of China (CPC) for all his achievements, and feels that his knowledge and career are the result of the education and training provided by the CPC. On the 9th of November 1971, he submits an application to join the CPC and formally becomes a member of the CPC on the 15th of May 1973.

（10）1979年，在改革开放春风的吹拂下，随着乡镇企业蓬勃兴起，张宝荣满怀投身实业、造福乡里的热情组建嘉兴洛东第一家乡办集体服装企业——洛东服装厂，从一名厂医转变为服装厂核心人员，并于1981年担任厂长。他亲自研究市场需求，和徒弟背着样衣长途跋涉，一个城市、一个柜台地出样签约。

Baorong joins in the setup of the first local collectively-owned township garment enterprise, Luodong Garment Factory, in 1979, and becomes director of the factory. He personally brings garment samples from one city to another seeking potential collaboration with retailers.

（11）张宝荣凡事严于律己，敢于迎难而上，创业期间跑供销的路途千辛万苦，饿了他吃几个廉价的苹果和出门自带的煮鸡蛋，困了找个最廉价的地下旅社将就过夜。张宝荣凭着那份韧劲，为厂里挣得了许多服装生产的订单。

Baorong is known to be frugal, self-disciplined and undaunted by challenges. Starting up is tough, and on each business trip, his typical meal includes cheap apples from local fruit stalls and boiled eggs. He also always chooses to stay in the cheapest hostel.

（12）张宝荣从不溺爱孩子，他用自己勤勉的言行教育和影响孩子。只要有空，他会坐下来和孩子们聊一些工作中的趣事。每次跑销售回来，他会把每一个去处的风土人情、地域特点告诉孩子，让孩子们感受到国的版图之大、河山之美。而儿辈们在深沉的父爱中，感受最多的是：不要忘本，懂得感恩。

Baorong never spoils his children and believes that actions speak louder than words in education. In his free time, he will spend time to tell his children about his business trips and they would understand the importance of "staying modest and being grateful".

（13）在参与洛东服装生产的管理和经营这前后七八年的时间里，张宝荣夙兴夜寐，兢兢付出。不愿受制于乡办集体企业的管理体制，踌躇满志的张宝荣在1988年极其艰苦的条件下承包经营洛东红政服装厂，以生产男士衬衫和丝绸加工为主。

Unwilling to compromise his beliefs under the system of township-run enterprises, Baorong makes a tough but visionary decision in 1988 to undertake the ownership of Luodong Hongzheng Garment Factory to manufacture men's shirts and silk clothing.

（14）面临服装厂起步阶段的诸多困难，张宝荣与职工同甘共苦。当年他会和员工一起排版放样，减少浪费。而张宝荣的真诚和干事的激情赢得了像王惠明那样的一批铁杆员工。

Facing many difficulties in the initial stage of the start-up, Baorong sticks with his workers through thick and thin. Baorong joins his worker to do pattern making and fittings, ensuring they save fabric to reduce cost wherever possible. Baorong's integrity and passion would win him a group of loyal employees like Wang Huiming.

（15）精诚所至金石为开，张宝荣在创业初期屡经艰难，幸得贵人相助。1990年12月3日，当时的嘉兴同兴丝绸有限公司与洛东红政服装厂签订合约，红政加挂丝绸公司第四服装厂牌子。洛东红政同时获得同兴出借的40台缝纫机和电力设备，生产力显著提高。

Where there's a will, there's a way. Baorong is fortunate to have the help of people that think alike on his arduous journey, such as Jiaxing Tongxing Silk Company that loans him industrial sewing machines and power equipments in 1990. As a result, the factory production capacity increases greatly.

(16) 1990年张华明高中毕业加入红政。张宝荣交给儿子的第一个重要任务是与他一道前往重庆催要一笔20万元的应收款。当时交通落后，宝荣父子先后搭乘火车、小巴，辗转从上海到贵定、贵阳，舟车劳顿终抵重庆，又经2个多月的坚持终于拿回应收款，这让张华明得到了至今受用的学习锻炼。

Baorong's youngest son, Zhang Hwaming, graduates from senior high school in 1990 and his father assigns him his first task to Chongqing. Public transport was extremely poor then and they had to transfer between multiple train and minibus rides across Shanghai, Guiding and Guiyang, before finally arriving in Chongqing.

17

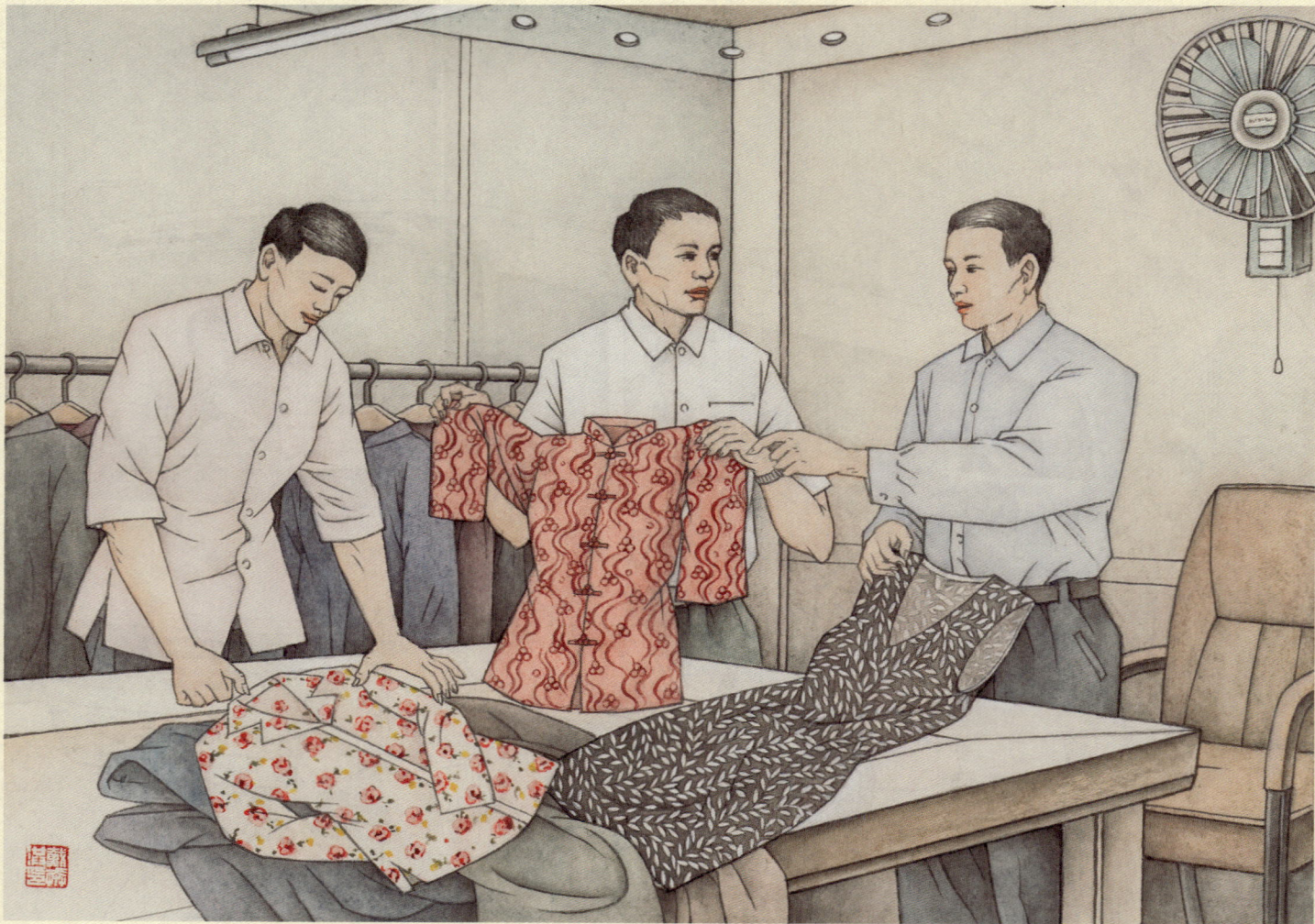

（17）1991年张宝荣派张华明北上开拓市场，凭借务实的为人，张华明携手戴雪明陆续达成北京15家商贸城的合作，积累了一定的服装销售和现代商品经营的技巧。他们洞悉市场，了解消费者的需求，发现丝绸服装尤受北京人喜欢的商机。经由张宝荣支持，大力生产丝绸服装迎来产销两旺的喜人局面。

In 1991, Hwaming and Xueming travels to Beijing to expand the business. Together they successfully open stores in 15 retail malls, produce silk garments that the local women love, and achieve new heights in production and sales.

（18）1994年年初，真丝衬衫经营取得阶段性成果，经张华明提议，张宝荣同意进一步扩大企业规模，将已经更名为洛东制衣厂的红政服装厂，再次升级为"嘉兴市永利来时装有限责任公司"。创业10多年的张宝荣，终于有了一个真正属于自己的名副其实的时装生产企业。

Business continues to boom. In 1994, Baorong accepts Hwaming's proposal for further expansion and upgrades the company to become Jiaxing Yonglilai Fashion Co., Ltd. After a decade, Baorong finally owns his own fashion company.

《张宝荣生平》连环画作品，精选自张宝荣故居陈展画册
Zhang Baorong, A Comic Strip Memoir, 2018,
featuring selected artworks from Zhang Baorong Memorial Album exhibited in his Memorial Hall

地发展。红政村当时已办有一家服装厂，正希望找更有成功经验的人来承包经营，于是他鼓励张宝荣以个人身份投资村集体企业，也就是以承包经营的方式，与红政一起来办好这家服装厂。

张宝荣欣然同意了这个建议。已跟随父亲在洛东服装厂工作两年，眼见父亲壮志难酬的张建明，也很支持父亲另起炉灶："（服装加工）技术我也熟悉了，我不怕！我们一起走！"

于是，张宝荣一边努力处理自己在洛东服装厂负责事务的善后工作，一边投入承包经营的筹备中。1988 年 3 月 8 日，张宝荣计划承包经营的洛东红政服装厂正式以新的身份运行了。1989 年 1 月 11 日，处理好善后工作的张宝荣告别洛东服装厂，正式担任了洛东红政服装厂法人代表及厂长。

1989 年 5 月 29 日，红庵里（隶属洛东红政的自然村落）牡丹盛开的季节，张宝荣以个人投资村集体企业的方式与洛东红政服装厂正式签订了投资协议，他用自己省吃俭用的积累和向亲戚朋友筹措的共计 20299.20 元，投资控股洛东红政服装厂 59.9%，承包经营，也是自主经营了洛东红政服装厂。

在投身服装业的第十年，就像再次出航的船老大，张宝荣又一次握住了船舵——雅莹真正的前身：洛东红政服装厂，正式扬帆起航。

his aspiration to open a new factory on his own. Hesheng knew Baorong well since childhood, and had every confidence in Baorong's capability and character, naturally giving his full support. He knew of a garment factory in Hongzheng that was looking for a buyer with successful management experience. Hesheng suggested that Baorong could become an investor in the factory and take over its management and operations.

Baorong readily took him up on his idea. Jianming, who had been working with his father in Luodong Garment Factory for two years, shared his father's sentiments on breaking new ground and ardently expressed his support, "I am good at what I am doing [tailoring] now, let's do it together!"

On March 8, 1988, Baorong officially launched Luodong Hongzheng Garment Factory's new operations. A few months later on January 11, 1989, he was formally appointed as legal representative and director of the factory. The factory was nestled in Hong'anli, a tightly knit community in Hongzheng, known for its unique century-old peonies; it would be symbolic that Baorong's ownership of the factory would too come into bloom in May. On May 20, Baorong became a major shareholder of the factory, investing a total of 20,299.20 CNY, that included savings he painstakingly put together and contributions from family and friends. In his 10-year milestone in the garment industry, Baorong, like a captain holding tight the rudder of his ship named Hongzheng Garment Factory, he would raise the sails and set the course, and begin on a new journey.

第一篇

CHAPTER 1

筚路蓝缕，
以启山林

1988~1998
AN ENTREPRENEURIAL ADVENTURE
SPARKED BY AMBITIOUS DREAMS

在改革开放春风的吹拂下，企业创始人张宝荣以勇于担当、艰苦奋斗的作风，历经挑战，从一名厂医转变为服装厂厂长，再从集体乡办企业走向自主承包经营。从此，张宝荣先生秉持"想要做好事，先要做好人"的原则，真正为雅莹美丽事业的发展开启梦想的篇章。

From the village's "barefoot doctor", to director of the town's garment enterprise, to shared owner of Luodong Hongzheng Garment Factory, Zhang Baorong continued to forge ahead with courage, determination and commitment amidst China's deepening reform and opening-up. His ethos of "being a virtuous person if you want to succeed in life" would become embedded in the company's culture and inspire the company as it moved forward.

怀揣梦想，自主创业
STRIKING OUT ON HIS OWN

感受到时代的春意，私营经济发展被进一步认可，一腔热血的张宝荣带着经验、智慧、才干和亲友的支持，走向自主的创业发展，以个人投资的方式承包经营了洛东红政服装厂，也为后来创办雅莹迈出最关键的一步，完成最重要的积累。

The times had called and Zhang Baorong had responded. He was a trailblazer who remained an enthusiastic learner and won the hearts of many. As private enterprises continued to grow in significance, Baorong broke new ground by undertaking the management of Luodong Hongzheng Factory, a significant milestone in the development of today's EP YAYING.

> "
> 1988 年 3 月 8 日，34 名员工，340 平方米的厂房，
> 18 台家用缝纫机的嗒嗒声中，洛东红政服装厂正式开张了。
> "

上页：
1988 年，嘉兴市洛东红政服装厂

右页：
1988 年，洛东红政服装厂生产车间

PREVIOUS
Luodong Hongzheng Garment Factory in
Jiaxing City, 1988

OPPOSITE
Production space in Luodong Hongzheng
Garment Factory, 1988

敢为人先，站稳脚跟
A PATH LESS TRAVELLED

1988 年 3 月 8 日，34 名员工，340 平米的厂房，18 台家用缝纫机的嗒嗒声中，洛东红政服装厂正式开张了。其中的缝纫机是工人们从家里搬来的，厂房是借红庵里曾经的小学校舍改成的。

没有开工仪式，不放鞭炮，不请领导，不摆酒席，张宝荣的创业就这样开始了。

虽然已有相当的经验，但那个年代初创企业能遇到的各种艰辛，张宝荣还是尝了个遍。首先是社会观念的障碍，以及由此导致的工作阻力。当时，私营经济依然不被普遍接受，甚至被争议、受歧视，这给私营的红政服装厂带来不少的困扰。曾经有一段时间，在能源紧张的情况下，工厂用电常常排不上号，被拉闸限电的事时有发生，甚至无法维持正常的生产秩序。直到张宝荣向当时的嘉兴市供电局局长说明情况，得到局长的支持——"监狱里都可以用电，私营厂怎么不可以用电？"用电才有了基本保障。

其次就是生产和生意的重重困难。起步阶段，工时效率和产能都很低。红政服装厂以男士衬衫、丝绸加工为主，也兼顾其他服装的加工，有滑雪衣、男女童装、绒布衬衣、织锦缎女式包衫、男女保暖衬衣、丝绸衬衫等，样杂量少，供需不一。开业后很长一段时间，公司订单难接，而且订单的质量也不好。

Luodong Hongzheng Garment Factory officially opened on March 8, 1988, with 34 craftspeople working behind 18 household sewing machines that they had brought from their own homes. The workplace was a 340-square-metre workshop, which was originally a primary school for the village. There was no opening ceremony, no firecrackers, no invited government officials or entertainment. This is how Zhang Baorong's entrepreneurial adventure would begin.

Although Baorong had accrued considerable work experience, nothing could prepare him for the numerous challenges that a start-up could face in his time. The public perception of the private sector was the first and foremost issue. At that time, individual and private enterprises were not generally accepted and were even discriminated against, which caused many issues for the factory. For example, there was a period of time when the power supply to the factory was often cut off, which persisted until Baorong reported the situation to the then director of Jiaxing Power Supply Bureau and gained his support. "Even prisons have access to power, why can't a private factory?" the director asked. From that time onwards, the power supply to the factory became relatively stable.

Production and orders also posed a challenge. In the beginning, the factory focused on the production of men's shirts and the processing of silk garments, but gradually became more disorganised, resulting in a chaotic jumble of menswear, childrenswear and womenswear. Orders became hard to come by and the quality of these orders also became poorer.

下图：
1988 年，洛东红政服装厂正式成立时，员工从家里搬来的 18 台家用缝纫机之一（捐赠人：老员工秦兴艳）

BELOW
One of the 18 household sewing machines donated by an employee during the start-up of Luodong Hongzheng Garment Factory, 1988

开业的第一单是为一个股东的童装厂做一款童装薄棉袄。因为第一次做，又以家用缝纫机做难度较高的绗缝，生产完成，生意却亏了。为了让工厂继续运转起来，张建明通过熟人拿到一份童装绒布衬衫订单，但也是每件的加工费还不到一元钱，同样没什么钱赚。

过程中，张宝荣还因为轻信他人而遭遇诈骗。他经人介绍，拿到一笔来自香港的手袋加工业务，金额150万元。签完合同，预付了高息筹集的5万元定金，却几个月迟迟不见加工订单和原料采购预付款。之后，张宝荣通过调查打听才知道这是个骗局。虽然后来通过法律途径讨回了定金，但耽误的工期，以及对他和员工们的精神打击，都加重了工厂的困难。

即便这样，张宝荣依然保持信心，在可能的范围内尽最大努力，按做到最好的标准推动工厂继续向前。他在上海找到优秀的技师、版师，三顾茅庐，请对方利用星期天的时间到工厂，像老师一样提供技术指导，帮助工厂优化生产的方式与技巧，尽可能地改善工厂生产的品质。

同时，他还请到时任嘉兴丝绸服装总厂技术质管科长的仇瑛等人，为工厂开展质量检测及技术培训。他坚毅执着、为人厚道的好品质，不但打动了仇瑛，还打动了仇瑛的老总周国建，后者帮助工厂与浙江同兴丝绸有限公司建立了外贸加工合作联营关系。

The first order came from a shareholder requesting production of children's lightweight quilted jackets. Quilting with household sewing machines for the first time proved to be difficult, and it was a loss-making order. In order to keep the factory running, Jianming went searching for new prospects and obtained a request through an acquaintance for the production of children's flannel shirts. However, the fee for each shirt was less than one yuan, and once again, the profit margin was nearly zero. In these early stages, Baorong even encountered several fraudulent orders. He was introduced to an order from Hong Kong for handbag processing said to be worth 1.5 million yuan. After the contract signing and a 50,000 CNY deposit, which he had to borrow at high interest rates, the order and the advance payment for the raw material procurement remained nowhere to be seen for months — at which point Baorong realised the order fraudulent. Although he managed to recover the deposit through legal proceedings, the wasted time, as well as the emotional shock to him and the employees, left an indelible mark.

左页左图：
1990 年 12 月，由张宝荣（左二）代表的洛东红政服装厂与当时的嘉兴同兴丝绸有限公司签约

左页右图：
在签署现场，张宝荣（左）与当时的工厂员工王海林

OPPOSITE LEFT
Zhang Baorong (second from left) represents Luodong Hongzheng Garment Factory to sign a partnership with the Jiaxing-based Tongxing Silk company, December 1990

OPPOSITE RIGHT
Zhang Baorong (left) and Wang Hailin, former employee, at the signing ceremony

1990 年 12 月 3 日，张宝荣代表洛东红政服装厂与嘉兴同兴丝绸有限公司签订合约，也给红政服装厂加挂了一块同兴丝绸公司第四服装厂牌子。同时，周国建还安排同兴公司出借 40 台工业缝纫机和电力设备，进一步提高洛东红政的生产能力，促使生产计划稳定实施。

为了提高工厂的经营管理效益，张宝荣还积极走出去，定期到上海、杭州与一些优秀同行交流，到其工厂参观，学习对方的生产、管理、经营之道。这让他不断在经营管理上进步。职工们都评价他："工作很认真，能吃苦，脑子也很聪明，会经营也会创新！"

千辛万苦的努力，让红政服装的经营走入了正轨，但刚入正轨，新的问题又来了。不过，张宝荣把问题变成了机会。

Baorong kept his head up and tried everything he could to keep the factory running without compromising on quality. He consulted the best craftsman and patternmakers in Shanghai and invited them over on their rest days to provide trainings as he continued to improve the factory's processes.

Meanwhile, he persuaded Qiu Ying, who had risen to chief of Technical Development and Quality at Jiaxing's Silk Mill, to provide quality control training. His persevering and honest character not only moved Qiu Ying, but also her general manager, Zhou Guojian, who further helped to connect the factory with Zhejiang Tongxing Silk Company for a long-term collaboration in 1990. In that same year, Guojian also loaned 40 industrial sewing machines and other electrical equipment to the factory, greatly increasing its quality and production capacity.

In order to improve operational efficiency, Baorong continued to visit his peers at their factories in Shanghai and Hangzhou to learn more about production and business management. His staff all shared similar sentiments: "He is hard-working, intelligent and innovative!" Thereafter, the factory's operations and business continued to gather pace and grow steadily.

上图 / 右页：
1980 年代末，洛东红政服装厂早期生
产的蓝、粉色盘扣提花缎面女士上衣

ABOVE / OPPOSITE
Blue and pink floral jacquard women's
shirts with Chinese knot buttons produced
by Luodong Hongzheng Garment Factory,
late 1980s

化危为机，巧解用工难题
TWO SIDES OF A COIN

20 世纪 90 年代初，以家庭为单位的小作坊开始在嘉兴等地流行。村民们发现自己在家织布卖给工厂，比在工厂当工人挣得更多，时间也更自由。很多工人因此离职单干，一度造成工厂的用工荒。

张宝荣历来重视合作伙伴、员工的利益关切和关系维护。他深知企业的成功离不开合作伙伴的支持，更离不开全厂员工的齐心合力。每到年底，他都把合作伙伴、员工全部叫齐，专门请来厨师烹羊宰猪，大鱼大肉，全鸡全鸭，和大家一起吃年夜饭。该给合作伙伴的利益，该给员工的工资和奖金也是一分不少地如数发给每一个职工。

张宝荣的这些举措令员工们很感激并珍惜在厂里的工作，让红政的用工压力相对小一些。其中，王惠明就是最早入职的员工之一。1988 年 3 月加入工厂后一直在生产一线工作直到退休的她就曾回忆："选择留在雅莹有感情方面的原因。当时的老厂长像家人一样关心着我们；服装厂刚开的时候，我女儿还在喝奶，如果我带小孩子到厂里，他都会来看看小孩子，我女儿也叫他爷爷，很开心。我的感觉就跟家人一样。"

但这股工人回家热潮还是给员工主要都是本地人的红政服装厂带来不小的挑战。面对新的问题，张宝荣勤思变通。他祝福那些希望出去单干的员工，感谢留下来的员工，并给大家鼓劲，要在工厂获得比自己单干更好的成就。

In the early 1990s, small family-based workshops became popular in Jiaxing and nearby cities. Instead of working in big factories, villagers found that they could generate better earnings with more flexible hours by sewing from home and selling to factories. As a result, many vacated their jobs, which left factories with a shortage of workers.

Workers at Luodong Hongzheng Garment Factory, however, treasured their place at the factory, and this all came down to Baorong's sincerity. He was a person who strongly valued his relationships with employees, business partners and relevant stakeholders — knowing that progress would not be possible without their support and a united effort. Each year during New Year's Eve, he would host a great banquet prepared by professional chefs for all his partners and employees, as well as their families. Dividends, wages and year-end bonuses would never be dragged past the new year, which created a strong sense of trust within the factory.

Wang Huiming, one of the original 34 craftspeople who joined the factory in 1988 and remained there until she retired, recalled: "I decided to stay because our late factory director treated me like family. I was still nursing my baby daughter when I joined the factory, and whenever I took her to the factory, he would come to see her, and she would grow to call him grandfather. We were really happy at the factory, like a big family."

However, as Baorong's factory was largely staffed by locals, the trend of workers choosing to work from home still posed a big challenge for him. As with all challenges he faced, he kept a sincere heart and an innovative mind. He wished the best for those whose chose to leave and encouraged those who stayed to achieve something bigger together so that everyone could become better off than working alone. He would think outside the box by personally leaving the city

最重要的，他找到从根本上解决问题的办法：到浙江相对边远的地区，以及江西、四川、贵州等人工成本低的地区招工，并从方方面面体贴和照顾这些远道而来的工人，甚至体贴到帮助外地员工在当地找对象、组建家庭，达到先"安居"后"乐业"的目的。

至今还在雅莹工作，负责原材料管理的张松英就曾回忆："老厂长给我们的关怀和照顾，真的跟对自己孩子一样。印象最深的是，每年春天，他都开车去边远的地方招工。那时招工挺难的，招过来的工人都住在一个厂区，老厂长晚上经常一个一个宿舍地去跟他们拉家常。因为招来的工人都还很年轻，老厂长觉得他们可能会想家、想父母，经常会跟他们聊天，关心他们，无微不至。"

除了工作和生活上关注员工，张宝荣还很善于激发人、鼓舞人。比如，他经常组织大家开展生产比赛，并且对优秀者给予鼓励、表彰。"大家都是熟练工了，对于能够做得比别人快和比别人好会感到非常光荣。所以厂里的生产热情非常高涨。"

初生的企业，各种的不完善、不具备，让红政服装厂一直处于紧张的状态。作为厂长的张宝荣一边全国各地跑业务、拉订单，一边操着生产、管理方方面面的心，总有解决不完的问题在排队等他，但无论多么困难，他都从未想过放弃。

红政服装厂也在他的永不言弃中，步步扎实，坚定向前。这"永不言弃"的精神，也成为张宝荣留给两个儿子，留给日后雅莹的重要精神财富。

to recruit workers from relatively remote areas of Zhejiang Province, as well as other provinces with lower labour costs, such as Jiangxi, Sichuan and Guizhou. Baorong took care of these out-of-town workers, helping them acclimate to the local lifestyle so that they could truly feel comfortable both in and out of work.

Zhang Songying, one of the employees under Baorong at the time and who is currently in charge of fabrics at the Group's supply chain, recalled: "Our late factory director looked after us as if we were his own children. Every spring, he would drive to remote places to recruit staff, which was a tough thing to do at that time. The new workers all lived in the staff accommodation on site and he would often visit them after work for a casual chat, in case they were homesick or needed any help." In addition to taking care of his employees, Baorong excelled at bringing out the best in people. He would organise mini skill competitions from time to time and reward outstanding staff, fostering a passionate and driven culture among the workers.

The typical challenges faced by any start-up were no strangers to the factory. From winning new orders to hiring suitable candidates, from production to management, there were always problems waiting for Baorong to solve. In his mind, there were always two sides to a coin; he never thought of giving up and his persevering spirit would be carried on by his two sons.

薪火相传，雅莹诞生
PASSING ON THE TORCH, YAYING

雅是高雅的雅；莹字上面一个草，下面一个玉，是宝玉，寓意天然宝贵，晶莹剔透——雅莹两个字都代表了"美"。

Ya, (Chinese: 雅), represents elegance; while the character Ying, (Chinese: 莹), is a combination of the Chinese radicals for "grass" and "jade" — symbolising purity and perfection. Both words embody and exude all that is beautiful.

初入职场显身手
AN INVALUABLE FIRST LESSON

1990 年，二儿子张华明高中毕业，也加入红政服装厂。

张华明从小在服装行业耳濡目染。在他小的时候，父亲在当地的丝厂担任厂医，母亲史月英则在丝厂做女工。"我中午放学后的午饭，都常常是在缫丝厂吃的。"烧茧子的味道、抽丝剥茧的场景，是他童年最深刻的记忆。

小学四年级，张华明就穿上了父亲在厂里给他做的小西装，成为班上第一个穿西装的人。后来，他也曾跟着父亲到各大工厂参观，"在边上听着，听不懂也听"。高中时又去工厂帮忙，学着钉纽扣，也干一些打包、写编码的杂活，还把工厂做的假领头带到宿舍卖。有时候卖十块钱，父亲就留给他五块，让他养成经营的意识……

这些都让张华明对服装有着天然的亲近和偏爱，也促成了他与服装事业的缘分。

当年 10 月国庆期间，结束学业的张华明就跟随父亲及哥哥建明，到山西太原、阳泉等地考察市场，跑供销、谈合作、租赁销售柜台，熟悉市场，了解行业。这期间，张华明第一次知道了香菜这样一种特殊的食物，也对生意和父亲的艰辛有了更多的认识。

Zhang Hwaming, Baorong's youngest son, officially joined his father's factory after graduating from senior high school in 1990 at the age of 20. Having grown up around the silk reeling mill where his mother worked, and in the garment factory ran by his father, Hwaming had always been fascinated by the industry. The smell of cooking cocoons and the sight of silk reeling were some of his most memorable childhood experiences.

Hwaming had his first suit made by the factory when he was in Year 4 at primary school, and became the first boy in his class to wear a suit. Sometimes his father would bring him along on his visits to major factories around the city, believing that even if Hwaming could not understand what they were talking about, he could simply soak in the experience. When Hwaming reached senior high, he would spend his spare time at the factory learning how to sew a button, helping with packaging, or even contributing to the daily grind of product coding. Occasionally, he would take the factory's detachable men's shirt collars to sell at the factory dormitory and his father would take the opportunity to pass on some lessons in business by letting him keep half of the proceeds. He even joined his father and brother on one of their business trips out of Jiaxing, and would begin to learn more about the business and the hardships they faced.

上图：
《全家福》油画，2018 年，孙景刚
（右起：张宝荣，大儿子张建明，
小儿子张华明，妻子史月英）

ABOVE
Sun Jinggang, *Family Portrait*, 2018, Oil on canvas (From right to left: Zhang Baorong, eldest son Zhang Jianming, youngest son Zhang Hwaming, wife Shi Yueying)

正式进厂后，张宝荣交给儿子的第一个重要任务是，与他一道前往重庆向一个客户催要一笔 20 万元的欠款。当时的红政服装厂困难重重，这笔款项关系着企业的生死存亡。这一趟工作，也让张华明得到了至今难忘也受用的学习和锻炼。

当时的交通条件非常落后，给张宝荣这样雄心勃勃要把生意做到全国的企业家造成很大挑战。而张华明和父亲的这趟重庆之行，更是让他深刻体会到创业之艰。

他们计划的是，先从上海坐火车到贵阳，再从贵阳转火车至重庆，整个行程需要长达 56 个小时。这在现在看来，已经是不可想象的辛苦，但在当时，就连这 56 个小时的行程，也经常因为意外而得不到保障。火车才开到离贵阳还有几个小时的贵定，因火车严重晚点，接到上海铁路局的回程令，所有乘客只能在贵定下车。

贵定是一座小城，离贵阳还有几个小时车程。而当时已是下午 3 点多，为赶时间，又累又饿的张华明和父亲来不及吃饭就赶紧找车去贵阳。"费尽周折才找到一辆小巴，没有坐票，但也只能站了。一路全是盘山公路，途中几次差点晕倒，浑身直冒冷汗。"张华明回忆说。颠簸两个多小时后，终于到了贵阳。按常理，应该找个招待所住一晚，但一心想尽早赶到重庆的张宝荣父子，只是简单吃了点东西，就又坐上了从昆明出发经停贵阳前往重庆的火车。

At that time, the recovery of receivables was often a matter of life-and-death for small and medium-sized firms. With an outstanding payment of 200,000 CNY owed by a Chongqing client being constantly delayed, Hwaming and his father embarked on a debt-collection journey.

Public transport at the time was extremely inconvenient and the outbound journey took them over 70 hours. Their train from Shanghai to Guiyang terminated at Guiding County, and they had to rush to take the minibus with standing-only tickets from Guiding to Guiyang, before transferring to another overnight train to Chongqing. "We searched frantically around for an available minibus, before finding one with only standing tickets left. The road we took was winding and hilly with many twists and turns, ups and downs, that it left me nauseous throughout the journey. I almost fainted a few times," recalled Hwaming. The long and arduous journey left Hwaming famished, drained and in cold sweat for many parts of the trip, as he even chose to sleep on a newspaper under the train seat. However, he would experience first-hand one of the many trials his father had to go through.

在前往重庆的火车上，张华明已是极度困倦了。"直接在车座下面贴着报纸就睡着了，睡了一夜。"又是六七个小时的颠簸后，他们终于在第二天清早赶到了重庆，好不容易找到一个招待所准备休息一下，但招待所却还没有腾出房间。

无奈之下，已经颠簸了70多个小时的张华明，只得将行李放在招待所，在等待入住期间，父子俩强打着精神，在招待所附近的长江大桥拍摄了一张纪念照。几十年过去，依然可以看出照片中年方二十的张华明风尘仆仆，神情疲惫。

重庆的客户当时也是经营困难，即便张宝荣已经催债上门，也无法偿还款项。而家里的工厂事务众多，于是，张宝荣将张华明介绍给客户之后，便赶回了嘉兴，留张华明在重庆，等待客户想办法筹款归还。

张华明虽然欠缺经验，但他坚定地接受了父亲交付给他的任务，并且充满信心地相信自己可以做好。认真了解调查之后，张华明发现，客户并非不讲诚信，而是的确拿不出钱来。接下来该怎么办？遵循父亲"要做好事，先要做好人"的原则，他决定给客户宽限时间，让客户去想办法，自己则尽可能帮客户做一些事情，大家一起想办法，渡难关。

Upon arriving at the hostel in Chongqing in the early hours of the morning and expecting to finally have a good rest, they were told that there were no available rooms and had to wait for the earliest checkout. The photo they took together at the nearby Chongqing Yangtze River Bridge, with extreme fatigue and disinterest written all over Hwaming's face while waiting for the room, would turn out to be a nostalgic memory of a father and son's entrepreneurial adventure together.

Their client's business happened to be in trouble at the time and was not able to pay off the debt immediately. Baorong had to rush back to his factory, so he handed Hwaming his first official task — ensure the successful collection of the outstanding payment. Hwaming had little experience in business but he nevertheless accepted the task without hesitation. He followed his father's teachings, placed himself in his father's shoes, and remained humble and sincere in his dealings with the client. He did not rush his client, knowing that he had his own frustrations and dilemmas too, and even decided to help the client with his business.

筚路蓝缕，以启山林

上图：
1990 年 11 月，张宝荣与小儿子张华明赴重庆催要应收款时在重庆长江大桥边合影

右图：
1990 年代，张宝荣出差路途上常用的行李箱

ABOVE
Zhang Baorong and his youngest son, Zhang Hwaming, by the Chongqing Yangtze River Bridge, travels to Chongqing to collect an outstanding payment, November 1990

RIGHT
The suitcase that Zhang Baorong used during his business trips, 1990s

他住进重庆陕西北路 47 号的一间招待所，白天去客户公司，帮忙接电话、搞卫生、倒茶水，有时候还帮客户一起出摊；周末，他又到客户家中，"他们打打麻将，我倒倒水，关系处得很好。"同时，他还让父亲一直写信，跟客户说明工厂当前的情形。父亲的信写到第三封，对方被感动了。"小张，你们父子这么好，我们觉得对不起你们。我再困难，也要把钱凑一凑，给你打一张支票。"两个月后，客户兑现诺言，还特意为张华明买了一张回程的卧铺票。

就这样，凭着这颗赤诚坚毅的心，张华明结束了原可能遥遥无期的催款之旅。回忆当时，张华明颇为感慨。但凡在事上未曾怀抱纯澈、简单的憧憬，或许待人接物的方式，也就不会是这样的。"这就是做好人的力量！"短短两月，张华明把对方当成贵人，因为这是他第一次凭借自己的能力为工厂贡献，也建立了可贵的自信。这次经历，真切地让张华明理解了父亲那句"要做好事，先做好人"的信仰，并在日后以此为人生指引，影响着雅莹的点点滴滴。

重庆的回款让工厂解了燃眉之急，让张宝荣看到了年仅 20 岁小儿子的能力。同时，这也大大鼓舞了历经两次高考失利的张华明，让他以更大的热情参与到企业中，从家族事业的旁观者变成了参与者。

1991 年，刚刚在北京设立首个外省经营办事处的张宝荣，又委张华明以重任：去北京开拓市场。

Hwaming stayed in Chongqing for two whole months, helping his client with taking calls and manning the store, even helping to clean the office and make drinks. Hwaming also had the idea to have his father write letters to the client from Jiaxing, informing the client of their conditions at the factory, so that the client would also understand the challenges they too were facing. By the third letter, the client was so moved by both Baorong and Hwaming's efforts and spirit, that he not only paid off the debt, but also paid for Hwaming's return ticket.

The debt recovery greatly helped to address the factory's immediate need for funds and allowed Baorong to learn what his son was made of. Most importantly, it established the young man's confidence in tackling future challenges. Hwaming had accomplished an almost impossible task at that time and he felt so strongly the power of being kind and virtuous, that affirmed his belief in his father's ethos of "being a virtuous person if we want to succeed in life." Until today, he continues to speak of this Chongqing client, grateful to the client for giving him such a valuable experience both in work and as a person.

In 1991, Baorong assigned him the next important task: developing the Beijing market.

做出零售新高度
RETAIL NEW HEIGHTS

1991 年 6 月，张宝荣承包经营的"嘉兴洛东红政服装厂"已小有起色，并更名为"嘉兴洛东制衣厂"。父亲努力发展生产经营的同时，21 岁的张华明也被派以新的重任：去北京发展。

他的任务是，接手经营父亲与两个合伙人在北京大栅栏福隆商场合租的柜台。进店的第一天，张华明要大干一番的热情就被浇了冷水：他们所拥有的说是商场柜台，其实只是角落里的一个小卖档；货品参差不齐，门可罗雀。

"男士衬衫卖不掉，童装卖不掉，很多东西都卖不掉。"但自己来了，就得解决问题。张华明一一分析后，认为当务之急是要想办法让销售转动起来。一番深入思考后，他想出了破解的办法：主动走出去，参加展销会，寻找更多的销售机会。

于是，他一边安排柜台员工卖货，一边到处打探各种展销会的消息，然后带着大包小包地在各个服装展销会推销。当时快要入冬，大家开始卖冬装，张华明手里只有一堆库存的尾货，没有冬天的衣服，于是他又回嘉兴进了一批羊毛衫。利用嘉兴羊毛衫在市场上的知名度，他在福隆商场试图把生意维持下去，也在维持中继续寻找机会。

这个过程中，张华明还遇到过不少挑战。对店里的营业员充分了解后，他觉得父亲请来的某个四川妹子工作态度和能力有问题，想要辞退对方。但福隆商场的老书记知道后，对他说了不，还教育了他一顿。"老书记正正规规的，不同意，说这是你爸爸来当时钦点的要她做营业员，你怎么有权力……我几乎跟他吵架，后来还在他家里面听他悉心教导。"

In June 1991, Hongzheng's business started to pick up, and it took on a new name: Luodong Clothing Manufacturing Factory. 21-year-old Hwaming was assigned the new task of developing the Beijing market. His father and two partners had rented a retail counter in the Fulong Department Store in Beijing, but Hwaming felt deflated as soon as he took over its management. The retail counter was more like a grocery store, as both the counter and the storage area were a mess: men's, women's, children's clothing, thick or thin, were all piled and mixed together, without a single item selling well. Furthermore, the counter was located in a corner with weak traffic.

With issues abound, Hwaming began to review the problems one by one, and like his father, thought outside the box, concluding that instead of being passive and waiting for customers to come by, they needed to expand their sales channels. He began carrying bags of garments to pitch to organisers of various trade fairs and exhibitions, seeking opportunities to join. As winter approached, he realised the counter did not have any winter clothes, and rather than simply waiting it out, he returned to Jiaxing to bring the city's well-known wool sweaters to Beijing.

左图：

1990 年，张宝荣与创业伙伴为开拓新渠道，在北京大栅栏福隆商店租下柜台。1991 年，他派张华明接手经营，发展北京市场

LEFT

Zhang Baorong and his partners begin to seek new retail channels and venture into Beijing in 1990. Thereafter, he sends Zhang Hwaming to expand the company's Beijing market in 1991

但张华明以一个好心态（沉住气），跟老书记一条一条地把道理讲清楚，最终双方听取各自的意见，以情动人，找到问题的根源，跟四川妹子耐心沟通，反而让业绩做得更好了。老书记还因此跟张华明建立了很好的关系，觉得这个年轻人不但有想法、有办法，而且处理事情也很周到。

主动走出去的过程中，一个偶然的机会，张华明找到了打开北京市场的更好法宝，也让他感受到主动与人打交道，主动建立人脉，以真诚待人的力量，再一次体会到"先做好人，才能做好事"的真谛。

当时，北京城乡贸易中心正筹备开业。这是后来在相当长一段时间内北京最为热门的商场之一，专注于拓展销售渠道的张华明热切地希望自己能入驻其中。苦于入驻无门之际，他在福隆商场经营的人脉帮助了他：北京城乡贸易中心开业之前，也曾在福隆商场开过专柜；当张华明找到城乡贸易中心招商负责人副总经理黄雷女提出进驻请求时，黄雷女听说他来自福隆商场，便打电话给福隆商场经理王建英了解张华明的情

Hwaming was also a good communicator. His efforts in proactively talking with people and treating them with sincerity and respect soon won rewards. Beijing Urban and Rural Trade Centre was due to open, which would later become one of the most popular department stores in Beijing for a long time. Hwaming had astutely identified the trade centre's potential, and on one of his many attempts to lease a space, Huang Lei, the then Leasing deputy general manager, made a routine verification call to Fulong Department Store's general manager, Wang Jian Ying, who recommended Hwaming with confidence: "Hwaming is a good man, with strong integrity and capabilities."

上图：
1990 年代早期，张华明与戴雪明
在北京共同开拓市场期间于天安门
广场合影

ABOVE
Zhang Hwaming and Dai Xueming at
the Tiananmen Square during their
venture in Beijing, early 1990s

况。而这位王建英当时已是张华明非常好的朋友，接到电话便对黄雷女说："华明这个人很好啊，人品好，又能干。"更巧的是，黄雷女还是杭州人。一番交谈下来，她心中也对这位小老乡充满了欣赏之情。于是，张华明很顺利地就进驻到了城乡贸易中心，实现了一个对当时的他来说，堪称伟大的飞跃：一举打入了北京商场的"至高点"。

当时的张华明还只是一个服装销售的个体户，却能与很多大品牌一样，在北京最好的商场，也是中国最好的商场拥有自己的一席之地。这得益于他敢于力争上游的开拓进取精神，也显示出这位年轻经营者的视野、雄心和格局，早已超越了小生意人的层级。攻入"至高点"的成功，不光让张华明有了一个崭新的、更高层级的舞台，而且给他带来巨大的无形资产：在商场拓展的领域，一旦进入一家"至高点"式的商场，就有了背书，也有了敲开其他商场的成功筹码。

心思敏锐、一心想要求得更好、更快发展的张华明，很快便有了新目标：北京另一家热门商场——复兴商业城。相对成熟的复兴商业城当时已很难打进，张华明多番努力后，才在

Hwaming would successfully open shop in the trade centre, achieving a rare feat by joining the ranks among many established brands despite being a self-employed garment retailer. His vision and ambition were beyond most small businesses' dreams.

This critical step had not only taken the business to new heights, but also served as a glowing reference and a stepping-stone to even more top-quality department stores. Hwaming soon set a new goal, eyeing Fuxing Department Store, another popular venue in Beijing. He managed to rent a counter about 4 metres wide and 1.5 metres deep, and despite its small size, the counter was the exact opportunity he needed to open more doors. He had come to realise that a factory must own its own retail channels to move forward and believed in the importance of selling directly to customers — a belief that would later spur the company's transformational growth.

"

以渠道发展带动服装销售，
以畅销产品推动销售业绩，
以销售业绩再推动渠道，
这一系列的动作下来，
张华明为日后的品牌发展、渠道模式探索积累了宝贵的经验。

"

一个角落处获得一个约 4 米宽 1.5 米进深的柜台，但他也愉快地接受了。他不把这个 6 平方米的柜台当成柜台看，而是当成一个全新的机会去看。他要的，就是机会。他相信，给自己一扇窗，他终会打开整扇门。

那时，张华明已经意识到服装工厂必须自建渠道，必须直接面向消费者的重要性，这是他在北京最大的收获之一，也至今是雅莹的核心策略之一。这几平方米，就是他的新渠道。几平方米，而且在角落，如何才能获得成功？张华明在决定进入之时，就有了清晰的主意：将有限的资金和柜台，都运用到上市即可大卖的产品上。也就是选择最受欢迎的商品卖，走"爆款"拉动路线——虽然那时还没有"爆款"这个词。

从福隆商场开始，张华明便已深刻意识到商品对商贸的重要性。"如果没有好的商品，再好的销售策略和场地，也无法取得好的销售业绩。"这让他养成商品至上的经营思维，也就是现在企业家们强调的产品力精神。正值 1993 年秋末，张华明仔细观察购物的消费者，发现一款高翻领羊毛衫很受欢迎。嘉兴本就盛产羊毛衫，于是，他立即回家采购一批高翻领羊毛衫，并且得到贵人支持。当时嘉兴毛纺总厂下属生产服务公司的门店负责人徐华与张宝荣相识，也和张华明很是投缘，很支持张华明的想法。

后来加入雅莹做过厂长的徐华当时主动表示，可以帮助张华明组织生产，确保供应。在他的支持下，张华明一口气购进了 25 种颜色的高翻领羊毛衫，并且给每种颜色配了两个尺码——适合北方人的大号与中号。最终，张华明确定了黑色、藏青色、香蕉黄、玫红和咖啡色五种颜色作为重点，其他作

Hwaming's experiences had deepened his understanding about the significance of good products in retail. "It is impossible to increase sales without good products, no matter how great the sales strategy or venue." He therefore attached great importance to product management — a term that is extremely relevant to entrepreneurs today — while gradually cultivating an acute sense of judgement for product forecasting and planning.

With his limited funds and space, he decided to focus only on popular products favoured by customers. It was the end of autumn and beginning of winter, and Hwaming found that wool turtleneck sweaters were popular with women. Furthermore, Jiaxing was home to high-quality wool sweaters, and he received strong support from close friend, Xu Hua, a store manager for one of the outlets under Jiaxing Wool Textile Factory, who agreed to supply him with sweaters. Hwaming decided to launch the wool turtleneck sweaters in 25 colours at once, with only two sizes per colour, which were the closest fit for local women. He recalled, "I continued to closely observe, taking note of which colours and sizes sold best. We would then focus our efforts on the popular colours."

Gradually, Hwaming streamlined the products to five colours: black, navy blue, banana yellow, rose red and coffee. As expected, the sales revenue was outstanding, at over 250,000 CNY per month. It was unbelievable that a small counter in a small corner could perform much better than prominent retail areas in the mall, and the department store management took notice, offering Hwaming a bigger and better space. Good retail channels create sales opportunities, popular products drive sales and strong sales performance attracts more retail channels. This cycle of growth was a key learning that Hwaming took with him from his venture in Beijing.

左页左图：
1990 年代的北京复兴商业城

OPPOSITE LEFT
Beijing Fuxing department store, 1990s

左页右图：
1993 年，公司在北京复兴商业城热销的 25 色高翻领毛衣

OPPOSITE RIGHT
The company's popular wool turtleneck sweater sold in 25 colours in Beijing Fuxing department store, 1993

为陪衬，集中力量推向市场。如其所料，这批羊毛衫的销售业绩出奇的好，每月销售额超过 25 万元。一个角落里的柜台坪效竟比其他显要位置的柜台要高出很多。看到这个成绩的复兴商场对张华明也是信心大增，马上给了他更大、更好的位置。以渠道发展带动时装销售，以畅销产品推动销售业绩，以销售业绩再推动渠道，这一系列的动作下来，张华明为日后的品牌发展、渠道模式探索积累了宝贵的经验。

秋冬时装有着落了，春夏季时装怎么办？1993 年 8 月，张宝荣的一个同行，嘉兴栖真的一家厂商生产了一批桑波缎（真丝提花）材料的圆领衬衫却销售无门，于是找到张华明代为销售。"当时感觉产品一般，我也没太注意，只是放在长安商场柜台顺便卖一下。大概两个星期，我过去一看，卖光了。"

这个意料之外的成绩，让张华明喜出望外，"我发现北京的顾客非常喜欢这种真丝面料，好像发现一个新大陆。"这也让他看到一个新的重要商机——在北京加大江南丝绸服饰的销售。杭嘉湖（杭州、嘉兴和湖州）素来有着"丝绸之府"的美誉，但当时的嘉兴丝绸大多做外贸。受栖真真丝衬衫销售成功的启发，张华明认为，伴随国内诸如北京这样大城市的消费水平和需求提升，嘉兴丝绸服装这样的优质产品，也应该分享给国内消费者。

这个新大陆的发现，让张华明找到了春夏季时装的着落，也找到了不同于一般同行的经营新路径，并且奠定了以丝绸为开端，坚持高品质面料与服饰的文化，开创出商品经营的新高峰。他的商品、渠道思维和本领，也一天天更加成熟、领先，为他日后带领雅莹打下坚实的基础。

Having enjoyed a successful Autumn-Winter season, Hwaming turned his attention to the upcoming Spring-Summer season. In August 1993, one of his peers in the town of Qizhen, Jiaxing, found that his round-neck silk jacquard tops for women were difficult to sell locally, so he turned to Hwaming for help. "I felt that the product was average and I didn't pay much attention. After two weeks, I checked and found that they had been sold out."

Hwaming was delighted by the unexpected result: "Clearly, women in Beijing adore the silk fabric, as if they discovered a new world!" It also allowed him to see an important new business opportunity — increasing the sale of Jiangnan silk garments in Beijing. Hangzhou, Jiaxing and Huzhou had always been known as the "Home of Silk", but Jiaxing's silk was mostly sold for export. Inspired by the successful sales of the silk garments, Hwaming believed that with the increase in consumption and demand from large cities such as Beijing, fine materials and Chinese products — such as Jiaxing's silk garments — should also be shared with local Chinese consumers.

Thereafter, Hwaming would embark on a different path from his peers. He would focus on silk products, high-quality materials and fashionable creations, establishing new retail and product strategies that would begin laying an important foundation for the company's future growth.

顾客思维, 商品经营
CUSTOMER-CENTRIC PRODUCT MANAGEMENT

有了将优质真丝桑波缎加工成真丝衬衣，面向北京市场销售的设想后，张华明快速地采取了行动。一旦看准机会，便抓紧落实，这也是张华明一贯的风格。

他向叔叔以两分的利息借了两万贷款，采购到一批真丝面料，交给洛东制衣厂生产真丝衬衫，由自己到北京销售。"打听到海宁长安镇长安丝织厂有一批零料销售，10 块钱一米，一共2000 米，都不是成品，是 10 米以内的零料，我租了一辆夏利车，全给买下来，拉回家生产了。"

张宝荣知道消息后，还一度批评张华明不该购买零料。"他说我买的是零料，做不了衣服，打电话给我，问我是没长眼睛还是怎么了的。"但后来，洛东制衣厂解决了生产问题，一共生产了 1800 多件真丝衣服，发到北京，很快销售一空 。之后，张宝荣继续加大对真丝衬衫的投入，而张华明则继续创造着很好的销售业绩。

这也是张华明第一次将自己的销售能力、渠道和父亲的洛东厂结合起来，第一次从纯粹的进货再转卖，转向自己采购面料，自己设计生产，然后自己销售。

张华明探索出的真丝衬衫的成功，也引起了复兴商场经理沈林秀的注意 。她希望进一步扩大商场对真丝衬衫的经营，于是找到张华明，希望他帮助商场采购更多的产品。张华明愉快地同意了，及时联系了一个厂家：江苏金坛晨风集团，约好和沈林秀一起前往采购。

With his eyes set on selling high-quality silk garments in Beijing, Hwaming acted swiftly, which was also one of his father's character traits — seizing opportunities at every chance. He borrowed 20,000 CNY from his uncle, ordered a batch of silk fabric, had his father's factory manufacture the silk tops and personally brought them over to Beijing. He recalled, "My father was initially angry with me because the silk fabric I had purchased were leftovers that he believed were useless for making any garments, even chiding me for being blind." However, the factory managed to solve the problem and produced more than 1,800 silk tops which quickly sold out — winning over Baorong, who increased production, allowing Hwaming to continue setting new sales records. Hwaming had upgraded the factory's purchase-and-resale model into an end-to-end business model that included procurement, production, design and sales, all built on the foundation of a consumer-centric product management strategy.

Hwaming's success also attracted the attention of Shen Linxiu, manager at Fuxing Department Store. Linxiu wanted the store to provide consumers with more silk tops, so she approached Hwaming to help her to bring in more silk products. Hwaming happily agreed and made an appointment with the manufacturer, personally accompanying Linxiu for procurement.

上图：
1990 年代，公司在北京商场热销的真丝女装

ABOVE
The company's best-selling women's silk
apparel in Beijing department stores, 1990s

"我们在嘉兴市叫了辆出租车，大概 5 个小时到了晨风集团。沈经理随身带了几十万的汇票，到了工厂，却被告知没有现货，我们只能空手回嘉兴，一路倾盆大雨。沈经理在车上就跟我说，'华明啊，我们拿着汇票，长途跋涉，买不到货。你要争口气，给我好好干！'"

好好干的最后结果就是，沈林秀应张华明的邀请，考察了张宝荣的洛东制衣厂，然后决定分两次，每次预付给张华明 50 万元，由他全权组织采购，由洛东制衣厂生产，落实真丝衬衫的经营，钱则由张华明在商品销售之后从销售款中扣还。

一个柜台和商场建立这样的合作，这在复兴商场还从没有过，张华明也因此把渠道经营做到了更高境界。而沈林秀之所以如此支持张华明，很重要的原因是出于对张华明经营能力和品德的信任。众多柜台供应商中，张华明是一个"异类"；他从不靠送礼、请吃饭、KTV 唱歌、喝酒来拉业务，除了忙工作，他几乎把所有业余时间都用于读书和整理自己的业务了。沈林

"It took us about 5 hours by taxi from Jiaxing to arrive at the factory. Manager Shen took hundreds of thousands from the bank only to be told that there was no stock. We had to return empty-handed. Furthermore, it rained heavily throughout our journey. Manager Shen said to me in the car, 'Hwaming, we travelled all this way in vain. There must be some other way!'"

This other way involved inviting Linxiu to his father's factory. After inspecting the factory, Linxiu was very impressed and promptly agreed to pay Hwaming 500,000 CNY in advance each time. Hwaming would take the full responsibility of procurement, production and sales, and the advance payment could be deducted later from the sales revenue. This kind of collaboration between a retail counter and a department store was unheard of at Fuxing Shopping Centre, and was clearly an innovative business model. Linxiu supported Hwaming because she trusted him completely. She felt that Hwaming was an outlier among the retailers, as he never tried to win business with gifts or entertainment. Instead, he spent his spare time reading and thinking about his business.

66

'我每天在长安街上走，
至少可以看到十多个顾客穿着我们的衣服。'
如今再谈起北京这段往事，
张华明还是难掩得意。

99

秀回忆，当时北京服装市场的消费者购买力还较为低下，以中低端产品为主流，品牌意识薄弱，外包装简单粗陋，但张华明的服装都是叠放整齐、包装精美，连特别定制的装衣袋、展示陈列的衣架都准备齐全。如此事无巨细的考量带来的美好产品形象，深深打动了她。"我们看到了这个老板'行'！这促使我们决心与他合作！"沈林秀说。

得到这个巨大的支持后，张华明说服父亲借一笔钱，提升了工厂的生产能力。1994 年夏天，洛东制衣厂如期完成了这批真丝衬衫的生产，发往北京后很快销售一空。在此基础上，北京王府井等几家最有名的商场主动上门谈合作，让父亲继续扩大生产，一战成名。"我每天在长安街上走，至少可以看到十多个顾客穿着我们的衣服。"如今再谈起北京这段往事，张华明还是难掩得意。

洛东制衣厂也经由张华明这些创新开拓的推动，告别贴牌为主或者只能生产相对低端大路货的模式，走向产销一体而且将产品打入高端市场的新道路。这是一个具有重大质变意义的突破，堪称伟大的转折：1991 年到 1994 年，工厂的销售收入从 21.67 万元增加到 256.81 万元，翻了 10 多倍。熬过万事开头难的洛东制衣厂终于开始盈利。尤其是 1994 年，在真丝衬衫的支持下，洛东制衣厂即便发生了被盗窃 800 件成衣的事故，依然获得了可观的利润。

Linxiu was also impressed with how Hwaming organised his retail counter: everything from the garment folding, to the customised packaging, to the arrangement of the clothing hangers, was neat and stylish. This was in stark contrast to most of the other counters that had poor brand awareness and packaging.

Hwaming persuaded his father to take out a loan to increase the factory's production capacity to meet the new demands of this collaboration. In the summer of 1994, the factory completed the order of silk tops as scheduled, which then sold out almost immediately. Several of the most famous department stores in Beijing, such as Wangfujing, came forward to discuss similar collaborations.

Hwaming would always be overwhelmed with pride when he shared his Beijing experience, "Every day, when I walked along Chang'an Avenue, I could see at least a dozen customers wearing our clothes."

The factory finally bid farewell to the OEM model of mass production of low-end garments and moved towards integration of production and sales, making a strategic leap into the higher-end market.

张华明在北京开辟了新天地，张宝荣和张建明也在大本营打开了新局面。他们先是很好地完成了真丝衬衫的生产，然后还将其带到南方销售，取得不错的成绩，让洛东制衣厂在春夏季有了成熟的产品和市场。同时，他们也带领洛东制衣厂在开发、生产秋冬产品上进行了新的探索。1994 年，一位朋友带给张宝荣一款使用双层衬衫面料、配有可脱卸衬衫领的金属棉新型男式衬衫。衬衫领口与袖口是最容易弄脏的地方，当时，大部分人都还没有经济能力买太多衬衫，可脱卸式领口与袖口的设计，可以兼顾讲卫生和经济实惠的需求。一向对服装款式敏感的张宝荣立即嗅出了其中的商机，决定自己也生产这种衬衫。

张华明对父亲的这个决定并不看好，因为金属棉衬衫的加工难度远高于真丝衬衫，洛东制衣厂的设备和工艺相对落后，按照当时的市场情况估算，就算做出来也难有好的利润。但工厂需要有产品来支持秋冬季的生产，于是也支持父亲一试。"我从头到尾都不看好金属棉这个产品，但没办法，你夏季做得再好，突然歇着也是不行的，你不能不做事。"

This was a ground-breaking milestone for the business: from 1991 to 1994, its sales revenue grew more than ten-fold from 216,700 to 2,568,100 CNY. In 1994, the factory made a handsome profit which was underpinned by the soaring sales of its silk tops.

While Hwaming was busy breaking into new markets, Baorong and Jianming also made exciting progress at the factory. They successfully completed Beijing's order of silk tops and even achieved strong results by selling these tops to cities in the south. Baorong also continued to expand the factory's product offerings. In 1994, a friend brought him a new type of men's double-layered poly-cotton shirt with detachable collars and cuffs. At that time, most people could not afford to buy multiple shirts, hence, these detachable collars and cuff designs helped solved hygiene issues and represented more value for money. Baorong decided to invest in the opportunity.

在大家的共同努力下，洛东制衣厂最终开发、生产出了自己的金属棉衬衫，并且还进一步创新：增配了一套领口和袖口以便替换。张宝荣对这款产品信心十足。他派出营销主力王阿六和杨和英攻坚市场。王、杨在集体工厂时就与张宝荣结识，作为洛东制衣厂的员工，也是张宝荣最得力的左膀右臂。在他们的齐心协力之下，金属棉衬衫虽然果真如张华明所料，没有什么利润，但也渐渐打开销路，令工厂在秋冬也有了稳定的产品方向。

经由这一轮的发展，张家父子的分工更为明确；父亲全面领导，哥哥张建明主要负责产品开发和设计，弟弟张华明主要负责市场和销售。在两代人一步步的探索和创新下，洛东制衣厂也逐渐摆脱困境，走上正轨。

最让张宝荣欣慰的还是张华明在北京市场的表现。短短几年，张华明就把一个半死不活的小柜台生意化腐朽为神奇，不但陆续和北京15家著名商场达成合作，销售业绩也蒸蒸日上。

However, Hwaming was not as optimistic as his father about the new shirts. First, the production was more difficult than the silk tops. Second, the cost was greater and production less profitable. Nonetheless, he supported his father's decision because the factory needed products for the autumn and winter season, and despite the smaller profit margin, it provided a steady income.

The roles between father and sons became clearer as they cleared hurdle after hurdle and ensured the factory's continuous growth. Baorong led the team; his elder son, Jianming, looked after product development and design; and his younger son, Hwaming, focused on marketing and sales, making his father especially proud by successfully capturing retail spaces in 15 high-end department stores in Beijing in a short span of time.

情系服装创未来
A FASHION LOVE STORY

在这一时期，张华明还遇到了他创业路上，也是雅莹创业史上的一位重要人物——他的太太、雅莹集团现任副总裁戴雪明。

张华明和戴雪明，因为一次偶然相遇，而有了一生的幸运缘分。1992 年正月初十，戴雪明的父亲煲了一锅鸡汤，让她送到平时在北京做生意，难得回一趟家的姐姐家，让姐姐补养身体。当戴雪明赶到姐姐家时，姐姐姐夫正在家里宴请两位在北京做生意并与之合租在一个四合院的两位客人，而客人之中的一位，正是当时刚刚 20 岁出头回到家乡的张华明。

之后，张华明与戴雪明开始了交往，并相互欢喜，开始了恋爱。第二年，张华明到戴雪明家过了春节，两人正式确定了关系。戴雪明性格直爽干脆，家中从事着羊毛衫生意，也是从小对服装和生意耳濡目染。之后，她第一时间跟随张华明到了北京，开始了携手打拼的岁月。

当时，戴雪明还不到 20 岁，只有八九十斤的体重，但一到北京就成为张华明的得力搭档。她吃苦耐劳，常常一个人拖着三四箱货坐地铁四处奔走；她聪明伶俐，很快就熟悉了各个商场动态，并且练出很好的销售本领，面对客户，她都会先在心里打好腹稿，把产品的优势和顾客的需求结合起来，尽可能将产品卖到最好。特别要提到当时热销的真丝时装，戴雪明和张华明一致认为："那时候的丝绸在江浙一带非常有名，这些最好的丝绸全部出口到国外很可惜，要把好的材料、好的产品分享给中国的顾客！"

It was also during this period that Hwaming met his wife, Dai Xueming, another important figure in the company's development, and now vice president and deputy CEO of EP YAYING Fashion Group.

A chance encounter brought the two together. Hwaming and Xueming met each other on the 13th of February 1992, when Xueming's father asked her to bring a pot of chicken soup over to her elder sister, who worked in Beijing and was on a rare trip back home. When she brought the soup over, her sister and brother-in-law were hosting two guests from Beijing. One of the guests was the 22-year-old Hwaming.

The two soon started dating and fell in love. The following year, Hwaming went to Xueming's house for Spring Festival and the two officially confirmed their relationship. Xueming's family ran a wool knitwear business, and she too had been fascinated by the garment industry and the idea of running a business since childhood. Xueming had a forthright personality and quickly made the decision to join Hwaming in his venture in Beijing, where the two would begin an unforgettable entrepreneurial journey together.

Despite outward appearances with her slight frame and being under 20, Xueming became Hwaming's best business partner in Beijing. She was a strong-willed person who never wilted under pressure, often hauling three or four boxes of products through the metro around Beijing. She was an intelligent girl with a great personality, quickly familiarising herself with the ins and outs of the various department stores and developing strong sales skills. Before meeting store managers, she would always prepare her proposal thoroughly and rehearse many times in her head, ensuring that the product features were aligned closely with their needs. Especially with silk

上图：
1990 年代早期，张华明与戴雪明在
北京共同开拓市场期间于北京世界
公园合影

下图：
1990 年代早期，张华明与戴雪明在
北京共同开拓市场期间于香山合影

ABOVE

Zhang Hwaming and Dai Xueming at the
Beijing World Park during their venture
in Beijing, early 1990s

BELOW

Zhang Hwaming and Dai Xueming at the
Fragrant Hills Park during their venture
in Beijing, early 1990s

> "
> 当时丝绸在江浙一带非常有名，
> 这些最好的丝绸全部出口到国外很可惜，
> 要把好的材料、好的产品
> 分享给中国的顾客！
> "

最重要的是，戴雪明不但有奋斗精神和事业使命，还是真正将劳动创造视为快乐、光荣和生命价值的人。她性格豪爽，待人真诚，开放、包容、热情、刻苦，聪明智慧，热爱钻研服装本身，常有奇思妙想，在业务经营中侧重负责产品创意的部分，并享受于此。"好玩儿"是她的口头禅。她曾说，自己从来不觉得干活是苦的，一直到现在，某件衣服卖得好，或者做出一件顾客喜欢的衣服，她依然觉得很有价值、很有成就感，是件值得开心的事……

当时，虽然生意还不错，但张华明和戴雪明都非常节俭。他们居住在只有十几平方米的四合院隔出来的简易房里，昏暗、闭塞。但艰苦的条件并没有影响他们的信心，反而激发他们要更努力。到今天，戴雪明还很为当年的选择、坚持感到欣慰。她说："一定要记得让自己强大起来，这比什么都重要，因为未来的路是要靠自己去走的，没有人能帮你一辈子。在保持自我的同时，根据环境改变自己才是最重要的，但前提是要做对的选择，选择好了就去做。而且自己要为自己的选择买单，没人有权利或义务为你的选择负责！"

这份笃定，这份艰难中建立的感情，奠定了俩人在北京打拼的深厚情缘，也为雅莹日后的发展塑造了彼此携手前行、无惧无畏的勇气和根基。

garments, she shared Hwaming sentiments: "At that time, silk from Jiangsu and Zhejiang province were very famous, hence, it was such a pity that such good items were all exported. We wanted to let Chinese consumers also enjoy these fine products as well."

Xueming not only worked hard, but also had a strong sense of purpose and enjoyed the grind. She felt fulfilled and proud of her work. In one of her interviews, she shared that she never found work tiring because she loved making clothes that women would fall in love with. She was passionate about fashion, enjoying the entire creative process and often coming up with fun and interesting ideas. "Fun" became her pet phrase.

Despite business doing well, Xueming and Hwaming lived a frugal lifestyle in Beijing. They lived in a small, dim and stuffy room that was only a dozen square metres in size, but the tough conditions never discouraged them, and only served to motivate them to work harder. Xueming never regretted her choice. She said: "One must learn to become stronger and this is more important than anything else, because your own fate is in your hands and nobody can take care of you forever. Stick to your beliefs and remain firm, but also remain flexible and adaptable to changes. If you make a mistake, take full responsibility and move forward, because no one is obliged to take blame for you."

Xueming and Hwaming would develop a relationship of both friendship and love that saw them stick together through thick and thin. Their strong bond, determination, courage and fearlessness would lay an unshakable foundation for the company that they would eventually establish.

在戴雪明的支持下，张华明也在更高的层面思考起实业的未来方向。综合真丝衬衫和金属棉衬衫的成功，他将工厂和北京的经验结合起来，也将生产和销售结合起来思考服装厂的未来，并提出两大发展方向：第一，不再采用之前倒进卖出的纯贸易销售方式，而是利用自己的工厂优势，走自产自销的道路；第二，打破传统工厂"以产定销"模式，而是根据市场上消费者的反馈，按照什么好卖做什么的方式来给工厂下单。

戴雪明认可张华明的这一判断，并跟随他一起，推动事业朝此方向进步。这两大核心理念，也在后来的雅莹得到延续和深化，并最终形成雅莹"以客户为中心"的经营理念，可谓是张华明从做生意迈向真正做企业的开端。

在张华明的推动下，体察和体贴消费者的需求，为消费者创造更好产品的"以销定产"，日渐成为洛东制衣厂的基本理念，并升级着整个"自产自销"作业运营系统。也是从那时开始，张华明就高度重视起供应链的建设，将其作为贯彻市场意识的重要一环——把握住时间，意味着把握住了时机，提高效率就意味着提高了市场的占有率。

"比如星期四我提出要某种款式的衣服，然后通知工厂，工厂星期四下午和晚上就要加班做出来。星期五早晨把产品送上嘉兴到北京的火车。星期六上午我就要从车站把衣服接出来，比快递都快。第二天中午12点以前基本都送到全商场，正好赶上周六、周日的销售日，这个供应链非常快。嘉兴工厂的广播也会每天播送北京市场需求的信息，以便后端及时对前端市场做出反馈。"张华明这样解释他的"以销定产"。

当时，国内的服装企业大都还以代加工为主，基本是批发模式，只追求量的规模，不重视市场需求，张华明的这些创新无疑走在了行业前列，而他这一阶段以"自产自销"模式对洛东服装的推动，也为日后的雅莹从一家有贴牌加工做贴牌加工，没贴牌加工就自己做品牌，缺乏明确发展战略的一般性服装小厂，向以自有品牌、自有店铺一体化模式为核心战略的现代化时尚企业快速发展，打下了坚实基础。但张华明认为，只做这些还不够，要真正可持续并且大有作为，还必须做更多的努力和进步：一是要创造自己的品牌，二是进一步优化自己的产品结构。

With Xueming's full support, Hwaming began to think about the factory's next stage of growth. From his insights on the sale of the women's silk shirts and men's poly-cotton shirts, he proposed that, first, instead of purchasing and processing finished or semi-finished garments and reselling them, the factory should produce and sell only their own products. Second, the current "made-to-stock" model should be replaced by a customer-centric retailing strategy, producing only according to what was popular with customers. Xueming agreed with Hwaming's judgements and worked closely with him to implement his ideas. These two ideas would gradually evolve into the customer-centric management philosophy at the core of the Group's strategy today.

The concept of setting production according to sales forecasts based on consumer insights began to slowly materialise in the factory under Hwaming's management, as the company was slowly working towards producing and selling only their own products. Hwaming paid close attention to supply chain development, as the speed of responses from the supply chain would greatly affect the ability to seize any market opportunities.

"For instance, if I notified the factory on a Thursday morning about manufacturing a batch of garments, the order would be completed and ready for delivery on Friday morning and arrive at Beijing's train station the next morning, where I would pick them up. This was faster than a courier! By noon, all the products would have been delivered to all our retail counters, just in time for the peak weekend sales period. This was the speed of our supply chain. Every day, the Beijing team would also update the factory in Jiaxing regarding any new demands, ensuring their timely response."

These innovative measures were undoubtedly miles ahead of the competition when most domestic garment companies were merely pursuing quantity and scale, rather than quality or market demands. However, in Hwaming's mind, these measures were still not enough for the business to maintain stable growth or expand. They had to work hard and improve: "First, we have to create our own brand. Second, we have to improve our product mix."

规模实力更上层楼
GOING FASHION

北京的经历，极大地拓展了张华明的视野，也放大了他的格局和事业心。

1994 年初，真丝衬衫经营取得阶段性成果时，张华明就有了进一步扩张事业的雄心：他建议父亲将乡里的洛东服装二厂买下来，进一步扩大企业规模。

虽然张宝荣已经算是非常有进取心的创业者，并继北京首个经营办事处之后，相继在沈阳、南京等地设立了经营部，为走向全国完成了万事开头难的关键步伐，但鉴于洛东制衣厂整体规模还很小，他最初还是无不悲观地对张华明表示，收购洛东服装二厂，还只能是一个遥不可及的梦想。

最终，张华明在北京的真丝衬衫大获成功，不但极大地鼓舞了张宝荣扩张事业的信心，也让张宝荣对收购建议有了认真考虑。1994 年获得全年经营业绩的突破之后，张宝荣开始把张华明的建议提上日程了。"有一天，父亲竟然主动告诉我，要把二厂买下来，当时我还在北京，很是吃惊。因为此前他还对这件事相当保守，这让我觉得我们那一两年真的是很成功。"

The experience in Beijing greatly broadened Hwaming's perspective and fuelled his ambition for greater success. In the beginning of 1994, when production of their silk shirts began to hit stride, Hwaming started to think about expansion and suggested to his father that they should consider acquiring the town garment factory's second facility to increase production capacity.

At that time, their factory was still in its infancy, and Baorong thought a second factory was surely an unattainable dream. Nonetheless, it did not stop Baorong from opening offices in Shenyang and Nanjing, a key step in his plan to improve sales across the country. However, Hwaming's success in Beijing made Baorong rethink his initial proposal and he surprised his son with a move to purchase the facility, an indication of their success at that time.

"
永利来时装的诞生，也是一个重要的里程碑。
从此，张家的服装事业走向了
自行设计、自主品牌、自主生产和自主销售的产供销体系，
走向市场，走进百姓。
"

1994 年 9 月，张宝荣最终以 71.8 万元的总价从洛东乡工业办公室买下了洛东服装二厂，将洛东的厂房面积扩大到 5150 平方米。随后，他还向嘉兴市郊区工商行政管理局申请成立了"嘉兴市永利来时装有限责任公司"作为工厂对外的招牌，公司也从红政村搬到洛东镇上，规模、实力都更上层楼。早就具有品牌意识的张宝荣，还同时以"永利来"为名提出了商标申请。

"永利来"寓意永远有利润滚滚而来、紫气东来，但这个商标申请最终却没能成功，因为北京已有一个同类的商标提前占位了。"永利来时装"里的"时装"二字，是张氏父子三人对公司未来的期许——成为一个集设计、品牌、生产与销售一体的全价值链品牌公司；而"有限责任公司"的形式，则意味着永利来正式成为一个以现代企业制度运作的公司，拥有了董事会、监事会。张宝荣为董事长、总经理。

永利来时装的诞生，也是一个重要的里程碑。从此，张家的服装事业走向了自行设计、自主品牌、自主生产和自主销售的产供销体系，走向市场，走进百姓。创业 10 多年的张宝荣，终于有了一家真正属于自己的名副其实的时装生产企业。

In September of 1994, Baorong successfully completed the purchase of the second facility for a total price of 718,000 CNY, expanding his production space to 5,150 square metres. Later, he merged his factory and the new facility, applying to the Jiaxing Suburban Administration of Industry & Commerce to set up a company named Jiaxing Yonglilai Fashion Co., Ltd. He relocated the factory from Hongzheng Village to Luodong Town, signifying a milestone increase in scale and performance. "Yonglilai" in Chinese means "profits keep rolling in," while the word "fashion" reflected Baorong and his sons' vison for the company's future — to become a fashion brand with its own end-to-end value-chain. The private limited company business structure reflected its official transformation into a modern company with a board of directors and a supervisory committee. Baorong was appointed chairman and general manager.

The creation of Yonglilai Fashion was another major milestone for the family business. In a short span of ten or so years, Baorong had grown from trying his hand at setting up a garment factory, to becoming a private owner, to owning a fashion company. His three-part entrepreneurial journey laid a strong foundation in the company's continual transformation into a modern company. With the business now stable, the first thing that entered Baorong's mind was not improving his personal lifestyle, but reinvesting in the company — upgrading production equipment and improving employee welfare. Every penny counted, and his selfless personality once again shone through.

新公司，新气象，而拥有了更大实力和更多利润之后的张宝荣，首先想的不是改善个人生活，而是将钱和资源继续投入公司的发展，并且要用在刀刃上——升级工厂设备，改善员工待遇。

他购入了一批当时比较高端且价格昂贵的设备——大烫设备、电剪刀、大型粘合机、小烫台、圆头锁眼机、撬边机，不但让工厂更具现代企业气质，也大幅提升品质和效率。当时，许多私营工厂都只有大烫机在服装包装前进行整烫，让衣服看上去挺括即可，永利来的小烫台则将熨烫做到衣服的每个关键部位，比如领子、袖窿、门襟等，制衣过程中每缝合一个部位都要熨一次，大幅提升了衣服各个部位与人体之间的服帖感，也让整件衣服最后看上去非常有型。

那一时期，永利来的主要产品依然是衬衫。除了富有创新的金属棉可拆卸式衬衫，张宝荣还以顾客需求导向原则，持续丰富着各种款式，尤其是加大了女式真丝服装的生产，让公司加速向时装化逐步迈进。更好的设备也让产能和品质都得到了极大的提升。

He procured high-end equipment, including pressing machinery, electric sewing scissors, glue filling machines, small ironing stations, eyelet buttonhole sewing machines and blind stitch hemmers, which not only added a sense of modernity to the workplace, but also greatly improved quality and efficiency. At that time, many private factories only pressed their garments once before packaging, but Yonglilai pressed each garment with care and precision throughout the production process — collars, sleeves and plackets. Each component was ironed once before assembly, which effectively improved the fit of the garments and made the finished products look more stylish.

Shirts remained the core products of Yonglilai. In addition to the double-layered detachable poly-cotton shirts, Baorong continued to develop other products and styles based on the demands of customers, such as using cotton and silk blend material for increasing comfort and production of its women's silk shirts.

同样具有创新突破意义的，还包括在员工待遇上的改善。1995年，张宝荣就在全员范围内实行了13薪制度，在当时，连国有企业都鲜有这样的福利。在张宝荣看来，宁可公司不赚钱，也要保障员工的利益，平时讲求按时发薪，年终的13薪也会选择在春节放假前发放，绝不拖延。员工得到更好的报酬，自然更努力投入工作，而公司日新月异的发展，也令大家对未来充满希望。综合因素的推动下，永利来很快进入快速发展阶段。

产能、品质和团队提升的同时，张宝荣父子也继续在市场拓展上创新进取。除了巩固好原有的销售网点，他们还采取了以巩固北京销售主战场为基点，进一步延伸销售面的战略思想，先后在湖南长沙、辽宁沈阳、江苏南京、山西太原、河北石家庄等地，增设网点、窗口、专柜、联合销售和代销点共80多处，一步步扩大着永利来在全国的影响力。

Another new measure was directed at employee welfare. In 1995, Baorong was one of the first to introduce the 13-month salary scheme, unheard of even at most state-owned enterprises. In his view, the interests of employees came first, and in both good and bad years, they should always be remunerated promptly for their work. Better pay and the rapid growth of the company filled everyone at the company with hope and confidence in the future.

此外，张宝荣也依然在品牌经营上执着努力并获得突破。当时，因为温州、义乌一些假冒伪劣产品的影响，全国市场对浙江商品抱有偏见，连雅戈尔等品牌都受到负面影响，但对北京、上海等地的产品格外高看一眼。张宝荣早年就对此有过应对，从上海购买过商标使用权。张华明当初去重庆催款的订单，使用的就是上海迪丽衬衫厂的吊牌。"浙江产品当时被称为 Y（歪）货，火车到义乌时，会被说成是全国最大的 Y 货市场到了。所以，我们用嘉兴的牌子是卖不掉的，父亲于是就想出这个办法，说白了就是买别人的牌子用，而且是临时的，不是买商标，是人家仅授权你使用。一套吊牌两毛钱。"

永利来成立，申请商标失败后，张宝荣还告别过去买吊牌的模式，专门收购了一个上海商标华丽牌的永久使用权，继续借"上海"出海，不断扩大销售的面和量。他的这一举措，不但对永利来当时的市场销售起到极大的拉动作用，也同时让张宝荣自己，以及张华明进一步看到了品牌的价值。这些努力让永利来进入高速增长期。

With improvements made in production capacity, product quality and people management, Baorong and his sons began to spearhead new market expansion plans. They consolidated existing sales in Beijing and expanded further to other key cities, such as Changsha in Hunan Province, Shenyang in Liaoning Province, Nanjing in Jiangsu Province, Taiyuan in Shanxi Province, and Shijiazhuang in Hebei Province, with over 80 retail outlets, gradually increasing the brand's influence across the country.

Yonglilai Fashion was expanding rapidly and would welcome the company's next milestone.

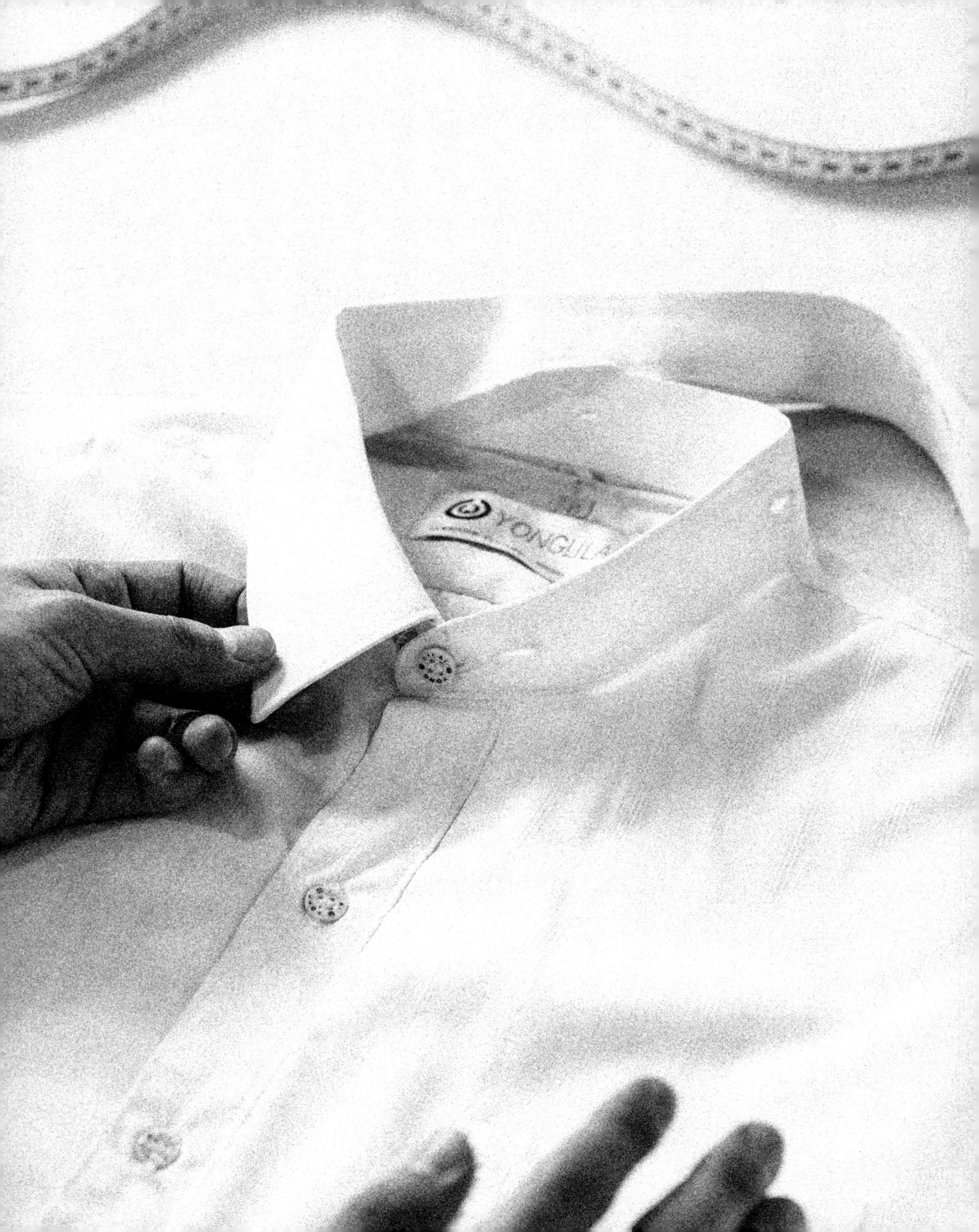

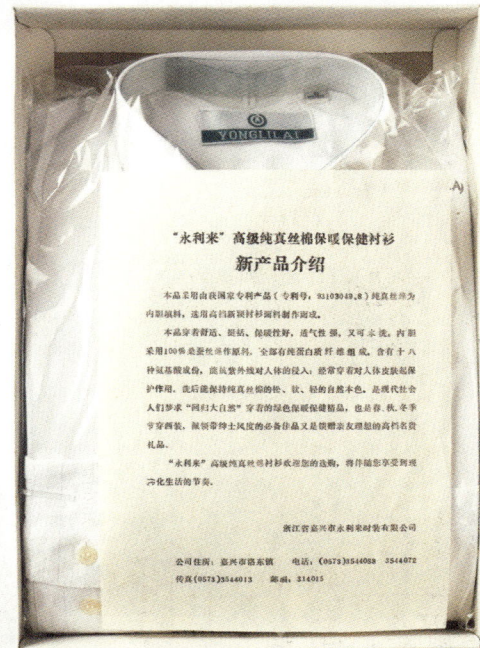

左页 / 上图：

1995 年，永利来自行设计生产的男式金属棉可拆卸式衬衫及包装

OPPOSITE / ABOVE

Men's poly cotton detachable shirt and packaging. Yonglilai Fashion 1995

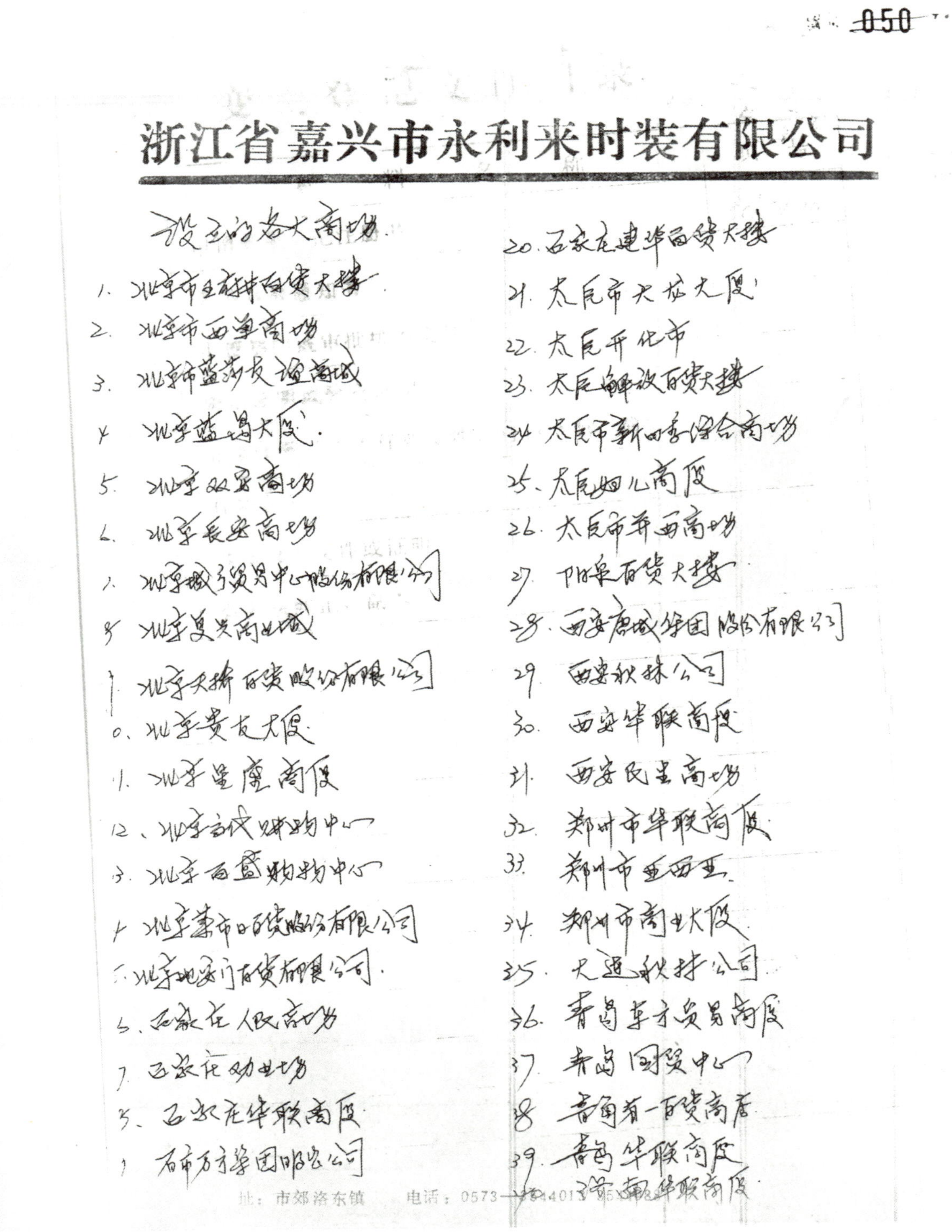

050

浙江省嘉兴市永利来时装有限公司

设立的各大商场

1. 北京市王府井百货大楼
2. 北京市西单商场
3. 北京蓝莎友谊商城
4. 北京蓝岛大厦
5. 北京双安商场
6. 北京长安商场
7. 北京城乡贸易中心股份有限公司
8. 北京复兴商业城
9. 北京天桥百货股份有限公司
10. 北京贵友大厦
11. 北京盈鹰商厦
12. 北京当代购物中心
13. 北京百盛购物中心
14. 北京菜市口百货股份有限公司
15. 北京地安门百货有限公司
16. 石家庄人民商场
17. 石家庄北国商场
18. 石家庄华联商厦
19. 石市万方集团明公司

20. 石家庄建华百货大楼
21. 太原市大华大厦
22. 太原开化市
23. 太原解放百货大楼
24. 太原市新时每综合商场
25. 太原妇儿商厦
26. 太原市开西商场
27. 阳泉百货大楼
28. 西安唐城集团股份有限公司
29. 西安秋林公司
30. 西安华联商厦
31. 西安民生商场
32. 郑州市华联商厦
33. 郑州市亚西亚
34. 郑州市商业大厦
35. 天通秋林公司
36. 青岛丰才贸易商厦
37. 青岛国贸中心
38. 青岛第一百货商店
39. 青岛华联商厦
40. 济南华联商厦

址：市郊洛东镇　　电话：0573—84014013

左页：
1990 年代，永利来时装生产车间

上图：
1993~1997 年，永利来时装全国部分
销售网点分布

OPPOSITE
Yonglilai Fashion's production workshop, 1990s

ABOVE
Yonglilai Fashion's retail locations across China
from 1993 to 1997

雅莹丝绸，展现女性真我风采
YAYING, SILK AND WOMEN'S FASHION

1995 年，在创业状态奋斗了 10 多年的张宝荣，终因长期操劳导致体力不支，且病症在身，他决心交班下一代。

当年 8 月，一番深思熟虑后，他打电话给在北京的张华明，令其从北京回家接班。张建明、张华明兄弟，都继承了张宝荣朴实、仁义、坚毅的品质，但张宝荣认为，性格外向、在经商方面颇有天赋，而且在北京闯出崭新天地的张华明，更能引领公司的未来。

在父亲的召唤下，张华明决定放下自己在北京干得风生水起的事业，以及在大城市闯出大未来的梦想，回到嘉兴接班。但离开北京之前，他做了两件极其重要的事。现在回头看，这也可当是他要新官上任，为未来的布局。

一是侧重女性时装市场，并且注册了"雅莹"商标。

在北京期间，张华明观察并得出一个结论：虽然当时国内的大型时装企业多以男性时装为主，但女性时装市场的空间和潜力更大。因为女性与生俱来地更注重对美与时尚的追求，女性时装有如鲜花般姿态万千、四季更替，其置装需求普遍比男性更高，也更愿意为此消费。

通过这个结论，张华明当时就已对服装厂的未来有了新的想法：转到女性时装领域，既抓住女性时装的机遇，也与当时已经在男装领域非常成功的雅戈尔等企业错位竞争。

In 1995, after more than a decade of dedication and devotion to the business he loved, Baorong, facing health issues, decided to hand the family business over to the next generation. In August 1995, Baorong asked Hwaming to return home from Beijing to take over the company. Both of his sons had inherited their father's integrity, benevolence and determination. However, Baorong believed that Hwaming, with a more personable character and a great talent for business, was better equipped to lead the company into the future. At his father's call, Hwaming put aside his successful work in Beijing and returned home. Before leaving Beijing, he took two actions, which in retrospect, were incredibly significant for the company's future growth.

First, he decided to focus on women's fashion and went on to register the "yaying" trademark.

Hwaming made this momentous decision based on his observations and experience during his five years in Beijing. Although China's dominant garment players at the time focused on men's fashion, he felt that the women's fashion market had greater potential and room to grow. Women love fashion, and they generally have greater needs for clothing than men, along with greater willingness to spend. The successful response to his silk shirts was also a life-changing experience, as not only did he feel pride in his hometown's silk, but he also felt a growing motivation to develop local fabrics specifically for the local market. "Using high-quality materials to make good clothing and bring beauty to women" therefore became the company's aspiration and the future brand direction.

右页：
1995 年 9 月，在北京注册的"雅莹"商标申报资料

OPPOSITE
yaying trademark application in Beijing, September 1995

中國商標事務所
CHINA TRADEMARK SERVICE

嘉兴市永利来时装有限责任公司：

你厂（公司）于 1995 年 9 月 15 日申报的第 25 类商品的"雅莹"商标，经中国商标事务所代理，国家工商局商标局已受理。目前此商标正在审理中。特此证明。

Yaying 雅莹

中国商标事务所

1995 年 9 月 15 日

yaying

雅莹

L
165/90B

"

雅是高雅的雅；莹字上面一个草，下面一个玉，
是宝玉，寓意天然宝贵，晶莹剔透——雅莹两个字都代表'美'。
中国所有美好的含义都表达在这两个字当中。
无论是做产品、做事业，还是做人，这都应该是我们的初心。

"

这也就是后来雅莹的初心：

"用好的材料做好的衣服，为女性顾客带去美。"

好的材料方面，张华明首先确定的重点就是家乡引以为傲的
丝绸，这也是他在北京就有的经营理念的延续：中国时装要
优先中国本土优势的面料去创新发展。确定要做好女性时装
的目标后，张华明第一个想到的就是，要有自己的品牌。

这是父亲留给他的经验，也是他自己在市场深刻的体会。尤
其是在北京打拼多年之后，他有了对更好未来明晰的憧憬。
然而眼下手上并没有最合宜的商标可现成使用；永利来的申
请并未获得商标注册，而上海华丽仅拥有使用权。这些不太
完美的现况，促成了张华明更急切地要解决自主品牌问题。

首先，好的品牌当然要有好名字。自己也对用什么名字拿捏
不准的张华明，于是去到当时的北京"中国商标事务所"，提
了几个关于商标取名的要求，请接待他的事务所工作人员柴莉
女士帮助自己取一个合适的好名字。他的要求是："必须是女
性喜欢的；必须是与天然的、高档的面料相关。"在商标事务
所的协助下，他最终获得了一个好名字：

雅是高雅的雅；莹字上面一个草，下面一个玉，是宝玉，寓
意天然宝贵，晶莹剔透——雅莹两个字都代表"美"。

With this new strategy, the next priority was to have his own brand. This was one of the most important lessons he had learnt from his father and his early years in Beijing. A strong brand comes with a great name, but he did not yet have a good brand name and trademark. At a loss for ideas, he went directly to the China Trademark Office in Beijing to enquire, even asking a staff member of the office, Miss Chai Li, to help come up with a good name. "Generally speaking, it must be adored by women, and it must refer to nature and high-quality fabric," Hwaming told her. With her help, they came up with yaying (Chinese: 雅莹): Ya, (Chinese: 雅), represents elegance; while the character Ying, (Chinese: 莹), is a combination of the Chinese radicals for "grass" and "jade", symbolising purity and perfection. Both words embody and exude all that is beautiful.

It was Hwaming's wish that more and more women could dress elegantly, comfortably and exquisitely. "All that is fine and good in the world is contained in these two Chinese characters, whether it is making a product, doing business or growing as a person. These two characters embody our original aspiration." He further recalled that back then he had not thought too deeply about the name, but simply fell in love with it.

Hwaming's second move as he left Beijing was focused on improving himself.

His experience in the city taught him the importance of knowledge and allowed him to witness the trends of modern business management. With the company's management and operation now resting on his shoulders, he knew that he had to keep up with the times, improve the quality of management at the company, increase awareness of the brand and make his father proud.

左页：
1996 年春夏，贴有"雅莹"商标的
真丝服装

OPPOSITE
yaying brand label, Spring-Summer 1996

"

用好的材料做好的衣服，为女性顾客带去美。

"

插页 1：
1995 年，雅莹丝绸系列，中式盘扣立领
真丝衬衫

插页 2：
1995 年，雅莹丝绸系列，无领真丝衬衫

插页 3：
1996 年，雅莹丝绸系列，重磅真丝套装

插页 4：
1999 年，雅莹丝绸系列，真丝双绉衬衫

插页 5：
1999 年，雅莹丝绸系列，真丝印花双绉
吊带连衣裙

插页 6：
1999 年，雅莹丝绸系列，真丝印花双绉
连衣裙

插页 7：
1999 年，雅莹丝绸系列，真丝弹力桑波
缎衬衫

右页：
1994 年以来，雅莹丝绸系列的经典款式

INSERT 1
Mandarin collar silk shirt with Chinese button knot,
yaying 1995, *Silk collection*

INSERT 2
Collarless silk shirt, yaying 1995, *Silk collection*

INSERT 3
Suit made with heavy sillk, yaying 1996, *Silk collection*

INSERT 4
Silk crepe de chine shirt, yaying 1999, *Silk collection*

INSERT 5
Spaghetti strap floral silk crepe de chine dress, yaying
1999, *Silk collection*

INSERT 6
Floral silk crepe de chine dress, yaying 1999, *Silk collection*

INSERT 7
Stretch silk jacquard shirt, yaying 1999, *Silk collection*

OPPOSITE
Iconic selections from yaying's silk collection since 1994

上图 / 右图 / 右页：
1994 年，公司在北京热销的真丝四维呢衬衫

ABOVE / RIGHT / OPPOSITE
The company's popular spun silk shirt in Beijing, 1994

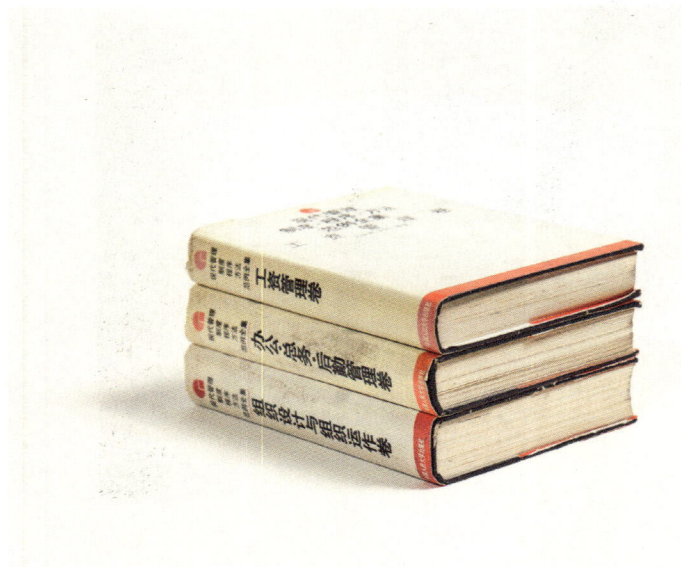

在张华明心中，未来就是让更多女性穿上优雅的、天然舒适的、精致时装。"中国所有美好的含义都表达在这两个字当中。无论是做产品、做事业，还是做人，这都应该是我们的初心。"他回忆说，虽然当时并没有现在这样的深层思考，甚至不理解这两个字的内涵，但他还是一眼就喜欢上了这个商标。

张华明做的第二件事，是对自己的全面提升。在北京的经历，让他深刻认识到知识的力量，以及整个企业经营已快速向现代化的经营管理转型的趋势。身负接班重任的他，希望自己能够跟上时代，提升企业的经营管理水平，打响自己的品牌，在父亲的基础上更创辉煌。

于是，离开北京之前，他特意去王府井外文书店花上万块钱买了一整套 15 本的《现代管理制度·程序·方法范例全集》，一批由美国、日本、中国台湾专家学者等出版的著作，如《企业形象文化识别系统》，以及大陆专家包政、彭剑锋等出版的《人力资源管理全套》等经管书籍带回嘉兴——当时人们的工资才几十块，他的这个投入可谓是相当的大手笔。而且，他不只是舍得花钱，更是舍得花时间和精力。

父亲住院期间，张华明陪夜时抱着那些从北京买回的厚厚的专业书籍啃，什么是公司架构，什么是营销，什么是人力资源，看不懂就反复看，自己琢磨。白天，他就开始对标思考，如何在永利来开展现代企业经营管理，并将永利来"改造"成他希望的雅莹。

With this in mind, he spent tens of thousands of yuan on a complete 15-volume set of *The System, Procedure, Methodology and Case Studies of Modern Corporate Management*, which he brought with him back to Jiaxing. At that time, the average monthly salary of a worker was in the tens of yuan, so this was a huge investment by Hwaming, not only in terms of the monetary cost, but in time and effort that he would put into studying.

During his father's hospitalisation, Hwaming accompanied him at night and spent time reading these books, learning about company structure, marketing, human resources and more. When he did not understand a concept, he read it over and over again. During the day, he would apply his learnings to the plans he drew up for the transformation of the company.

In January 1996, Baorong stepped down from the general manager role but continued to serve as the chairman of Jiaxing Yonglilai Fashion Co., Ltd., with Hwaming as the newly appointed general manager. Hwaming restructured the company and purchased new office furniture, improving the office and production environment, as he believed that a fashion company must look and feel the part.

The company started launching new products, but Hwaming grew frustrated with its conventional way of setting prices. "If you don't understand market-based pricing strategies, you won't be able to make money despite your efforts." Combining what he learned in books and years of retail experience, he designed a set of pyramid models for product pricing based on his insights of different customer segments.

1996 年 1 月，经公司股东会议决议，张宝荣任嘉兴永利来时装有限公司董事长，不再担任公司总经理，张华明正式接任公司总经理一职。肩负重任后，张华明开始把自己的经验积累结合最新学习到的知识应用出来，推动企业再一次转型升级。

他把办公室分好部门，新买了桌椅家具，并且大力推动办公、生产环境的升级与优化，因为"开会要有开会的样子"，"一家时装公司要有一家时装公司的形象"。

新产品上市，工厂按照传统方式定价，张华明也不赞成。"不懂市场定价，再怎么做都挣不了钱。"结合书中所学，加上自己多年做零售的经验，他根据产品的成本，参考市场同类产品的价格以及顾客可以接受的价格等多个维度，为产品线的价格体系设计出一套金字塔模型——在一个从数十元到两三百元的价格体系中，将相邻产品拉开档差。

在新的设计下，底层价格的产品，主打薄利多销，意在拉拢更多顾客；金字塔尖的产品，则专注于树立品牌形象。通过这种品质和价格的定位差，公司得以既满足不同层次消费者的需求，扩大顾客群体，又拉开了与以平均价格定价的竞争品牌的差异。这种定价方法，如今已经非常普遍，但在当时相当超前。

According to his new pricing strategy, lower-priced products, despite their lower profit margin, were intended to attract more customers, whilst high-end products were aimed at branding and image building. Through price differentiation, the company could not only expand the customer base by meeting the needs of different consumers with varying degrees of purchasing power, but also distinguish itself from its competitors who were mostly employing average cost pricing strategies at that time. Although such price differentiation strategies are commonplace today, Hwaming was ahead of his time.

The marriage of silk from Jiangnan with women's fashion set the focus of the brand. In 1996, Hwaming set up an R&D centre in Shanghai to enable his Luodong-based company to keep pace with trends of the international metropolis. Meanwhile, he also invited professional designers and pattern designers to infuse the brand with more creative and contemporary ideas and concepts. Together, they launched yaying's silk collection.

This casual chic silk clothing became a huge hit, providing more high-quality, comfortable, and beautiful fashion choices for women. In March 1996, Hwaming launched a marketing campaign — yaying Silk, Bring Out the Real Woman in You — in a Beijing local newspaper, which attracted many department stores to reach out to the brand for collaboration.

北京队饮恨东莞排名第四

全国男篮甲级联赛预赛结束

本报东莞今晨专电（记者孙保生）555全国男篮甲级联赛昨晚战罢第22轮，北京首钢队以60比68负于广东宏远队，最终排在预赛第4名的位置。

昨晚的战幕一拉开，双方都表现得非常紧张拘谨。北京队开局单靠强攻篮下，首开纪录。宏远队张勇军回敬一球，2平。之后，比分交替上升，京队盯人防守十分严密，尤其是防宏远队外围寸步不离。宏远队见外围投篮困难，便将球喂给高中锋策应，造成京队腰部犯规。宏远队多次获得罚球机会，但命中率很低。京队双中锋缺乏身高优势，被对方打乱了阵脚。

易边后，京队发挥出快速反击的特色，频频发起快攻，7分钟时一鼓作气将比分追成40比41。宏远队再度把比分拉开至54比47。京队顽强抗争，单靠巴特尔轮番强攻，17分钟时又把比分追成60比64，最后1分钟，单靠在抢篮板时被判第5次犯规下场。最终京队以8分之差饮恨东莞。

至此，预赛22轮赛完，八一队、宏远队、辽宁队、北京首钢队分获预赛前四名，比赛复赛于10日开始，北京首钢队将在主场迎战八一队，宏远队赴鞍山挑战辽宁队。

王利发：宏远之胜加篮板球没吃亏

——京广男篮教练赛后谈

北京首钢队主教练谈

全国男篮甲级联赛预赛积分表

队　名	比赛场次	胜场	负场	积分	名次
八　一	22	22	0	44	1
广东宏远	22	18	4	40	2
辽宁鞍钢	22	18	4	40	3
北京首钢	22	17	5	39	4
山　东	22	12	10	34	5
浙江中欣	22	10	12	32	6
济南军区	22	9	13	31	7
沈阳军区	22	8	14	30	8
空　军	22	7	15	29	9
江　苏	22	6	18	28	10
南京军区	22	4	18	26	11
前　卫	22	1	21	23	12

（注：广东宏远队与辽宁鞍钢队积分相同，但两队相互之间得失分率宏远队列前。）

特约体育新闻

一汽北京

进军奥运　先过津门

——国家游泳队教练冯上豹一席谈

（本报昆明今晨专电）杨大遒

国安队信心十足

体能测试在即

本报昆明专电（记者孙永广）对即将到来的甲A联赛体能测试，这样我就有了10天的时间。……据教练们介绍，目前北京队体能测试困难较大……他们先参加9日12分钟跑，然后于20日再参加折返跑测试……

老将王汝南再克杨晖八段

本报讯　在"大国手"围棋擂台赛八段竞逐中，老将王汝南再次守擂成功，战胜杨晖八段。

刘小光先拔头筹马晓春失守天元

围棋天元赛第二盘战罢

本报上海专电　第十届中国围棋天元赛第2局的比赛……

（汪晓青）

中国国奥队战胜伊拉克队

争夺奥运入场券前热身赛

新华社广州3月6日电（记者林和）中国奥林匹克队在今晚于南海举行的国际足球挑战赛中，以4：1胜伊拉克奥林匹克队。

体操名宿张健高健

《金牌看台》今晚介绍

本报讯　今晚9点北京电视台21频道介绍体操名宿张健和高健。

（孙力）

右图：

1996 年 3 月，雅莹在《北京晚报》刊登的丝绸系列广告

RIGHY

yaying Silk collection advertisement in *Beijing Evening Standard*, March 1996

北京晚报

BEIJING EVENING NEWS

代号 1—14

1996年3月 7 星期四
农历丙子年 正月十八
第8713号

市天气象台预报　今夜 晴　降水概率0%　北风三四级　低温 零下5℃
明天 晴　降水概率0%　北风四五级　高温 6℃

便民电话　市长:3088080　消协:3011234　急救:120　投诉:4923392　市话:3088467　邮编:3037131

李鹏总理与北京代表共商国是

本报综合消息　国务院总理李鹏昨天上午来到人民大会堂北京厅，作为北京代表团的代表参加北京代表团的全团讨论，并听取代表们对《关于国民经济和社会发展"九五"计划和2010年远景目标纲要的报告》的意见。

吴树青、江小珂、梅祖彦、罗益锋、国林、严仁英、胡亚美、仉振亮等代表先后发言。他们认为，李鹏总理代表国务院所作的报告，勾画出了我国跨世纪的发展蓝图，令人振奋。同时，报告提出的未来15年的发展目标是实事求是的，经过全国人民的共同努力是可以实现的。

参加讨论的尉健行、李锡铭等代表专注地倾听着发言。

在代表们发言过程中，李鹏总理一边认真听取大家的意见，一边不时记下代表们所提建议和意见的要点。代表们发言后，李鹏也发表了自己的意见。

李鹏十分关心北京的各项建设。他说，北京市要适当发展第三产业，加强城市改造。要控制高楼大厦的建设，多发展城市居民盼望的中低档住宅，多搞安居工程。他希望北京建设更多的商业网点，方便市民的生活。要减少中间环节，使商品能够直接同消费者见面。

关于社会治安问题，李鹏说，广大人民群众对社会治安十分关心，希望安居乐业，有一个良好的工作、学习、生活环境。在维护治安方面，公安干警做了大量工作，但问题仍然存在。他指出，解决社会治安问题要靠广大公安干警的思想觉悟和业务素质，靠全社会的综合治理，靠人民群众的共同参与，同时还要靠发挥科学技术的作用。北京市作为首都要进一步加强社会治安工作，并为公安机关配备先进的设备。

挥洒汗水勇于创业

——记市"三八红旗奖章"获得者宋红玲

华东汽车配件厂党支部书记、市"三八红旗奖章"获得者宋红玲1982年刚到华东汽车配件厂时，这里仅有60人，只能生产汽车制动蹄板。职工对她都不很信任。为了让工人们挣到钱、吃上饭，她跑到乡里要来了修养水池的工程，带着全厂职工在冰天雪地里苦战了两个月，年底终于让工人们每人拿了300多元。工人们开始信任她了。

到1991年，这个作坊式的小企业已渐渐发展壮大起来，拥有职工100多人，32种冲压件和车架分装等制造任务，建起了自己的职工食堂……正在全厂一心"摽着膀子干"的时候，乡里提出让华东厂兼并一个300多人的亏损企业。宋红玲犯难了：这家亏损企业没有一间像样的厂房，300多工人也都了没有纪律观念……兼并了它，就像小马套上大车，够难受的。可这关系到全乡的利益，不能只算小帐不顾大家呀。

经过反复思量，宋红玲和厂领导班子以大局为重，终于答应了乡里的要求。一时间，破烂的车间被夷为平地，旷野上拔起了成片的厂房，一个现代化的企业破土而出，紧接着是制订并监督实行各种严格的制度、纪律。

如今，那个分不清车床、冲床、铣床的"门外"书记已变成了汽车配件行业的行家里手，华东汽车配件厂也变成了拥有600多职工、4万多平方米面积的大厂，去年它向国家上交税收1200多万元。　本报记者　杨威

京华女杰

本报讯（记者邓京湘）用现代手段实现信息便捷的沟通与提取，是今年"两会"的新特点。3月3日零时，"全国政协委员语音信箱"在港澳京驻地投入运行。

据悉，这是全国政协会议史上的首次尝试。其主要功能是通过电话随时将委员建议存储到语音信箱内，由工作人员来收集提取汇总。它为委员们参政议政提供了一条新渠道，便于及时反映社情民意，下情上达得到委员们的欢迎。3日零时开通，零时1分，邓伟志委员便打进了第一个电话。到昨天，已储存信息30余条。

"政协委员语音信箱"开通

两会飞鸿

本报讯　北京图书馆自筹资金开发馆藏文献，完成了"国家书目数据光盘研制"项目，通过了文化部组织的成果鉴定会。鉴定委员会的专家对该项成果光盘给予了高度评价，认为该成果光盘涵盖了1988-1995年上半年的251112条书目记录，提供了10个检索点，平均单项检索时效在2秒左右，是我国目前数据覆盖范围最大、编制质量最好的书目数据库，解决了快速检索的问题，系统实用有效，便于推广。认为光盘的诞生填补了我国书目数据光盘生产的一项空白，达到了国内领先水平。

北京图书馆还大力推动自动化建设，通过先进的技术手段和丰富的馆藏，优质高效地向全社会提供各类电子信息服务，在全国率先创办开辟了电子阅览室，以收藏计算机磁盘、光盘为信息载体的电子出版物为主，拥有丰富的信息库，数据近亿条。

北图研制书目数据光盘

本报讯　据市气象台报告，进入三月份以来，由于没有强冷空气影响，本市平原地区的平均气温达5～6℃，比常年同期偏高3℃左右。受蒙古地区强冷空气南下影响，本市从昨天夜间开始

本市出现大风降温

出现了5～6级偏北风，短时阵风达到7级，气温有所下降。从昨晚天气形势分析，入夜后风力将逐渐减弱到3～4级，明天白天仍有4～5级偏北风，请有关单位注意防风防冻。　（高树德）

首都气象事业上新台阶

风雨雷电早知道

本报讯　"八五"期间，本市把建立现代化天气监测、预报、服务和人工影响天气系统放在十分重要的位置，经过广大气象工作者的辛勤努力，国产第一部全相参脉冲多普勒天气雷达、城市有线自动雨量监测网、中尺度数值预报业务系统等一批现代化设备先后投入使用，在天气和气象监测、防灾减灾中发挥巨大作用。

1991年6月6日至11日，密云、怀柔出现暴雨，1994年7月12日至13日北京东部地区的暴雨，气象部门均提前两天做出了预报，对减轻灾害损失作出了贡献。

由于先进设备的投入使用，使预报的准确率明显提高。五年来，气象工作者成功为第七届全国运动会、远南运动会、第四次世妇会和首都纪念世界反法西斯战争和抗日战争胜利50周年等重大活动提供气象服务，受到社会各界的普遍赞誉。　（胡祥凯）

回首八五

本市命名三八红旗标兵

本报讯（记者杨威）昨天，本市"三八"红旗奖章获得者、"三八"红旗集体标兵和"五好"家庭的代表、女状元、女能手和高校女教授等各界妇女近3000人欢聚在北展剧场，共同欢庆自己的节日。全国妇联副主席黄启璪及北京市领导陈广文、孟志元、胡昭广、陈大白等出席了昨天"三八"妇女节纪念大会。

市妇联主席李巧云在昨天的大会上宣布命名陈济生、陶敏芹等98位同志为市"三八"红旗奖章获得者，复兴医院心脏重症监护病房和北京女子体操队等99个单位为市"三八"红旗集体标兵；命名房山区岳各庄下中阴村"三八"果园等80个单位为市"双学双比"先进集体，顺义县王玉凤等100位农村妇女为市"双学双比"女状元，命名东城区朝阳门街道妇联、延庆县康庄镇妇联等270个妇联为市妇联系统基层妇女组织先进集体，粟惠明、李秀琴等200位同志为市妇联系统基层妇女组织先进个人。

金吉列自愿抚养烈士家属

本报讯（记者张明非）昨天下午，沈金柱烈士的老父亲沈家琪接受了北京市金吉列企业集团自愿代烈士交纳的第一笔赡养费——6000元人民币。同时，这家企业还向沈金柱烈士的幼子沈英鑫，给付了第一笔6000元的抚养费。该企业将每月向烈士遗孤发放500元抚养费。

本报今天座谈"刘罗锅"

本报讯　一条白绫把和珅送上了西天，刘墉则返老还童，和小孩子一块儿玩起了弹球游戏……昨天晚上，40集电视连续剧《宰相刘罗锅》就这样和观众告别了。但是，关于这部电视剧的话题也许才刚刚展开，随着这部电视剧的播映，人们发现拍摄历史题材的电视剧可以另辟蹊径，《宰相刘罗锅》就是一个很好的例子。

本报今天上午特邀了该剧的摄制单位——北京文化艺术音像出版社总编辑张和平、该剧导演张子恩和韩刚、编剧秦培春、主演王刚等与部分专家、学者及普通观众举行了电视连续剧《宰相刘罗锅》座谈会。有关座谈会的详细情况请阅明天的本报文化新闻版。

京华扫描

妇女法律热线开通

本报讯　一条妇女法律热线861．7687近日开通。这条法律热线是北京大学妇女研究中心法律部设立的，它将免费为妇女解答法律问题，提供法律帮助。　（纪从周）

骨质增生专家义诊

本报讯　3月8日至10日在东城区滨河路1号每天为60名骨质增生、颈椎病、腰椎间盘突出等症患者进行义诊。

维护妇女儿童合法权益现场咨询

本报讯　3月8日，北京电台教育台与市女法官协会将在劳动人民文化宫联合举办"维护妇女、儿童合法权益"现场咨询活动。届时，一批女院长、女庭长、女法官将到现场解答问题。同时，从事补碘研究工作的专家、教授也将来到咨询现场解答妇女儿童补碘的问题。

接班之前就有的转入女装生产，以及以丝绸为核心做高端面料服饰的产品品牌发展战略，也在张华明的推动下有序地进行着，这也是他接任后最大的改变。

1996 年，在张华明的带领下，公司全面启动了女装品牌发展战略，并在上海专门设立了产品设计研发中心，让当时尚处于偏远地区的洛东小厂和国际大都市完成接轨。同时，他还引入专业设计师和版师，帮助雅莹以丝绸为原料，在女装开发上形成初步的规范，让雅莹的产品更具时尚服饰的概念。由他在此期间主导推出的"雅莹丝绸系列"也在市场大受欢迎，进一步奠定了雅莹高端优质的经营理念与品牌基因。

1996 年 2 月 2 日，张华明还将之前的沈阳经营部升级为沈阳分公司，并将分公司设址在沈阳团结路 60 号。永利来由此迈出历史性一步：第一家驻外分公司正式成立。同时，张华明趁热打铁，在自己闯出一片天地的北京，拿出 3 万多在《北京晚报》做起了广告，"雅莹丝绸系列，穿出女性真我风采"，引来京城不少商场的争相合作。

In September 1997, the company moved its management and operations from Luodong town to the office floor of the Diamond Hotel, one of the most high-end commercial buildings in the heart of Jiaxing. On October 18 of the same year, the company was renamed to "Jiaxing Yaying Fashion Co., Ltd." sharing the same name with its brand.

Some of Hwaming's new reforms, such as replacing old office furniture or relocating the office, were initially strongly opposed by Baorong, who lived frugally throughout his life. Baorong believed that one should never forget where he came from and that spending lavishly on what he viewed were superficial appearances was totally unnecessary.

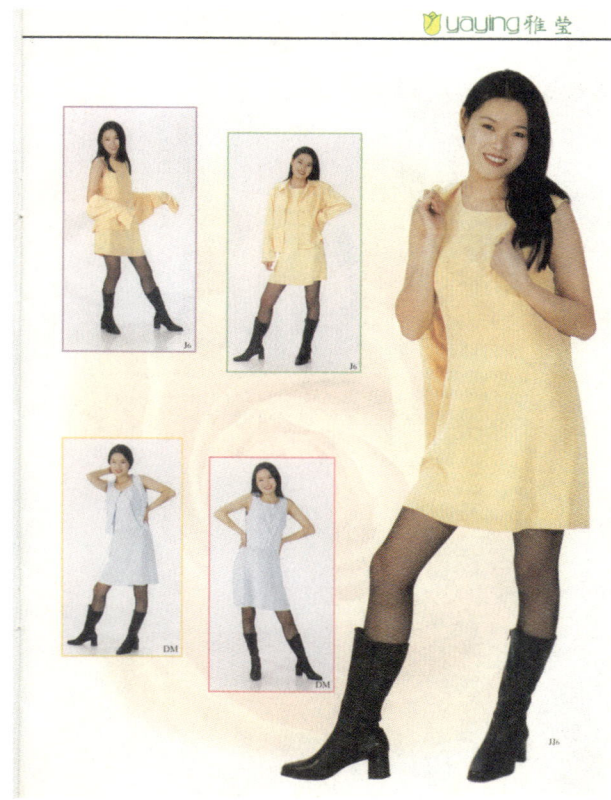

1997 年，张华明还将公司总部从洛东乡搬往嘉兴市区最高档的写字楼——戴梦得大酒店，建立雅莹商业运营中心。同年 10 月 18 日，张华明将公司改名为"嘉兴雅莹服装有限公司"，实现公司名称和品牌名称的统一。

对张华明的一些改革举措，比如换掉旧的办公桌椅，建设新的办公环境，包括租赁新的办公大楼，一生节俭的张宝荣起初都是极力反对。他认为，千辛万苦才有今天的事业基础，大家都是苦日子过来的，不应该忘本，不能把挣来的钱花在这些表面的东西上。

Hwaming, however, had higher expectations for the company, and he aimed to grow yaying into a renowned fashion brand in China. He told his father that to achieve this goal, they must create a strong image, and office decor and location are both part of that image. Hwaming explained patiently and his father began to accept these new perspectives. Actions speak louder than words, and the company's performance under Hwaming's leadership would eventually convince his father completely.

左页：
1997 年 9 月，公司商业运营中心迁往嘉兴市中心戴梦得大酒店 9 楼。雅莹在嘉兴戴梦得大酒店张贴的巨幅商业广告

上图左：
1997 年，雅莹首次发布的春夏产品手册

上图右：
1997 年，戴雪明参与雅莹当季春夏系列产品发布推广，亲自身穿春夏系列产品

OPPOSITE
yaying's billboard outside Jiaxing Diamond Hotel, 1997. In September 1997, the company moves its management and operations to Diamond Hotel located in the heart of Jiaxing

ABOVE LEFT
yaying's first lookbook, Spring-Summer 1997

ABOVE RIGHT
Dai Xueming modelling yaying's Spring-Summer 1997 collection

'97 6 23

莹真丝时装真诚回馈

'98 7 29

但张华明对雅莹有更高期待——他希望雅莹成为中国著名的时装品牌。他告诉父亲，要达到这样的目标，就必须有与之匹配的形象，无论是地理位置，还是内部装修，这都是品牌形象的一部分。在他耐心的沟通解释下，父亲慢慢接受了他的这些新理念和新思维。

但真正让父亲对他彻底放心和信任的，还是他的改变所取得的优异成绩。依靠新的产品和价格体系，1996 年和 1997 年两年，"雅莹"品牌女装便累计创造了将近 2000 万的销售额，而且在北京、上海、天津、太原、南京等市场都大受欢迎。

这也是从未有过的业绩纪录。

到 1997 年时，公司的销售收入已从 1994 年的 256.81 万元上升至 1117.05 万元。从 1988 年承包经营红政服装厂到改名洛东制衣厂，再到成立永利来并从永利来时装升级成为雅莹，从服装制衣升级到时装生产；从红政村家门口办厂到洛东集镇西文桥再到在嘉兴最黄金的市中心有了一片天地，经过十年磨一剑的三部曲，张宝荣两代人终于算是苦尽甘来。

雅莹服装正式成立后，张华明担任公司总经理，戴雪明出任公司销售经理。10 月 18 日从此作为雅莹发展的周年纪念日。也是雅莹创立的这一年，1997 年 3 月 18 日，张华明与戴雪明正式注册登记，结为夫妻。

一个新的时代，雅莹的时代由此开启。

With new products and pricing strategies, yaying's womenswear collection brought in record sales revenue of nearly 20 million CNY in 1996 and 1997, and was well-received in big cities such as Beijing, Shanghai, Tianjin, Taiyuan and Nanjing.

By 1997, the company's turnover had risen to 11.1705 million CNY , up from 2.5681 million CNY in 1994. From trying his hand at the management of Hongzheng Garment Factory in 1988, to setting up Yonglilai Fashion and transforming the company into a modern yaying; from garment processing to creating fashion; and from Hongzheng village to Luodong town to downtown Jiaxing, this was an entrepreneurial journey that spanned over a decade and two generations.

The hard work of the Zhang family had finally blossomed into a new era for yaying.

第二篇
CHAPTER 2

固本培元，
过关晋级

1998~2008
SETTING THE ROADMAP
FOR A NEW MILLENIUM

走过1988~1998年初创10年的"求生存"之后，雅莹进入"图发展"的第二个10年。这10年，是雅莹跟随中国经济崛起为腾飞发展打下坚实基础的10年；也是雅莹从父子"铁三角"向张华明、戴雪明"夫妻档"转变的10年，是张华明从商人向企业家转变的关键10年。通过这10年，雅莹不但在市场上站到更高位置，也进一步确立了品牌核心、建立了核心竞争力。这也是雅莹在更大挑战与挫折中百折不挠且创新精神激荡的前进。

Following yaying's initial 10-year period of "survival mode" from 1988 to 1998, the company entered a "flourishing" period. The decade from 1998 to 2008 saw yaying riding the wave of China's economic growth and laying a new foundation for the next phase of growth. It saw the leadership transition from the "Golden Trio" of father and sons to the "Golden Couple" of Zhang Hwaming and Dai Xueming, and it also saw Hwaming's transformation from a businessman into a corporate leader. During this period, yaying not only increased its market share but also further established its core strengths and competitive advantages. This was a time when yaying rose to greater challenges while remaining relentless and innovative in its pursuits.

逆境重生，更上层楼
REBIRTH OUT OF ADVERSITY

"要有真正的发展之道，要有坚定的信心、坚强的毅力并且坦诚，遇到问题自己要有想法，别人才能相助成行，要知道要如何改进、如何调整，要脚踏实地，亲力亲为，最终将一切落到实处！"

"You must have a vision and unbreakable faith. If you remain sincere and resilient, even when facing tests and trials, help shall follow. If you remain flexible and eager to go the extra mile, if you keep your feet on the ground and you roll up your sleeves to get down to work, you will eventually make things happen."

局势突变，临危新生
EVERY CLOUD HAS A SILVER LINING

张华明从小喜欢下军棋，经营公司之后，他越发感觉到商场也是有如棋局。棋局的思维让他更懂得把握优势、趁胜追击，也更懂得化危为机，反败为胜。

1998 年，雅莹的棋局就突然大变了。刚刚营收迈进千万台阶，踌躇满志的张华明也迎来堪称致命的一击：公司上半年还有几百万元净资产，年底却变成了负债 400 多万元，而账面上已经没有流动资金了，库存价值也不到 100 万元，走到资不抵债的绝境。

这是雅莹的至暗时刻，也是内忧外患、祸不单行的一年。于外，亚洲金融风暴令国内服装业受到重创，不少企业应声倒台；于内，公司为了应对危机研发的新产品在大货工艺上出了意外；已经病中的创始人张宝荣也不幸病逝，更令一切雪上加霜。

现在回头看，这也是雅莹从服装工厂升级到时装公司必不可少的阵痛。1996 年时，张华明从北京撤回后，雅莹的主要业务又回到了衬衫等服装的代加工，并且在秋冬季"粮荒"。好不容易做出一个金属棉衬衫，既无品牌优势，又无成本优势。"我正式接手以后就决定停止金属棉衬衫的生产，因为它成本将近 90 块，我们也只能卖 90 块，没有利润空间，也竞争不过宁波的雅戈尔等男装厂家。"

Hwaming enjoyed playing military chess since childhood, and taking charge of the company made him increasingly feel like he was playing a game of chess. Chess strategies had taught him concepts such as seizing the upper hand and how turn to the tides in one's favour.

These concepts would be tested as 1998 brought sudden drastic change to yaying. While the company's revenue had just crossed the ten-million-yuan milestone, Hwaming, who was proud of what he had achieved, now faced a dire predicament. Though the company had several million yuan in net assets in the first half of the year, they were in debt of more than 4 million yuan at year end, with poor operating cash flow, and on the brink of bankruptcy. This was yaying's darkest moment — a year with both internal and external misfortunes. Externally, the Asian financial crisis had severely impacted China's domestic apparel industry and left many companies bankrupt; internally, the company's new products had failed badly, leading to heavy losses. Above all else, Hwaming had to deal with the loss of his father.

In retrospect, these issues represented yaying's growing pains of transforming from a garment processing factory to a fashion brand. In 1996, when Hwaming took over the company, he gradually stopped production of men's poly-cotton shirts, as it was not profitable, and it was almost impossible to compete with the other more experienced menswear manufacturers. Hence, the company suffered a "vacuum" of products for autumn and winter wear. Based on his observation of the market trends at that time, Hwaming decided to make cashmere the new star product, as he was "keen to fill this winter product gap." In late 1997, he spent two million yuan to purchase high-quality cashmere blend fabrics from Shanghai Yingchun Wool Factory. This was a huge investment and it did not turn out well for yaying.

逐步停止原来没有利润空间的生产销售，但新的出路在哪里呢？一番市场调查后，张华明决定选择当时热门的羊绒大衣作为主打。"我要把秋冬的时装做出来。"1997 年秋冬季，他先后花费 200 万元从上海瀛春毛纺厂采购了一批含羊绒的上好面料，由雅莹来生产。200 万元对当时的雅莹来说，是一笔巨大的数字。但这次尝试却并不成功。

长期以丝绸加工为主的雅莹没有做大衣加工的经验。丝绸属于薄料，质地柔软，羊绒大衣属于厚料，质地偏硬，无论是制版还是制作工艺，都是天差地别。雅莹的工艺、设备都不成熟，原本被寄予厚望的新品被做成了次品，肩宽严重超过正常尺寸。压力顿时扑面而来。更糟糕的是，因为羊绒大衣的生产，工厂打破了原来的生产节奏和安排，雅莹在自己原本擅长的真丝等生产方面，也是接连出问题。内部忧患不断的同时，亚洲金融风暴的爆发让外部环境也恶劣起来，让雅莹连做外贸代工的机会也没有了。

巨大的压力之下，两个选择放到张华明面前：一是将这批羊绒大衣作为次品降价处理，只要他愿意，马上有人提货交钱，公司会把损失降到最低；二是坚持做最好的信念，不合格的大衣，绝不推向市场。若在平时，不用思考，张华明就会选择后者，但现在资金对雅莹太重要了，选择后者，雅莹可能就此关门。

yaying, an expert in silk, was new to overcoats. Compared with lightweight and delicate silk fabrics, cashmere was heavy and stiff, completely going against what the company knew about pattern making and the production process. The company was also poorly equipped professionally to produce this new product, and what was meant to be a lucrative inaugural Autumn-Winter womenswear launch ended up resulting in overcoats that had severely disproportionate shoulders. Now, the pressure from all directions was overwhelming. Worse still, to prepare for a successful launch, the company had to sacrifice its usual production schedule, putting off the production of its star silk products. Meanwhile, the outbreak of the Asian financial crisis aggravated the external business environment and wiped out any possibility of pivoting to OEM to generate cashflow.

Hwaming was left with two choices: either sell the coats at a discount so that the company could have immediate cash flow, or stick to his original aspiration of using high-quality materials to make good clothing — if quality was not good, yaying would not sell. Hwaming did not hesitate in his decision and stared bankruptcy in the eye. His belief, his character, his will and his expertise were all put to the test. He had not only put nearly all of the company's capital into the production of this cashmere coat, but he had also even taken out a loan. Now, not only were all his efforts in vain, but the company faced a massive debt problem. Yet none of these challenges could be worse than what was to come.

艰难的抉择考验着张华明的意志和智慧，也考验着他的品格与信仰。最终，他做出了宁可雅莹关门，也不自毁信誉的选择。为了这批大衣，张华明不但押上了自己几乎所有的资金，还借了钱，现在却几乎是颗粒无收，雅莹随即陷入巨大经营困境，尤其资金困境。但这还不是最困难的。

1998 年 7 月，沈阳一家经销商因资金断链，将店铺盘给正四处催债的雅莹作为补偿。为尽快获得现金流，张华明决定接过店铺自己做销售，并亲自前往处理。抵达沈阳当天，他便和同事一起与经销商交接。事情忙完回到酒店已是晚上 10 点左右，累了一天的他还未来得及洗漱，就接到家里电话：病重的父亲，与世长辞。

放下电话，张华明陷入无尽的悲痛，甚至绝望之中。

An exclusive retailer in Shenyang requested to transfer the ownership of its store back to yaying, and at that time, desperate for the company to receive more cash flow, Hwaming travelled to Shenyang in person for the handover. On the day of arrival, Hwaming and his colleagues went straight to meet the retailer, and it was already ten at night when he returned to his hotel. After nearly a full day on the road, and just as he was about to catch his breath, he received a phone call: "Father has passed away." In that moment, Hwaming's world collapsed into a pit of despair.

"My father was the son of farmers, and this background and his hometown shaped his character: resilient, focused, inventive and compassionate. At each phase of his career, he knew, regardless of all the hardship, that his success was closely associated with the country's growth and the call of the times. He knew, without complacency or doubt, that he was following his dream. His spirit is embedded in our genes and we will remain true to where we started."

"

父亲是农家的儿子，
清贫家境和江南水土造就了他
坚毅、专注、创新、善良的人格品质。
在他事业发展的每一个阶段中，
虽然步履之艰辛，付出之辛苦，
但他深知他的每一段事业
都是和国家的发展、时代的召唤联系在一起的。
知道自己的秉性，不懈怠不彷徨，不用扬鞭自奋蹄。
这样的基因传承下来，
这是我们的血液，这是我们的原点。

"

反败为胜，引领时尚冬季
THE ALPACA COAT, A WINTER VICTORY

悲痛中料理完父亲后事的第一时间，张华明咬紧牙关寻找着雅莹的解困之道。

虽然身处内忧外患，张华明内心依然乐观。他告诉自己，越是困难的时候越是考验一个企业、一个人的时候，哪里摔倒哪里爬起来，绝不能丧失信心。"我始终勉励自己，只要积极调整，找到明确的改变措施，再把这些措施一一落到实处，就能挺过难关，而且再升一级。"他回忆说。

虽然大儿子刚刚出生不久，家里需要自己照顾，但张华明几乎把所有时间都放到了企业上。他独自背上行李，沿着改革开放的南巡路线，先坐火车到温州，然后又赶夜班车到福州、厦门、深圳，沿着海岸线往南走了一圈，一出去就是半个月没回家。在这些时尚行业的前沿阵地，他白天看市场、找机会，晚上睡在大巴里赶路，睡不着就翻来覆去地思考：如果换成是父亲，他会怎么做？雅莹未来的路在哪里？

悲伤、玉抑、困顿、挖空心思的"炼狱"中，张华明在最困难时刻爆发出最大力量。等到从南方回家时，他已有了清晰的自救思路——羊绒大衣的失败，并非市场选择的失败，而是技术和产品选择的失败，所以，他决定继续生产羊绒大衣，而且选择了当时最热门也最新式的阿尔巴卡大衣作为东山再起的筹码。于是这一年，张华明计划以每米 200~400 元的高价，从喜盈盈（原湖州第二毛纺厂），即宋世楹手中买下了货值几百万的阿尔巴卡面料，大手笔推出雅莹阿尔巴卡面料冬衣。

After the loss of his father, the grieving Hwaming kept his head and swore to find a way forward for the company. Through all the lows, he remained optimistic. In his heart, he knew that difficult times are measures of a person and even a company's strength. Giving up was never an option; the only option was identifying the problems and solving them one by one.

At that point in time, Hwaming also welcomed the birth of his son. It was a difficult choice to make, but he would spend almost all of his time working, doing all he could to save the company. He travelled to major coastal cities in southern China to research the leading fashion markets, taking a train to Wenzhou first, and then night buses to several other cities including Fuzhou, Xiamen and Shenzhen. Ultimately, Hwaming spent half a month on the road. During the day, he would walk through the markets and at night, he would continue his trip so as not to waste any time. He never had a good night's sleep, but would ask himself repeatedly: "What would my father do in this situation? What is yaying's future?"

He was in a dark place, but sorrow, distress and soul-searching seemed to unleash Hwaming's full potential. When he finally returned home, he had a clear vision of what to do to lead the company out of crisis. He concluded that the failure of the cashmere coat was not because the product was unpopular, but because of poor production skills and product selection.

He decided to make a comeback with Peruvian Alpaca wool fabric — the newest material in style at that time — for the brand's winter coat launch. As was his style, Hwaming made a considerable one-time investment for a large order of Alpaca wool, for which the market price had reached nearly 200 to 400 yuan per metre at that

右页 / 127 - 131 页：
2000 年代，雅莹不同色系与创意的
阿尔巴卡女士大衣

OPPOSITE / 127-131

yaying's Alpaca wool coats in different
colours and style, 2000s

YAYINGCLASSICAL

雅鉴 ®
C·O·L·L·E·C·T·I·O·N
WINTERCOLLECTION

阿尔巴卡俗称"秘鲁羊驼"，其纤维强度与保暖性可达羊绒的3倍与1.5倍，价格也比羊绒高很多。1996年，京派服装强企"罗曼"将其引入中国，交由浙江喜盈盈开发成功之后，很快成为市场上最炙手可热的紧俏品。

张华明相信，如果能成功开发这款产品，雅莹一定可以翻身。产品路线确定了，当务之急是要解决好羊绒大衣秋冬生产技术，补足急需的资金，购买新面料，尤其重要的是，要努力做好产品，激活市场，让生产出来的东西必须很快变现。但此时的雅莹深陷困境之中，单靠自身已无能解决这些问题。最艰难的时刻，雅莹只能靠王阿六在哈尔滨的批发生意维持，"每天把卖掉的钱就马上打回来了，否则工资都发不出了。就是靠老王守着哈尔滨的档口，每天把流水打回来。"

time, with a supplier called Zhejiang Xiyingying Textile (former Huzhou No.2 Wool Mill). Alpaca wool is 3 times stronger and 1.5 times warmer than cashmere, and therefore much more expensive. Hwaming believed that if yaying could successfully produce this Alpaca coat, they could reverse the company's fortunes. His next step was to bring in the skillsets and funds needed.

At that time, yaying's survival hinged on the income generated from the wholesale business ran by Wang Aliu, the late Baorong's trusted aide, who was the sales and marketing manager at that time and based in Harbin. Hwaming recalled, "The sales revenue had to be transferred back on a daily basis or else the company could not afford to pay the staff."

There is a Chinese saying, "Adding icing on the cake is an easy gesture, but sending coal for warmth during snowy weather reveals true friendship." Many people came forward to help yaying, thanks to the trust and respect won by Baorong who was known for his good-heartedness, and thanks to the company's credibility earned under Hwaming's leadership. This goodwill proved to be yaying's most valuable asset in Hwaming's hour of distress.

右页：
雅莹2000年冬季大片，中国超模佟晨洁身着雅莹皮毛拼接撞色包边的阿尔巴卡大衣

OPPOSITE
Chinese supermodel Tong Chenjie in yaying's Alpaca coat with contrasting fur lining, yaying Winter 2000 ad campaign

右页：

雅莹 2000 年冬季大片，中国超模佟
晨洁身着雅莹米色阿尔巴卡大衣

OPPOSITE

Chinese supermodel Tong Chenjie
in yaying's beige Alpaca coat, yaying
Winter 2000 ad campaign

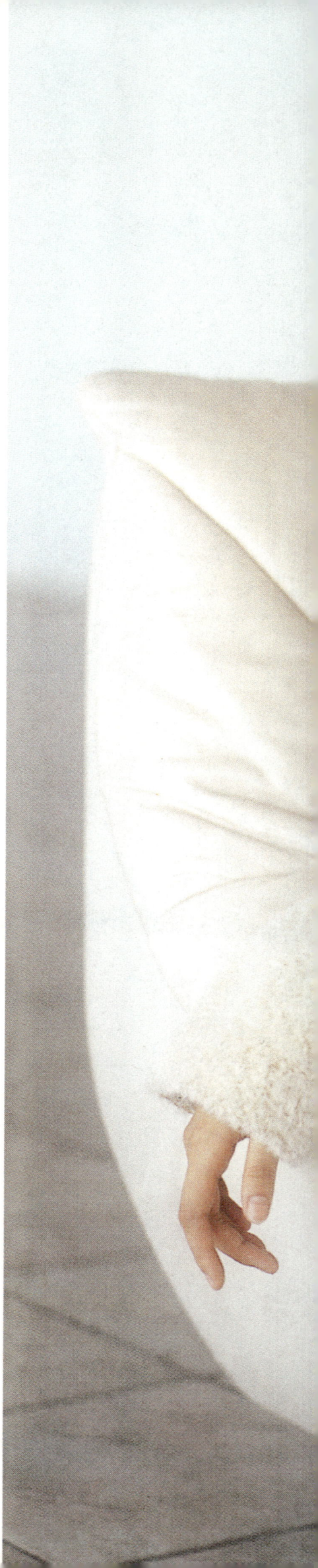

左页 / 上图：
2000 年秋冬，雅莹蓝灰色阿尔巴卡大衣

OPPOSITE / ABOVE
Blue-grey Alpaca coat, yaying Autumn-Winter
2000 ad campaign

上图：
2000 年，在嘉兴首届产（商）品质量跟踪展评会上展示的雅莹阿尔巴卡冬装

左图：
2000 年，在嘉兴首届产（商）品质量跟踪展评会上悬挂的巨幅雅莹冬装阿尔巴卡广告

ABOVE
yaying's Winter Alpaca coats on display at the first "Jiaxing Exhibition of Quality Products Show", 2000

LEFT
yaying Alpaca coats' billboard at the first "Jiaxing Exhibition of Quality Products Show", 2000

俗话说"让人锦上添花易，让人雪中送炭难"。谁来给雪中的雅莹送碳呢？最终，从父亲到自己多年坚持的"要想做好事，先要做好人"所积累的人脉和信任，尤其是遇到困难后，宁愿生意关门也要坚持做好的品格和信誉，这些不被记在企业资产表上，也常常被人认为虚无的东西，在关键时刻成了张华明最重要的无形资产，让他得道多助，也让重启雅莹的前三个问题得到解决。

很多人站了出来，成了他的贵人。而这些人选择支持他的原因几乎都是："雅莹虽然小，但是华明和雪明他们人很不错。"这些当年帮助自己的贵人，张华明至今牢记在心：好朋友嘉兴市蓝翔航天器材厂庞家俊总经理为雅莹担保，中国银行嘉兴分行放贷业务负责人黄龙新鼎力支持，让雅莹从中国银行嘉兴分行获得 100 万银行贷款；戴雪明的姐姐姐夫以及公司当时最早的英才顾海明的姨夫等也在关键时刻慷慨解囊……他们的合力帮助，让雅莹解决了资金的燃眉之急。

据黄龙新回忆，当时市场上普遍资金紧张，贷款困难，给雅莹这样的企业贷款 100 万在当时是天文数字，但大家都是看着张华明父子一步步做起来的，对他们的能力和品德都有信心，所以特别支持。"觉得他们很实在——不唱歌、不跳舞、不喝酒，都是一心一意发展公司而且有能力。"

雅莹第一次做羊绒大衣的失败是技术问题，但归根到底还是缺少大衣版型技术的优秀人才。而过去的人脉积累又一次帮助了雅莹：当时人在重庆、学过制版的雅莹代理商梁贤安是张华明的挚友，为帮张华明解决制版难题，他常常一个月到嘉兴四次，每次都在雅莹戴梦得总部与张华明同吃同住，挑灯夜战地在样衣室研究如何把版型调到更好。后来，张华明又找到与父亲熟识并且有过加工合作的嘉兴著名女装制版专家李成林，前往工厂帮忙。

Pang Jiajun, the general manager of Lanxiang Aviation Equipment, a native of Luodong town and a long-time friend of Hwaming's, became a guarantor for yaying's bank loan. Huang Longxin, who worked at the Bank of China, patiently assisted with his loan application, and praised the couple, saying: "They had really good character and were true entrepreneurs. We never saw them pass their days drinking or partying, instead, they threw themselves wholeheartedly into the development of the company." Xueming's sister, Dai Xueying, and her husband not only provided financial support to the company, but also put aside their own business to help yaying. Even the uncle of Gu Haiming, one of the earliest management trainees in yaying, came forward to help.

The failure of yaying's cashmere overcoat was largely a matter of skill shortage and Hwaming received significant help in solving this issue. Liang Xian'an, who became an agent of yaying's silk products after discovering the brand at a China Fashion Expo in 1997, travelled to Jiaxing four times a month from his base in Chongqing, to help work on the pattern making, often staying overnight in Hwaming's office to work on the coats; Li Chenglin, a well-known expert in womenswear pattern making and an acquaintance of Hwaming's father, boldly shut down his own factory and transferred his equipment into yaying, and his expertise and support would help yaying achieve a breakthrough. With the much-needed capital, technology and skills, Hwaming also received further support from Song Shiying, chairman of Xiyingying, who provided yaying with a complimentary batch of high-end Alpaca wool.

资金有了，人才有了，技术有了，重启生产的关键时刻，从哪里跌倒就从哪里站起的张华明，又得到了喜盈盈董事长宋世楹的支持——为雅莹慷慨提供了价值 300 多万元的精品阿尔巴卡高档羊绒面料……

各路伙伴、好友的支持下，雅莹的生产重启了，张华明接着转身投入市场的开拓，这也是他擅长的。权衡之后，张华明决定以"零售＋批发"两条腿走路的方针重整旗鼓，理由是："第一从长远考虑，我不能不做品牌，所以一定要到商场里做零售；第二我也不得不做批发，如果全在商场压款，资金周转不过来，这是当前形势下的权宜之计。"

策略既定，张华明保留了雅莹南京、无锡等零售根据地，然后北上冬衣重镇哈尔滨，在红博服装批发市场租下柜台，努力把每一个机会变成现实的业绩。成效很快显现：市场火热时，仅仅每天从哈尔滨批发市场回收的货款，就已足够维持公司的日常开销。

yaying finally resumed production and Hwaming soon shifted his focus to marketing, his area of expertise. He decided to pursue both retailing and wholesaling, "walking on two legs." As he recalled: "In-mall retailing will help increase brand awareness in the long term, while wholesaling is critical for positive cashflow. It is the best way forward under the circumstances." Beyond the existing retailing bases in Nanjing and Wuxi, Hwaming went north to Harbin, a major market for winter apparel in China. He rented a counter at Hongbo Wholesale Clothing Market and worked hard to seize every opportunity.

After continuous study and experimentation of nearly a year, all of yaying's efforts soon paid off. In the second half of 1999, the design and production of yaying's Alpaca coat began to see results, especially in Harbin. yaying's Alpaca coats sold for up to 3,000 yuan, and the daily revenue from Harbin alone was sufficient to cover the company's daily expenses. yaying had not only turned losses into profits, but also created an historic new sales record for the company.

1999 年下半年，凭借从 1998 年秋冬就开始尝试、调整，到 1999 年时已相当成熟的阿尔巴卡大衣，张华明打了一场漂亮的翻身仗——大衣卖到 3000 元一件依然产销两旺。货如轮转中，雅莹不但扭亏为盈，还走上新的快车道，创造了业绩新高。

1999 年 10 月 18 日，喘过气来的张华明决定召开一次特别的会议，一是感谢大家在过去两年对自己和雅莹的支持；二是好好交代、检讨过去两年的情况并展望未来。曾经相助过雅莹的银行、供应商、销售伙伴、员工干部等 200 人都一一到场开了会。会上，张华明细数了存在的问题、漏洞，介绍了眼下的境况，坦诚了自己的策略，也分享了自己对未来发展的思考。其诚意和智慧、担当精神和事业心，得到一致的支持。不少伙伴当场表示，要与雅莹风雨同舟，并肩前进。曾经多次仗义相助的喜盈盈宋董事长就当场表示，"我看重华明的为人，我们的仓库就是雅莹的仓库！"

也是当年，雅莹成了全国阿尔巴卡大衣市场销售额最大的品牌之一。

On October 18, 1999, Hwaming called for a special meeting to thank everyone who supported the company during its darkest moments and to review the company's performance while sharing its future plans. Around 200 people, including suppliers, sales partners and staff representatives were invited to the meeting, and as Hwaming shared his insights and vision for the future, many were inspired, expressing their willingness to stick with yaying through thick and thin.

It was this year that yaying became one of the top brands for Alpaca coats.

一鼓作气, 服装四季
FOUR SEASONS OF FASHION

雅莹成立伊始，张华明就有一个明确的目标：要把雅莹打造成为一个时尚品牌。走出困境，并靠"阿尔巴卡大衣"东山再起后，雅莹开始朝向这个目标继续努力，并通过创新面料研发以及毛衣时装化等，令雅莹进一步从单季走向四季的品类发展。

时装的源头是面料，没有好的面料，就没有好的服装。一心要做好服装的张华明对面料极其重视。早在 1996 年，雅莹就在上海设立了产品研发设计中心。其中的一个重点就是面料研发，1999 年春夏，张华明与杭州天成丝织厂胡文威合作，开创采用真丝＋莱卡结合的弹力桑波缎面料获得成功，而张华明看好并最终打了胜仗的阿尔巴卡大衣，也首先是因为看准了面料。决定从单季走向四季后，他也以更大力度在面料研发上投入并不断突破，甚至为此不惜成本。

1999 年年底，阿尔巴卡大衣大获成功之际，重庆代理商梁贤安从台湾买了一件素色雪纺裙子样衣。看到面料的张华明，凭借多年市场经验立刻判断——这种雪纺面料一定会受欢迎。此后，他几次找人开发面料都不成功，但依然不放弃，最终在深圳一布料市场通过朱适、朱佩君兄妹找到最接近的进口面料。与台湾雪纺面料相比，深圳这款面料垂感稍显不足，但张华明仍然坚信自己的眼光，并大胆押注自己的判断：把整个市场几十种颜色的这款面料全部买了下来。

Hwaming had a clear aim for the company from day one: to transform yaying into a fashion brand. Having survived his first crisis and making a comeback with the Alpaca coat, Hwaming returned his focus to this aim. Good materials are both the beginning and end-product of fashion, and Hwaming always emphasised the use of high-quality materials.

As early as 1996, he had set up a product research and design centre in Shanghai, with a major focus on textile innovation. In the early summer of 1999, he reached an agreement with Hu Wenwei, director of Hangzhou Tiancheng Silk Factory, to jointly develop stretch silk jacquard fabric by combining silk jacquard with lycra. This would become one of the many breakthrough fabric innovations by yaying at that time, as it pushed to develop four seasons of products.

At the end of 1999, following the success of the Alpaca coats, Liang Xian'an brought a new type of material to Hwaming: a plain chiffon dress sample from Taiwan. Hwaming, based on his years of experience, instantly saw huge potential in the fabric. He attempted to recreate the fabric several times without success, as the R&D process was difficult, and it was not until the end of 2001 that the

这批雪纺面料制成的衣服很快就售罄了。张华明于是进一步创新，找到之前的一家厂商继续合作研发。又是一番努力后，这次终于成功了，并从次品率高达 30% 的水平步步提升，在 2001 年年末实现了品质的稳定。

素色雪纺品质稳定之后，张华明又继续创新——在素色面料上尝试印花工艺。这是难度非常大的挑战，因为雪纺印花的缩率极难控制。但张华明信心笃定，百折不挠，他和时任采购部经理刘瑾找到苏州的两家韩资企业苏州大宇和日新，经过多次实验终于研发出了雪纺印花工艺。新研发的雪纺印花花型多样，为更多款式设计、版型、生产制作提供了更大的空间。提到这种面料，张华明至今赞赏有加："这就像真丝乔其纱那样漂亮，洗完之后又不硬，手感很好，穿在身上透气，价格也不贵。雕花的效果是真丝做不出的。"

后来，由雅莹推动研发的这款印花雪纺还成了整个服装业的一个革命级创新，不但领先了市场，还提升了整个市场的雪纺工艺水平。雅莹自身的雪纺面料市场也被快速培养起来，很快达到每年 200 万~300 万米的采购量，并在相当长一段时间里处于该领域的垄断地位。

真丝弹力桑波缎的创新，让雅莹在真丝市场获得巨大的成功；阿尔巴卡让雅莹填补了秋冬的薄弱，充实了雅莹的产品线。对面料的重视和创新，让雅莹获得超越同行的成绩，但

quality of the brand's chiffon fabric gradually stabilised. In the meantime, he also found another batch of imported chiffon fabric through Zhu Shi and Zhu Peijun, who had been working with the company on key fabrics from 1997. Although not as good as the ones from Taiwan, Hwaming still bought over 10 different colours.

After 2001, Hwaming continued to innovate with the fabric, working on floral prints led by Liu Jin, then purchasing manager, and partnering with Suzhou Dayu and Nissin, two Korean-funded enterprises in Suzhou. yaying's new chiffon collections featured a variety of a floral print patterns and became well-known in the market for their outstanding texture, colour and breathability.

The newly developed printed chiffon fabrics allowed more creative room for designers, pattern makers and dressmakers. To this day, Hwaming is full of praise for the material whenever people talk about it, saying: "It is as beautiful as silk georgette. It is always soft to the touch, even after washing. It is highly breathable and most importantly, affordable too. These floral prints are also not possible with silk."

"

服装的源头是面料，没有好的面料，就没有好的服装。

"

2000 年，雅莹自主开发出印花雪纺面料

OPPOSITE

yaying successfully develops the floral print
chiffon fabric, 2000

这些面料的创新，依然还局限在市场已有产品的范围之内，雪纺面料的开发，则让雅莹在面料上一举实现重大突破：直接走上了自主研发、开创市场的道路，也让雅莹更大程度地分享了市场的红利。"尤其是雪纺面料，它什么都可以做。衬衫、短袖、连衣裙、裤子，什么都可以做。印花、素色都可以。最重要的是，顾客都翘大拇指。我们整整卖了三年，产品在全国市场可以说是所向披靡，甚至包装都不用打开，就被抢掉了。"

雪纺面料的开发，也是坚持好材料的雅莹在材料创新上的一个大突破。张华明回忆，他一接触到雪纺面料就被其深深折服，并希望用这样的面料做出更好的产品。但当时，这种面料还被国外垄断且很难采购到，国内也没有其他中资企业在做，于是他只能自己来创新。

不过，张华明最初也并非要自主研发雪纺，而是想用真丝来做替代，可多种尝试后，依然失败，最后才与两家韩资企业合作。'真丝做不出白色（偏黄）且容易皱，因此花了三年，在当时的情况下挤出上百万研发费用，自己去研发雪纺。材料的纱感、垂坠度都很好。"

The market share of yaying's chiffon creations skyrocketed and the company's annual usage of the fabric reached a high of nearly 2 to 3 million metres. "The versatility of chiffon allowed us to expand our product mix — shirts, short sleeves blouses, dresses and pants, in plain colour or a variety of colours, and we received much positive feedback from our customers. We were the leading brand for chiffon fabric at that time."

From yaying's launch of fine silk for the Chinese market, to its extensive silk collection range, to its astute choice of high-end Alpaca wool, to its R&D of chiffon fabric, the company had demonstrated the importance it placed on using high-quality materials. This continuous investment and innovation in fabrics placed it miles ahead of its competition.

Whilst Hwaming was busy developing chiffon fabric, his wife, Dai Xueming, was also making breakthroughs in product development. After returning to Jiaxing from Beijing, she began to oversee the production process, paying meticulous attention to every detail, from style to size, and from invoice to delivery, as she worked in the warehouse until 10 at night every day.

右页：
雅莹 2000 年春季大片，印花雪纺衬衫

OPPOSITE
Floral print chiffon blouse, yaying Spring 2000 ad campaign

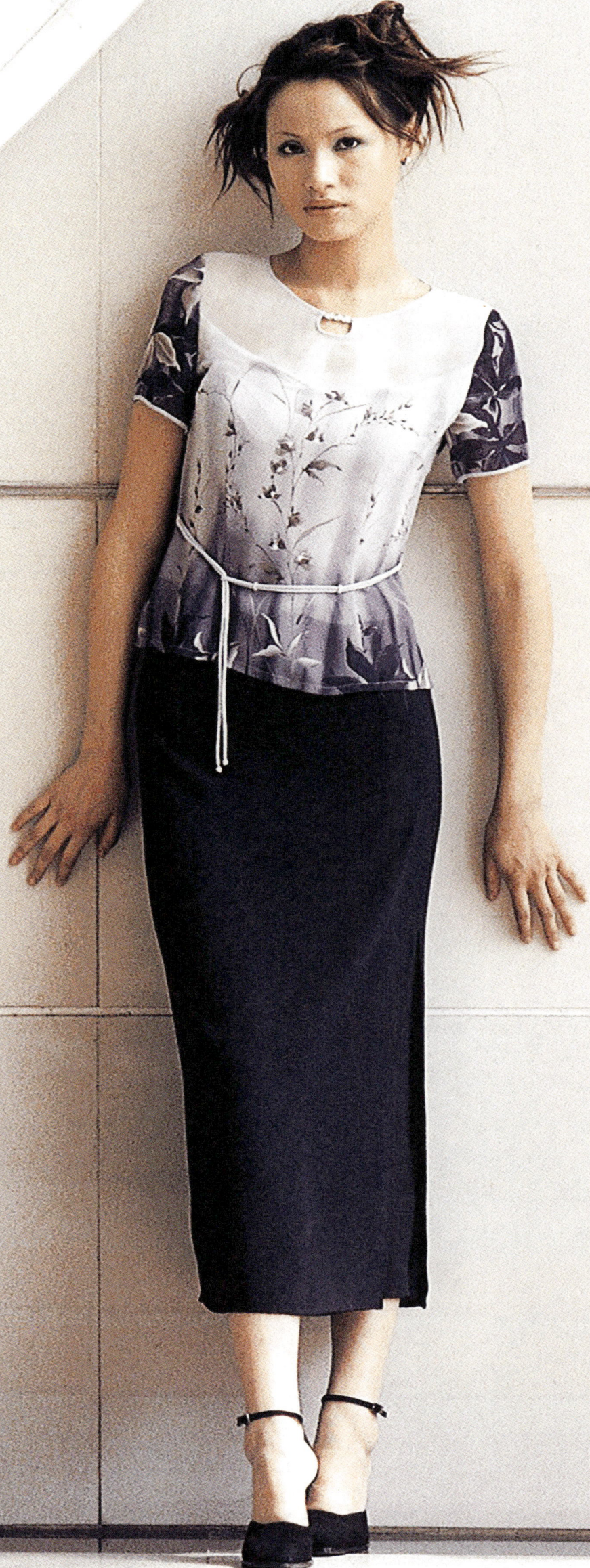

左页：
雅莹 2001 年春夏大片，印花雪纺衬衫及半裙

右图：
2001年春夏，雅莹印花雪纺衬衫及半裙设
计原稿

OPPOSITE
Floral pr nt chiffon blouse and skirt, yaying Spring
2000 ad campaign

RIGHT
Original design sketches of yaying Spring 2000
floral print chiffon blouse and skirt

DESIGN依賴書

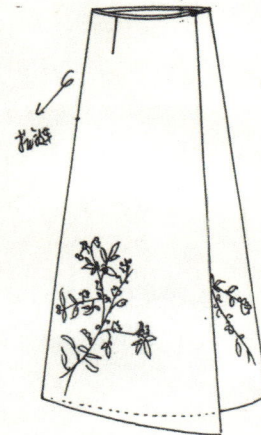

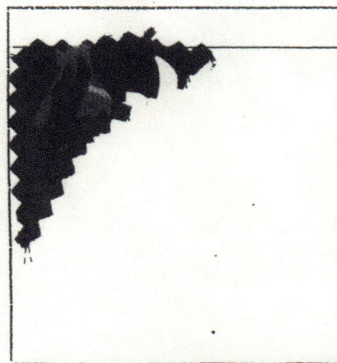

DESIGN GROUP

直到今天，由雅莹创新研发的这款面料依然还很畅销，这次成功，也大大鼓舞了张华明的创新勇气和信心，并无意间对中国雪纺（化纤）领域的材料进步做出了里程碑式的贡献。

张华明开发雪纺面料的同时，太太戴雪明也在产品开发上获得突破性进展。跟着张华明在北京开拓市场期间，性格开朗的戴雪明就主动走出去，协助打点生意以及各种人际关系。回到嘉兴后，她也在大后方管生产，事无巨细，每一个款式、每一个尺码、每一个单子、每一批发货都亲自坐镇，每天在库房忙到晚上十点。

这些事情看起来普通，但非常琐碎，连张华明都觉得是"要命的事"，戴雪明却能一一理顺。张华明说，戴雪明对公司的发展起到了巨大的作用，1998 年发生的困难，包括大货工艺出了问题，很大程度上就是因为 1997 年第一个孩子出生后，戴雪明放下业务回家带孩子，让他缺少了贤内助："当时就是因为妻子在家里带孩子，我们几个大男人管工厂，做起来都大大咧咧。结果，一些细节问题没有管控好，就出事了。"戴雪明自己也开玩笑说："我就跟张华明说了，你把我用好，公司就能好。"

These tasks seemed marginal, but even Hwaming found them complex, whilst Xueming sorted them out one by one with ease. "Xueming has always played an instrumental role in the company's development," said Hwaming, as he reflected on the company's crisis in 1998, a time when his wife was not by his side as she had just given birth to their son. "At that time, my wife was taking care of the child at home, leaving us, a group of men, to take care of both production and warehousing. We were not as meticulous as she is, and as a result, things went wrong," said Hwaming. "I've told Hwaming that if he knows how to plan my role well, the company will definitely do well," Xueming joked in her reply.

Xueming returned to work in 1999, providing a major lift for the company. Xueming was born into a family that produced sweaters, and she had learned knitting and embroidering at the age of 10. In 2000, a former neighbour who was also in the business of sweater production, approached Xueming, hoping to sell her products in yaying's store. Xueming agreed and the good response inspired her.

右页：
2000 年代早期，雅莹经典雪纺系列

OPPOSITE
Iconic selections from yaying's chiffon series, early 2000s

150

左图：
雅莹 2001 年春夏订货会雪纺时装

右页：
雅莹 2001 年春夏大片，真丝数码
印花无袖衬衫

ABOVE
Chiffon pieces at yaying's Spring-Summer
2001 trade fair

OPPOSITE
Floral print sleeveless silk blouse, yaying
Summer 2000 ad campaign

> "
>
> 夏季有丝绸，冬季有大衣，春秋有毛衣，
> 雅莹的产品线因此得以丰富，
> 成为一年四季都有当季主打产品上市的时装企业。
> 这一变化对雅莹的扩张发展意义重大，
> 也为雅莹迈向品牌化打下了最重要的基础。
>
> "

1999 年，戴雪明重新回到公司，更是给雅莹和张华明带来巨大的助力。戴雪明从小就接触毛衣，10 岁就开始自己织毛衣、绣花。2000 年，之前一个做毛衣的邻居找上戴雪明，希望将自己的货放在雅莹店里卖，她同意了，结果销量不错。

这启发戴雪明有了进一步的思考：当时，毛衣的主要功能还是保暖，戴雪明认为，毛衣也可以做得很漂亮，跟雅莹的定位结合起来，有优雅美丽的设计和品味。于是，她大胆创新，将毛衣设计成短袖、无袖、连衣裙等各种流行样式，推向市场。戴雪明的创新受到了市场的欢迎。当时，还没有一家毛衣品牌的公司像雅莹这么做。这一创新让雅莹开创出一个新商孔——将毛衣时装化，也让雅莹成为中国毛衣时装化的创新先驱。

夏季有丝绸，冬季有大衣，春秋有毛衣，雅莹的产品线因此得以丰富，成为一年四季都有当季主打产品上市的时装企业。这一变化对雅莹的扩张发展意义重大，也为雅莹迈向品牌化打下了最重要的基础。

Sweaters had been cold-weather essentials only but Xueming saw that they could be a byword for the sense of fashion and style which yaying was pursuing. Moving forward, she boldly innovated with a variety of fresh sweater designs — including short sleeves, sleeveless and dresses — becoming a pioneer of fashionable sweaters in the Chinese fashion market.

By the turn of the 21st century, yaying's product mix included silk in the summer, overcoats in the winter, and sweaters in the spring and autumn, successfully extending its product line from a single season to all four seasons.

右页：
2000 年秋冬，中国超模佟晨洁身着
雅莹高领无袖毛衣

OPPOSITE
Chinese supermodel Tong Chenjie in
yaying's turtleneck sleeveless sweater,
Autumn-Winter 2000

左页：
2000 年秋冬，雅莹紫色长袖针织衫

右图：
2000 年秋冬，雅莹棕色短袖高领针织衫

OPPOSITE
Purple long sleeve sweater, yaying
Autumn-Winter 2000

RIGHT
Brown turtleneck short sleeve sweater,
yaying Autumn-Winter 2000

2000-2001 AUTUMN & WINTER

雅莹

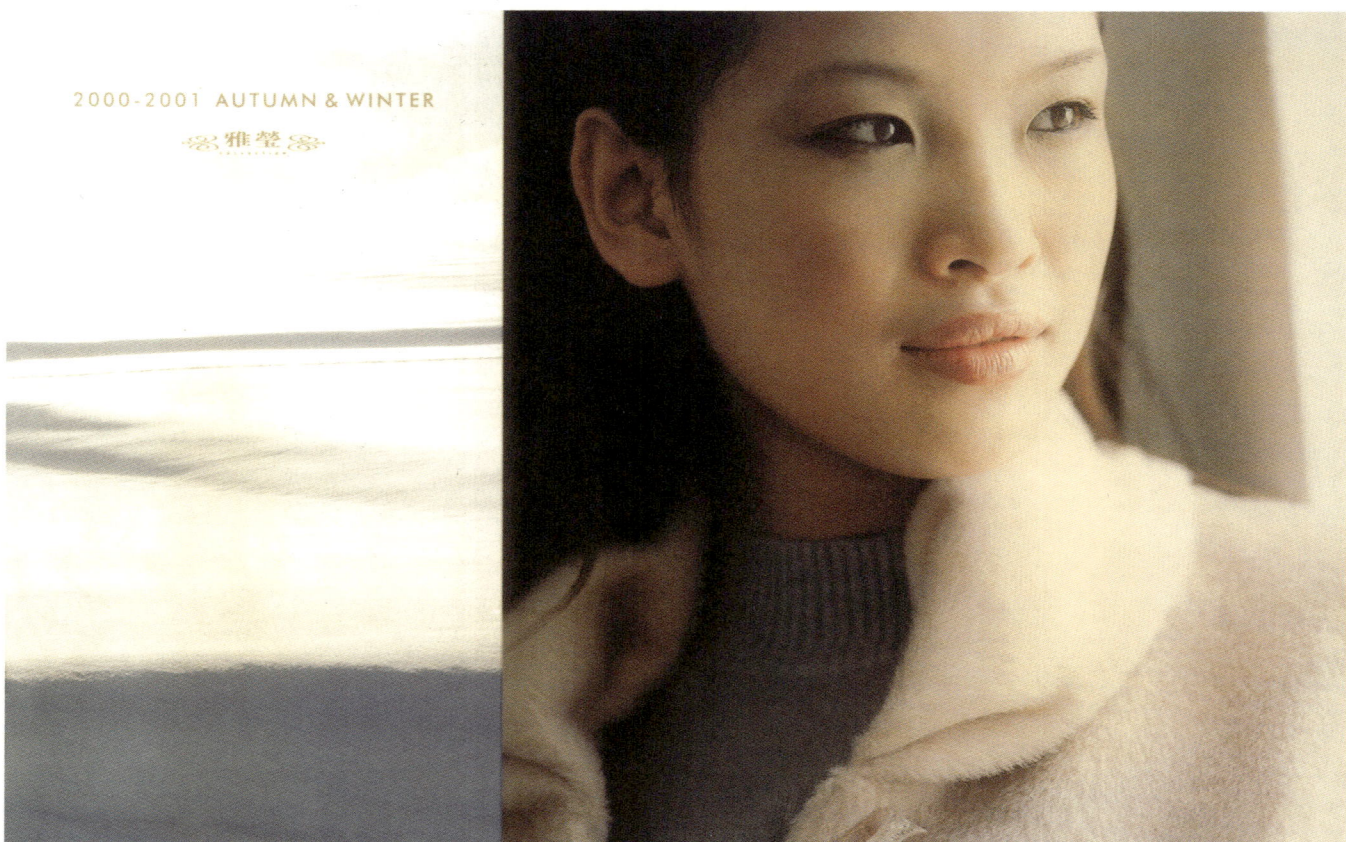

上图 / 右页：

雅莹 2000 年秋冬产品手册，中国超模
佟晨洁领衔呈现雅莹阿尔巴卡大衣系
列，以及雅莹创新毛衣时装化系列

ABOVE / OPPOSITE

yaying's lookbook, Autumn-Winter 2000,
featuring Chinese supermodel Tong
Chenjie in yaying's Alpaca coat collection
and designer sweaters

ELEGANT.PROSPER

BLUE

159

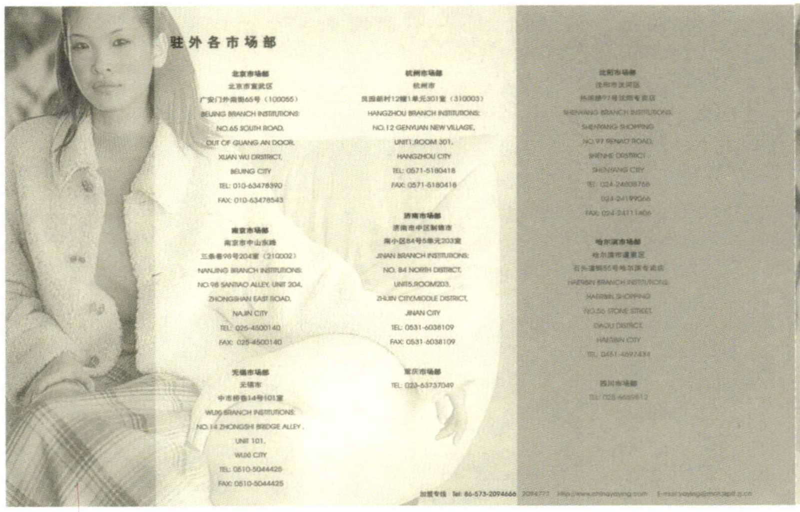

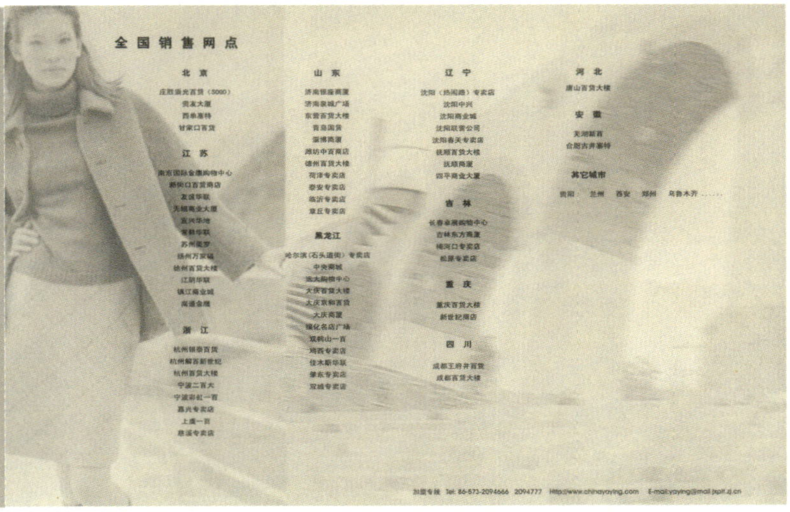

上图 / 右页：
雅莹 2001 年春夏产品手册

ABOVE / OPPOSITE
yaying's lookbook, Spring-Summer 2001

BLACK

Den Alltag hinter sich lassen, die Unabhängigkeit leben.
Lebenslanges Glück.

GAMBOGE

Ich vertraue meiner Intuition und treffe klare Entscheidungen.
Ich genieße es, Frau zu sein.

BLACK

新建本部，脱胎换骨

CREATING NEW SYNERGY WITH A NEW HEADQUARTERS

2000 年，不但恢复了元气，规模实力还更上层楼之后，张华明开始布局雅莹新一轮的发展。他在北京设了仓库，并提出一个具有里程碑意义，也奠基雅莹日后发展的重要计划：自己盖楼兴建本部生产基地。

雅莹的实力还不足以支持这一计划的完成，伙伴与朋友再一次大力地支持了他，让他梦想得以圆满实现。其中，喜盈盈董事长宋世楹主动为他担保，中国银行嘉兴分行主任孙林燕鼎力支持，让雅莹获得贷款 500 万元。政府也特别看好雅莹的发展，在嘉兴华云路特批出售了将近 17 亩的土地给雅莹。利用这些有利条件，张华明在当时还相对荒郊的嘉北地区盖起了一座三层大楼：一楼为办公区、仓库，二楼为设计师、版师工作区，三楼则是生产车间。

为确保新基地建成后能尽快正常生产，基地尚在建时，张华明就安排时任负责人资招聘的李炜中提前招纳了 35 名基础不错的员工，提前进行培训。基地没有地方，他就把课堂设到洛东工厂，每天安排车辆接送前往，直到正式入驻华云路。这次超前的人力培植，也是张华明从现代人力资源管理的学习中收获到的一个硕果：这些班组长，再后来都成了雅莹的得力骨干。

精心准备和紧锣密鼓的筹备下，2001 年，雅莹告别租住了 3 年零 3 个月的戴梦得大楼，搬进了真正属于自己的本部，一个集产销研于一体的时尚女装企业由此初具雏形。也是在 2001 年，张华明将公司品牌由雅莹升级为根据雅莹英文翻译的 Elegant Prosper，寓意优雅美好、晶莹繁盛。新品牌名随即被沿用于公司大厅及当时的各大门店。以此为标志，雅莹开

yaying continued to grow in scale and strength, and Hwaming started to plan for a new phase of expansion with a new headquarters. With support from partners and friends, and even a confidence-boosting backing from the local government who sold them nearly 17 acres of land, yaying began construction on a three-storey building along Huayun Road in Jiabei district (now known as Xiuzhou district). The new headquarters housed its administrative offices and warehouse on the first floor, its design workspace on the second floor and its production workshop on the third floor.

Planning ahead, Hwaming also began recruiting new talents for the headquarters, hiring 35 individuals, many of whom hold important positions in the company to this day and have become acclaimed professionals in their fields. While construction was ongoing, Li Weizhong, who oversaw human resources at that time, would provide new hires with training at the company's factory in Luodong, and also provide transport between the office and their homes until the new headquarters was completed.

In 2001, yaying bid farewell to their office in the Diamond Hotel, which they had rented for over 3 years, and moved into its very own new headquarters. A modern women's fashion enterprise bringing its design, manufacturing and retail functions together to improve synergy began to take shape. It was also in the same year that Hwaming officially launched yaying's new English brand name — Elegant Prosper.

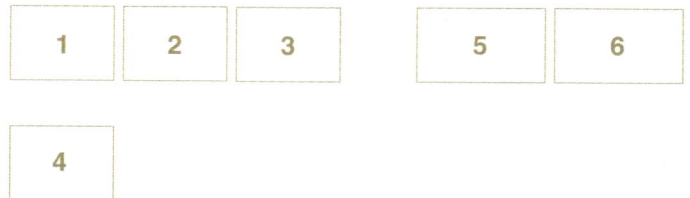

上图 / 左图 / 右页：

1. 雅莹本部前台，展示全新英文品牌名称 Elegant Prosper

2-3. 办公区

4. 设计师版师工作区

5-6. 生产车间

ABOVE / LEFT / OPPOSITE

1. Front desk with yaying's new English brand name — Elegant Prosper, 2001

2-3. Office space

4. Design workspace

5-6. Production workshop

| 1 | 2 | 3 | | 5 | 6 |

| 4 |

始了全新的发展与提升。

雅莹，从此真正有了自己的一片天地，也是真正的根基。

兴建总部是雅莹区别于一般服装经营者，真正迈向现代服装企业的关键里程碑，也体现出张华明有别于普通商人的远大目光和志向。而当时已经在北京、上海有过成功经历的张华明，没有像一些同行那样迷恋北京、上海这样的大城市，甚至是图求大城市的体面和风光，而是选择继续留在嘉兴兴办工厂和实业，则是他务实、低调作风使然。

这奠定了雅莹今日发展的扎实根基，也让雅莹通过自己的发展对家乡、嘉兴的发展起到更积极的作用和贡献。如今，雅莹总部除华云路之外，还在毗邻的几处兴建办公区域，整体占地面积至210亩左右，员工近5000名，而且先后设立了时尚产业园、独立的生产基地等。但若没有张华明当年的勇敢一跃，建立自己的根据地、大本营，依旧租用办公楼，一切或许又是另一番局面了。

如今回忆起那几年，张华明和戴雪明印象最深的还是1998~1999年的艰难。他们都把这段经历比作雅莹的"长征"。这"长征"不但让雅莹具备了更强的风险意识和抗风险能力，也让张华明夫妇对父亲一直告诫的"要想做好事，先要做好人"有了更切肤的体会，并将其当成信仰去坚持。

Having its own headquarters was a key milestone for yaying in its pursuit to stand out in the industry and truly become a modern fashion enterprise. It also reflected Hwaming's entrepreneurial vision and ambition. Hwaming already had experience and success in Beijing and Shanghai, but he was not obsessed with big cities or the comfort and splendour that came with them. Instead, he preferred to stay in Jiaxing and focus on strengthening the company, a decision very much in line with his pragmatic personality and low-key style.

Looking back, the toughest times in 1998 and 1999 would be forever engraved in the minds and hearts of Hwaming and Xueming. They would refer these times to the "Long March", but this Long March had made them stronger, with better risk awareness and management abilities. It also left them with a deeper experience of Hwaming's father's teachings of being virtuous, a key value that they continue to pass on.

Hwaming would always say, "Without all the support, yaying would have gone bankrupt and closed in 1998." Those who were willing to help them when they were at their lowest point not only had faith in the couple's character and capabilities, but also had confidence in yaying's future.

那些帮助雅莹走出困境的人，也被张华明夫妇视作自己和雅莹的贵人一生感恩。雅莹每一次对发展历程的回顾，张华明都会对当年帮助雅莹走出低谷的贵人们一一点名感谢。2018年10月18日，在雅莹集团30周年的励志庆典上，他也是一字一句地强调："这里要特别感谢浙江喜盈盈集团的宋世楹总经理当时慷慨提供了价值300多万元的精品阿尔巴卡高档面料，让我们继续生产秋冬大衣；还有嘉兴市蓝翔航天器材厂庞家俊总经理冒着巨大的风险主动帮我们担保。还有中国银行的孙林燕和黄龙新的积极放贷。"

张华明说，如果不是这些贵人的相助，雅莹在1998年就已破产关门了。这些贵人们，也都是看好张华明夫妇的能力和品行，看好雅莹的发展，才在关键时刻给予雅莹和张华明帮助。

如果想要得到他人的信任和支持，必须付出百分之一千的真诚和努力，而且不光要是好人，还要是有能力的好人。"要有真正的发展之道，要有坚定的信心、坚强的毅力并且坦诚，遇到问题自己要有想法，别人才能相助成行，要知道如何改进、如何调整，要脚踏实地，亲力亲为，最终将一切落到实处！"他强调。

此番逆境重生，不但让雅莹发展到了更高层级，也让张华明对未来更有了信心。他说："人生需要考验，如果一直一帆风顺就会有问题。经过这样考验，一旦逾越过难关便是脱胎换骨！"也幸亏有这样的脱胎换骨，雅莹才安然度过在此之后的又一次危机，并且把危险变成了巨大的机会。

Hwaming believed that if one wants to win the trust of another, one needs to go above and beyond the call of duty and possess both integrity and capability to earn it. "You must have a vision and unbreakable faith. If you remain sincere and resilient, even when facing tests and trials, help shall follow. If you remain flexible and eager to go the extra mile, if you keep your feet on the ground and you roll up your sleeves to get down to work, you will eventually make things happen."

He added, "Life has never been and shouldn't be all smooth sailing, because that would create problems. Everyone at some point in his or her life needs to be tested so that they can be reborn a better person!" Pulling through the toughest of times, yaying was reborn from adversity and Hwaming became more confident about the future.

1	2	3	4	5
6	7	8		

右页：
1997 至 2001 年之际，雅莹历经挑战，获得众多贵人襄助（部分）：
1. 宋世楹 2. 黄龙新 3. 庞家俊 4. 梁贤安 5. 李成林 6. 戴雪英、张建明夫妇 7. 朱适、朱佩俊兄妹 8. 孙林燕

OPPOSITE
The company received wide support from its partners in its times of need from 1997 to 2001 (not all-inclusive):
1. Song Shiying 2. Huang Longxin 3. Pang Jiajun 4. Liang Xian'an 5. Li Chenglin 6. Dai Xueying and her husband, Zhang Jianming 7. Zhu Shi and Zhu Peijun 8. Sun Linyan

> 要有真正的发展之道，
> 要有坚定的信心、坚强的毅力并且坦诚，
> 遇到问题自己要有想法，别人才能相助成行，
> 要知道要如何改进、如何调整，
> 要脚踏实地，亲力亲为，最终将一切落到实处！

非典悟道，固本培元
SARS AND LAYING A NEW FOUNDATION

"企业业绩下滑或破产的根本原因是，不能为目标顾客提供符合需求的优质产品和服务"，这成为张华明的座右铭。以顾客为中心的经营信念，也在此间被雅莹确立下来，成为企业的核心文化。

"The fundamental reason that a company declines or fails is that it can no longer provide high-quality products and services that meet consumer demands." This is one of Hwaming's key beliefs. Placing customers at the core of its business philosophy became a top priority for Elegant Prosper.

宝贵的100天
CRITICAL 100 DAYS

2003 年，雅莹刚新建本部大楼，物流中心正着手建设，投入巨大，而此时又一场灾难降临了：全国陷入非典病毒的笼罩，零售业一时间满眼尽是萧条。

雅莹的销售也跌入冰点："整个公司一天最多两三万的营业额"，新建本部基地的喜悦，也渐渐被新的忧患所取代。

与此前面临危机不同的是，经过上次命悬一线又反败为胜的历练，面对这次挫折的张华明并没有慌张，反而意识到这是一个机会："就像每一个困难都会给你机会，叫你痛定思痛，让你升级，这次的挑战也是这样，让我有机会停下来深度思考和检讨，进一步看清企业的弱点。"开源节流，是企业度过危机的通行办法。非典里的雅莹也是如此，总部办公人员还主动降薪与企业共渡难关。有了稳定的大后方，张华明进一步在团队的支持下，站在更高层面以更长远的眼光审视雅莹，也为企业未来的发展再强根基。

其中最重要的举措是，利用因为非典影响而相对"空闲"下来的时间，从深圳和香港请来业内的专家和老师，带领全员展开为期 100 天的内部学习和系统提升。这 100 多天的学习、反思、感悟，让张华明和团队对企业的发展与经营，尤其是卓越品牌的建设有了全新的认知，也让雅莹向现代先进品牌企业的进程有了质的飞跃。

"企业业绩下滑或破产的根本原因是不能为目标顾客提供符合需求的优质产品和服务！不了解顾客真实需求！"张华明说。这次学习的最大收益就是，促使他和雅莹对到底什么是优质产品和服务进行了再思考与再定义："我们的服装风格、卖

It wasn't long after Elegant Prosper had moved into its new headquarters and was riding the momentum towards improved growth, that the SARS outbreak occurred in 2003. The outbreak caused an economic downturn across China, posing a serious test for retail businesses. During this period, companies that rose to the challenges survived, further expanded and opened to new horizons.

Nearly all of Elegant Prosper's retail stores had to close and company sales fell dramatically. "The turnover of the entire company was around 20,000 to 30,000 yuan per day at best." The joy of moving into the new headquarters was soon replaced by new worries. However, Hwaming had grown from previous experiences, and this time he was comparatively calm and saw the crisis as an opportunity. "Just as each adversity before had taught us something and gave us a chance to improve, this time was no exception. It made me stop and reflect on what could have been done better," said Hwaming.

Increasing sources of income and reducing expenditures were common ways for companies to survive such a crisis. During the epidemic, the head office staff also took the initiative to take a pay cut. Everyone had faith in Hwaming and the company to pull through the downturn, and with everyone's support, Hwaming took a strategic and longer-term perspective in response. He invited a diverse panel of industry experts from Shenzhen and Hong Kong to provide a 100-day team training, sharing their knowledge and insights into customers and markets, which enabled a quantum leap for the company on its journey towards becoming a leading fashion brand. The industry-wide shutdown gave the team a chance to reflect on what could be improved, and how to strengthen its risk management and sustainable development.

"我们雅莹连锁总部是生产什么产品的？企业业绩下滑或破产的根本原因：不能为目标顾客提供符合需求的优质产品和服务！不了解她们的真实需求！我们生产的产品是雅莹终端门店，包括我们风格的服装、温馨的卖场形象、卓越的服务、提供卓越服务的人和品牌价值感受！它们都是我们产品的组成部分！其中服装产品是最核心的！

场形象、服务、提供服务的人和品牌价值感受，它们都是我们产品的组成部分。服装产品当然是最核心的，但不是全部！"

通过非典期间的培训和自我悟道，雅莹明确了自己为顾客提供的"产品"要由6部分组成：(1) 终端门店；(2) 服装品类与风格；(3) 卖场形象；(4) 服务；(5) 提供服务的人；(6) 品牌价值感受。

以顾客为中心的经营理念，从此被雅莹确立下来，成为企业的核心文化。

随后，张华明围绕这6大部分，来创建一个卓越品牌，并在此之下，推动雅莹全面转型升级，助力品牌开始大步阔进。不仅实现了单品到系列的突破，也在商业模式创新、渠道模式创新、供应链建设、人力资源建设、信息化管理等多方面引领变革，为集团化运作打下扎实的基础。

"The fundamental reason that a company declines or fails is that it can no longer provide high-quality products and services that meet consumer demands. The brand has lost understanding of its customers," Hwaming believed. He and his team found that the training was extremely helpful in opening up new perspectives and inspiring everyone to rethink and redefine what constitutes an exceptional product or service. "Our fashion style, store image, service, people and brand perception are all part of us. Our clothes themselves are of course the core, but clothes alone are not everything!"

The team concluded its learnings with a customer-centric business strategy that laid out the six critical elements of an exceptional product: (1) retail stores; (2) product categories and styles; (3) store image; (4) service; (5) service people; and (6) brand value. Customer centricity has since then become the key to Elegant Prosper's continuous growth.

The company pursued a comprehensive transformation after the SARS period by implementing an upgraded business model and investing in branding, production lines, sales channels, supply chain, information technology and corporate management, all of which laid a new foundation for growth.

上图：
2003 年非典期间，开展百天培训学习后，总结出产品由 6 大部分组成

ABOVE
Zhang Hwaming summarising the 6 critical elements of an exceptional product at its 100-day team training during the SARS period in 2003

左图：
2004 年 8 月，张华明与戴雪明代表雅莹与意大利 MiroglioSpA 公司正式合资签约

LEFT
The company formally signs a joint venture agreement with Italian Fashion Group Miroglio S.p.A in August 2004

右图：
2004 年 10 月，庆贺浙江雅莹服装有限公司正式成立之际，张华明总经理现场发布致辞

RIGHT
Zhang Hwaming speaking at the formal launch of the company's joint venture in October 2004

"非典悟道"后，雅莹还第一次"走出去"，向世界先进同行学习，向国际化迈出步伐。期间，张华明夫妇带着团队去到了世界时装之都意大利，他们深入其间与当地同行学习、交流，并且找到合作的机会：2004 年，雅莹与意大利 Miroglio S.p.A 公司合资，共同组建浙江雅莹服装有限公司，让雅莹进入国际化资本与资源合作发展的崭新阶段。

Mircglio S.p.A 此前就与雅莹有过合作，曾是雅莹的面料供应商。2003 年启动新战略后，张华明深刻意识到要让雅莹发展得更好，在越来越激烈的竞争中，把握住中国经济快速发展的机会，必须以更加开放的视野和格局，快速提升自我。于是，他先是前往欧洲学习，认认真真地学习当地优秀企业的商业模式和经营管理，然后萌生了与 Miroglio S.p.A 合作的想法，希望借助对方先进的管理经验，帮助雅莹真正走上接轨世界的发展与行业潮流之中。

这次合作让雅莹成为国内首家与意大利合资的女装企业。虽然后来因为 Miroglio S.p.A 家族变化，双方逐步结束了合资，但张华明依然对这次合资持高度评价，并感恩对方在此期间给雅莹带来的宝贵经验。也是通过这期间变被动为主动的发展与提升，张华明将危险变成机会，用时间换了空间，以固

Hwaming and Xueming, together with a small team, also decided to travel abroad to learn from leading companies of the fashion world. A team led by Hwaming and Xueming first arrived in Italy, the world's fashion capital, where they exchanged knowledge and experience with local counterparts, and agreed on a new collaboration opportunity. In 2004, the company and the Italian fashion group, Miroglio S.p.A, set up a joint venture — China's first Sino-Italian joint venture for womenswear — marking a new stage of international development for the company.

Miroglio S.p.A was previously a fabric supplier for the company and in Hwaming's new growth plan from 2003, he realised that international collaboration was necessary amidst the ever-increasing competition of the fast-growing China market. He went to Europe to study and learn about business strategies and corporate management, and developed the idea of upgrading his business model to partner with a top foreign fashion company. The aim was to transform Elegant Prosper into a truly international brand that could become more involved in the global fashion industry.

Hwaming seized the advantage in a downturn and turned uncertainties into opportunities. "In good times, the risk of organisational restructuring is higher because if you fail, it's probably game over. However, in a market downturn, everyone is pretty much on an equal footing, and it allows you the time to explore and experiment, with the chance of success being higher," said Hwaming.

本培元的再修炼让雅莹完成了从一家服装厂到一家现代时装品牌公司的关键一跃。

"当大家都好时，你来转型风险比较大，要是你转得不好但别人依然好，可能你就出局了；如果大家都不好，都卖不出去，就给了你一个喘息的机会，反正大家都不好，你慢慢转型、探索，成功的可能性比较大。"张华明说，如果没有非典让雅莹停下来思考自己的不足并及时调整，大概也就没有以后的成功了。

非典一百天确立的转型方针被张华明称为"非典悟道"。雅莹所有的经营方针都在这一时期被定下来，此后的发展都是围绕此全面持续发力，从未偏移。尤其重要的还包括，通过非典的自我进化与提升，雅莹还收获了一个更团结一致、同频共振、同心同德的团队，张华明的领导力和管理力也都有了质的进步。

2003 年加入公司，当时负责雅莹生产供应链的仇瑛，一到雅莹就赶上非典，生意因此萧条，但雅莹上下的表现令她至今想来都感到温暖、有力。"我们管理层员工自己提出来工资减半，但给基层员工承诺不减工资。张总、戴总则带着我们努力到外面找订单，维持员工的正常生产。大家都是一心一意跟着企业一起发展，同甘共苦，同进共退。"

2001 年加入工厂任小组长的沈美文也回忆，即便当时服装行业的大环境很不好，实体都不好，工厂一线工人都没有降工资，而且依然多劳多得，这也让一线的员工都非常感动，珍惜这样的老板和公司。"大家也因此更有信心，知道公司不会因为有点困难，就放弃我们，或者减少我们的收入。"沈美文认为，这要归功于张华明在关键时刻的正确策略，但最重要的，还是有赖于雅莹长期对员工友善的文化贯彻，得益于张华明夫妇的胸怀、格局和品德。

"他是很真诚地对待我们的，也很照顾我们的利益，让我们对公司充满了信心。所以，我们都是更加努力地工作。后来市场一复苏，我们就很快恢复了业务，而且做得更好。"

The SARS period offered valuable time for the company to pause, reflect and adjust. In different circumstances, Elegant Prosper would probably not have been able to achieve today's success. The strategies established during the 100 days of the epidemic were dubbed the "SARS enlightenment" by Hwaming. He had continued to grow in terms of his leadership and management competencies, and many of his business strategies were inspired by this period. Most importantly, by pulling through the tough time together, the team became more united and determined.

Qiu Ying joined the company in 2003 to oversee the company's supply chain not long before the SARS outbreak. Qiu Ying remains moved by the solidarity and selflessness of the people to this day: "Our management team took the initiative to take a pay cut and the company promised the rest of us full wages. Mr. Zhang and Ms. Dai proactively looked for new orders to maintain production. Everyone chose to stick together with the company."

Shen Meiwen, who joined the factory as a team leader in 2001, recalled that although the overall environment for the apparel industry was difficult at the time, the front-line workers did not have their wages reduced and those who did more continued to get more pay. All the employees felt truly valued working at Elegant Prosper. "Our confidence was boosted by knowing that the company would not compromise us in difficult times." There is no doubt that Hwaming's business strategies played a key role in the company's accomplishments but Meiwen believed that Elegant Prosper's success was due most importantly to its "people-oriented" culture, and the good heart and morals of Hwaming and Xueming.

"He always treated us sincerely and would ensure our benefits. This made us feel confident in the company. Therefore, we all worked harder. As soon as the market recovered, we resumed business rather quickly and achieved much better results," Meiwen continued.

从四季单品走向系列产品
MORE STYLES, MORE COLLECTIONS, MORE CATEGORIES

到 2003 年，雅莹已经形成了衬衫、大衣、毛衣等连接四季的时装单品。非典的培训，尤其是对如何经营卓越品牌的深刻反思，以及到国外的考察，让张华明和戴雪明认识到单品的不足，进而进一步对服装产品进行了再拓展。

2004 年开始，雅莹通过对国外设计企划的学习和自身探索，在符合品牌整体调性即优雅时尚的前提下，增加产品线，推出了系列化产品，促进了品牌的张力和活力，也让公司再次走在了国内同行的前列。

此时加入雅莹不久的田玲、高鹰等设计人才是推动这一工程的核心人物。曾在上海一家台资企业工作的高鹰和田玲也是夫妻档，因为一次合作与张华明认识。颇具戏剧性的是，那次合作让雅莹遭遇了不小的亏损，但张华明却在此间与高鹰、田玲很是投机，继而于 2002 年邀请他们一起加入雅莹一直工作到现在，让双方的相遇、相识成了意外的机缘。

By 2003, Elegant Prosper had developed signature pieces across four seasons — shirts, overcoats and sweaters. However, Hwaming and Xueming understood from their experience and time abroad that they had to continue expanding their product lines. Tian Ling and Gao Ying, who had recently joined the company, became the core figures behind the project. The couple used to work for a Taiwanese company based in Shanghai and had met Hwaming through a collaboration. They enjoyed working together and Hwaming invited them to join Elegant Prosper in 2002. They remain in charge of the brand's designs and product mix today. Tian Ling and Gao Ying were an inventive couple who enjoyed trying out fresh new ideas. They worked closely with Hwaming and Xueming, and successfully enriched the Elegant Prosper's product line with more creative styles, collections and categories.

左图 / 右页：
2004 年春夏，雅莹首创女士 POLO
衫系列

LEFT / OPPOSITE
Elegant Prosper launches polo shirts for women, becoming the first local brand to do so. Spring-Summer 2004

左图：

2005 年秋冬，雅莹开启 Sports 运动系列

右图：

2007 年秋冬，雅莹发布 Elegant 高端优雅系列

LEFT

Elegant Prosper launches its Sports series, Autumn-Winter 2005

RIGHT

Elegant Prosper launches its high-end Elegant series, Autumn-Winter 2007

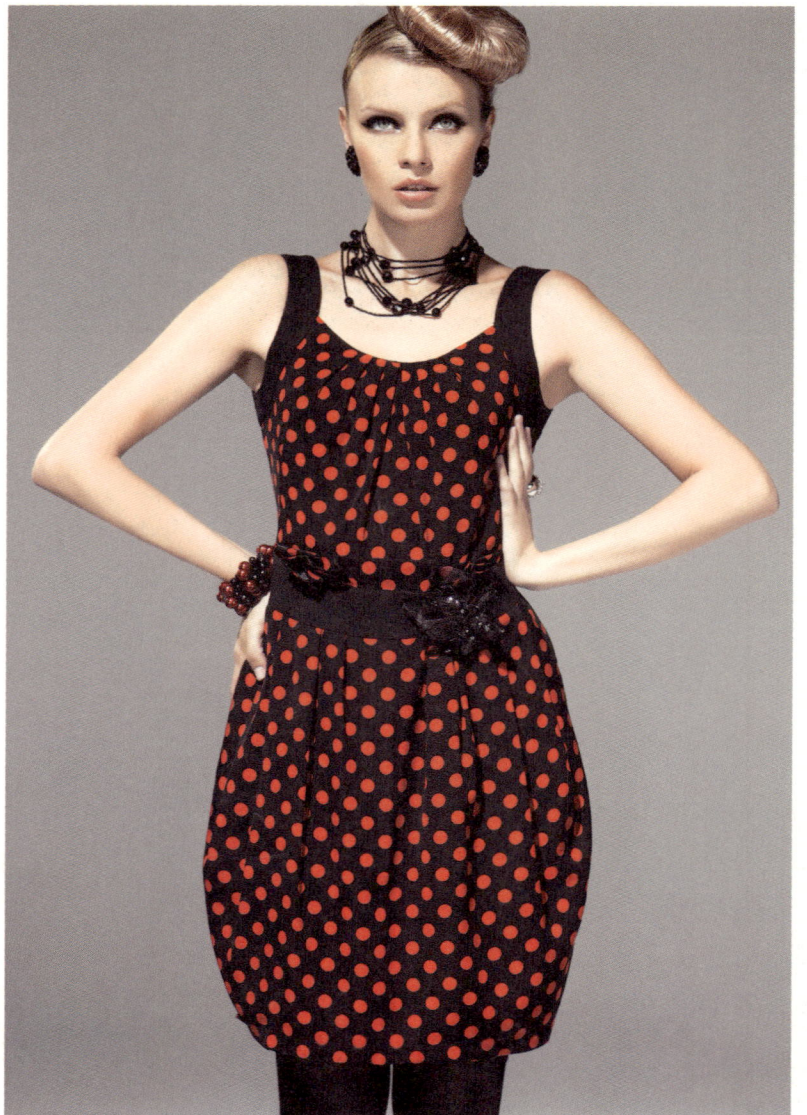

张华明还因此感叹："生命中有些事情也许早都安排好了。"

田玲和高鹰加入雅莹后，主要负责系列化产品的企划。他们既善于学习，又富有创新开拓精神，合力与张华明夫妇将雅莹的时装从品类到设计都提升到新的境界。

一个例子是，当时国外的男士 Polo 衫很流行。雅莹团队看好这一趋势，但又不满足只是跟风模仿，于是在消化吸收的基础上创新，创新设计出一系列女士 Polo 衫，推出市场后在国内大受欢迎。运动风尚流行后，雅莹又接着推出了运动产品线，以张扬运动元素，推出了 Sports 系列，同样大获成功。

广泛地学习，尽可能了解一切优秀的成果并在此基础上前进，但最终一定要做出自己的特色与差异化价值，这是张华明向来的作风。在时装产品线的建立上，他也如此，这让雅莹的自主创新再上台阶：例如，Sports 系列之后推出的高端优雅 Elegant 系列、度假 Holiday 系列，就是设计团队从生活中找到的灵感。既勤劳刻苦，又极富创新精神的戴雪明，更在其间发挥了特别的作用。她发现，公司到海边度假或开年会时，一些同事穿的也是上班时的黑色套装、高跟鞋，感觉非常不搭，于是产生创意和灵感，带领设计团队开发度假系列。

"做衣服不仅是要把一块面料设计成一件好衣服，而且要去想象这件衣服穿在消费者身上，不仅要让她美，也要让她和整个环境相匹配。在家里、在公司里、去度假，衣着都应该和整个环境更和谐。"Elegant 系列、Holiday 系列的研发和成功让戴雪明对设计有了新的认识，也让雅莹的时装研发理念再升级：融入生活方式，根据不同生活场景细分系列，引导顾客进行正确搭配。

依靠持续的探索与创新，那一时期的雅莹还形成了 Daily、Party、Sports、Elegant、Holiday 等系列多元化产品，而且在多元化的同时继续专业化，让每条线都有专职的设计师专攻研发，保证了数量与质量的双提升。

多元化产品线的打造，让雅莹既更好地把握了不同的潮流趋势，也更好地满足了女性消费者更加多样化的需求。品质、设计、渠道、产品线等一一厚实积累之后，张华明也将雅莹的品牌塑造与推广提升到新的高度，并走上全国顶级的品牌秀殿堂。

One of their innovations dealt with men's Polo shirts from the west. The company became the first local brand to launch women's Polo shirts as part of its Spring-Summer 2004 collection, and they continued to explore new horizons by launching a stylish *Sports* series in the Autumn-Winter 2005 collection. The high-end *Elegant* and *Holiday* collections that followed the Sports series continued to showcase Elegant Prosper's creativity and innovative spirit.

The design team would always find inspiration from everyday life. Xueming, for instance, found inspiration for the colourful and vibrant Holiday collection after seeing how strange it was for colleagues to wear office-style black suits and high heels to seaside resorts for their holiday trips.

"Dressmaking is not just about converting a fine piece of cloth into fine clothes, it's about imagining what your clothes say about your customers wearing them. It's not only intended to make them feel beautiful but to fit them perfectly in different contexts, be it at home, in the office or on holiday," said Xueming. The success of the Elegant and Holiday collections injected a new perspective into the brand and made the team realise that design must always be about exploring, embracing and serving the diverse lifestyles and needs of customers in markedly new ways.

The team would go on to create the *Daily* and *Party* collections with dedicated designs for each series. Step by step, Elegant Prosper built a diversified product portfolio that met the various needs of modern women. Creative design, high quality materials, captivating marketing and great product choices led to Elegant Prosper's increased renown across the country.

2005年3月25至31日，备受业内外瞩目的中国国际时装周05/06秋冬系列发布会在北京饭店宴会大厅隆重举行。3月30日，雅莹与意大利百年服装企业 Miroglio S.p.A 集团合资并具有浓厚"意大利风潮"的 Elegant.Prosper 隆重亮相于国际时装周，展示其全新的品牌魅力。姜培琳、常春晓、王阳、Monica 等国内外顶级超模联袂演绎了 Elegant.Prosper 的精彩与经典。中国服装协会常务副会长蒋衡杰、中国设计师协会主席王庆应邀出席，全国各主要城市顶级商场的相关领导、时尚媒体及高级合作商 500 余人参加了盛会。

雅莹本次时尚发布分 Collection、Sports 两大系列，由深海幽蓝、晨曦霞光、秋日浓情、剧院魅影等七个章节组成，恰到好处地演绎了现代都会女性的高贵典雅、知性浪漫，塑造了她们热爱生活、活力无限的阳光形象，也令雅莹整个品牌形象大放异彩。

这是雅莹第一次登陆中国国际时装周，国家级、国际级也由此成为雅莹品牌的新属性。雅莹还曾在后续的几届发布会上相继扩大了发布会的规模与影响力，包括邀约李艾、熊黛林等国内顶级模特领衔诠释产品，进一步彰显品牌作为国内女装行业领军品牌的地位。

品牌升级的同时，商业模式、渠道拓展、供应链建设、信息管理、人力资源建设等方面的全面创新提升，也在"非典悟道"的新战略之下，被张华明稳扎稳打地推进。

Elegant Prosper staged its first fashion show at China International Fashion Week's Autumn-Winter 2005/2006. Jiang Peilin, Chang Chunxiao, Wang Yang, Monica and other local and foreign supermodels showcased the brand's upcoming Autumn-Winter collection inspired by the latest Italian trends, which reflected the sophisticated elegance, romantic charm and passionate energy of the modern woman. The show also featured Jiang Hengjie, executive vice president of China Fashion Association, and Wang Qing, chairman of the Chinese Designers Association, along with over 500 guests from high-end shopping malls, fashion media and VIP partners from across the country.

Riding on the success of its inaugural fashion show, from 2006 to 2008, Elegant Prosper continued to debut its collections at China International Fashion Week, with top supermodels such as Li Ai and Xiong Dailin walking down the show's runway. The size of the shows and its brand influence increased year by year, the brand began to gain notice as a top Chinese fashion brand, with a great potential to make an impact on the world's fashion stage.

"

做衣服不仅是把一块面料设计成一件好衣服，
而且要去想象这件衣服穿在消费者身上，
不仅要让她美，也要让她和整个环境相匹配。
在家里、在公司里、去度假，
衣着都应该和整个环境相匹配。

"

Elegant.Prosper®
SPORTS

Elegant.Prosper®
COLLECTION

China International Fashion Week

2005 年中国国际时装周

China International Fashion Week

2006 年中国国际时装周

China   International   Fashion   Week

2007 年中国国际时装周

ELEGANT.PROSPER

2005

2007

2006

2008

渠道创新，形象提升
RETAIL SUCCESS

渠道，始终是张华明最关心的重点工程。他说："渠道最直接关系市场，好的产品要依靠合适的渠道抵达消费者，产品的研发创新也要好的渠道所掌握的消费者反馈来支撑。渠道不创新，一切都是空话。"

渠道，也是张华明在北京时就已经开始创新修炼，也至今仍在持续修炼的功夫，是雅莹的成功基石，是张华明在服装行业最具创新引领的核心竞争力之一。

张华明正式执掌雅莹后，在渠道上的一次大突破是：1999 年在嘉兴市勤俭路与少年路交叉口开出了第一家专卖店。虽然它的面积才 50 多平方米（两层），但这是雅莹一个质的飞跃：从单一的百货渠道变成双渠道营销，并为后来的多渠道营销做了铺垫，也让雅莹的自营连锁化有了开端。

在渠道方面，张华明也总是极具前瞻性。他似乎对与之有关的新事物有天然的敏感，也乐于并且敢于去创新。21 世纪初，兴起于美国的购物中心（shopping mall）模式登陆北上广深等大城市。张华明第一时间注意到这个新事物，认定这是未来的趋势，必将在中国流行，于是决定把雅莹开进其中。

Hwaming had always attached great importance to retail. "Retail is consumer facing. Our products need retail to reach our customers. Our design and production need retail to provide us with customer feedback. Retail is key to everything." Retail was also where Hwaming honed his skills and the laid the foundation of the company's success, making for one of the brand's key competitive advantages.

Hwaming's first retail innovation after taking over the company was to open the brand's first specialty store in Jiaxing in 1999. The store had two floors with a total space of about 50 square metres. It was a pivotal moment in the brand's retail development as it made the transition from a simple department store counter to a multi-dimensional retail space, and it kick-started the company's aggressive and diverse retail expansion strategy.

右页：
1999 年 8 月，雅莹全国首家专卖店在嘉兴开业

OPPOSITE
yaying's first specialty store in China opens in Jiaxing, August 1999

当时，北京和上海这类大城市的 shopping mall 都更喜欢国际大牌。雅莹这样的本土品牌进入的可能性非常小，即便进入其中，消费市场的接受度也很低。于是，张华明决定先从深圳、广州等本土时尚品牌氛围更好的市场打开局面。就像当年从福隆商场到北京城乡再到复兴商业城一样：先找一个机会做出标杆来，然后一一复制。

深圳、广州市场本土服装品牌众多，打入其中同样难度不小，但张华明认准目标，以坚毅、果敢、不放弃的精神最终获得了成功：2005 年，雅莹正式入驻当时亚洲最大购物中心广州正佳广场，开启了首家 shopping mall 店，再次丰富了雅莹的零售渠道形式，其渠道多元化策略也由此开启。

南方告捷之后，手握成绩单的张华明按计划挺进北京、上海，也都陆续获得了成功。这南北格局的形成，以及随后的一系列拓展，也让雅莹彻底领先了同行们一大把。当时，六型购物中心在中国还没有真正开始，张华明的行为因此被很多同行大呼"看不懂"，并被认为不可行。

而等大型购物中心真正星火燎原，同行们都纷纷跟进时，张华明早已将其在全国复制——成都、武汉、西安、上海、北京，七大区域联合拓展，三下五除二就把品牌专卖铺向了全国主要市场，不仅大幅拓展提升了渠道的规模和层次，还借此抢占了本土品牌俘获中高端市场的先机。

过程中的一个插曲是：一家大型商城考虑到雅莹已在另一家购物中心开了店，拒绝了雅莹的入驻申请。对自己有信心的张华明没再继续争取，转而在这家商城附近开出了一家专卖

Hwaming was a forward-looking strategist in retail. He seemed naturally astute to potential gaps in the market and most importantly, he dared to take bold actions with new approaches.

In the beginning of the 21st century, the shopping mall model that was popular in America had entered the big cities of Beijing, Shanghai, Guangzhou and Shenzhen. It caught Hwaming's attention immediately, as he saw its future in China. In the beginning, these shopping malls in Beijing and Shanghai preferred top international brands, whist local brands like Elegant Prosper were unlikely to be given space. Even if these local brands managed to secure a space, customers would generally not pay much attention. Therefore, Hwaming decided to start instead in Shenzhen and Guangzhou, where the market was more friendly to local brands. His experience in Beijing in the early 1990s also taught him that he needed a good track record to gain momentum.

However, the competition in Shenzhen and Guangzhou was not necessarily any lower, as there were still many high-performing apparel brands. Unsurprisingly, this did not stop Hwaming from opening a store in the Guangzhou Grandview Mall, the largest shopping centre in Asia at the time.

He continued to slowly but surely gain a foothold in cities in the south and eventually, in Beijing, Shanghai and many other major cities across the country. He was a first mover when it came to shopping malls and he was brave enough to take the chance when many others did not understand the shopping mall concept; for this reason, he became a market leader.

店："直接开一个楼，我们来看看行不行。"结果，专卖店的成绩很好，这家商城很快就主动找张华明合作了。这也是张华明处理争议，包括面对质疑时的风格之一：不争论，做出来证明给你看。

购物中心大获成功之后，凡是能进的又符合雅莹定位与调性的渠道模式，都成了张华明积极尝试的对象，并最终构筑起一个囊括专卖店、旗舰店、百货商场、街头生活馆等多元模式在内的渠道矩阵。

一手指挥全国扩张的同时，张华明的另一只手还同步按下暂停键——收缩批发业务。此前，雅莹为渡难关定下零售和批发两条腿走路的战略，而随着其品牌化经营与走向全国，张华明主动撤掉了北方的批发点，尽管它们为雅莹贡献了不少利润。继续批发业务，不利于品牌的建设，得到短期利益却损害长远利益。"那时候是生存需要，现在我们要做品牌，不可能经常搞批发。"张华明说，"我们把这段路走完就完了，何必恋战呢？"

停掉批发业务，构建渠道矩阵的期间，张华明还腾出精力持续提升门店形象。2007 年，雅莹就在大本营开出雅莹嘉兴时尚生活馆，正式开启了大店模式。张华明认为，门店与陈设形象，是争夺顾客第一印象的窗口，对品牌体验至关重要，也是雅莹向顾客传递品牌美好的关键。因而，他始终致力于打造更具吸引力、时尚高端的门店形象，雅莹的店铺形象也一次次被他升级、优化。

至 2008 年，雅莹的形象店已历经四次迭代。

In one example that showcases Hwaming's grit, a large shopping mall turned him down because he had opened a store in a competitor's mall. Hwaming, who always had strong self-confidence, did not pursue the matter further; instead, he opened Elegant Prosper's specialty store in the same neighbourhood. Before long, the management team at the shopping mall changed their minds in view of the brand's stellar performance and they even took the initiative to contact Hwaming. This was typical Hwaming — he believed that actions speak louder than words, especially when facing disputes or doubts.

Following the success of the shopping mall expansion, Hwaming did not stop there. He seized each opportunity that the times had to offer and successfully forged a comprehensive and diverse retail network, comprised of flagship stores, large lifestyle experience stores, retail outlets in shopping malls and department stores, and specialty stores.

He also terminated the company's wholesale business to fully focus on the brand's positioning as a fashion brand and he continued to upgrade its store image every few years, with the aim of creating and delivering better and better experiences for customers. By 2008, the brand's store concept had undergone four redesigns.

右图：

1999 年，雅莹全国首家专卖店在嘉兴启幕，它代表了第一个时期的店铺风格。外观简洁大方，整体采用米白色基调，给人以亲近自然的感觉

RIGHT

In 1999, yaying opens its first speciality store in Jiaxing and would represent the brand's first generation store concept. The design is simple and class, adopting a beige tone to give customers an inviting and cozy feel

右图：

第二代形象于 2002 至 2005 年推出。第二代形象店在色彩上增加了黑白对比，强调了标识与模特的组合应用，灯光色彩以舒适、明亮温馨为主基调。并以玻璃及反射面效果的材质为主制作货柜和层板，整体突显出优雅迷人的商业空间。2005 年雅莹正式入驻广州正佳，开设全国首家购物中心店

RIGHT

The second generation store concept spans from 2002 to 2005, with bright, yet warm and comfortable ambient lighting. Glass and reflective surfaces in black and white are used to exude elegance and class. In 2005, Elegant Prosper opens its inaugural shopping mall store in Guangzhou's Zhengjia (Grandview Plaza)

右图

以 2005 年嘉兴时尚生活馆为代表的第三代店铺，着重增加了国际流行元素，为品牌赋予国际化的现代时尚气息，也为雅莹奠定了生活馆理念

RIGHT

Elegant Prosper launches its lifestyle concept store in Jiaxing in 2005. This third generation store focuses on creating an expansive store space that is international and fashionable, continuing the use of modern black tones, whilst adding premium varnished shelvings

右图：

2008 年开始，北京华贸生活馆、成都生活馆、武汉生活馆相继开业，作为第四代形象店铺的北京华贸从门店到陈列都着重展现雅莹对优雅、温馨、爱的诠释。作为突破性的提升，店铺首次使用了皮革及镜钢材质等道具，塑造出更高品质的氛围。同时，第四代店铺还将品牌标识的四方连续图案作为视觉元素应用其中

BELOW

Elegant Prosper continues the opening of its lifestyle concept stores in Beijing, Chengdu and Wuhan from 2008. Beijing Huamao Center becomes the brand's fourth generation signature concept store and aims to strengthen the brand's style of elegance, warmth and love. The concept combines the use of leather and reflective surfaces that elevates the brand's image, and gradually incorporates the EP monogram in the store design in 2009

感动服务, 品牌跃起
HEARTFELT SERVICE

"非典悟道"对张华明特别大的一个启发是，服务也是成就品牌的核心。只有好的服务，匹配好的产品，才会给顾客真正好的体验，进而为品牌加分。

服务从哪里来？最终归结到"人"身上，即提供服务的人。张华明说，作为一份美的事业，零售一线的伙伴扮演着美的传递者，对如何提供优质的服务至关重要。

为将服务做到更好，雅莹在 2007 年提出了"感动服务"的理念，并将此作为品牌形象的一部分。具体包括：将导购更名为客户经理，并对仪容、仪表提出统一标准；通过对销售流程各个环节服务标准的建立和把控，确保销售与服务品质的稳定输出；收集客户的个性化信息，通过更个性与细致化的管理和执行，不但满足顾客所需，而且为顾客创造意外惊喜，最终让顾客获得超出预期的感动。

为培养好服务团队，将"感动服务"落到实处。张华明还启动了一项史无前例的培训工程：他将全国近 100 位店长召回本部一起培训，并亲自和店长深入展开细枝末节的沟通，增加大家对工作的使命感和信心，同时，也提升大家服务的能力和技巧。

"我们是做什么的？我们从事的是美丽的事业，我们是传递美丽的使者。想要真正感动顾客，先要从改变自己开始！"张华明反复在培训中强调这样的精神，也以品牌再塑造让大家切身感受雅莹的尊荣。

比如，2005 年起雅莹连续多年参加中国服装协会在北京举办的中国国际时装周大型专场时装发布会，就大幅提升了品牌

Hwaming's experience during the SARS period made him realise that service is also a culture and core value of a brand. Only when a product of superior quality is married with exceptional service can it deliver a genuinely outstanding customer experience that adds value to the brand.

Exceptional service is essentially and ultimately centred around "people." Hwaming noted: "We work in a beautiful industry. Each and every service person is a brand ambassador who communicates and delivers beauty to our customers every day. They play key roles in offering outstanding customer experiences."

To this end, Elegant Prosper launched the concept of *Heartfelt Service* in 2007. Firstly, service personnel were renamed as customer care managers and given service etiquette standards to meet. Secondly, clear service quality benchmarks and after-sales service processes were established to ensure that service quality standards remained stable across different stores. And thirdly, customer care managers were directed to provide customers with more personalised services to not only meet their needs, but to exceed their expectations.

To strengthen the service team, Hwaming called nearly 100 customer care managers from different stores across the country back to headquarters for training, and talked with each of them in person to learn about their first-hand experiences and observations. He also spoke to them about the value of changing oneself before influencing others, and how each and every staff member serves a brand ambassador that delivers beauty to customers every day. This session not only improved their knowledge and skills, but also instilled even more confidence and passion for the fashion industry.

上图：
2002 年，身着统一制服的雅莹营业员

中图：
2007 年，雅莹推行"感动服务"，与顾客
建立更深层沟通与服务

下图：
2008 年，雅莹"感动服务"下，推行高标
准的仪容、仪表管理

ABOVE
Elegant Prosper service staff, 2002

MIDDLE
Elegant Prosper launches a service campaign
called "Heartfelt Service" in 2007 to establish
deeper communications and connections with
customers

BELOW
As part of its "Heartfelt Service" campaign,
Elegant Prosper upgrades its service standards
from appearance maintenance to communication
skill sets, 2008

> " 我们从事的是美丽的事业，
> 我们是传递美丽的使者。
> 想要真正感动顾客，
> 先要从改变自己开始!
> "

影响，也对提升店员的品牌自信起到相当的支持。

"感动服务"之下，雅莹全国的店铺发生了很多"感动"的故事。列如，有的销售人员为其 VIP 客户庆祝生日，有的销售人员帮客户烹饪，还有的销售人员陪客户到医院就诊。总结起来就是，把客户当家人般贴心入微地关照，而不只是向他们销售产品。

感动之下，雅莹的品牌精神润物无声地融进消费者的心中，不但大幅提升了顾客的品牌忠诚度，也树立口碑，逐步建立起自己在服装产品之外的竞争壁垒，真正开始了依靠优质产品加卓越服务的品牌价值发展之道。

而这条道路能够走得通畅并且越走越宽广，则有赖于顾客看不见的更多基础修炼的支撑。雅莹集团副总裁顾海明曾在雅莹集团 30 周年庆典上感恩顾客时致辞分享："新的时代下，我们要不断和顾客建立起心与心的链接，让我们品牌时刻保持着和顾客的心的互动。这就是多年来雅莹立于不败之地的秘诀，也是我们未来还要坚持的原则。正是顾客的优雅美丽使我们所有雅莹人不断前进，这是我们为之奋斗的最大动力。很感谢顾客给我们服务的机会，这是我们最好的成长机会。"作为雅莹 1996 年培养的第一代英才之一，顾海明曾与老一辈营销人学习零售业务，始终致力于与团队将美不断传递给更多人。

The Heartfelt Service campaign generated many touching stories between customers and Elegant Prosper customer care managers across the country. The managers all viewed their customers as extended family and worked to build long-standing bonds with them, well beyond the simple seller-and-buyer relationship. Elegant Prosper continued to win customers' hearts, which not only increased brand loyalty among existing customers but also created very positive word-of-mouth.

Brand building is the sum of multiple, often intangible, elements. "Times are changing. If you want to take your brand to the next level, you need a sense of purpose that your customers truly connect to, something bigger than the products or services you offer. This relationship has ultimately become the driving force behind our success and a core strategy for our future development. It is the elegance and beauty of our customers that keeps all of us at EP YAYING inspired, growing and moving forward,"said Gu Haiming, deputy CEO of EP YAYING Fashion Group, as he thanked customers at the Group's 30th Anniversary celebration in 2018. Haiming was one of the first management trainees of the Group in 1996, learning the ropes of retail from the company's first generation of employees and continuing to pass beauty on to more people.

右页：
2007 至 2009 年收集的"感动服务"故事（部分）

OPPOSITE
Some of the Moving "Heartfelt Service" stories collected from 2007 to 2009

"2007 年 2 月 14 日，有位顾客走进雅莹店里，对其中的几套春装有了购买意向，得知没有促销优惠，顾客有些意兴阑珊。就在这时，她女儿打电话过来说中午要吃干菜肉，她嫌太麻烦。听了她的话，客户经理凌娟赶忙接口说：是挺麻烦的，烧得不好，味道就出不来，我烧干菜肉挺入味的，我给你烧吧。随后，她边和凌娟拉家常，边把单给买了。第二天凌娟烧好干菜肉配了蔬菜带给顾客，顾客非常感动。并一再感叹这样周到和温馨的服务。"

"阴雨绵绵的早上，一位年纪三十七八岁的女士，一只手推着宝宝车，拿着几袋东西，另一只手拿着伞，远处散落一地的橙子。雨点大起来了，她弯下腰想捡起身边的橙子，但宝宝又在哭，又怕淋到宝宝。二话不说地跑过去帮忙的雅莹店员引起了她的注意，她一边感激地连声道谢，一边忙着哄宝宝。分别之后的第二天晚上，3 个年纪相仿衣着华丽的女人出现在了雅莹店里，其中一位就是那天店员帮助过的女士。就这样，这位女士成了雅莹店里的常客。以小小的举动帮助有需要的人，也会有意外的收获，而收获的不仅是回报，更多的是日常生活中人与人之间一种爱的传递。"

"顾客小娜是一次偶然的机会接触到雅莹的，她个子不高，体型较为丰腴。她经常表示自己太胖买不到衣服。'再胖的人也能穿出很漂亮的衣服，只是您还没有找到适合您的衣服！我帮您介绍几款吧？'在和顾客的闲谈间，店员已经准备了几款能修饰小娜身材的衣服。那一次小娜下单了好几件，她说她从来没有买过那么多。每个顾客的潜力都是无限的，为了感谢顾客，也为了让顾客在雅莹找到更多的自信，店员事后特意为她和她的家人织了毛线拖鞋。虽然不是名贵的礼物，但用心准备和送出的诚意是我们和顾客感情最好的维系。"

"有一位顾客带着她的老母亲来到店铺，凭着日常训练有素的服务水准，店员一边照看好老母亲，另一边为顾客进行服装的推选和试穿。几件衣服试穿下来，顾客提议再去别处看看，就带着老人走了。送走客人，店员清理试衣间，发现了装满现金的小包。因为不确定是哪位顾客丢失的，就和领导报备，并和柜长对了钱数，便把包包收好。很快这位顾客带着老太太就来找包，经过正常询问，便把包包还给了她。以为事情到此结束了，没承想到了晚上，顾客带着先生再度来到店里，白天试穿的衣服都买了单。她赞扬雅莹的员工就是不一样，拾金不昧的人越来越少了！"

2006 年夏天的一个晚上，汪女士和女儿一次偶然的商场购物，就被雅莹店铺里陈列的色彩搭配所吸引，随即进店试穿了一件上衣，发现风格喜欢、穿着舒适，就这样简单直接地开启了与品牌的缘分。至今十几年，汪女士直言："雅莹的衣服，工艺品质考究，设计超前，所以这些衣服我都藏在衣柜不舍得送人。我喜欢雅莹多元设计和精致工艺带来的适合不同场合穿着的服饰，比如日常装轻松舒适，随性有活力，特别场合也有高级典雅的选择。服装上的花朵、动物、建筑图案寓意美好，刺绣珠片都令人神往。特别是客户经理专业的上门服务，每次对我的风格喜好总是十分了解，这是让我成为品牌忠实粉丝的原因！"

郭女士与雅莹结缘是在 2006 年。身为银行职员的她，无论是工作还是生活都十分严谨，而她在平日的穿搭中则体现了自己的个性和对时尚的见解，每次到店她都是自己挑选中意的服饰。同时，她还是一个很热情的人，常在店里帮着其他顾客推荐衣服。郭女士对雅莹的钟爱，除了时尚优雅的服饰，还有雅莹优秀的文化氛围。在她看来，雅莹的纸袋设计也饱含了雅莹精神。她从第一次购买雅莹产品开始，都会把纸袋保存好，这些年收集的纸袋已厚厚一沓，而这些纸袋也足以体现她十几年如一日对雅莹的支持！

开心地说着"我是忠实雅粉"的江女士，距离第一次走进雅莹店铺已经十多年了。"记得是买了一件裙子，直到今天基本衣服都穿雅莹的。"她喜欢品牌的风格，最重要的是适合自己，而雅莹不断的进化也让她欣喜："近几年变得越来越年轻时尚，雅莹的服务态度让我印象深刻，工作人员非常热情，很贴心！在雅莹店铺，我不会有局促感，每一次和店员的谈话都自然又舒服，她们总是知道我想要的是什么。未来，希望雅莹能设计出更多元化的时装，帮助女性消费者不管在什么场合、年龄都能展现出最美的一面。"

强化供应链，夯实根基
SUPPLY CHAIN, A PILLAR OF STRENGTH

渠道创新和品牌升级背后的底气是产品创新——只有产品足够丰富且优质，才能支撑渠道的快速扩张，才是保障消费体验的根本核心。而这些最终都是对企业研发、生产和经营能力的大考验，需要先进的供应链体系支撑。

前方在打仗，后方的配套和及时供给也要跟上。为扩张企业规模实力，也更专业化集中与分工，开启全国品牌化的 2005 年，雅莹同步在毗邻华云路的东升西路 966 号启动了专门的生产、物流中心——雅莹时尚园的建设，并于 2007 年 7 月正式投入使用。至今，它依然是雅莹生产、物流的大本营。

在此之前，雅莹的生产被安排在华云路本部的一厂，以及由原洛东制衣厂生产车间改成的二厂进行。其中，华云路本部的一厂在雅莹本部大楼的二、三楼分 6 个小组生产，二楼是剪裁仓库，三楼是车间。雅莹时尚园启动后，华云路本部被作为整个体系运作的中枢大脑，承载着设计研发、商业管理与行政决策职能，时尚园则集中负责生产、物流等功能。这样的区隔，让雅莹的新格局由此构成，也让雅莹对产业和企业的精细化运作得到进一步提升。

也是 2005 年，张华明还请来一家瑞典咨询公司为公司做供应链建设，并梳理出两条供应链齐头并进：一条是常规计划供应链，从制订计划到上货以半年为一个周期；一条是快速反应供应链，最快可在半个月内让产品从设计开始，经由生产制造和物流运输最终进入终端店铺。

但相比速度，雅莹对品质的要求更高。

Every innovation in retail and upgrade in brand needs to be backed by an expansive range of creative products, especially when it comes to supporting the rapid expansion in retail channels and providing customers with a quality experience. And behind these creations, it all comes down to the R&D, production and operational competencies of its supply chain.

Production and supply continued to be a pillar of strength of the brand. In order to achieve further expansion, the company decided to build a dedicated production and logistics centre, *Fashion Park*, in 2005. This centre was located near its headquarters at 966 Dongsheng West Road and was officially completed in July 2007. The company's production was previously divided across two factories, one at its headquarters on Huayun Road and one at its previous location of Luodong Garment factory. With Fashion Park, the company could not only expand the design and retail team at its headquarters but also develop its production and logistics system, thereby improving the company's division of labour.

Also in 2005, the company invited a Swedish consulting company to improve its supply chain operations in order to meet the demands of its omnichannel retailing strategy. The company would go on to add a secondary fast response supply chain — capable of meeting timelines of 15 days from design to delivery — to meet some un-forecasted demands. Despite its speed and efficiency, Elegant Prosper was better known for their great attention to quality control.

上图：

2007 年 9 月，雅莹时尚园生产物流中心，嘉兴市东升西路 966 号

右图：

2002 年，雅莹供应链管理骨干在新塍集镇的生产二厂前合影

ABOVE

Elegant Prosper Fashion Park Production and Logistics Centre, No.966 Dongsheng West Road, Jiaxing City, September 2007

RIGHT

Elegant Prosper supply chain employees in front of the former factory in Xincheng Town, 2002

2000 年以前，张华明就特别聘请了嘉兴著名的服装运营专家顾亚薇老师为公司导入 ISO9000 体系，经过一年多的努力，2001 年，雅莹首次通过了 ISO9000 质量管理体系认证。

张华明认为，认证仅仅是一个开始，更关键的是，真正按照这一体系提升自己的管理和质量。于是，他还进一步鼓励包括当时负责仓储管理的倪美华等人，也要多向工厂员工组织培训，把品质理念向全厂强化。同时，他还推出定时定期检查、抽查制度，并亲自出任内审员，确保从设计到生产再到销售，在环环相扣的每个节点上精益求精。他自己还担当品质的第一责任人，带头落实和保障质量，促进品质意识成为雅莹的核心文化之一。

"整个 ISO9000 就是以顾客为中心的国际标准管理体系，这个管理体系用在工厂的时候怎么来做，用在服务业怎么来做，要融会贯通！把品质体现在方方面面！"张华明说。

2005 年启动供应链升级时，雅莹的品质管理也进一步提升。为确保核心产品的高品质和绝对可控，张华明将连衣裙、大衣、外套等核心单品全部自己生产，其他非核心产品才交给外协工厂加工，而且对外协工厂也是高标准、严要求。为确保产品都是精品，张华明还将雅莹最好的员工分成快速反应组、小单组等若干核心小组专做高端产品，在以精益生产做好品质的同时，引进 SPS（单件流水系统）项目、GT108 标准工时系统，以自动化科技提升效率和规范化水平，一步步与时俱进，推动公司迈入现代智慧化时代。为让整个供应链体系高标准地高效运转，张华明还致力推行各环节的精细化管理，以现代化企业营造透明的管理及运营环境，使企业的一切都处于清晰可控状态。

2006 年 12 月，雅莹还在管理实践中导入 6S 系统——整理 (Seiri)、整顿 (Seiton)、清扫 (Seiso)、清洁 (Seiketsu)、素养 (Shitsuke) 和安全 (Security)，组织开展多种形式的 6S

Before 2000, Hwaming invited Gu Yawei, a well-known quality management specialist in the industry, to help the company set up its ISO9000 quality management system. A year later, Elegant Prosper would receive the ISO9000 certification for their quality management. This was only the beginning of a string of ultra-meticulous and methodical approaches to quality management.

Hwaming was a strong advocate of the consistent involvement of staff at all levels. No one was too big or too small for quality control. He asked Ni Meihua, who was in charge of warehousing at that time, and other key team members to provide regular trainings to all employees at the factory and to strengthen everyone's awareness of quality management. Meanwhile, he introduced both random and regular inspection procedures to ensure that Elegant Prosper embodied excellence across all aspects of the brand, not only in production, but also in design and retail. Through their collective efforts led by Hwaming, quality excellence became a core cultural element of the company.

"The entire ISO9000 system of quality management is a customer-centric management standard for companies. When it comes to implementing this system on the production floor or across any customer-facing touchpoint, we must know the standards inside out and apply them to all aspects of our brand!" said Hwaming.

These high-quality management standards also applied to the company's extended family of suppliers who were selected based on the most stringent of criteria. To improve on the brand's high-end garments, Hwaming also split the production team into smaller and more specialised groups. He introduced SPS (Single Piece Flow System) production and the GT108 standard working hour system, taking advantage of automation technology to improve efficiency and standardisation, and keeping pace with an era of increasing technological advances.

> "
> 从产品到店铺再到管理，
> 每个环节都要掌握主动并确保品质理念，
> 这在一定程度上限制了雅莹的快速扩张，
> 但给雅莹的品质和长远发展打下坚实基础。
> "

培训与学习，进一步改善现场办公环境，提升工作效率，优化公司的整体形象。期间，张华明和 6S 推行委员会成员一起组织会议，参与检查 6S 整理、整顿和整洁的工作落实。"为了以身作则，我们的干部包括我，8 点上班，7 点 30 分开始在大厅口迎接员工，跟员工问好！"他回忆说。

在管理团队的带头示范下，雅莹的风貌更加焕然一新。员工上班时，都规范佩带着工作证进入公司，面带微笑、热情地开始新一天；进入工作现场后，会自觉对责任区域进行整理及清洁；上班了，大家会在主管的组织下进行早会，根据当日工作内容及时更新看板；在工作中，离开座位时会主动将坐椅归位，并在各自标示清楚的文件夹中便捷取用各类文件资料；同事间也多了温馨的提示，多了快乐的洋溢……

从产品到店铺再到管理，每个环节都要掌握主动并确保品质与管理水准，这在一定程度上限制了雅莹的快速扩张，但给雅莹的品质和长远发展打下坚实基础。

In December 2006, the company implemented the 6S criteria for manufacturing to improve its productivity: Sort (Seiri), Straighten (Seiton), Shine (Seiso), Standardise (Seiketsu), Sustain (Sitsuke) and Security. Hwaming was personally involved throughout the implementation process, saying, "In order to set a good example, the 6S leaders and I would wait to greet our employees at the entrance at 7:30 every morning!" Consequently, the workplace environment greatly improved, along with the morale and spirit of the staff. A typical day started with a meeting to discuss and plan ahead, with the expectations for everyone being made abundantly clear. Any chair that was used would always be returned to its place and the workplace cleaned after use; documents were properly filed and could be easily accessed.

These very high standards of quality control set by the company across its value chain may have occasionally restricted a faster expansion but they helped to establish more sustainable growth built on quality excellence.

引入 ERP，拥抱信息化
ERP AND DATA-BASED INNOVATION

当年离开北京，不是带了一大堆特产或奢侈品，而是带了一大堆现代管理书籍回家的张华明，在后期的经营发展中也始终坚持认为，企业要走向一定的规模，内部的管理和文化是根基。外在所展现的一道道美丽风景背后，都需要后台文化建设和系统管理为载体。

雅莹从 2003 年就开始逐步对内部进行系统性的现代化升级建设。升级工程从企业文化梳理、人力资源管理、领导力提升、供应链建设和信息化建设等多方面入手，每年至少瞄准一个核心领域完成一个大项目。借此，公司进一步提升了员工和干部素质，提升了企业的凝聚力和文化氛围，也提升了企业整体运营素质和效率。

2006 年，张华明将大项目锁定在了企业信息化管理升级上。那也是雅莹现任党委书记、时任供应链总监仇瑛非常繁忙的一年。这一年，雅莹在意大利合作公司的推荐下，携手全球领先的美国 Lawson（路顺）公司开始建立 ERP（企业资源计划）系统，成为业内最早上 ERP 的公司之一。

ERP 出现于 20 世纪 90 年代，至 20 世纪末已被国外大公司普遍使用。其作用是集信息技术与先进管理思想于一体，是为企业员工及决策层提供决策手段的信息管理平台。简而言之，就是把企业的采购、生产、销售等环节数据线上化，实现资源共享，以让每个环节的工作人员都可根据自己和其他环节的数据进行科学计划与决策安排。

Enterprise Resource Planning (ERP) was the focus for the company in 2006. That year, the company began upgrading its information management system by collaborating with Lawson, the world's leading ERP supplier, becoming one of the first companies in the industry to apply such a system. The ERP system was created in the 1990s and had been widely used by large international companies at the end of the 20th century. With integrated and data-based management applications, it provided a continuously updated view of core business processes, enabling decision making at all levels of an organisation. Enterprises could track procurement, production capacity, purchase orders and other business activities to facilitate information flow across all functions.

ERP was brand new in China back in 2006 and while many people remained sceptical, Hwaming saw its potential. "We introduced ERP not for the sake of just trying something new. We aimed to provide customers with the things they wanted, not the things we liked. Likewise, with ERP, we needed a more scientific method of planning production and delivery, and enforcing quality management," said Hwaming.

The company invested heavily in the project. "At that time, some companies would only spend a few hundred thousand at maximum on an ERP system. We spent 7 million yuan for phase one. This was a major project for us," Qiu Ying recalled. As the outlay of the system was not limited to financial resources only, it required a huge commitment in manpower. "ERP implementation in the apparel industry is a real challenge because a product life cycle is normally too

2006 年时，ERP 还刚在国内兴起，不少人都认为其华而不实，没有太大价值，但张华明认定其对提升效率和品质将有巨大帮助。他说："我们不是为了做 ERP 而做 ERP。最终的目的是要给消费者更需要的东西，而不是自己喜欢的东西。ERP 也一样，如果不做就没法更科学地确定规模化的生产计划、交付期、品质管理。"

认准目标后，雅莹不惜成本地推动这项工程。"当时人家上一个 ERP 才几十万，我们第一期就 700 万，这是很大的工程。"仇瑛回忆说。而且，成本还不只是财力，更包括人力的巨大投入。"服装企业 ERP 非常困难，因为产品寿命周期太短，种类多，BOM（物料清单）也多，我们一年要做到三四千个 BOM。一个多的 BOM 有三四百个物料，一件衣服要多少米线，包装袋要多少，事无巨细都要输入系统。大家白天做自己的事情，晚上都是 ERP 之夜，集体去熟悉操作程序，梳理流程、制定规则，用了将近一年时间理顺了。"回忆当年情景，仇瑛至今很是感慨。

在张华明的坚定支持下，雅莹最终完成了这一计划。效果也很快显现：ERP 对于提高生产效率和帮助决策效果显著，为公司品牌化、规模化提供了坚实的支持。"我们发扬了雅莹人的专注、创新、拥抱变化的核心文化。2006 年公司销售还不到 5 个亿，一般人家说上 10 亿了才上 ERP，但也正是因为我们超前的领先的战略，才让企业发展这么快。"仇瑛说。

short, and there are numerous types and BOMs (bills of materials). We have three to four thousand BOMs every year and a single BOM may include three to four hundred materials. Every detail, including how many metres of thread and how many packaging bags are required to produce a garment, must be entered into the system. We had to work overtime for ERP, familiarising ourselves with the system and resolving any issues, because our daytime work was too packed. This carried on for about a year," Qiu Ying recalled.

With the gradual implementation of the system, its benefits were evident. The system played an indispensable role in improving production efficiency and assisting with decision-making, and its implementation at Elegant Prosper even became an important case-study brand for Lawson. "Our people are dedicated, innovative and progressive. In 2006, the company's sales were less than 5 million yuan and most people said that a company would only need ERP when its sales revenue exceeded 1 billion yuan. However, our success shows that a forward-looking vision is perhaps the most important attribute for a company to unlock its potential for growth," said Qiu Ying.

> ❝
> 只有传统的思想，没有传统的产业，
> 传统产业也能插上科技和创新的翅膀。
> ❞

这次信息化升级，还让雅莹成了路顺公司的全球标杆示范企业，在国内引起同行竞相学习和效仿。尝到 ERP 的甜头后，雅莹又正式成立信息管理部，员工达到 60 多人，并同时引入标准工时软件、SGS（质量检测系统）、PMS（工程生产管理系统）等计划管理系统，与 ERP 配合使用，还在 2009 年就上了云平台，让公司信息化程度越来越高，系统管理也越来越完善。同年，雅莹也开始了电子商务渠道的发展，开创了国内同类中高端女装网络渠道建设的先河。

也是 2009 年，雅莹被评为国家高新企业，成为服装行业第一家国家高新企业。

期间，张华明还被叫到北京回答：一家传统服装企业为什么是高新企业？他带了厚厚一本资料和一句动人的话，亲自去说明了雅莹如何把信息化和生产制造结合在一起，以及为什么应该是高新企业。

他说："只有传统的思想，没有传统的产业，传统产业也能插上科技和创新的翅膀。"

This echoed Hwaming's belief that corporate management and organisational culture are essential for an enterprise to flourish, and that culture and management are vehicles for a brand's creations.

Since 2003, the company has implemented systematic modernisations to its internal management system and has come a long way in improving its operational efficiency and supporting employee professional development. Building on this momentum, the company formally established an information management department with more than 60 employees, and successively introduced a series of other management systems, including a new quality management system from SGS and the Product Management System (PMS).

In recognition of its innovation in the traditionally conservative garment manufacturing industry, the company was awarded the accolade of National High-tech Enterprise by the government in 2009 — the first in China's apparel industry.

Hwaming was also invited to Beijing to share his insights with government departments on how a traditional apparel company could also be a high-tech company. His answer was simple: "There is only traditional thinking, no traditional industries. A so-called traditional industry can also grow wings of technology and innovation."

左页：
2009 年，雅莹生产供应链数字化看板

OPPOSITE
One of the digital information boards in Elegant
Prosper's supply chain, 2009

打造最佳雇主品牌
PEOPLE-CENTRIC MANAGEMENT

张华明能推动这一系列升级目标的完成，得益于雅莹管理团队和员二的上下一心。这有赖于他和戴雪明对人力资源的重视，对员工利益的关切，舍得对"人"投入。

对"人"重视，以人为本，这也是雅莹生来就有的基因。张宝荣时期，雅莹就对员工非常关照，并给张华明留下了深刻印象。张华明上任后，追求现代管理的他不但没有丢掉父亲善待员工的老传统，还对其进一步发扬，包括让当时还在洛东老厂的雅莹领市场之先，开始发放 13 薪；之前不规范时，有员工不愿缴纳养老金，后来政策要求缴满 15 年，张华明又让公司一一配合员工补全。

一直与公司员工关系亲密的戴雪明，也春风化雨地将对人的关切融入雅莹的点点滴滴。熟悉的人都评价，戴雪明就像是公司的黏合剂，能把所有人的心力聚合在一起。她说："我心中最根本的工作就是人的部分，这些年来没有变过。"很多员工提到她，都会做出的评价是："像家人一样。"同时，张华明、戴雪明夫妇还以艰苦奋斗的作风感召着雅莹的创业精神。2000 年雅莹的业绩与利润跨入规模化发展阶段，公司很多管理人员都在嘉兴买了房，但张华明夫妇在员工宿舍一直住到2003 年，"孩子都是在宿舍里长大的。"

雅莹的人才观是信任人、培养人、善用人、成就人——成就员工就是成就公司。一个例子是，雅莹对门店一线销售人员进行"微笑培训"——不仅提升了销售人员服务客户的水平，让其自身业绩提升、收入增加，也让公司的整体销售额上去了。

"如果一个员工到我公司工作了七八年还买不起房子、买不起

The solidarity of the people at Elegant Prosper had become a prized asset and a symbol of what the company had achieved over the years. Hwaming and Xueming attached great importance to people andinvesting their success and growth.

People-centric management had been embedded in the DNA of the company from day one. Baorong, the late founder of the company, cared deeply for his employees, which had a strong influence on Hwaming's leadership. When Hwaming took over the company, he combined his father's love of his employees with modern management methods, including providing workplace pension contributions at a time when government policies were still not in place.

Xueming, who had always been very close to the employees, cared about all the aspects of their lives. Many people say that she served as the glue that held the team together. "The most fundamental aspect of this job has always been the human part. This has not changed over the years," said Xueming, who employees have viewed as a "family member."

Hwaming and Xueming were the face of the company's entrepreneurial culture, and their determination in difficult times combined with their personal frugality in better times served as an inspiration to many. In 2000, when the company overcame its challenges and achieved a quantum leap in growth, many among the higher management team bought new houses in Jiaxing but the couple continued to live in the staff dormitory until 2003.

右图：
2007 年 9 月，雅莹携手美国翰威特
树立人力资源战略，建立国内领先
的人才开发体系

RIGHT
The company collaborates with Aon
Hewitt to work on it human resources
strategy and established a leading talent
development system, September 2007

车子，我会感到羞愧。你的员工如果得不到成长就是你的责任。"这是张华明在房价刚刚上涨之时谈到员工发展问题时最喜欢说的话，也是他对自己的要求。在房价大涨之初，雅莹的很多年轻人加入公司之后，也的确都用不了多久就买车、买房，实现了安居乐业。如今，虽然房价涨得实在太快，几乎无一家企业可实现这样的目标，但张华明依然努力确保员工获得同比更加优越的生活水平。

2005 年，雅莹就在内部推动成立了由公司和员工共同出资设立的互助基金，主要用于员工婚丧礼金、疾病及生育探望费、春节困难员工慰问、员工重疾及临时紧急困难资助等。近 3 年，雅莹互助基金累计受益人群达到 669 余人次。

2007 年，雅莹又跟美国顶级人力资源服务商翰威特合作：打造最佳雇主品牌。第一期首先规范了公司的岗职薪酬绩效体系，这是人力资源最基础的部分；2009 年开始的第二期则着重于搭建员工领导力模型，致力提升公司的中高层人才和管理水平。

人力资源部门的变迁反映了雅莹对人的重视，以及人对雅莹发展的支撑。当时整个人力资源部门仅 3 人，相关的人力资源管理、规章都不够成熟。请专人建专业的人力资源部门，那也是雅莹腾飞发展的起点。自己摸索两年后，张华明带着当时的人力资源骨干吕虹等人引进翰威特系统，从薪酬激励到领导力模型等项目，把所有与人有关的事项一件件捋清楚，同时不断学习尝试新的东西，人力资源体系也逐渐完善，发展到现在已是有 50 多位员工的专业部门。

Elegant Prosper remains a place where people are trusted and motivated, where they grow and achieve success. Even a simple smile can make a difference. In one of the service campaigns that taught customer care managers on how to smile, managers not only found their service quality improved but were able to sell more clothes and achieve their targets. Their quality of life was equally important.

In 2005, the company set up a mutual aid fund jointly funded by the company and employees, with the aim of helping employees in need — supporting them during the passing of a family member, offering sickness pay, maternity leave pay, accident and critical illness assistance and other emergency relief. In the three years from August 2018 to August 2021, the fund has helped more than 669 employees.

In 2007, the company collaborated with Aon Hewitt, a US-based provider of human capital and management consulting services, to bolster its employer branding. Phase one formalised the Performance-related Pay (PRP) system, the foundation of human resources management; and phase two commenced from 2009, with a focus on developing the leadership and management skills of middle-to-senior level managers. The collaboration was a catalyst for the upgrade of the company's human resources department, growing from a handful of apprentices who had to "do it all" to a team equipped with the systems and specialisations necessary to meet the increasing needs of a fast-growing company.

党建引领，助推企业建设
PARTY DEVELOPMENT AND SOCAIL COHESION

通过加强党建提升企业凝聚力，也是雅莹的重要的特色之一。

2007 年 9 月，雅莹就成立了自己的党支部，并由当时的行政管理负责人李炜中出任第一任党支部书记。这个成立之初仅有 7 名党员的支部，很快成为凝聚雅莹人的一个纽带。在李书记和党组成员的共同努力下，党支部开展了学习周、文体赛、红色教育、赈灾献爱心、帮扶困难职工等党员主题活动，不但将集团已有党员的积极性调动起来，还持续吸引员工积极加入党组织，让党员人数从最初 7 人迅速发展至数十人。

雅莹的党建文化也随此愈加浓厚，并且提出了打造"党建强、发展强"的双强企业目标。立足于此，公司自主建立了"360度测评"体系，通过全方位、立体式、多维度、细分化的考评激励党员争先创优，并以"将骨干发展为党员，将党员发展为骨干"为理念，进一步提升党组织的影响力和驱动力，让党员力量对企业发挥关键作用。

One of the key elements of the company's culture is its successful Party development.

In 2007, the company formally established its Communist Party of China (CPC) branch with 7 members. Soon, led by Li Weizhong, the then head of administrative management and the first Party secretary for the company, the branch organised a series of team-building activities. These included cultural and sports competitions, learning and reading sessions, assistance for needy employees and community involvement programs, which gradually attracted additional Party members to join the branch.

In 2011, the committee launched a campaign called the "Five Integrities" — covering aspirational integrity, youth integrity, brand integrity, service integrity and social enterprise integrity — all of which aim to strengthen the company and improve social cohesion. The company's CPC branch continued to grow from strength to strength and upgraded to establish a larger committee made up of 4 different branches in 2013.

左页：
2007 年 9 月，雅莹党支部成立初期的 7 位党员

右图：
2018 年 4 月，雅莹党员们在南湖革命纪念馆开展重走"一大路"，重温入党誓词的主题党日活动

OPPOSITE
The company's CPC branch is formally established with 7 members, September 2007

RIGHT
The company's CPC committee celebrates its 10th anniversary in 2018 and visits the CPC's South Lake Revolutionary Memorial Hall in Jiaxing, April 2018

2011 年，雅莹党组织又提出了创"五美党建"品牌的理念，其"五美"由梦想之美、青春之美、形象之梦、服务之美和关怀之美组成，每一项"美"中都包含丰富的内容，并与企业经营发展深度融合，以达成用美丽党建助力美丽事业的目标。

如今，雅莹集团的核心高管等都被发展成了党员。与此相辅相成的是，还有不少先进党员，凭借努力成为企业不同岗位上的骨干。雅莹的"五美党建"已成为一张响亮的红色名片，雅莹也并被列为嘉兴市委党校教育示范点，既提升了公司的社会影响力，也推动企业在更高层面与社会同频共振。

"曾经听人说，党建是企业最亮的品牌、最好的资源。这句话我是赞同的。"雅莹现任党委书记仇瑛介绍说，"现在最主要的工作是搭建平台，不仅让我们的党员能够在这个平台上，实现人生的价值，也要建设成更加关注社会责任、关注环境卫生、关注所有需要帮助的人的一个平台，这样才能使企业走得更远。未来 30 年，乃至更长的时间，都一直这样走下去。"张华明也始终认为，公司的发展必须顺势而为，跟随时代的前进而前进。

1988 年，企业创始人、老党员张宝荣在红庵里创业起步，秉承"想要做好事，先要做好人"的原则，发挥共产党员的先锋模范作用，带领全体员工创业前行。更具现代意识和管理能力的张华明更是与时俱进，不但把握住了 1998 至 2008 这 10 年中国消费与产业蓬勃发展，本土创新和本土品牌持续茁壮的时代机遇，让雅莹获得了腾飞式的发展，也为雅莹在随后 10 年成为中国时装业的领军者进一步夯实了根基。

Today, many CPC members have become the backbone of the company and the "Five Integrities" campaign. This has served as a benchmark for the Party development of many other companies, and a driving force behind the company's social influence and commitment to creating more value for society.

"I've heard people say that strong Party development leads to strong company growth. I agree with them," said Qiu Ying, the current Party secretary of the company. She added, "Our main priority now is to help the company build a workplace where not only the Party members, but also anyone who deeply cares about social responsibility, protecting the environment and helping those in need, can come forward and contribute. Only in this way can the company's growth continue to be sustainable for the next 30 years and even longer."

The company's late founder, Baorong, was a senior Party member who selflessly led the team to build the company from scratch based on his ethos of being a virtuous person if you want to succeed in life; and he inspired all who followed him. He was a man ahead of his times, one who dared to be the first to try, one who dared push the boundaries. Hwaming inherited his innovative spirit, and took up the baton, not only laying a strong foundation for the company, but taking it further ahead of its times — seizing the opportunities presented by the decade from 1998 to 2008 and propelling the brand's next decade of growth as a leading Chinese fashion brand.

第三篇

CHAPTER 3

根植文化，
锻造经典

2008~2018
ROOTED IN CULTURE,
TIMELESS IN FASHION

2008年5月，雅莹在北京最具地标性的购物中心——华贸中心开设的"雅莹生活馆"正式开业。以此为标志，雅莹开始向更高目标挑战。此后10年，在经济全球化、互联网+、人们消费能力与消费观念不断提升的大背景下，雅莹的规模实力和品牌都得到历史性的提升：不但全面深化EP雅莹主品牌经营，而且陆续创建了DOUBLOVE 贝爱（2009）、GraceLand雅斓名店（2013）、N.Paia恩派雅（2013）、DA YA JIA大雅家(2016)、LITTLE SPACE小雅童装(2017)等新品牌，助推公司朝向多元化时尚集团发展，同时还与米兰世博会中国馆、世界互联网大会携手合作，作为中国时装的典范，向世界展示了中国时尚之美。

The opening of Elegant Prosper's lifestyle concept store in the iconic Beijing Huamao Centre in 2008 opened another new chapter for the company's growth. In the following 10 years, with an increasingly open market, the soaring influence of the Internet and the increasing rise of consumer power, the company's growth reached previously unmatched heights. This was led by Elegant Prosper's deep revamp with the new "EP" brand name, and the company's evolution into a global fashion group, named "EP YAYING Fashion Group", with a diverse portfolio of fashion and retail brands: DOUBLOVE (2009), GraceLand (2013), N.Paia (2013), DA YA JIA (2016) and LITTLE SPACE (2017). Meanwhile, its collaboration with Expo Milano and the World Internet Conference further enhanced the global prestige of Chinese brands and shared the beauty of Chinese fashion to the world.

深化品牌，强化内涵
A BRAND'S INNER VALUES

"有了爱，有了平衡，幸福也就有了保证。

做品牌就是做情感。爱，就是雅莹希望传递出的情感。"

"Love has the power to balance, naturally, happiness will follow.
Brands are about emotions, EP is about love."

品牌新主张：平衡·爱·幸福
BALANCE, LOVE AND HAPPINESS

2008 的"金融海啸"令全球实体经济受到冲击，也让包括服装在内的诸多实体企业陷入艰难，有的企业甚至因此破产。2003 年"非典悟道"的经验，则让张华明将大环境之"危"变成了改善自我微观小环境的"机"，并令雅莹借机更上层楼。

变革的起点是：深度调研与思考后，张华明断定中国的消费市场已经发生了切实的变化，各行各业已陆续进入过剩的环境，且同质化竞争越来越激烈。消费者对产品的选择不再只是关注品质和价格，更关注品牌本身的个性与底蕴，品牌必须更有个性魅力才能赢得人心。这让张华明对雅莹的发展有了新的考虑：相比开设更多的门店、投入更多的产量，此时更需要的是加强品牌文化底蕴的建设，通过品牌的优化为公司建构新的竞争力。

也是在 2008 年，北京奥运会召开，中国的进一步开放、世界的包容、文化的交汇，更让雅莹深知打好品牌根基的重要。从此出发，雅莹开始了又一个 10 年的探索与升级。从最初的单季单品到四季单品再到四季系列化，在升级过程中，雅莹始终在围绕一个核心迈开步伐——从消费者出发，从市场出发，更好满足消费者多元化的需求。2009 年，敏锐洞察着消费趋势演绎的雅莹，在业内率先提出了"时尚生活方式"的概念——将生活化场景带入产品分类设置中，让产品更加体贴消费者的生活场景与个性化偏好，公司的发展也从提供好产品、好服务，升级到帮助消费者更好生活的新阶段。

与此同时，2009 年 1 月，雅莹正式启动"EP"新标志，升级原先的"Elegant Prosper"英文组合为全新的大写"EP"缩写标志。张华明也明确提出了目标：成为代表中国时装形象

The financial crisis of 2008 had a great impact on the global economy, once again driving many retail companies, including those in the apparel industry, into dire straits. But Hwaming, who had been through many crises, especially the trying SARS period, knew from experience to take a step back to gain new perspectives, and turn crisis into new opportunities.

The starting point for dealing with any new circumstance is to understand and define what has actually changed. With careful research and reflection, Hwaming concluded that China's consumer market had undergone deep-seated transformation, with excess supply across almost all sectors and increasingly homogeneous competition. Modern consumers were no longer concerned only with price and quality, they had started to care more about a brand's values and culture, and strong brand personalities would win the hearts of customers.

It was also in 2008 that the Olympic Games were successfully held in Beijing. With the country's further opening-up and increasing cross-cultural exchanges, the world's attention towards China reached a level never seen before, and Hwaming saw the significance of cultural strength. He accordingly developed a new perspective: instead of opening more stores and producing "more", what was genuinely needed at that point was to build and strengthen the brand's cultural groundwork.

In January 2009, the company officially launched the new *EP* trademark and brand name, replacing the previous *Elegant Prosper*. Hwaming and the company began a decade-long deep revamp of the brand, with further study into Chinese culture and fashion. The brand was no longer satisfied with only providing outstanding products and services; instead, it aimed to contribute to a better life for its customers. EP put forward the concept of "fashion lifestyle" in 2009, bringing various real-life settings into its creative process and product mix, as a response to its customers' real-life needs and personalised preferences.

的经典品牌。作为已经深耕女性时装 20 年的专业企业，雅莹也开始围绕发现与表达女性之美进行更深层次的思考与探索，期望带给女性消费者更独特的价值与体验。

将近两年的探索，戴雪明和一干设计师人才经常坐在一起头脑风暴，梳理继而再思考，最终根植于雅莹对完美女性的理想，以及自身在生活和工作中的体验，于 2011 年，大家碰撞出了雅莹品牌的新主张："平衡·爱·幸福"。

这三个关键词，也是戴雪明对现代女性如何成就美好事业、家庭与生活的理解与诠释。她说："在一个家庭里，如果女人幸福了，全家人都会幸福，如果她不幸福，这家庭会很折腾。"

"服装是生产美的行业。雅莹追求气质优雅之美、心地晶莹之美，但最终的目标是要帮助女性实现在方方面面的和谐平衡，以此获得幸福，拥有美丽人生。因为她既要平衡好工作，又要平衡好家庭，还要在这个过程中既要赋予爱，又要获得幸福，把幸福传递给周边的人。"戴雪明如此解释让女人幸福的理念。她认为，欲望驱使我们为目标而全力以赴，梦想激发我们的心灵优雅绽放。我们需要平衡欲望和梦想，我们还需要平衡现在和未来，平衡当下的机会和未来的发展。

戴雪明总结，当今的女性不仅要平衡方方面面，更要内外兼修，既追求外表的美丽时尚，也追求内心的丰盈能量。爱，则是平衡好一切的原动力。有了爱，有了平衡，幸福也就有了保证。她说："做品牌就是做情感，如果人都没有情感，品牌可以做得出情感？"

爱，就是雅莹希望传递出的情感。

Meanwhile, as a Chinese fashion brand that had been specifically focused on womenswear for more than 10 years, the brand began to delve deeper into the concept of feminine beauty, seeking to create more value and improve its experience for its female customers. Modern women became increasingly confident and calm, and their quest for quality and beauty had become more discerning and diversified. To reflect the evolving way women interact with the world, EP launched its new value proposition — Balance, Love and Happiness — in 2011, conceptualised by Xueming and a team of designers who spent nearly 2 years brainstorming and piecing together the insights of women balancing their careers, families and lives.

These three keywords also reflected Xueming's thoughts on how a working Chinese woman achieved work-life balance in a modernising society. She said, "Happy wife, happy life."

"The fashion industry is the creator of beautiful things. EP tirelessly pursues both elegant styles that enhance beauty on the outside and natural beauty that radiates from within. But our ultimate role is to support women to live harmonious, happy and beautiful lives. This is so important at a time when women have to balance work and family. A woman's happiness and love are vital to creating an environment of positive energy around herself," said Xueming. She also added the concept of balance: "Desire can drive us to go above and beyond to get what we want, whilst dreams can inspire our souls. We need to find the balance between our desires and our dreams, and even more so, between the present and the future — the opportunities present to us now and our future development."

Xueming concluded: "Today's women have too much to balance in their lives, but the most important balance is between what is within and what is without. Yes, pursuing fashion aims to make one look beautiful, but it can also uncover a beautiful inner self. Love has the power to balance, naturally, happiness will follow. Brands are about emotions, EP is about love."

> "
>
> 平衡
> ——
>
> 当下：工作、生活，
> 未来：梦想、欲望；
> 商业、原创，
> 西方的运作、东方的智慧
>
>
> 爱
> ——
>
> 一种付出、一份责任
>
>
> 幸福
> ——
>
> 幸福没有准则，充满爱心的人最幸福，
> 人生若能被人需要，为人付出，
> 就是最幸福的人生；
> 这些价值观在影响着思维
>
> "

右页：
精选自 EP 2012 年春夏 "平衡·爱·幸
福" 大片创意策划

OPPOSITE
Selected pages from EP Spring-Summer
2012 "Balance, Love and Happiness" theme
ad campaign

"

平衡
——

当下：工作、生活，
未来：梦想、欲望；
商业、原创，
西方的运作、东方的智慧

爱
——

一种付出、一份责任

幸福
——

幸福没有准则，充满爱心的人最幸福，
人生若能被人需要，为人付出，
就是最幸福的人生；
这些价值观在影响着思维

"

右页：
精选自 EP 2012 年春夏"平衡·爱·幸
福"大片创意策划

OPPOSITE
Selected pages from EP Spring-Summer
2012 "Balance, Love and Happiness" theme
ad campaign

的经典品牌。作为已经深耕女性时装 20 年的专业企业，雅莹也开始围绕发现与表达女性之美进行更深层次的思考与探索，期望带给女性消费者更独特的价值与体验。

将近两年的探索，戴雪明和一干设计师人才经常坐在一起头脑风暴，梳理继而再思考，最终根植于雅莹对完美女性的理想，以及自身在生活和工作中的体验，于 2011 年，大家碰撞出了雅莹品牌的新主张："平衡·爱·幸福"。

这三个关键词，也是戴雪明对现代女性如何成就美好事业、家庭与生活的理解与诠释。她说："在一个家庭里，如果女人幸福了，全家人都会幸福，如果她不幸福，这家庭会很折腾。"

"服装是生产美的行业。雅莹追求气质优雅之美、心地晶莹之美，但最终的目标是要帮助女性实现在方方面面的和谐平衡，以此获得幸福，拥有美丽人生。因为她既要平衡好工作，又要平衡好家庭，还要在这个过程中既要赋予爱，又要获得幸福，把幸福传递给周边的人。"戴雪明如此解释让女人幸福的理念。她认为，欲望驱使我们为目标而全力以赴，梦想激发我们的心灵优雅绽放。我们需要平衡欲望和梦想，我们还需要平衡现在和未来，平衡当下的机会和未来的发展。

戴雪明总结，当今的女性不仅要平衡方方面面，更要内外兼修，既追求外表的美丽时尚，也追求内心的丰盈能量。爱，则是平衡好一切的原动力。有了爱，有了平衡，幸福也就有了保证。她说："做品牌就是做情感，如果人都没有情感，品牌可以做得出情感？"

爱，就是雅莹希望传递出的情感。

Meanwhile, as a Chinese fashion brand that had been specifically focused on womenswear for more than 10 years, the brand began to delve deeper into the concept of feminine beauty, seeking to create more value and improve its experience for its female customers. Modern women became increasingly confident and calm, and their quest for quality and beauty had become more discerning and diversified. To reflect the evolving way women interact with the world, EP launched its new value proposition — Balance, Love and Happiness — in 2011, conceptualised by Xueming and a team of designers who spent nearly 2 years brainstorming and piecing together the insights of women balancing their careers, families and lives.

These three keywords also reflected Xueming's thoughts on how a working Chinese woman achieved work-life balance in a modernising society. She said, "Happy wife, happy life."

"The fashion industry is the creator of beautiful things. EP tirelessly pursues both elegant styles that enhance beauty on the outside and natural beauty that radiates from within. But our ultimate role is to support women to live harmonious, happy and beautiful lives. This is so important at a time when women have to balance work and family. A woman's happiness and love are vital to creating an environment of positive energy around herself," said Xueming. She also added the concept of balance: "Desire can drive us to go above and beyond to get what we want, whilst dreams can inspire our souls. We need to find the balance between our desires and our dreams, and even more so, between the present and the future — the opportunities present to us now and our future development."

Xueming concluded: "Today's women have too much to balance in their lives, but the most important balance is between what is within and what is without. Yes, pursuing fashion aims to make one look beautiful, but it can also uncover a beautiful inner self. Love has the power to balance, naturally, happiness will follow. Brands are about emotions, EP is about love."

"万物的和谐在于秩序的平衡，
秩序就是把事物安排在，
各自适当的位置上。"

——古罗马思想家奥古斯丁

"幸福就是你的所思、所言及所行
皆达至平衡和谐。"

——圣雄甘地

"没有一种化妆品比幸福更能让人美丽。"

——19世纪爱尔兰作家
Lady Blessington

"表象的美只能取悦一时，
内心的美才能经久不衰。"

——大文豪歌德

"情感与理性平衡所以最美，
因为是最上乘的人生哲学，
生活艺术。"

——天人翻译大家傅雷

"人类的生命，
并不能以时间长短来衡量，
心中充满爱时，
刹那即永恒。"

——哲学家尼采

雅堂相信，
美丽的女人，
源自于平衡·爱·幸福。

美丽，
不只是姣好的容颜，
不只是漂亮的外衣，
不只是外在的完美无瑕，
更是由内而外的身心灵平衡美好。

不只在于自身能否拥有爱的光环，
更在于自身能否拥有能够给予爱
的无限能量。

不只关于幸福是否降临自身，
更关于是否幸福于
人间无所不在的永恒祈愿。

拥有平衡·爱·幸福的女人拥有强大的力量，
独当一面的女强人与温柔万能的女主人
她能同时胜任；
理性思维与感性思绪在她脑海里兼容并存。

21世纪的美丽女人拥有强大的力量，
由内而外，由外而内，循环不息，
平衡·爱·幸福是一种让世人无法不看见的，
专属于她的光采。

ACCESSORIES

CITY

CELEBRITY SOCIAL

BUSINESS SOCIAL

DAILY

PARTY

OFFICE

BUSINESS

FASHION SOCIAL

HOLIDAY

上图：
20"2 年春夏，在"平衡·爱·幸福"
价值主张下，EP 围绕女性生活方式
鞋出"十全十美"产品系列

右页：
2013 年春夏 EP 广告大片

ABOVE

EP launches a new product collection
— Perfect 10, in its Spring-Summer
2012, centred around the brand's
"Balance, Love and Happiness" value
proposition

OPPOSITE

EP Spring-Summer 2013 ad campaign

上图：

2015 年，雅莹集团邀约艺术家篆刻的"平衡·爱·幸福"印章，成为集团签发要文或书信的重要落款

ABOVE

EP YAYING Fashion Group collaborates with an artist to create a Chinese seal carved with the Chinese characters of "Balance, Love and Happiness", used as the Group's signature for important letters or documents, 2015

"

爱，则是平衡好一切的原动力。
有了爱，有了平衡，幸福也就有了保证。
做品牌就是做情感，
如果人都没有情感，品牌可以做得出情感？
爱，就是雅莹希望传递出的情感。

"

在"平衡·爱·幸福"价值主张的指引下，2012 年春夏，雅莹围绕女性生活方式提出"十全十美"新概念，以 EP 六条产品线（Party, Office, Daily, Business, Holiday, City）、Elegant Prosper 的三条高端产品线（Business Social, Fashion Social, Celebrity Social）与 EP Accessories 一起，组成一个"十全十美"产品线矩阵。

随着对品牌精神的深入贯彻，"平衡·爱·幸福"还一步步升级成为集团的经营哲学，引领雅莹发展至今。也是在这一时期，雅莹深入剖析自身文化与影响，并将牡丹确定为品牌基因。"唯有牡丹真国色。"牡丹，是中国国花，它常被形容为雍容华贵的贵妇人，也被认为是国运昌盛的标志，是幸福美满的象征，既具有自然美又有艺术美。

牡丹，与张华明的家族关系亲密。从 20 世纪开始回溯，这抹绽放的红就像被刻下的情怀，在冥冥中成为雅莹独特风格的重要注脚。早年，张华明生活的祖村红庵里就生长着一株百年牡丹，童年时期的他，经常在早晚上学、放学时，驻立花前，仰慕其娇艳花容的晶莹高贵。更巧合的是，这株百年牡丹，正与当年张宝荣承包经营的洛东红政服装厂紧紧相邻。仪态万千的牡丹随年月更替，历经贫寒一茬茬盛放；洛东红政服装厂，亦饱经风霜一日日成长。仿佛是生命的默契和共鸣，牡丹与张华明和雅莹的渊源也就此深深伏笔。

2011 年，张华明在一次采风途中，受异域文化启发，联想到

The brand's value proposition of *Balance, Love, and Happiness* would eventually become the Group's business philosophy, synonymous with the concept of Chinese beauty today.

Centred around the brand's new value proposition and the different lifestyles of modern women, EP launched a *Perfect 10* concept collection as part of its Spring-Summer 2012 campaign, featuring 10 product lines in 3 different categories. These included the *Party, Office, Daily, Business, Holiday* and *City* lines under the EP category; the *Business Social, Fashion Social* and *Celebrity Social* lines under the high-end Elegant Prosper category; and the *accessories* line as its own category.

It was also during this period that the Peony became ingrained into the brand's identity. The Peony holds an important place in the hearts of Hwaming's family, as their village of Hong'anli featured bushes of century-old Peony flowers, which the villagers called the *Hong'anli Peony*. These left a deep mark of beauty and prosperity on their otherwise plain and humble environment. During his childhood in the 1970s, Hwaming spent countless mornings and evenings before and after school admiring the beauty and charm of the flower. In 1988, Zhang Baorong's factory would, by fate, be situated beside these Hong'anli Peonies, and they accompanied the factory in rain and shine, and in winter and summer. Their growth and bloom each year served as a symbol of the factory's success.

During one of his overseas trips in 2011, Hwaming was inspired by the beauty of the local culture and realised how important it was for Chinese brands to possess their own unique cultural identity. He recalled the century-old Hong'anli Peonies beside the old factory, and how he loved them as a child — their poise and elegance forever

"

牡丹，在张华明的家族记忆中占据着重要的地位。
从 20 世纪开始回溯，
这抹绽放的红像被刻下的情怀，
且在冥冥中成为雅莹独特风格的重要注脚。

"

中国品牌当有属于东方的特色之美，又回想起当年陪伴着雅莹老厂发展壮大的百年红庵牡丹。从此，牡丹成为雅莹产品创作的重要元素，2013 年，牡丹被正式确立为雅莹的核心基因，视为雅莹"女性美"的典雅象征。牡丹根植于雅莹的血液，不但为其产品创作设计注入了美好而斑斓的灵感，也以其大气、优雅与高贵，为雅莹人的审美和修为注入独特气质，成就雅莹由内而外的独特精神内涵。

这一年，雅莹还首度与艺术家展开合作。专门邀请英国艺术家 Paul Alexander Thornton 运用圆珠笔以纯手绘形式解读雅莹的灵感之花——牡丹，并联手中国知名插画师雷梦婷，创作了一系列雅莹集团 25 周年限量版牡丹插画纪念品。这种链接全球优秀设计师、创意人才展开深度合作的方式，开启了雅莹为产品逐步注入更多艺术文化魅力的旅程，也为女性消费者带去了更多美和愉悦的艺术享受。

此后雅莹的诸多设计，都融入了牡丹元素。无论是精致的配饰细节，还是融合艺术创作的灵动纹样，在雅莹的精心创作下，牡丹成为一种内涵的精神，演绎着独属雅莹的东方浪漫和优雅。牡丹，还激发了雅莹对整个大自然之美的热忱，为创造美的事业不断蓄能。

etched into his heart and mind. He began inserting the Peony motif into the brand's designs, and gradually, the Peony became a recurring element in the brand's style — an icon celebrating women's confidence, dynamism and wisdom.

A famous poet from the Tang Dynasty once wrote, *The Peony is the real beauty of the nation with its bloom moving the capital.* The Peony is China's national flower, and its cultural and artistic connotations transcend time and culture. The flower also provided creative inspiration and unique oriental romance to EP's many creations and collaborations.

In 2013, EP launched its first collaboration with international artists, commissioning Paul Alexander Thornton, a British artist, to create a series of Peony designs for its pieces. He also worked together with another well-known Chinese illustrator, Lei Mengting, on a series of limited-edition collections for the brand's 25th anniversary. This kicked off a string of collaborations with creative talents around the world, injecting more artistic and cultural charm into EP's creations and bringing a more joyful experience to customers.

The Peony was more than just a design motif, it was also a strong influencer of the development of both the company and individuals. It reinforced the company's belief in beauty from within, of *Balance, Love and Happiness*, and further manifested into a passion for the grandeur of nature.

左页 / 右图：

2013 年秋冬，EP 首次与海外艺术家合作，英国艺术家 Paul Alexander Thornton 为 EP 绘制的牡丹花型系列

OPPOSITE / RIGHT

EP launches its first collaboration with international artists in 2013, commissioning Paul Alexander Thornton, a British artist, to create a series of Peony artworks

上图：
2013 年，EP 与数位艺术家合作手绘
花型的牡丹丝巾系列

ABOVE

EP launches a collection of silk scarves in
2013, each featuring unique hand-drawn
Peonies created by different artists

左图：
2014 年春夏 EP 广告大片，中国超
模杜鹃身着牡丹纹样连衣裙

LEFT
Chinese supermodel Du Juan in a
Peony-pattern dress, EP Spring-Summer
2014 ad campaign

上图 / 右页：
2015 年春夏，雅莹手工坊牡丹刺绣作品

ABOVE / OPPOSITE
Peony embroidery in EP's artisanal workshop,
Spring-Summer 2015

以东方美学彰显世界时尚
ORIENTAL AESTHETICS, INTERNATIONAL FASHION

雅莹在 2012 年春夏提出的"十全十美"产品系列满足消费者更多元化、多层次的消费需求，进而在更大范围扩展市场。但丰富的产品线同时也带来挑战：子产品和系列过多，淡化了主体风格，品牌精髓也因此变得模糊。幸运的是，张华明敏锐地感觉到了风险的存在，并及时对其进行了检讨、修正。

"卖场的体验会比较复杂，顾客进来之后，可能看不清楚你是谁。所以，到 2013 年的时候我们开始思考如何收一收。目标是更聚焦，把核心的东西凸显出来，兼顾生活场景的同时，在整体上有一个统一感和一致感，在产品的调性上再统一一些。"时任 EP 事业部产品总经理高鹰回忆说。

一轮深刻反思与检讨后，2013 年，雅莹对 10 条产品线重新梳理并瘦身聚焦为三大产品线——Elegant.Prosper（EP 高级线）、EP 线和 EP jeans；实现了产品分类更清晰，让顾客更简便了解雅莹的定位。更清晰的定位之后，雅莹开始在产品创新上更大胆地彰显自己的个性与精神，并尤其强调将设计根植于中国传统文化之中。这一策略也很快成为雅莹区别于其他从业者，尤其是国际同行的独特魅力与核心优势。

Elegant.Prosper 高级线就是雅莹深耕传统文化的一个起点。2009 年 Elegant.Prosper 高级线刚刚诞生，经过两三年摸索，雅莹在 2012 年 9 月为其建立了由具备几十年技艺的手工艺匠为核心的手工坊。这些手工艺匠都在刺绣、珠绣、编织和手绘等方面有丰富经验，通过传承和发展江南精湛手工技艺，助力了雅莹手工制品的臻美产出，也将服饰顶级的传统技艺不断发扬光大。

EP's *Perfect 10* product collection launched during its Spring-Summer 2012 season allowed EP to meet the more diverse and differentiated needs of women, but they also presented new challenges, as the product mix had become over-complicated without a clear and distinct style with which customers could remember the brand.

"The in-store experience became more complex. The many different product collections seemed to confuse the customers as they were left wondering what kind of a brand we were. Therefore, we started to consolidate different product lines around our key styles. We focused on the different lifestyle needs of our customers, but maintained a consistent and unique image," recalled Gao Ying, then EP general manager for product management.

By 2013, EP had narrowed its 10 product lines to 3, namely its main *EP* line, its *Elegant.Prosper* high-end line and a *EP jeans* line. It was the high-end line that would become a springboard for the brand's journey of cultural re-discovery.

As early as September 2012, the company had set up an artisanal workshop to boost its high-end category, led by craftspeople with decades of experience in embroidery, beading, weaving and many other handicraft skills. These craftspeople possessed the exquisite artisanal abilities well-known in the Jiangnan region, and they were key to instilling even more artistic and cultural value into the high-end collections. Through these fashion pieces, time-honoured craftsmanship and know-how could not only be preserved but passed on to future generations.

"

做手工艺要有不容出错的细致，
能在重复中不断练习，这样的坚持是很难的。
当我们用精湛的技艺打磨每一个环节，
塑造着每件服饰的艺术价值时，
看到在 T 台上熠熠发光的衣服就仿佛看着自己的孩子们一样。
雅莹在做的不但是传承，还是创新表达。

"

雅莹的工匠们凭借一双巧手、一颗匠心，以工匠之绝磨炼技艺、修炼身心。2012 年，雅莹耗时 150 天，游走半个地球，从法国巴黎到印度再到中国，在这个文明交流越来越方便的"地球村"里共同完成了一件华贵无比的大礼服。它是工匠精神的在线，凝聚了匠人孜孜不倦的好奇心，以及对惊喜永不停歇的追求。这件大礼服上，有玛丽皇后旧宫里夕阳映照下的漆金雕花，精致繁复又极富生命力；有恒河水荡漾来的润泽钉珠，星罗棋布，光彩夺目；有江南手艺人严丝合缝勾勒出的一二龙骨。精益求精的制作，展现了雅莹"平衡·爱·幸福"的理念，呈现出女性内外兼备，优雅而晶莹的力量感。

实践口，雅莹还推动手工坊坚持将极致的材料和传统工艺创新融合，以更完美也更挑战地呈现品牌的极致特质。比如，在一系列以中国传统文化元素为主打的产品中，用极致细小的珠片勾勒诸如仙鹤等图腾，以富有当代感的珍贵蓝色弹簧丝层叠嵌入，于色彩的完美折射中全新演绎蹙金礼服的传统纹样，并用 12 种刺绣针法使仙鹤的每个角度都呈现不同的光泽，让其呈现出栩栩而飞的神态。而这些，都最终成为 Elegant.Prosper 高级线的高级所在，体现尊贵。

"做手工艺要有不容出错的细致，能在重复中不断练习，这样的坚持是很难的。当我们用精湛的技艺打磨每一个环节，塑造着每件服饰的艺术价值时，看到在 T 台上熠熠发光的衣服就仿佛看着自己的孩子们一样。雅莹在做的不但是传承，还是创新表达。"拥有 20 多年手工经验的雅莹手工坊负责人郑爱梅表示，这些年，雅莹一直在致敬传统，致敬那些多年坚守传承和创新中国传统手工艺的匠心，不断推动品牌的艺术文化发展，并为社会文明发展蓄势赋能。

In the same year, the brand embarked on an extraordinary cultural journey — spending 150 days travelling around the world, from Paris to India, and then back to China — working with local craftspeople in each destination to complete a haute couture evening gown for the Autumn-Winter collection. The gown embodied meaningful cross-cultural exchange and was the result of a collective pursuit of exceptional craftsmanship. It featured patterns by French artisans that referenced the golden sophisticated carvings adorning the old palace of Queen Marie-Antoinette; the magical and brilliant beading of pearls by master craftsmen along the Ganges; and interior bonings gracefully put together by adept Jiangnan craftspeople. All of these culminated into an original work of art, culture and fashion.

EP began to marry high-quality materials with exquisite traditional craftsmanship, pursuing new mastery that showcased the brand's fashion pursuits. One of its many works of art included a beaded and embroidered piece, *A Crane in Flight*, which used extremely fine beads to outline the shape of the crane; adding extremely fine coloured wire embroidery for a contemporary touch; and finally using 12 different embroidery techniques to give its customers a different view of the crane from different angles, "almost lifelike in flight".

"Handicraft allows no room for error, and repeating the same action over and over again to hone one's skills requires extreme perseverance. However, when we see our creations slowly taking shape and coming to life, especially on the runway, there is a heart-warming sense of achievement, as if they were our own children. We not only pass down these valuable skills, but we also continue to innovate and develop these methods," said Zheng Aimei, who has over 20 years of handicraft experience and serves as the head of China YAYING's artisanal workshop today.

She added, "The brand continues to pay homage to the traditions and

追求"好衣"，既是雅莹的初心，也是历经多次成功和失误之后更加坚定的信念。就像张华明曾说，企业失败的根本原因，就是偏离了消费者，偏离了产品。这次立足核心再造品牌的过程中，雅莹也曾遭遇挑战，但这个初心和信念依然使其快速纠错并自我赋能，继而保持了朝向大目标的持续进化与优化。2014~2015 年，已连续 10 年高速成长的雅莹，一度在力推新品牌的过程中陷入扩张的困顿：核心品牌的销售开始下滑，整体增长减缓。"感到顾客的需求有点抓不住了，产品上开始偏向惯性的思维，有点偏老气。核心产品的研发上投入的精力不够，影响了核心产品在市场上的竞争力。"

2016 年 4 月的季度经营会议上，雅莹进一步明确了当前经营的困难，并再一次主动变革，从组织、产品、销售模式以及商品经营结构上应变、创新，并以破釜沉舟、迎刃而上之决心在当年实现逆势增长，创造令整个服装行业惊艳的业绩。在战略层面，张华明在公司发起走出"安全区"和"舒适区"的运动，要求全体重新定义成功与风险；具体到产品层面，戴雪明也提出了两个要求：第一，加强与国际流行趋势的关联性；第二，加大创新、创意和迭代。

与此同时，张华明对品牌实施了进一步的升级优化，推出 EP、中国雅莹双产品线战略，并提出新的品牌发展方向："世界的 EP，中国的雅莹。"其中，EP 融合东西方审美和艺术，从全球时尚视角出发，结合中国当代生活方式，突出国际风尚，塑造更加当代和摩登的产品风格；中国雅莹则回溯中国本源，强调东方美学，专注于对中国传统文化、美学、服饰、工艺不断探究与演绎，融合当代审美趣味，打造极具中国文化特色的高品质生活方式。

ingenuity of craftspeople, supporting arts and culture, and ensuring their integration with our society's development, each becoming one another's driving force."

Using high-quality materials to make good clothing, EP had never wavered in its vision, though it encountered many bumps along the way. The rapidly-changing Chinese fashion market meant that in 2014 and 2015, the company found its products once again hitting a plateau, as customers seemed to have lost interest.

"I felt that we were no longer able to capture the wants and needs of our customers. Our products seemed to become stuck in inertia, our products felt old. Where was our commitment to innovation?" Hwaming pondered. At the strategic level, Hwaming initiated a campaign across the company to urge everyone out of their comfort zones, insisting change at all levels. From the company's structure to the brand's designs, and from product mix to retail, everything had to be overturned.

In 2016, the company introduced a new brand development strategy and a revamped dual product line — "World EP" and "China YAYING". World EP represented a fusion of both Eastern and Western design that is inclusive, contemporary and international; China YAYING focused on the inheritance and evolution of Chinese traditional culture, aesthetics, fashion and craftsmanship that embodies the quintessential Chinese elegance.

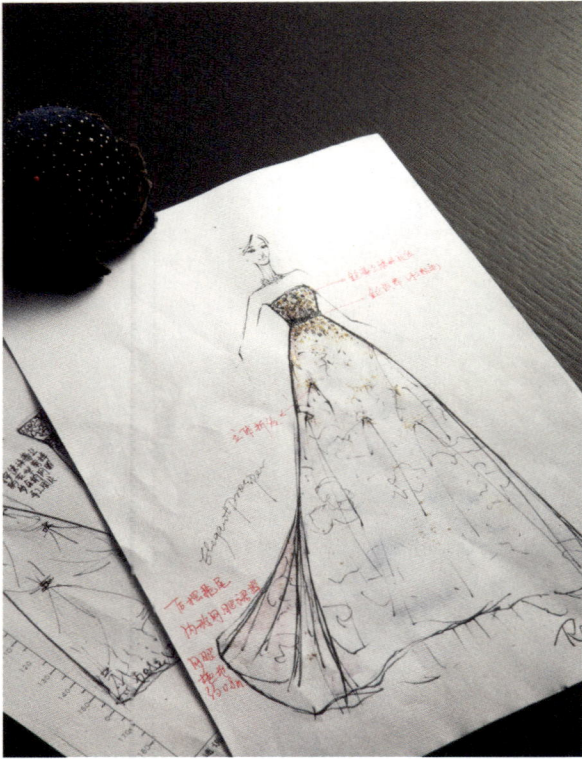

上图／右页：
2012 年秋冬，EP 推出高级定制礼服，辗转法国巴黎、印度、中国等地高级工坊，耗时 150 天制成

ABOVE / OPPOSITE

EP designs a haute couture evening gown, which took over 150 days to complete, making its way around artisanal workshops in Paris, India and China, Autumn-Winter 2012

根植文化，锻造经典

右图：
2012 年秋冬 EP 广告大片，高级定制礼服

品质，心造之境

Quality from the HEART

优雅的外表和莹洁的心灵是互相映衬的平衡，这是雅莹珍视的品牌之名，也是30年来不曾改变的起点和初心。雅莹集团始终视品质为重中之重，视品质为人品。雅莹重视承载时代精神的设计，更在意隐藏在美丽的衣装背后，写在一针一线中的工艺和品质。在创作中传承传统的精湛手工艺，以"匠心"自我要求，用专业的生产管理将这种高水平的工艺应用到工业生产中。不断革新工艺、优化流程，以每一个环节的精细管理，确保产品的卓越品质。技艺的革新背后，也是从事技艺之人内心对进步和完善的需求。雅莹珍视内心的力量，相信诚与善的心意是创造美好之物的源泉。精益求精带来考究的细节和含蓄的优雅，生生不息，韵味长久。而品质，则是用心创造的馈赠。

An elegant appearance and a pure soul are the balance of each other. This is also the meaning of the brand's Chinese name " 雅莹 ". It is also the starting point and the heart of the brand that has not changed in its 30 years. EP YAYING has always sought to maintain the highest standard of quality and alludes quality to character. Great importance is attached to designs bearing the spirit of the Times, and even more the craftsmanship and quality behind each needlework that create these beautiful garments. In every creating process, passing on these exquisite time-honoured skills, demanding the finest from oneself, complemented by modern professional production management and constant improvements to the process, ensure that excellence is continually passed on to our customers. Yet, behind all the techique and innovation, are the peoples' hearts and how much we ask of them to continue to push the limits of craft and even themselves. Excellence begets excellence. Beauty begets beauty. EP YAYING values the inner strength of all craftspeople and believes that sincerity and goodness are the source of creating beautiful things. Quality is a gift from the heart.

雅莹制造，品质保障

坐落于雅莹时尚园的精品工场，是雅莹服装制造工艺最高标准的体现。现代专业化的生产管理体系下，雅莹贯穿"匠心精神"，严于律己，不断革新工艺、优化流程，以每一个环节的精细管理，每一道工序的细心打磨，确保产品的卓越品质。

PREMIUM FACTORY

Located in EP YAYING Fashion Group's Fashion Park, its Premium Factory is the embodiment of the highest standard of quality production. Continuously tested and improved over the years, it operates under a modern and specialised production management system with strict attention to detail, combining craftsmanship spirit and self-discipline, with innovation and advanced technology to ensure the quality excellence of each garment.

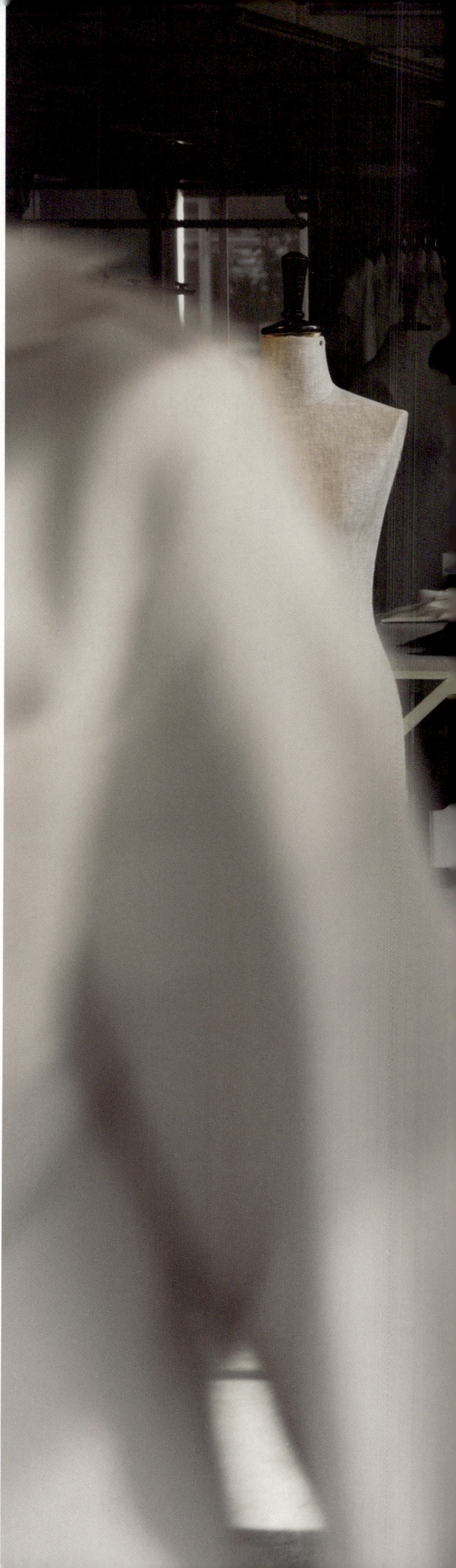

手工工坊

雅莹手工工坊代表了雅莹最精湛的手工技艺，平日里寂静无声，平均从业年龄在 10 年以上的技师们似乎在与针线对话，仔细听的话，还能听到富有节奏的，绣针穿过绷紧的丝绸，丝线摩擦布料的声音。雅莹手工工坊致力于传承和发展江南精湛手工技艺。丰厚的经验让工匠们得以以自由的姿态演绎和革新传统，将传统文化和美学融入当代精品服饰的创新演绎之中。

ARTISANAL WORKSHOP

EP YAYING's artisanal workshop epitomises the Group's most exquisite craftsmanship. The space is usually silent, if you listen hard enough, you can hear what is a heart-to-heart dialogue between the craftspeople and their needle and thread. And if you listen harder, the latter in a fascinating rhythm with the fabric. These craftspeople with decades of experience continue to pass on and develop their exquisite artisanal skills well-known in the Jiangnan region, and with their rich experience, are adept at instilling even more artistic and cultural value into EP YAYING's contemporary and exquisite collections.

刺绣与钉珠

以刺绣、钉珠为首的中国手工工艺不仅赋予每一件衣服独一无二的特质，更为其添加了无上的艺术风格，是服装价值体现的核心。雅莹的刺绣以苏绣为基础，集各家绣法之长，手工技师们展开想象力，在皮革、棉麻、针织、丝绒等不同材质的布料上钻研创作出最具表现力的刺绣方式和图案。钉珠也是如此，米粒珠、长珠、圆珠……不同形状的珠子在手工技师们手中变幻出多种造型，为服装增添立体而丰富的装饰。

EMBROIDERY AND BEADING

Embroidery and beading are iconic Chinese traditional handicrafts that not only endow each garment with its unique characteristics, but also add to it an infinite artistic style. These handicrafts are also the heart of EP YAYING's creations, each an expression of the craftsperson's imagination and fantasy, combining EP YAYING's signature Su embroidery style with a range of exciting embroidery styles, creative patterns, high-quality fabrics and snazzy beads.

制版与打样

制版是让纸面上的设计变成立体现实的关键步骤。设计给了衣服灵魂，制版则赋予衣服生命。雅莹的制版师们深知自己的使命，领口的角度、缝线的长短、拼接的位置……每一个细节都要与设计师反复琢磨。每一个款式确定之前，都要经过四轮确认和至少十次的打样。

PATTERN-MAKING AND PROTOTYPING

Pattern-making gives life to a designer's sketches. This is the responsibility that the pattern-makers at EP YAYING are well aware of, from the angles of the neckline to the length of each stitching line to the positioning of each pattern, every detail is examined and worked on repeatedly with the designers, with at least four rounds of confirmation and ten rounds of fittings required to achieve the perfect fit.

Love is the driving force for everything

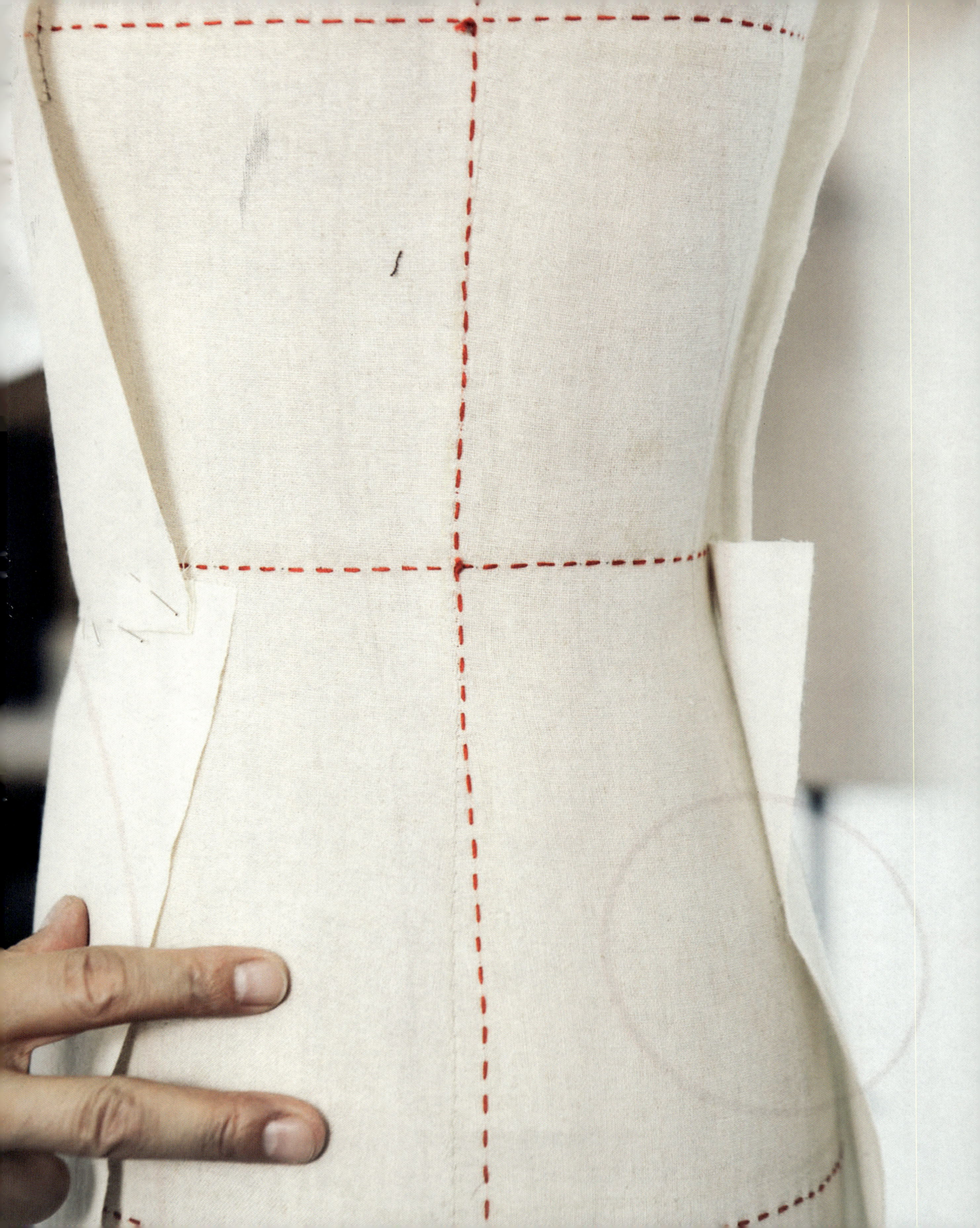

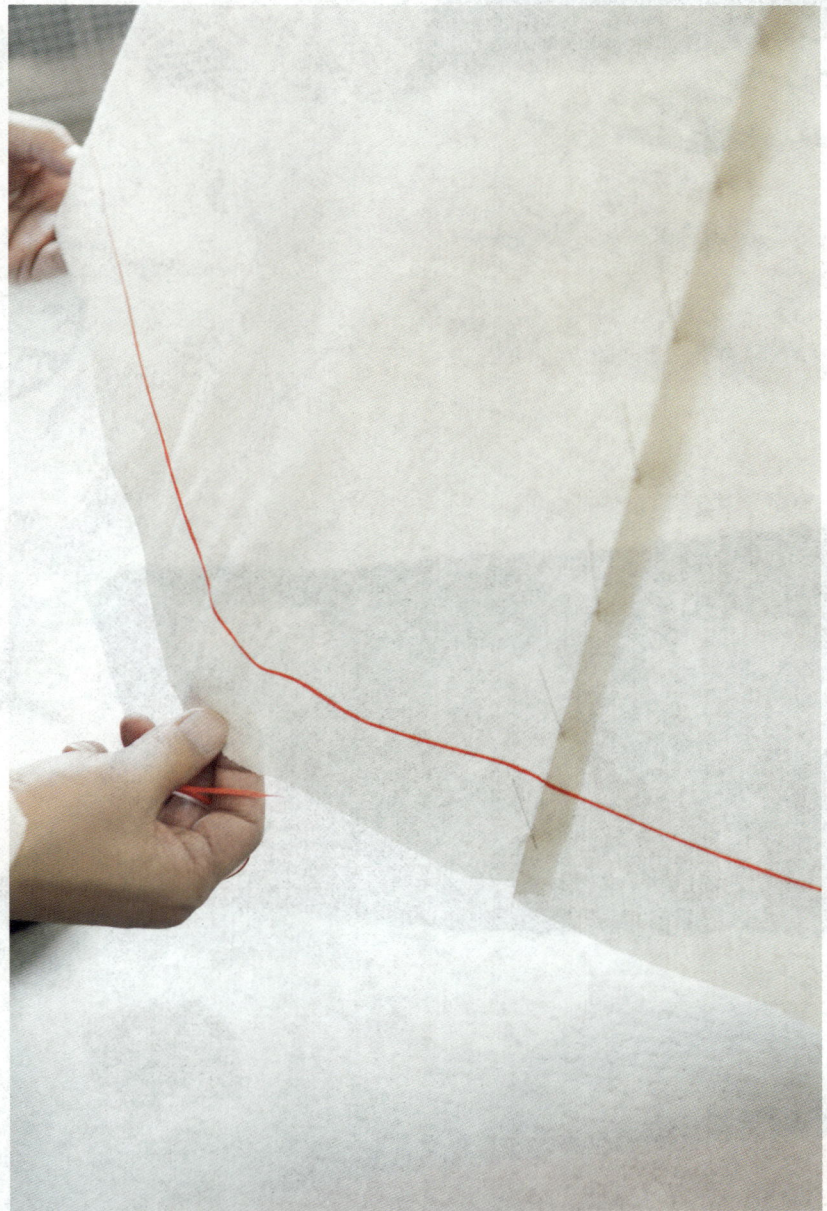

面料选择

自主理化实验室以科学严谨的态度，研究每一种布料的特性。制作衣物之前，布匹的 pH 值、色牢度、缩率、耐用性等都需经过检验。如今已有 33 种设备，可完成 25 种检验项目，并连续多年参与服装行业国家标准的制定。

FABRIC SELECTION

The chemical laboratory at the factory studies the characteristics of each fabric with a scientific and rigorous attitude. Before every production, the fabric's pH value, colour fastness, shrinkage and durability are tested. The laboratory has 33 kinds of equipment that can complete 25 different kinds of testing per industry standards.

肉眼检验

面料检验的指标有 20 多道，色差、疵点、抽丝、纬斜……这些细微的识别机器无法办到，而需要通过人工肉眼辨别。为了从源头上保证最终成品的品质，雅莹多年来坚持肉眼对比检验入库的每一寸面料。

FABRIC INSPECTION

There are more than 20 indicators for fabric inspection such as colour differences, snags and weft breakages. These subtle defects are not able to be identified by machines and can only be picked up by experienced human eyes. In order to guarantee the quality of the final product from the very beginning, EP YAYING has insisted on personal inspection of every inch of fabric for many years.

手工定位裁剪

特殊花型面料是雅莹服装的特色之一，为了保证同一款式的每一件成品拥有一致的花纹，雅莹在初裁之后，均用手及夹子将每一片裁片的花纹对齐压平，而后亲手用剪刀细微修剪调整，争取将误差减至最小。

FABRIC CUTTING

To ensure that each garment retain their designed style and pattern order, EP YAYING ensures precise fabric cutting, aligning the patterns of each fabric before and after each cutting to minimise the variations.

装袖

从裁片到成衣，中间隔着上百道工序，而其中尤以装领、装袖为至繁之步骤。雅莹的装袖工作要求由 10 年以上经验的制衣师完成。车缝、拉皱、修袖窿……一件袖子，需要经过 27 道工序，1298 个动作才能装制完成。

SLEEVE ASSEMBLY

From fabric cutting to the finished garment, there are still hundreds of processes in between. Details such as the amount of ease and fullness to give to set in the sleeves, are just part of at least 27 processes at this key stage that is completed by a dressmaker with at least 10 years of experience.

整体组合

在服装制作的过程中，雅莹的工匠们会多次将服装套上人台组合、试穿与调整。立体别烫、修裁以及别花，反复地台检、终检与抽检，只为最大程度地呈现服装与设计的立体感，保证顾客的穿着体验，还原衣服在最初设计中的优雅姿态。

FINAL ASSEMBLY

Many fittings and adjustments are undergone before the garment comes into shape. Each piece of fabric is assembled on a personalised 3D mannequin to mirror the different body shapes, each piece of fabric is pinned, sewn, pressed and trimmed, perfect to every millimeter. The final assembly process exemplifies the detail-oriented spirit of EP YAYING. From design to completion, elegance comes to life.

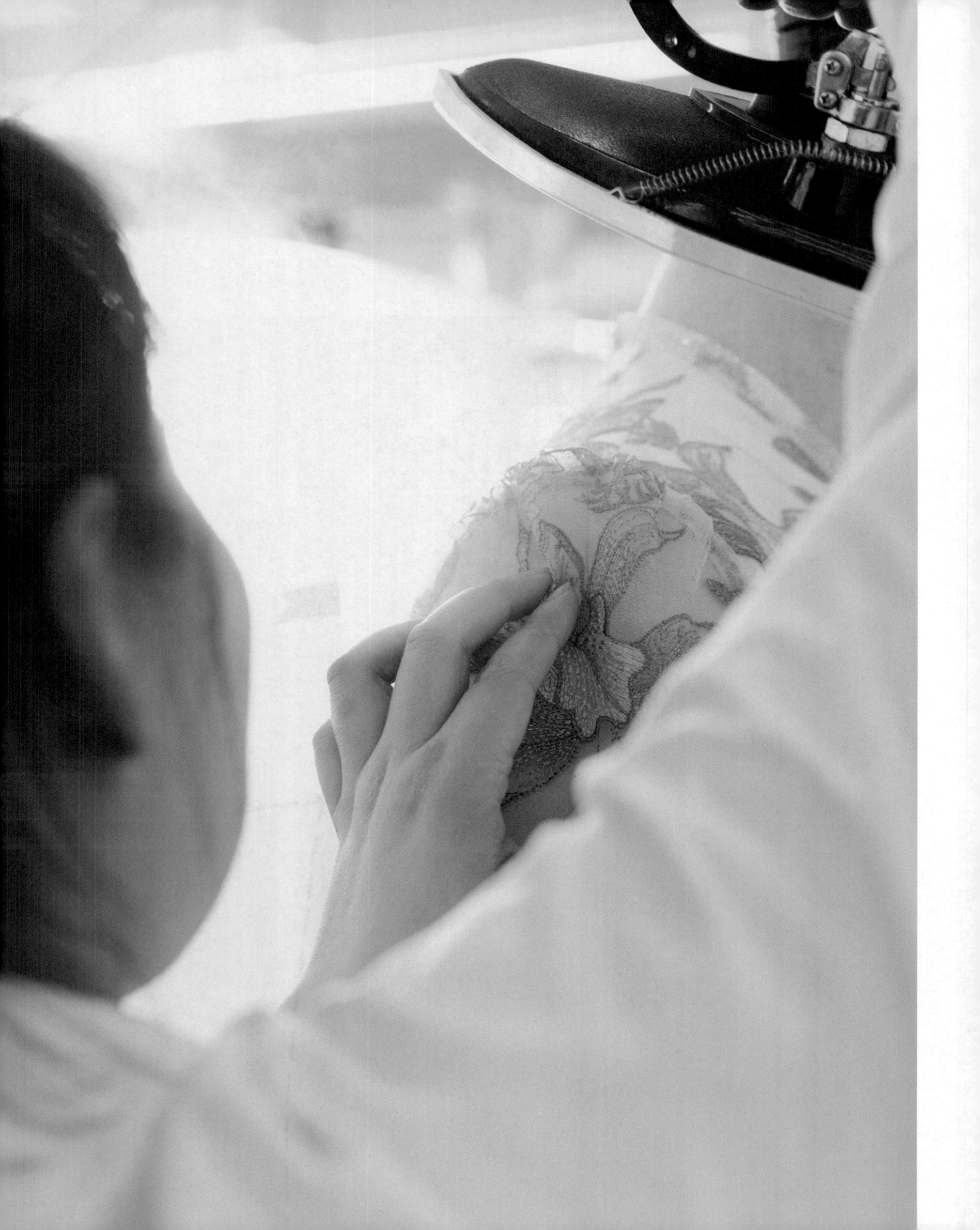

而当时担任雅莹顾问的爱马仕原全球执行副总裁 Christian Blanckaert 这样评价雅莹："EP 所代表的不单是产品，而是一种生活方式、一种精神、一种慷慨，是一个承载社会责任的品牌。EP 是中国式的魔术师，是一个让全世界人民崇拜的魔术师，她能够把多元化的风格融为一体。所有的女性都认可 EP 这个品牌，因为 EP 卖的不单是产品，她卖的是生活艺术，这种生活艺术让每位女性更加的优雅。我们透过服务也能感受到 EP 的这种品位，透过这个服务看到与其他品牌的区别，没有傲慢，只有开阔的思想，这使得这个品牌成功地超越世界上的大品牌，非常的中国化，也非常的自豪。EP 不单是品牌了，而是一个像丝绸一样的艺术品。"

新的变革下，中国雅莹强化了在产品创意中融入文化与艺术，在细节处彰显独特品味。雅莹还专门邀请篆刻大家韩天衡，以典雅优美的虫鸟篆印章形式，篆刻"雅莹"二字，构建自身独特的品牌标识。虫鸟篆被誉为"最优美的篆体之一"，刻印线条蜿蜒屈曲如虫，画首精巧饰以鸟状，落成一副生动的装饰纹样。温润的玉石，所刻下的虫鸟篆体线条柔美，曲直相映，繁简之间，游刃有余。中国雅莹这一独特品牌印记，既有取意印章所象征的责任、诚信之意，也折射了雅莹追求东方美学、匠心精神与自然传承的理念，代表着品牌对品质与内涵的不断深究。

值此，中国雅莹还在总部及核心门店所在商场，自 2017 年起陆续举办多场艺术展览，如"雕刻时光""盛唐华章""梦花镜源"等。雅莹注重将传统文化精粹、手艺与现代时尚不断交融，以东方美学倡导者的身份，积极探索古典与现代的碰撞。

Christian Blanckaert, former global executive vice president of Hermes, who served as EP's brand consultant from 2014 for several years and remains a close friend of Hwaming and Xueming today, described EP as a unique legened birthed from China: "EP does not represent just a single product, it is in fact a way of life, a spirit, a kind of generosity and a brand with a strong sense of social responsibility. With the ability to integrate a diversified range of styles together as one, EP is like a Chinese magician, one that is admired by the world. Women from around the world recognise the brand EP, as the brand is not selling a single product. Instead, it advocates the art of life and this lifestyle allows every woman to feel elegant. Through interaction with the brand, many can appreciate and resonate with EP. Unlike many other brands, EP is one without arrogance, only an open mind. This allows EP to surpass many other big brands around the world. It is a Chinese brand, one that is immensely proud of its origins. EP is not just a brand, but a type of art likened to silk."

Everyone at the company was excited by this unique change. China YAYING began to work on its new identity, seeking a deeper relationship with Chinese culture. It would go on to invite renowned seal carver, Master Han Tianheng, to create a logo in the form of a classically elegant "bird-worm" seal script. The "bird-worm" seal script is known to be one of the most beautiful seal characters, and has been used by kings and nobles as their personal seals. The intricate and alluring lines he carved in this script stand for the two Chinese characters of the brand 雅莹（yaying）. The unique seal not only symbolised promise and sincerity in traditional Chinese culture, but also reflected the brand's pursuit of oriental aesthetics, craftsmanship and culture.

Since 2017, China YAYING has successively held many fashion and cultural exhibitions in its headquarters and in selected shopping malls where the brand's major stores are located, including *Crafting*

"

EP 所代表的不单是产品，而是一种生活方式、一种精神、一种慷慨，
是一个承载社会责任的品牌。EP 是中国式的魔术师，
是一个让全世界人民崇拜的魔术师，她能够把多元化的风格融为一体。
所有的女性都认可 EP 这个品牌，因为 EP 卖的不单是产品，
她卖的是生活艺术，这种生活艺术让每位女性更加的优雅。
我们透过服务也能感受到 EP 的这种品位，透过这个服务看到与
其他品牌的区别，没有傲慢，只有开阔的思想，这使得这个品牌成功地
超越世界上的大品牌，非常的中国化，也非常的自豪。
EP 不单是品牌了，而是一个像丝绸一样的艺术品。

"

"

'世界的 EP，中国的雅莹。'
EP 融合东西方审美和艺术，从全球时尚视角出发，
中国雅莹回溯中国本源，专研东方美学。

"

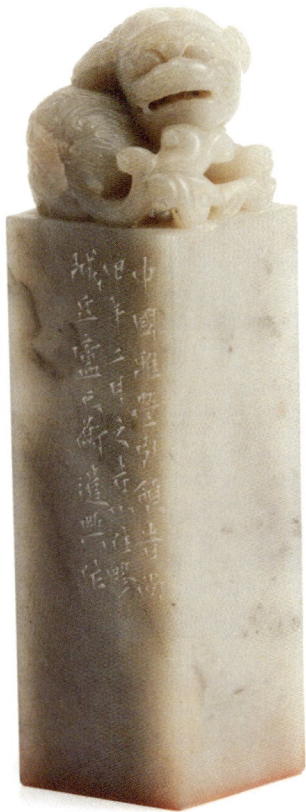

左图：

2014 年，公司邀请著名篆刻大家韩天衡，以典雅优美的虫鸟篆印章形式呈现"雅莹"二字，构建"中国雅莹"独特的标志

边款：中国雅莹引领时尚，甲午二月之吉小住鄮城，豆庐天衡遣兴作

LEFT

The Group invites renowned seal carver Han Tianheng to create a logo for its China YAYING collection in the form of the classically elegant "bird-worm" seal script, that depicts the Chinese characters of YAYING（雅莹）

YAYING

上页：

2017 年春夏中国雅莹广告大片，中国超模杜鹃演绎的中国雅莹龙袍系列，由新文人画摄影师孙郡掌镜。孙郡充满东方诗性的摄影表达，融入极具功底的细腻手绘，与中国雅莹"雅人深致"的精神完美契合，再经由杜鹃兼具中西的摩登演绎，将所有人带入新中式美学此间遐远的意境中去，如入画中，流连不已

左图：

2017 年秋冬中国雅莹广告大片，中国超模杜鹃身着清代《九阳消寒图》为灵感纹样的修身套装

PREVIOUS

Rising photographer Sun Jun captures Chinese supermodel Du Juan in China YAYING's dragon robe-inspired dress with his signature Chinese painting-styled photoshoot. China YAYING Autumn-Winter 2017 ad campaign

LEFT

Chinese supermodel Du Juan in a suit depicting a famous kesi tapestry artwork *Nine Yang Dispersing the Cold of Winter* from the Qing Dynasty, China YAYING Autumn-Winter 2017 ad campaign

左页／右图：
中国雅莹"雕刻时光"2017 年春夏时装
艺术展

OPPOSITE / RIGHT

"Crafting Time" Fashion & Arts Exhibition,
China YAYING Spring-Summer 2017

根植文化，锻造经典

右图：
中国雅莹"盛唐华章"2017 年秋冬
时装艺术展

"Prosperous Tang Dynasty" Fashion
& Arts Exhibition, China YAYING
Autumn-Winter 2017

左图：
中国雅莹 "梦花境源" 2018 年春夏时装艺术展

LEFT

"Arcadia of the East" Fashion & Arts Exhibition,
China YAYING Spring-Summer 2018

根植文化，锻造经典

右图：
中国雅莹"华章"2019 年春夏时装
艺术展

RIGHT
"A Beautiful Chinese Fable" Fashion &
Arts Exhibition. China YAYING Spring-
Summer 2019

264

同时中国雅莹还进一步将国际流行趋势与中华传统文化艺术紧密结合，令整个品牌更加优雅灵动并富内涵，也彰显出当代中国服装人继往开来，创新推动中国服饰文化与文明前进的社会责任。更清晰、高端与国际化的品牌定位之下，渠道管理、商业模式创新等系列新计划也陆续展开，推动雅莹持续成长，也将"平衡·爱·幸福"更好地传播到更广范围。

"世界的 EP，中国的雅莹"之下，雅莹还将 EP 品牌进一步区隔优化为 EP 主线、EP ZEN 和 EP LAB 三大系列。其中，EP 主线是 EP 品牌的主体，延续了雅莹一直以来坚持的精致、优雅风格，满足当代都市女性在工作与家庭生活中的着装需求；ZEN 是简约风，秉承东方美学，尊崇回归自然的价值理念，一般选用棉、麻、毛、丝等天然材质面料；LAB 则偏潮流，以牛仔裤、卫衣、衬衫、T 恤为主打品类，提供给消费者充满艺术、活力的潮流单品。

为使产品在兼顾生活场景的同时，更为聚焦，戴雪明还在产品创新上提出了新要求：除了横向产品线的开发和聚焦，还纵深到产品创意、原创性上进行深入研发，尝试每一季都和当代艺术家合作花型设计，在材质、版型上持续迭代，加快创新。

其中，在产品主打色的选择上，EP 选择了红、蓝两色。"EP 的红色，象征优雅、幸福、自信；EP 的蓝色，象征和谐、平衡、睿智。这两个颜色也象征着品牌的起源、发展与未来，透过它们的诠释，EP 讲述的是一个源自江南的时尚品牌，不断探索成长、积极进取的故事。"张华明解释说。

Time, Prosperous Tang Dynasty, Arcadia of the East and more. China YAYING worked to promote the integration of global fashion trends, and traditional Chinese culture and craftsmanship, not only providing a new look for the brand, but also renewing its purpose of representing a new generation of Chinese fashion practitioners who are committed to carrying forward past traditions and innovating for the future.

At the same time, the EP line was further differentiated into 3 themes: *EP, EP ZEN* and *EP LAB*. EP retained its exquisite chic style that continued to meet the demands of the modern woman both at work and at home; EP ZEN attracted nature lovers with a simpler design language inspired by oriental aesthetics and natural materials such as cotton, linen, wool and silk; and EP LAB dove into streetwear, involving jeans, sweaters and T-shirts with artistic and energetic designs. To ensure that the brand didn't lose steam again, Xueming called for more investment into its product R&D, which featured not only more collaborations with artists, but a deeper focus on materials and the tailoring of its garments.

In addition to these new design changes, EP also set its focus on two key colours — "EP Red" and "EP Blue". "EP Red symbolises elegance, happiness and confidence, while EP blue embodies harmony, poise and wisdom. These two colours are closely associated with the brand's origin, growth and future. Through these two colours, EP also tells the story of a Jiangnan-born fashion brand that is timeless and full of life," said Hwaming.

EP continued to open its doors to the world to create fashion and styles for hundreds of thousands of Asian women: they blend the grace and tenderness of the East with the modern and avant-garde of the West; and in the timelessness and harmony of the East, they share the freedom and diversity of the West. The brand's passionate journey, underlie its dedication to its life's philosophy — empowering women with "balance", "love" and "happiness" in life.

"

EP 红，象征优雅、幸福、自信；
EP 蓝，象征和谐、平衡、睿智。
这两个颜色象征着品牌的起源、发展与未来，
透过它们的诠释，EP 讲述的是一个源自江南的时尚品牌，
不断探索成长、积极进取的故事。

"

根植文化，锻造经典

左图：
2017 年秋冬 EP 广告大片

LEFT
EP Autumn-Winter 2017 ad campaign

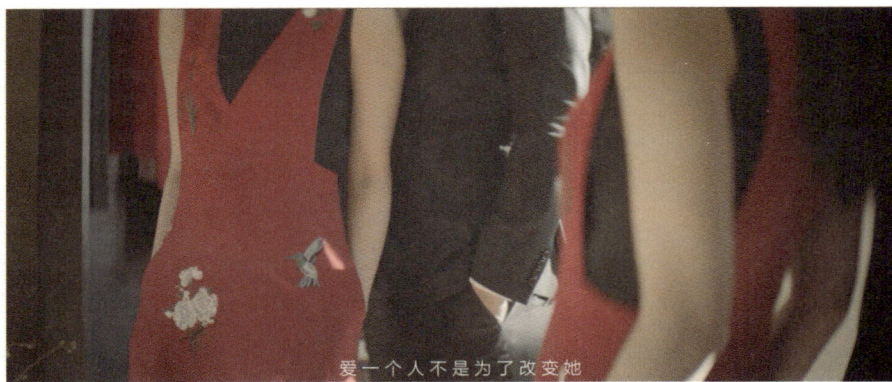

爱一个人不是为了改变她

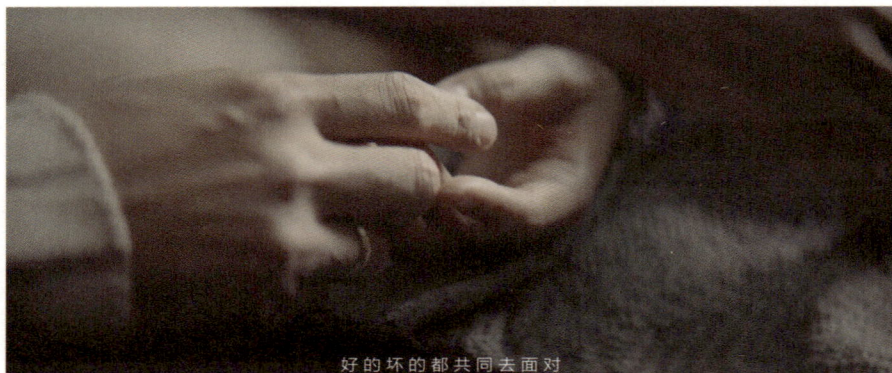

好的坏的都共同去面对　　　　　　　　　当然会

让我一直陪着你

现在最喜欢的是两个人一起去旅行

我们一起经历一切

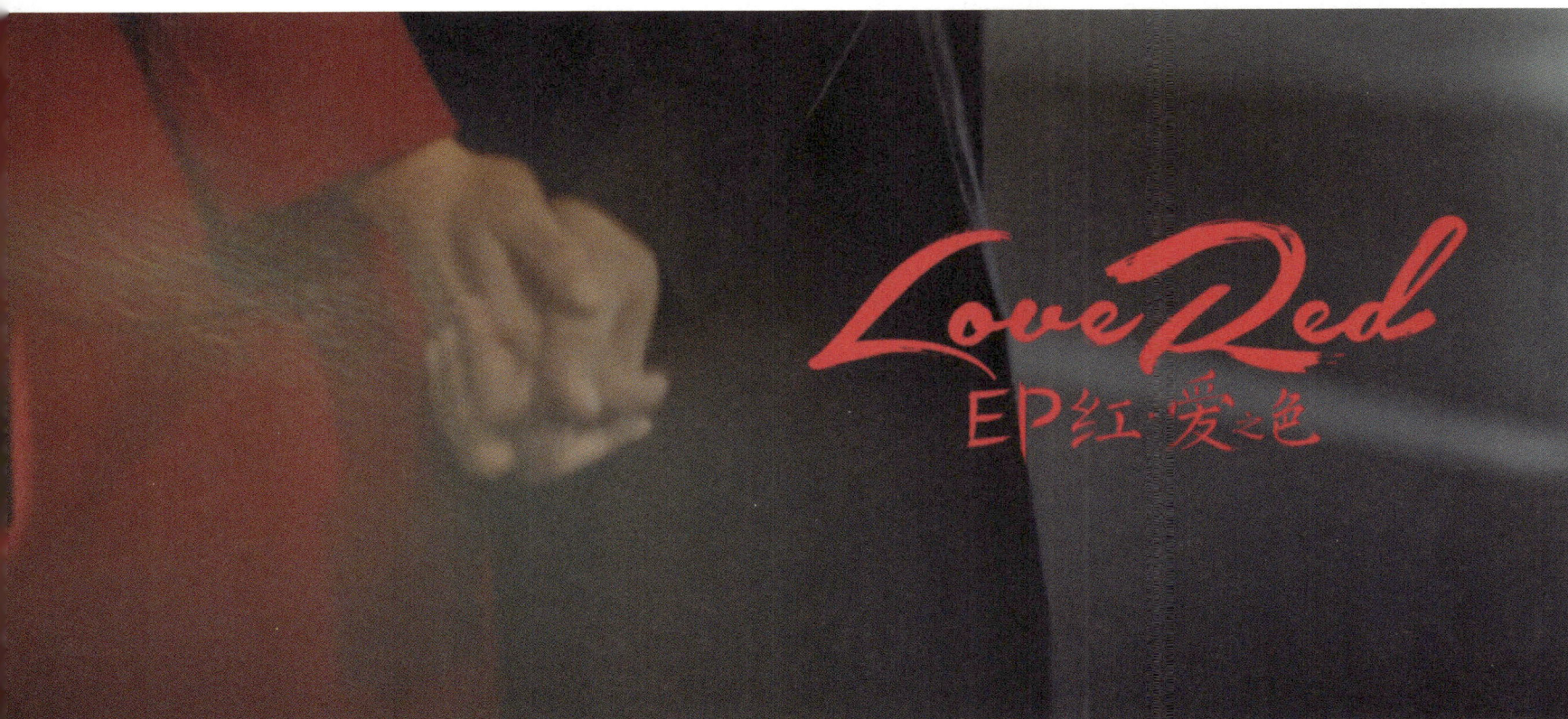

Love Red
EP 红·爱之色

左页 / 上图：
2016 年 11 月，"EP 红" 戓念微电影
《时间里的爱》发布

276 - 287 页：
2017 年秋冬 EP "豐·奢" 时尚发布
秀于中国乌镇举行

OPPOSITE / ABOVE
Love Red, a short film part of the EP Red
campaign, November 2016

276-287
EP Autumn-Winter 2017 fashion show,
Wuzhen

ELEGANT PROSPER

EP

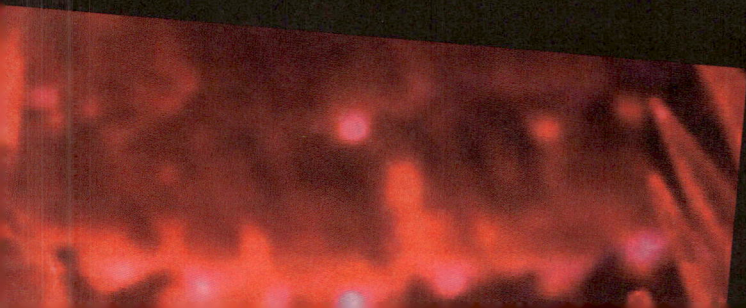

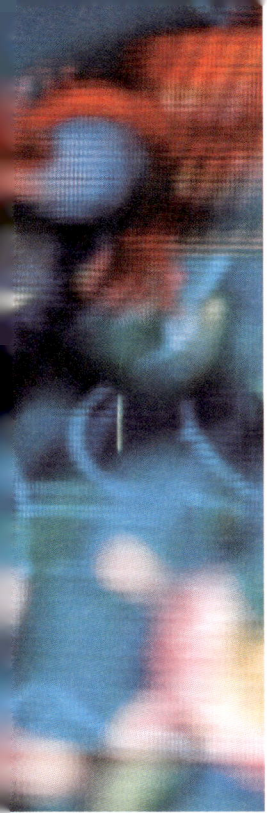

EP

288 - 295 页：
2018 年春夏 EP "灃 · 蘭" 时尚发布
秀于北京凤凰艺术中心举行

右页 / 298 - 305 页：
2018 年秋冬 EP "滢 · 泂" 时尚发布
秀于上海 1862 时尚艺术中心举行

288-295
EP Spring-Summer 2018 fashion show,
Phoenix International Media Centre, Beijing

OPPOSITE / 298-305
EP Spring-Summer 2018 fashion show, Mifa
1862, Shanghai

ROOTED IN CULTURE,
TIMELESS IN FASHION

2018 A/W

厚积薄发，成就名牌
THE FACE OF CHINESE FASHION

在第三个十年，雅莹还有一个显著的变化：以更大力度塑造和推广品牌。

相当长时间内，在中国大众群体中，相对很多销售业绩和利润都不如自己的大众品牌，雅莹都是令人相对陌生的。这与它的品牌定位有关，比如，其主品牌都是面向中高端消费群体；与它的品牌策略有关，比如，它注重通过渠道拓展实现品牌与消费者的触达，注重让消费者口耳相传形成品牌影响，很少投放品牌广告。最重要的，还是张华明对品牌发展节奏的掌控，他是一位强调什么阶段就做什么事的企业家，总是严格按照自己的时间表推进着雅莹发展，他会前瞻、超前，但不会冒进，对雅莹品牌的塑造尤其如此。

先把基础打好，是张华明坚持的理念。在更多通过渠道拓展品牌，通过消费者口碑建立品牌印象的时期，张华明把设计、品质和渠道形象作为品牌的基础。他尤其注重通过对门店形象、陈列、服务的不断升级强化品牌影响和印象。雅莹初创的 1997 年，他就坚持搬到最繁华的市区办公，并在后来开设生活馆，进入高端商圈的大店模式，这些都是对这一策略的贯彻。

当雅莹的产品、产品线、渠道和运营管理已足够支撑其冲刺向全国品牌之时，张华明才开始展现他的大牌雄心，改变几十年鸭子划水的姿态，向品牌升空进击。里程碑事件就是 2009 年 1 月，雅莹正式启动"EP"新标志，致力成为代表中国的、民族的经典品牌。

一系列品牌推广活动也随之展开：一方面在更广、更高层面塑造品牌影响，另一方面也以更加时尚的元素活化品牌。包括：通过赞助热门影视剧置入品牌形象，携手时尚媒体举办各类专题活动，向外传递品牌精神和态度，邀请大牌名模代言名牌等。

For quite some time, brand awareness of EP remained limited among the masses in China. This was because of its middle to high-end brand positioning, as well as the fact that its marketing strategy was focused on retail channels and word-of-mouth publicity. There was little reliance on advertising. Essentially, this was aligned with Hwaming's personality and work style, never flamboyant, and always down-to-earth.

Rome wasn't built in a day and Hwaming believed in waiting for the right time to do the right things. In the early years of brand building, Hwaming regarded design, quality and customer touchpoints as the foundation of the brand, and he stressed that each store, window display and element of customer service must reflect, reinforce and reiterate the brand's image. As early as 1997, when EP was newly founded and still known as yaying, Hwaming insisted on moving into the best office building in the most prestigious urban area of town; later he opened lifestyle concept stores and high-end flagship stores, all of which served as part of his strategy to transform the company into a fashion brand. When yaying's designs, product lines, retail channels and operations management reached new levels of competitiveness to support the brand's expansion across the country, he embarked on another deep revamp of the company to cement its positioning as a Chinese fashion brand.

This included launching a series of branding campaigns to increase top-of-mind awareness and expand the brand's influence.

"EP's core customers were white-collar office workers, and accordingly, our brand was relatively conservative and low-key in our marketing. We were known as a dark horse in the industry. However, with our revamp, we increased our marketing and communications activities, especially with the fashion media, to increase the brand's influence and perception," recalled Tian Ling, the then EP design director.

"之前 EP 的核心消费层集中在社会的中坚阶层，年龄层偏大，我们在品牌上相对保守，也一直非常低调，没有对外发声，所以业界说我们像一匹黑马。品牌升级后，我们加大了推广，并且更多与时尚融汇。我们希望通过这些形式，提升品牌影响力，也希望更加时尚，所以开始往这个方向发展。"时任 EP 设计总监田玲回忆。

两三年间，雅莹就先后赞助支持了《我愿意》《媳妇的美好宣言》《一不小心爱上你》《回家的诱惑》《摇摆 de 婚约》《张小玉的春天》《婆婆来了》《青春四十》《疼痛的幸福》等热播剧，通过作品中一个个优雅、自信的都市女性形象，生动展现了 EP 的品牌形象与魅力。

同时，EP 也与多家时尚媒体建立长期合作，曾先后参与《瑞丽》OL 榜样力量、*ELLE* 风尚大典等大型媒体活动，并加大与明星、名模的合作，不仅邀请唐嫣、陈数、袁姗姗等知名演员作为特别嘉宾观看 EP 多届大秀，携手杨澜、海清、朱丹、宋轶等参与品牌推广，还先后邀请到杜鹃、秦舒培、贺聪等多位一线超模担纲演绎其东方大牌风采，直至成为与国内超模合作关系最为频繁、密切和前沿的时尚品牌之一。

一系列的品牌塑造活动，让雅莹配合店铺的扩张，快速成为国内女性服装行业的新势力，但这成就的取得令张华明感受到的是更大的压力，而不是轻松。"越多人关注，越是要头脑清醒；越想在外部赢得长久，越是要在内部稳定根基。"

于是，外部发力的同时，雅莹的"内功"也不断加码提升。

With its new EP visual identity, the brand collaborated widely with international and local fashion media, and sponsored several films and TV shows celebrating stylish, confident and independent women, including *I Do, A Beautiful Daughter-in-law Era, Fall in Love, Home Temptation, Love in Cosmo, Zhang Xiaowu's Spring, My Mother-in-law's Coming, As Young as Forty* and *Painful Happiness*.

The brand also co-organised fashion events such as *Finding the Model OL* campaign with Chinese fashion magazine, *Rayli*, from 2009 to 2010. It even received the *ELLE China Stars: Most Beautiful Fashion* award at the annual ELLE China Style Awards 2010.

Step by step, EP got to know more and more celebrities and supermodels, and began working extensively with them and forming deep bonds. Famous Chinese actresses including Tiffany Tang, Chen Shu and Mabel Yuan were invited as special guests to EP's fashion shows; famous TV personalities such as Yang Lan, and celebrities including Haiqing, Dani Zhu and Song Yi joined in EP's promotional campaigns; and A-list supermodels from Du Juan and Qin Shupei to He Cong endorsed the brand. EP had become a leading Chinese fashion brand.

The company's rise to become a new leading force of Chinese fashion made Hwaming feel even greater pressure and responsibility. "Greater attention calls for a cooler mind and lasting victory requires sound preparation," said Hwaming. Like always, he kept his head down and continued to work.

根植文化，锻造经典

上图：
2018年11月2日，EP 诚邀陈碧舸、
王雯琴、佟晨洁等一路陪伴品牌成
长的名模好友参加 30 周年"EP 雅
莹之夜"时尚发布秀

右页：
2017 年至 2018 年，EP 先后邀请
知名影星唐嫣、袁姗姗、陈数参加
品牌时尚发布秀

ABOVE

EP's iconic Chinese supermodels over the
years, such as Bonnie Chen, Anna Wang
and Tong Chenjie, at the brand's 30th
Anniversary 2019 Spring-Summer fashion
show, 2 November 2018

OPPOSITE

Chinese famous actresses Tiffany Tang,
Mabel Yuan and Chen Shu at EP's fashion
show from 2017 to 2018

312

强化运营，全面提升
CREATING VALUE

以顾客为中心，是雅莹持续进步的关键支撑。每一个经营环节的持续创新优化方能促成对顾客最为优质的关照与关切，而这背后，是品牌、渠道和服务素质以及供应链、人力素质等整套运营体系的再强化。

Customer-centricity was key to EP's continuous growth. Every improvement in the customer experience was underpinned by holistic and meticulous upgrades across the entire value chain — whether customer-facing in branding, retail and service, or behind-the-scenes in supply chain and human resources.

线下线上，渠道再升级
OFFLINE AND ONLINE

2007 年，在渠道上颇有心得的张华明对渠道进行了又一次创新与升级：在自己的大本营嘉兴开出了雅莹首个时尚生活馆，以此探索像国际大牌那般拓展迈进的大店模式。

2008 年，那个 10 多年前天天在北京跑街串巷推销衣服的张华明又来北京了，但身份已经改变：在当年北京最具地标性与高端影响的华贸购物中心，为"雅莹生活馆"揭幕。

作为雅莹第四代门店形象的代表，"雅莹生活馆"不但以丰富的产品系列彰显出本土品牌的创新活力与魅力，而且从门店到陈列都一一展现着雅莹对优雅、温馨、爱的诠释，将雅莹的品牌形象和消费者认知都推向了新高。

2009 年，经过两年的实践后，张华明启动了"大店航母战略"，即在核心城市开设旗舰大店，将其作为夯实雅莹市场根基，提升 EP 品牌段位，拓展品牌市场规模的核心策略，拱卫和推动雅莹的整体发展。当时，正值全球金融海啸后期，行业依然处于低迷之中，互联网电商对线下零售业的影响持续加深。此种背景下，张华明却逆势而上，大开线下大店，一度备受质疑。但市场再一次证明了张华明这位渠道和商品经营大师对市场的精准把握，"大店航母战略"启动的当年，EP 就在其品牌影响提升和店铺规模扩张中实现了跨越式发展。

至 2009 年，EP 旗下包括自营、加盟、五季在内的店铺就达到 352 家，并且在新的策略下实现了门店形象、服务品质等综合提升，不但令 EP 的市场能见度得到巨大提升，也令 EP 的市场美誉度得到显著提升。尤其是高端百货门店的发展，更让 EP 品牌形象实现了脱颖而出的超越。最重要的是，它让

In 2007, Hwaming tested the idea of a lifestyle experience concept store in Jiaxing, a model that was very popular abroad, with a bigger space that focused on the customer experience. The successful reception of the new concept led him to officially open a permanent location in Beijing in 2008.

Beijing Huamao Centre, one of the most premium and iconic shopping malls in Beijing at that time, would witness the brand's fourth generation signature store — a lifestyle experience store with a greater variety of fashion choices, all amidst an elegant and warm ambience.

In 2009, EP continued to make big strides, launching a series of large high-end flagship stores in top cities around China, greatly elevating its market positioning and perception among customers.

In the aftermath of the 2008 global financial crisis, when the industry was still in a downturn, and the disruption of offline retail continued to deepen with the rise of e-commerce, Hwaming's decision to aggressively open new stores was questioned by many. However, the situation proved once again that Hwaming was a master of retail with an astute sense of the market. By 2009, EP owned 352 retail stores across China, which led to increased brand visibility and popularity.

EP's sophisticated retail network was the result of a proactive channel strategy and valuable experience accumulated over the years.

品牌抓住了中国百货商场和大型购物中心蓬勃发展的时代机遇，走出了一条与竞争对手截然不同的道路，让 EP 以中国式新优雅引领精致生活方式从光荣梦想变成璀璨现实。

一路以来，雅莹的渠道崛起，经过了积极的市场布局和多年的市场积累，构建了大型时尚生活馆、购物中心店、百货店、专卖店和网络商城等全方位、立体化的营销网络，成就了雅莹在全国各大城市构建的这一道道靓丽的风景线。

2011 年，EP 在深圳京基百纳 KK Mall 店、沈阳万象城店推出了五代门店。这一代门店采用更亲近顾客的"体验式"产品展示空间设计，首次使用"木饰面＋镜钢"材质并结合产品分类，分区演绎产品故事风格，展示"亲民轻奢"的品牌诉求，同时配合设定引导性动线在每个动线上设定出吸引点，让产品能够充分迎合顾客的视线，让店铺"会说话"：顾客进店即能最直观感受到 EP 传递的品牌精神与文化。

以大店化、大店的生活馆化推动品牌的高端化，是雅莹在这一时期渠道创新的核心与精髓。2012 年，EP 又以上海八佰伴为开端，开出了首家百货店里的生活馆，让其大店模式在更大范围、更多平台推进。同一时期，EP 还联合丹麦知名设计师合作推出 EPICENTER 概念店，于杭州文二西路的独栋别墅中臻美呈现，为顾客提供更精致的艺术体验的同时，强调了大店空间的艺术化与品牌概念。

在消费升级的趋势下，通过大店模式的升级，雅莹以顾客为中心的理念进一步贯彻落实：不仅以顾客为中心推动产品设计与研发，还将对顾客的体贴和尊重体现在每一件时装的每个细节，也在门店设计中为更好的顾客体验而竭尽所能。

In April 2010, EP opened its first airport store in Guangzhou Baiyun Airport, and in 2011, opened its fifth generation stores in Shenzhen's KK Mall and Shenyang's The MixC, aiming to bring an immersive shopping experience to customers. The combination of wood and stainless steel finishing highlighted this generation's design, and a greater focus was given to interaction with the products. Visual merchandising played a stronger role in accentuating the different product categories enabling the different zones to "speak" to visitors, thus improving the brand's connection with customers.

Meanwhile, EP collaborated with David Thulstrup, an award-winning Danish architect and interior designer, to launch its "EPICENTRE" design concept for its villa store on Wen'er West Road in Hangzhou in 2012. It was the first time the brand fully integrated art and space, showcasing a modern simplicity that was pure and alluring.

Driven by new levels of rising consumption, there was greater pressure on the brand to make deeper connections with its customers.

In 2013, during the 5th anniversary of its Beijing Huamao Centre store, EP upgraded the space to its sixth generation store concept, also known as "EP Mansion". This design integrated oriental charm and classic western modernism, as the new space showcased an exquisite and beautiful way of life. The elegant interiors and use of exquisite European materials accentuated the luxurious collection of EP's styles and accessories, and the space was filled with artistic interpretations of Peony motifs, Chinese art paper and crystal glass mosaic tiles that provided a romantic and elegant shopping experience.

上页：

2011 年，EP 沈阳万象城店。2011 年起，EP
深圳京基店、沈阳万象城店、上海第一八佰伴
店相继开业，作为第五代形象店铺，首次使用
"木饰面 + 镜钢"的材质组合，将品牌标志元
素融入店铺设计。同时首次结合产品分类及
顾客生活方式，分区演绎产品故事风格，融入
了更多富于生活气息的元素

上图 / 322 - 327 页：
2012 年 EP 上海第一八佰伴店

PREVIOUS

EP store, The MixC, Shenyang, 2011. EP launches
its fifth generation store concept from 2011,
including KK Mall in Shenzhen and the No.1
Yaohan Mall in Shanghai. The combination of
wood and stainless steel is a signature of this
generation. Visual merchandising plays a stronger
role, with more lifestyle elements and product
categorisation

ABOVE / 322-327
EP store, No.1 Yaohan Mall, Shanghai, 2012

上图 / 右页：

2012 年，EP 在杭州文二西路的独栋别墅，联合丹麦知名空间设计师 David Thulstrup 合作推出 EPICENTRE 概念店。首次充分将艺术与空间融合，通过运用尽量少的道具和更简洁的外形营造单纯、趣味、艺术化的店铺特色

ABOVE / OPPOSITE

EP collaborates with David Thulstrup, an award-winning Danish architect and interior designer, to launch its "EPICENTRE" design concept for its villa store on Wen'er West Road, Hangzhou, in 2012. It's the first time the brand fully integrates art and space, showcasing modern simplicity that is pure and alluring

左页 / 右图 / 332 - 333 页：
2013 年，第六代店铺"雅莹之家"
北京华贸店形象焕新。品牌首次将
牡丹元素融入店铺形象装饰，并以
结晶釉和马赛克结合的地面设计以
及宣纸包裹式的楼梯设计等细节，
充分展现东方古典韵味与西方精致
浪漫融合的艺术化风格

OPPOSITE / RIGHT / 332-333

EP begins to integrate oriental charm
and western classic modernism in its
sixth generation store concept, also
known as "EP Mansion", in 2013. The
revamped Beijing Huamao Centre store
features artistic interpretations of Peony motifs, Chinese art paper and crystal
glass mosaic tiles

2013 年，北京华贸 "EP 生活馆" 开业的第五年。雅莹再次以北京市场为平台，推出了自己的第六代店铺——"雅莹之家"。这一代店铺的设计以江南园林廊柱为灵感，以东方古典与西方浪漫主义相融的艺术化演绎，让东方文化与现代设计相互辉映，并首次将品牌基因元素——牡丹，以各种形式贯穿应用于店铺内，首次全部使用从欧洲等地搜寻而来的道具，体现 EP 对细节的注重、对精湛品质的追求，以及构建精致生活的匠心。

"雅莹之家" 也真正开启了 EP 品牌的中国化元年。第二年 10 月，EP 又将其杭州万象城 "雅莹生活馆" 成功升级为第二家 "雅莹之家"，然后依次在全国展开改造升级。大店拓展与升级的另一边，雅莹对渠道的创新拓展也依然在稳扎稳打地推进。2010 年 4 月，EP 在广州白云机场开出了第一家专卖店，开启机场渠道；同年，EP 还开启了奥特莱斯专卖战略，成为国内率先进驻奥特莱斯的时尚品牌之一。

进入奥特莱斯，也是张华明在渠道上的又一次具突破意义的创新。"当时，奥特莱斯在国内还是新事物，刚刚在北京和上海兴起，张总眼光非常超前，认为这是一片蓝海，我们要去卡位，成为行业领跑者，于是就成立团队开始接手做奥特莱斯。" 经后期参与奥特莱斯业务的负责人集团副总裁兼大雅家总经理陈伟健回忆。

张华明看好奥特莱斯，是因为他看到了奥特莱斯在中国的特别之处：不仅是卖尾货的地方。"中国奥特莱斯有中国特色，有溜冰场、超市和最好的电影院。对消费者来说不但可以买到高性价比的东西，还可以吃喝玩乐，这就是好的体验和服务。张总认为，这是未来的趋势。而且，我们相信奥特莱斯

Another highlight in EP's retail journey was the launch of its outlet store, becoming one of the first few Chinese fashion brands to take such a leap. "At that time, the concept of outlet malls was new in China and had just emerged in big cities like Beijing and Shanghai. Mr Zhang was very forward-looking and believed that we must explore this vast blue sea of opportunity and become the leader in this channel, so we quickly set up a team to open a store there," recalled Chen Weijian, who oversees the outlet business, and is also the Group's deputy CEO and DA YA JIA's general manager today.

Hwaming was optimistic about the outlet malls because he understood the special opportunity they presented in China and it was far from just selling end-of-line products. "The outlet malls in China were localised to provide a one-stop shopping and entertainment experience, including ice skating rinks, supermarkets, restaurants and the best cinemas. Customers were not only able to buy lower-priced luxury products, but also eat, drink and have fun. Mr Zhang believed that this was the future. Moreover, we did not think international luxury brands had as much of an advantage as local brands due to logistics and operational costs. We were very confident that local brands could become the leaders here," added Chen Weijian.

"

一路以来，雅莹的渠道崛起，
经过了积极的市场布局和多年的市场积累，
构建了大型时尚生活馆、购物中心店、百货店、专卖店和网络商城等
全方位、立体化的营销网络，
成就了雅莹在全国各大城市构建的这一道道靓丽的风景线。

"

只是奢侈品肯定不行。首先量不够，另外还会叫好不叫卖，开了店跟不上，只有当地的本土品牌才能够成为奥特莱斯的王者。"陈伟健说。

对雅莹来说，进入奥特莱斯还有一个很大的优势：相比大型商场，奥特莱斯的整体运营成本低，产品定价也更低。不仅可为其去库存、卖尾货提供支撑，还能以高性价比为切入口，成为雅莹体验和观察市场的窗口。为此，雅莹还开发了一条奥特莱斯的产品线专门服务——奥特莱斯市场。

线下持续升级的同时，一直对技术改变商业保持敏感与敬畏的张华明，也高度关注着互联网电商的发展。2009 年，当大多数实体企业还对线上零售冷漠或观望之时，雅莹就已开始了线上化尝试。当年年底，EP 第五季及 EM 品牌的奕尚网（SASACITY）官网旗舰店上线，正式开启了网络营销渠道。2010 年 3 月，淘宝商城刚刚正式启动独立域名，对 B 端开启品牌化之路，EP 第五季旗舰店便正式登陆其中，成为行业内最早与淘宝合作的商家之一。

自那之后的 10 年，是国内电商飞速发展的 10 年，是实体企业从最初到网上卖库存到后来线上专供，再到品牌化和规模化的 10 年，也是雅莹对线上渠道的开发和探索从电商营销一直走到线上线下一体化，走到重构人、货、场，走到拥抱和探索新零售的 10 年。跟大多数品牌一样，EP 一开始也是通过淘宝商城去库存、卖尾货，当天猫商城逐渐成熟，EP 又及时做起了天猫专供。微信普及后，EP 也在业内率先开始了微信营销。

While EP was expanding offline, Hwaming was also closely watching the development of e-commerce. In 2009 when most brick-and-mortar retailers were still indifferent or had a wait-and-see attitude towards internet retailing, EP started to sell online through its website, SASACITY, which it had set up for its EM line and past seasons' products. In March 2010, EP also became one of the first few fashion brands to collaborate with Taobao.

The following 10 years saw a rapid development of e-commerce in China, with brands transitioning from viewing it as a means to clear stock, to setting up exclusive products lines for online customers, to positioning it as a key brand building platform.

This was also a decade when EP fully embraced new retail and adopted an omnichannel retail strategy. Like most brands, EP started by selling past seasons' styles on Taobao and when Tmall became more established, EP quickly created an exclusive product line for the platform. Similarly, when WeChat launched in 2011, EP was one of the earliest adopters, testing the platform internally before using it as a marketing tool from 2013.

Unlike brands that either disregarded e-commerce or went entirely online, Hwaming was cautiously optimistic about the emerging trend. He had been closely monitoring the pace and scale of the development of online stores and constantly sought a balance between online and offline. The potential damage to the offline businesses concerned him. "The pricing of exclusive online products is generally lower, and the relatively lower-priced clothes in the Tmall store may confuse customers and affect our brand image. The higher the sales online, the higher the losses to our brand equity and profit margins in the long term," said Chen Weijian.

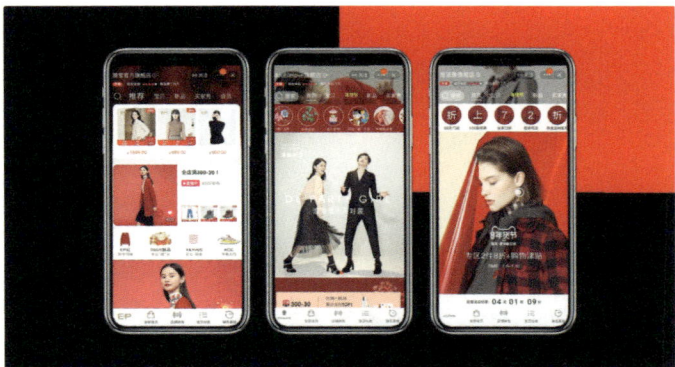

但与要么对互联网电商漠视，要么倾尽全力线上化的品牌企业不同，张华明对互联网电商的拥抱是在战术上积极探索，战略上保持警惕。相当长时间内，他都严格控制着电商的发展节奏和规模，在线上和线下间不断寻找着平衡。他担心过快、过猛的线上化，对线下业务和品牌产生负面影响。"专供产品的定价一般比线下低，消费者一进天猫看我们的衣服卖得便宜，会有认知的问题，甚至动摇品牌价值；卖得越多，红利透支越多。"陈伟健解释道。

这种克制一直保持到 2018 年，也只保持到 2018 年。当新零售浪潮风起之时，表面上按兵不动的雅莹就已对其进行着高度的关注和研究。2018 年，深思熟虑之后，张华明带领企业对电商渠道进行了再次升级，并提出品牌化的电商新战略。

新的定位下，线上不再仅是渠道，而是品牌战略的一部分，不再是销售产品和行销品牌，也是进一步贴近消费者、洞察需求的通路，是推动产品设计与研发的创新之源。为了实现这一目标，张华明还像当年为做品牌而砍掉批发专供零售业务一样，放弃已经成功实现的线上化短期利益——撤掉线上专供，让线上线下同步，EP 全部提供当季的正价产品，重新培养客群和生意。虽然这一举动起初的效果并不理想，但也很快展现出新的曙光。

更重要的是，团队对新的策略越来越自信——相信线上线下的同步，会让雅莹在又一个新的 10 年再上台阶。

The brand's e-commerce proceeded with great caution until 2018 when the concept of "new retail" began to gain traction, and Hwaming invested heavily to launch the company's omnichannel retail strategy. The team did not view e-commerce as simply a retail channel, but an extension of its brand strategy — a new way to gain insight into customers' needs and a key driver of product creativity and innovation.

To this end, Hwaming made a tough decision, similar to when he ceased the company's wholesale business in its early years: he decided to suspend the sale of past seasons' styles and lower priced products online. Although it had been profitable, it was not sustainable in the long term. Under its new omnichannel retail strategy, offline and online stores reflected the same image and products, and while the move was not well-received in the beginning, many began to see the fruits of this decision.

Most importantly, they saw EP's infinite potential in the coming digital era.

上图：
2010 年代，雅莹集团旗下品牌入驻多元的线上平台

ABOVE
EP ventures into e-commerce, 2010s

深化内功，综合能力再提升
SERVICE AND SUPPLY

以顾客为中心，是雅莹持续进步的关键支撑。渠道、店铺以及品牌的持续创新优化是其对顾客关照与关切的进化。而这背后，是品牌、渠道和服务素质以及供应链、人力素质等整套运营体系的再强化。

在新的 10 年，雅莹的顾客对雅莹持续进步的最直观印象，除了店铺的升级，就是服务上的不断惊喜了。期间，雅莹完成了"感动服务"到"管家式服务"再到"尊享服务"的进化。

这是由点点滴滴的改变积累的蜕变：2006 年开始，雅莹门店开始使用手写的顾客档案本记录顾客的姓名与联系电话；2008 年，雅莹开始要求店员增加记录顾客的性格、喜好等信息；2010 年开始，雅莹再次增加顾客消费信息及服务沟通信息并将记录形式信息化，同时引入 CRM 系统，让记录内容也更加全面精细，以便为顾客提供一对一的个性化服务……

同时，雅莹还大力推动"走出去服务"，相继推出衣橱整理、顾客探病等创新举措，不断加强对顾客从生活便利到情感维护的关照。"比如，很多人平常上班很忙，周末不想出门，就想在家里陪孩子，可能买衣服没有时间，我们帮她们解决这样的痛点，或者去顾客办公室，或者去家里，为她们提供上门服务。"顾海明解释。

服务是传递品牌文化和精神的"使者"，为顾客提供自然、舒适、"家"感觉的优雅体验，"现在消费者不一样了，不是因为缺衣服而买衣服，而是为了美。"于是，雅莹又主动应需而动，让店员更懂"美"：店员会和顾客聊一些流行时尚趋势，同时提供穿搭建议，在服务中带给顾客专业意见和参考。我们在零售培训中，也增加了大量关于时尚、行业信息等方面的内容，

In the new decade, EP never stopped improving its service, always placing the "people" factor at the heart of its retail experience improvement programs.

Following its first *Heartfelt Service* campaign in 2007, the company successively introduced its *Butler Service* and *Personalised Service* concepts. EP's service excellence was not the result of an overnight effort, but the sincere dedication of all its customer care managers day in day out, year in year out. In 2006, the managers started making handwritten records of customers' details; from 2008 onwards, they started to record more details of their customers including their personalities and preferences; from 2010, these handwritten notes became digitalised and the brand would officially implement the use of Customer Relationship Management (CRM) software, enabling more efficient data filing and analysis to provide more personalised services.

At the same time, EP launched an "out-of-store" service program that introduced innovative service measures for customers, such as wardrobe management services and assistance with some of their lifestyle needs. "For instance, many of our customers were so busy during the weekdays that they did not feel like stepping out during the weekends, or they may have just wanted to spend more time with their families at home. They simply did not have the time to shop for clothes. We helped by providing personal visits, whether at the office or at home, so that we could bring fashion to our customers," said Haiming.

Service is the "messenger" of a brand; through service, customers understand the brand's culture and identity. This is why EP has always placed customers at the heart of the brand, not only to provide them with a natural, comfortable and personal service experience, but also to satisfy their increasing need for exclusive and tailored fashion advice. "Consumers nowadays are not buying new clothes due to a lack of clothing, but to look more beautiful," said Haiming.

"

服务是传递品牌文化和精神的'使者',
为顾客提供自然、舒适、'家'感觉的优雅体验。

"

上页：
2018 年，专注呈现更优质门店体验的 EP 时尚顾问

左页 / 左图 / 下图：
EP 时尚顾问与顾客

PREVIOUS
An EP fashion consultant working on maintaining a quality store experience, 2018

OPPOSITE / LEFT / BELOW
EP fashion consultants working with customers in stores

让雅莹的每一个客户经理都成为传递美丽的使者，去满足顾客尊享式、个性化的时装需求，努力做到爱顾客、懂顾客、感动顾客。

专业度的提升对业绩的提升效果也是显著的。EP 南京德基广场店员葛静就讲述了这样一个故事："一天，一位穿着卓雅的顾客来到我们店，我立刻迎上去喊了句，'欢迎光临 EP 雅莹'，她很不屑地看了我一眼。我借着她戴的卡地亚指环是限量版与其聊天，赢得了她的好感。但她觉得 EP 的衣服颜色太深了，不适合她。我又笑着推荐了几款 3D 立体裁剪，并说上身了就能感觉到它的独特了，尝试让她换下其他的风格。她带着疑惑的眼光进了试衣间，出来时照了下镜子，看上去很高兴。我趁机跟上节奏多推荐了几套，而且赞赏衣服的美丽和她的年轻。她对推荐很满意，并要求我再给介绍两套职业装，这单一共成交了 15000 多元。"

优质服务的提升，背后是卓越供应链的支撑。在新的 10 年，雅莹对供应链的每个环节再检讨与优化，并以一套快速反应机制，严格控制每个关键点，通过持续技术研究、预防改善、精益创新和信息化等方法，不断提升每个环节的专业与效率，确保及时高效呈现给顾客卓越的产品和服务。

2012 年，雅莹提出精品工厂理念，以精细化管理和工匠精神打造精致产品。2013 年，公司又对自有工厂与外协工厂两种生产方式更优化组合：自产侧重追求高品质生产，外协侧重寻求有品质保证的快速反应，并同时将原考核一等品率的质量要求提升为考核优等品率。

为消费者提供高价值而非价格虚高的产品，是雅莹创立之初就有的理念。为确保其贯彻，这期间的雅莹也在成本控制上追根究底，比如，通过更合理、先进的面料管理、剪裁生产管理等方式，降低生产损耗，提高生产效率。"努力通过良好的成本控制，让消费者以可接受的价格，享受到一流品质的高价值商品。" 雅莹集团供应链总监倪美华解释说。

"The company organises regular trainings on fashion and the latest industry trends. This means our customer care managers are happy to talk to customers about fashion trends and provide professional advice on styling. Loving our customers, understanding our customers and offering them our sincerity are all part of EP's service DNA, and every single customer manager acts as a messenger of beauty, dedicated to offering exceptional and personalised services."

Professionalism shows. Ge Jing, a customer care manager at an EP store in Nanjing said: "One day, a customer wearing an outfit from another brand visited our store, and I immediately greeted her with 'Welcome to EP', but she looked at me with disregard. I soon took notice of her limited-edition Cartier ring and began to make small talk with her, and she began to warm up to me. However, she felt that EP's colours were too dark to suit her style. I responded with a smile and selected some dresses with sharper shapes and unique tailoring that would bring out her flair. She did not believe me at first, but was won over the moment she saw herself in the mirror. She was very satisfied with my recommendations and even asked me to pick another two workwear suits for her."

A high-performing frontline service team can only be sustained with an equally high-performing supply chain. In the new decade, EP reviewed and optimised each link of the supply chain, and also set up a rapid response mechanism to ensure quality control at every step, so as to deliver the highest quality to customers.

In 2012, the company upgraded the supply chain by launching a new premium factory that would specialise in more demanding products that required a higher level of craftsmanship. A year later, the company further consolidated its production, strengthening its in-house production line, and ensuring the quality and efficiency of its partners. The company also increased the benchmark for its product quality assessment criteria in a bid to deliver higher-quality products. Providing consumers with products of the highest value, rather than products of inflated pricing, has been the brand's commitment.

"We strive to deliver first-class quality products, while ensuring strict cost control, so that we do not pass on unnecessary costs to our customers and can offer the most value for their spending," said Ni Meihua, deputy CEO of the Group's supply chain today.

66

努力通过良好的成本控制，
让消费者以可接受的价格，
享受到一流品质的高价值商品。

99

上图：
2020 年，雅莹集团供应链生产技术中心

ABOVE
EP YAYING Fashion Group Supply Chain,
Technical Production Centre, 2020

347

ROOTED IN CULTURE,
TIMELESS IN FASHION

左页 / 下图：
2020 年，雅莹集团供应链生产技术中心

OPPOSITE / BELOW
EP YAYING Fashion Group Supply Chain,
Technical Production Centre, 2020

上图 / 右页：
2020 年，雅莹集团供应链生产技术中心

ABOVE / OPPOSITE
EP YAYING Fashion Group Supply Chain, Technical
Production Centre, 2020

上图：
2020 年，雅莹集团供应链生产技术中心辅料仓库

ABOVE
EP YAYING Fashion Group Supply Chain, Technical Production Centre, decorative embellishments storage, 2020

右页：
2020 年，雅莹集团供应链生产技术术中心面料仓库

OPPOSITE
EP YAYING Fashion Group Supply Chain, Technical Production Centre, fabric storage, 2020

从人力到人文，打造卓越团队
PEOPLE AND CULTURE

张华明说，"匠心品质的核心是品质即人品。"人品首先是品德，但也必须包括专业与能力。也就是既要有以顾客为中心的真心诚意，又要有为顾客创造价值的过硬本领。

2008 年以后，雅莹的人力资源建设也更紧密地围绕业务来进行。当时参与雅莹集团人力资源建设的吕虹说，在雅莹人资要说业务的语言，而不是人力资源的语言。"因为人力资源部门是为业务服务的，要让人力资源真正进入业务中。用专业术语来说就是，一个公司没有人力资源问题，都是业务的问题。"张华明解释。

2009 年，雅莹与翰威特合作开启了第二期人力发展计划——发展人，通过搭建人力资源系列的模型，例如建立领导力模型、销售胜任能力模型等，推动公司人力再造。

"首先是建模，以领导力计划为例，首先要知道雅莹的领导力是什么，要从成功人群中找到他们成功的特质，用阿里的话讲就是闻味道。"吕虹说，"通过努力，雅莹建立了一套符合自己实际的领导力建设模型，模型有若干题库可用作测评、对标检讨，找出领导力构建的关键点，以及需要什么资源，如何去实现。测评完之后就是做发展规划、实施。"

同年，雅莹还启动了长期人才储备与培养项目"英才计划"，为企业发展持续提供新鲜动力。2011 年，雅莹又与 IBM 合作推出发展领导力的专项，与德勤合作了长期激励计划。

通过这些专项，雅莹把招聘人、培养人、用好人、留住人和发展人都推向更专业也更可评估的程度，让公司的"以人为本"变成一本清晰的"账本"。与世界顶级专业公司的合作，

Hwaming once said, "At the core of quality excellence is quality character." This meant that behind its efforts to create value for customers, the company and its employees must first build character, ensure adherence to a professional code of ethics, and develop competencies to improve individual and organisational performance.

Since 2008, the company's human resources team has continued to work ever more closely with the operations team. According to Lv Hong, who was involved in the company's HR planning, the HR team became business partners, speaking of business instead of simply HR matters. Hwaming added, "The human resources department is built to support the business, so it is essential that HR is an integral part of the operations team. To put it simply, there are no HR issues in a company, only operational issues."

In 2009, the company kicked off phase two of its collaboration with Aon Hewitt, which aimed to develop the competencies of its talents, primarily the leadership and management skills of its middle-to-senior level teams. "Our first step was creating a leadership development model. We needed to know and understand what defines leadership at EP, and the traits shared by successful talents at EP. We would then go on to develop a model that was unique and relevant to the company's needs, before going about our action plan," said Lv Hong.

In the same year, the company launched its Management Trainee program, to identify and develop new talents. In 2011, the company worked with IBM to provide leadership training for its key management team and also collaborated with Deloitte to devise a long-term incentive scheme for employees.

上图：
2011 年 4 月，公司携手 IBM 开展高管团队战略性业务领导力提升专项培训

下图：
2017 年，雅莹集团第 8 届"英才计划"成员

下页：
2012 年，雅莹集团成立"人文关怀中心"，下设心灵关怀、健康关爱、文体活动和爱心传递执行组

ABOVE
The company works with IBM to organise a training on strategic leadership for the top management, April 2011

BELOW
EP YAYING Fashion Group 8th Management Trainee Program, 2017

NEXT
EP YAYING Fashion Group establishes an "Employee Well-Being Centre" consisting of four support pillars — spiritual care, health care, cultural and sports engagement, and charity, 2012

"
最好的文化是在所有员工感到幸福的基础上，
让员工可以从内心露出最真实的笑容。
"

和世界优质资源的联动，也对雅莹人从思维到能力与国际接
轨帮助巨大。

专业训练和提升的同时，雅莹也将公司的人性管理再强化。

伴随企业规模的扩大，雅莹的员工队伍在 10 余年间从 1000
多人增加到近 5000 人，这给管理，尤其是团队凝聚力建设，
以及企业文化的建设与传递都带来更大挑战。

为破解这一难题，2012 年，雅莹集团党、工、团、妇组织联
合成立了"人文关怀委员会"，并在委员会下设人文关怀中心，
在人文关怀中心下设心灵关怀、健康关怀、文体活动和爱心
传递等多个执行组，确定各部门秘书为联络员，建立联络员
制度，推动落实。不但通过人文关怀中心提升员工的向心力
和敬业精神，也推动员工更投入、热爱家庭与生活，最终实
现张华明提出的"乐业乐活"理念。这也是雅莹所认可和坚持
的——最好的文化是在所有员工感到幸福的基础上，让员工
可以从内心露出最真实的笑容。为此，公司相继推出了共享阅
读、幸福课堂、家庭日、活动俱乐部等丰富员工生活的项目，
并持续开展于日常工作中，不但大幅提升内部凝聚力，还成
为雅莹党建发挥表率、切实带动群团建设的典范之举。

从当年在父亲反对下整顿办公环境开始，张华明就有一个信
念：美好的环境才能成就美好的人，做出美好的产品。他
说："美是源于自然的，美是由内到外的，要成为引领美好生
活方式的人，得首先自己美好。"戴雪明也是与他高度地共鸣，

From recruitment to talent development and training, and from
engagement to retention, the HR team themselves continued to
mature and grow professionally. The close collaboration with
world-leading HR companies and individuals helped to further
broaden their horizons, and was also a catalyst for the growth of
the company's human capital. In 10 years, the company's headcount
grew from 1,000 to 5,000. This aggressive growth presented another
set of challenges to the company — building team cohesion and
corporate culture.

In 2012, the company jointly established the "Employee Well-Being
Centre" together with the organisation's Party Committee, Labour
Union, Youth League and Women's Union. The plan consisted
of four pillars — spiritual care, health care, cultural and sports
engagement, and charity.

The centre's initiatives not only greatly enhanced team cohesion but
also promoted work-life balance, echoing a phrase Hwaming would
often mention: "Joyful work and happy life." This was also in line
with the company's belief that the best corporate culture is built on
the well-being of all employees and the smiles that come from the
bottom of their hearts. Some of the centre's initiatives included a
book club, self-improvement classes, family day and sports clubs, all
to enrich employees' daily work and life.

打造卓越的环境也被二人当作雅莹提升人力和人文的核心项目推进。

2012 年，雅莹正式提出了创造艺术化办公环境的目标，从加强公司美学氛围，提升员工审美入手，升级公司的人文美学，并且专门设立了一个特别的部门——环境艺术部门，负责公司的艺术和环境氛围。为强化艺术氛围，2013 年起，公司将环境、艺术和文化建设上升到战略层面，并在产品创意设计及品牌建设上更加注重中国传统文化艺术的植入。

集团 25 周年庆之际，雅莹还第一次在集团设立了艺术展厅并举办了主题艺术展——"清雅华裳"清末民初女性服饰展，2014 至 2018 年间，又相继举办"华彩毅裳"少数民族服饰展、"火舞凤凰·时尚莲开"荷花主题书画艺术展、"东方意蕴·雅竹共赏"竹主题艺术展、"雅派韵致·写毅芳华"牡丹主题艺术展等展览，让美与艺术显于形，沁入人心，也为催生创意提供灵感。

EP 在产品设计上推崇的一个理念是："美源于自然。"其 2015 年成为米兰世博会中国馆全球合作伙伴，主打的就是"天地人和"的自然人文主题。其设计团队每年都会到全国各地采风，从大自然中汲取养分，寻找设计元素的灵感。比如，2017 年的彩云之南、呼伦贝尔；2018 年的江南水乡、稻城亚丁等。"你只有在那里生活过，感受过风从你耳畔掠过的速度，呼吸过空气里裹挟植物芬芳的气息，才能设计出那些饱含情感的时装单品。"时任 EP 设计总监田玲说。

From the time he took over the company and upgraded the office environment, Hwaming always believed that only in a beautiful environment can one create beautiful things. "Beauty comes from nature, beauty comes from inside out. If we want to promote a beautiful lifestyle, we must first live a beautiful life." Xueming couldn't agree more with him in this regard. Creating an engaging and beautiful workspace was therefore high on their agenda.

From 2012, the company began to refurbish its headquarters, establishing a dedicated team in charge of beautifying the office space with art and nature. By 2013, the company had made it a strategic priority to infuse elements of the environment, arts and culture into the company's ethos. Especially when it came to the creativity of its products and the development of its brand, Chinese traditional arts and culture were of the utmost importance.

In the same year, as part of its 25th Anniversary celebrations, the company held its first exhibition at its Arts Gallery, with the theme of *Elegant Chinese Costumes*, showcasing the different styles of women's clothing in the Late Qing Dynasty. From 2014 to 2018, the company successively organised several themed exhibitions that brought Chinese cultural heritage closer to employees and encouraged more artistic exchanges. These included *Colourful Cultural Costumes*, an exhibition on costumes from 56 Chinese Ethnic Groups; *Lotus in Bloom*, a lotus-themed painting and calligraphy exhibition; and *Youth and Elegance*, a Peony-themed art exhibition.

EP had a strong love of nature that showed in its work. For example, its unique creations for Expo Milano in 2015 were a tribute to Mother Nature; the design team would often travel to find inspiration each season in the most beautiful parts of China, including Yunnan Province and Hulunbuir in 2017, and Jiangnan and Yading, a national level reserve in Daocheng County, Sichuan Province, in 2018.

至今还在持续的办公环境艺术化，让雅莹成为"美"的"家园"，艺术的"家园"——满目绿意的花园、精心装点的艺术家画作、极具艺术感的雅聚餐厅，涵盖书法、瑜伽等不同内容的幸福课堂……自然和人文环境的塑造，让雅莹人更加优雅、晶莹，也让"平衡·爱·幸福"的品牌精神首先在内部融入血液，继而注入产品，传递给顾客，带给更广世界。

这些目之所见、耳之所闻、心之所感的多重角度，反映、塑造、影响着每一个雅莹人的内心世界，并润物无声地推动着他们向着更美、更好迈进。细微处的高度人性和人文关怀，再加上不断发展的事业、持续提供晋升发展的空间……这些因素的综合让雅莹团队始终和谐向上，并且具有非常好的稳定性。

雅莹的很多高管都在公司效力超过10年。根据采访总结，他们留在雅莹的原因都会包括：公司氛围和团队精神面貌好，有家的感觉。尤其是信任员工这一点，很多高管都提到，老板对下属给到了足够的信任。其次，发展空间很大，大家都把这份工作当作自己的事业在做。

这也是雅莹在快速变幻的时装市场，能够快速创新应变的根本保障。

"You must have lived there, felt the breeze blowing through your hair and breathed the air that carries the fragrance of nature, before you can create something full of life that resonates with customers," said Tian Ling, EP design director at that time.

The continuous improvement and enhancement of the workspace had transformed the company's headquarters into a "home of aesthetics" and an "artist's paradise".

Nature and culture became one — with lush gardens, colourful paintings and an artistic restaurant-canteen, as well as the various self-improvement classes from calligraphy to yoga. The workplace environment became an endless source of inspiration that reflected the brand's values of *Balance, Love and Happiness*. It was only natural that these values became more deeply ingrained in the people at EP, and that through their creations and service, they would share this with customers around the world every day.

The new sights and experiences, as well as the emotions they evoked, had a profound influence on everyone at EP. There was a greater sense of peace, harmony and positivity. Many of the senior management team at EP have been working at the company for over a decade and the main reasons behind their choice to stay year after year was simple: the beautiful environment and the beautiful team camaraderie made them feel like they are at home.

上图：
2020 年，雅莹集团嘉兴华云路本部前厅

ABOVE
Reception area at EP YAYING Fashion Group
headquarters, Huayun Road, Jiaxing, 2020

右页：
《家园》·油画·2013 年·王晓恩

OPPOSITE
Wang Xiao'en, *Home Garden*, 2013, oil on canvas

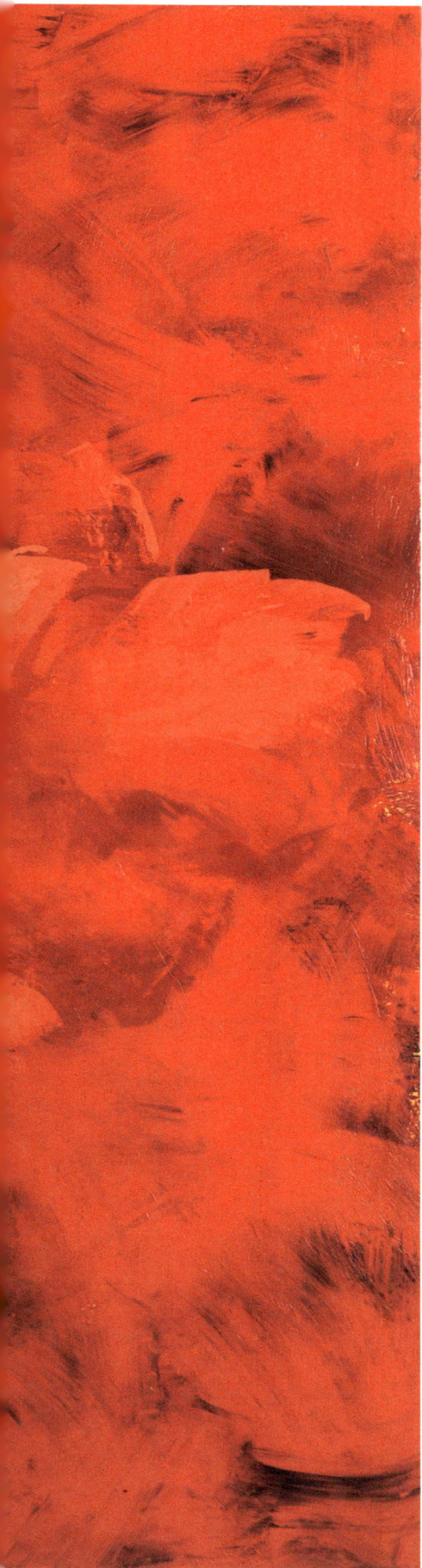

左页：
《银莲花初盛开》· 油画 · 2014 年 ·
Charles Belle（法国）

OPPOSITE
Charles Belle, *Yun now-anemone*, 2014, oil on
canvas

上图：
2020 年，雅莹集团嘉兴华云路本部
办公区

ABOVE
Office space at EP YAYING Fashion Group
headquarters, Huayun Road, Jiaxing, 2020

下页：
雅莹集团嘉兴华云路本部花园式办公
环境

NEXT
EP YAYING Fashion Group garden workspace at
its headquarters

左页上图：
2013 年，雅莹自办首期艺术展览
——"清雅华裳"，清末民初女性服饰展

左页下图：
2014 年"华彩毅裳"，民族服饰展

右图上：
2015 年"火舞凤凰·时尚莲开"，荷花
主题书画艺术展

右图下：
2017 年"雅派韵致·写毅芳华"，牡丹
主题艺术展

OPPOSITE ABOVE
"Elegant Chinese Costumes", the Group's
first art exhibition on women's clothing in
the Late Qing Dynasty, 2013

OPPOSITE BELOW
"Colourful Cultural Costumes", an exhibition on
costumes from Chinese Ethnic Groups, 2014

RIGHT ABOVE
"Lotus in Bloom", a Lotus-themed painting
and calligraphy exhibition, 2015

RIGHT BELOW
"Youth and Elegance", a Peony-themed art
exhibition, 2017

超越服装，构筑国际化时尚版图

A GLOBAL FASHION GROUP

除了在服装上致力引领新的生活方式，2009年后，实力更强的雅莹也以服装为媒介，向美好生活的更多领域衍生。

Starting in 2009, the company began to more deeply explore the concept of a beautiful life, and would go on to establish new brands with unique identities, and formed "EP YAYING Fashion Group".

多元精彩，助力美好生活
FASHION COLLECTIVE, BEAUTIFUL LIFE

美好生活，是新时代中国的关键词。

推崇"好人，好衣，好生活"理念的张华明，对美好生活的拥抱从创立雅莹就已开始。雅莹的第三个十年里，不但成就了时尚一线品牌的卓越，还做出了美好生活的新意思。

至此，雅莹人的名片背后，已赫然印着六个品牌的标志：EP、DOUBLOVE、N.Paia、GraceLand、大雅家、LITTLE SPACE。

张华明将这六个品牌比喻为雅莹的"六棵树"，也是雅莹奉献美好生活的业务版图。其中，EP 已是枝繁叶茂，大雅家、DOUBLOVE、N.Paia 正在茁壮成长，GraceLand、LITTLE SPACE 还是小树苗，但代表着未来的方向。

DOUBLOVE、N.Paia 以及雅莹的童装线，是雅莹在新十年为服务更广消费群体，尤其是年轻群体而着力培育的新品牌。在此之前，EP 的顾客群以优雅的熟女为主，DOUBLOVE、N.Paia 以及雅莹童装线着重加强对年轻消费者的关注，不仅在更广年龄层满足消费者需求，还提升了雅莹整体的年轻与活力。其中：

DOUBLOVE（贝爱）创立于 2009 年，由雅莹为吸引年轻的消费群体，携手韩国团队合作而倾心设计，并以 2012 年 10 月盛装亮相南京新城市广场为标志，跻身中国年轻女性高端时装品牌之列。

时任 DOUBLOVE 设计总监的曹青是资深设计师。品牌在创立之初起名为 Double Love，提出了"备受宠爱"的观点，希

A "better life" was the buzzword in China during the new era.

Virtuous people, good clothes, a beautiful life — this was how it all began for the Zhang family and how, over the course of 30 years, the company had not only established a top-tier fashion brand, but also worked hard to create beauty for customers and society.

Whilst EP mainly targeted middle to upper class women, the new brands that Hwaming would create in the next decade were focused on younger consumers, and this would be the beginning of the company's evolution into a global fashion group, changing its name to "EP YAYING Fashion Group".

DOUBLOVE was founded in 2009. Collaborating with a South Korean team, the brand aimed to design clothes for a younger group of women, with its first store officially opening in the New Town Plaza in Nanjing. Cao Qing, who was a senior designer at the outset of the brand's creation, put forward the concept of "love and be loved". From this ambition, the brand's original name "Double Love" was born, before undergoing a rebrand in 2018. The brand was launched with a new brand name "DOUBLOVE", that brought voice to a new generation's romantic nature and independent spirit, featuring collections that were cool and modern, yet warm and romantic at the same time.

"Today's young women are both little girls with romantic dreams and big girls with vision and professionalism. They bring a new charisma to this generation," she said. Therefore, DOUBLOVE strove to evoke young women's power of creation, where fashion becomes more than just pieces of apparel, but a real expression of their inner emotions and every beautiful moment in life. Xueming added, "Each brand has its own defined role to play in the company's strategy. DOUBLOVE is designed to be younger, trendy and carefree, in order to attract the younger generation customers."

"

当今女性既有少女般柔美、浪漫的一面，
又兼具大女人率性、干练的一面。
这些特质共同存在于都市女性身上，
令女性散发出前所未有的多重魅力。

"

根植文化，锻造经典

上页：
2018 年春夏 DOUBLOVE 广告大片

左页 / 下图 / 376 - 377 页：
2018 年秋冬 DOUBLOVE "遇见"
时尚发布秀于北京三里屯举行

PREVIOUS
DOUBLOVE Spring-Summer 2018 ad campaign

OPPOSITE / BELOW / 376-377
DOUBLOVE Autumn-Winter 2018 fashion
show, Sanlitun, Beijing

根植文化，锻造经典

上页 / 右图 / 382－383 页：
2019 年春夏 DOUBLOVE "绮想" 时
尚发布秀于上海龙美术馆举行

PREVIOUS / RIGHT / 382-383:
DOUBLOVE Spring-Summer 2019 fashion
show, Long Museum, Shanghai

望品牌以对当下女性的深刻理解，给予消费者加倍呵护。她说："当今女性既有少女般柔美、浪漫的一面，又兼具大女人率性、干练的一面。这些特质共同存在于现代女性身上，令女性散发出前所未有的多重魅力。"2018年，贝爱正式启用新标志"DOUBLOVE"，将原先的"Double Love"的品牌名升级为全新的"DOUBLOVE"英文组合，以"爱的进化论"为巧思，导入新锐视觉设计概念，以更精炼的设计语言、国际化的美学风格，既表达品牌对顾客的爱，也让顾客感受到爱和温度。

戴雪明对DOUBLOVE的诠释则是："每条产品线在品牌战略上都要扮演自己的角色。作为一个更有年轻感的产品线，它和潮流更加接近，给到更前端的消费者，或者是胆子更大的消费者，或者吸引一些年轻的消费者，这就是DOUBLOVE的战略角色。"

创立于2013年的N.Paia（恩派雅），是雅莹致力打造的当代设计师品牌。时任设计总监张声琴在服装行业有20多年的丰富经验，她在工作上保持低调但勇于创新，一直行走在时尚前沿，是极简主义的推崇者。其设计以简约、针织情怀为主张，以摩登、时尚、轻松、愉悦为内核，致力将实用功能理念与现代设计新工艺相结合。

"女人每天都在愁自己今天应该穿什么，其实这就是内心与服装之间的对话。"因循于此，张声琴要求自己的设计，极简于外，内在于丰——"少是复杂的升华，更加耐人寻味。"她希望N.Paia不仅要能穿上身，也要通过设计元素增进消费者的自信和优雅。

2018年，N.Paia走过五个年头，时任总经理王翔在品牌五周年的生日会上表示，恩派雅的"恩"是感恩的意思，感恩雅莹平台的源泉和力量，N.Paia的成立，意味着一个品牌的从无到有，需要倾注诸多心力。个人也好，品牌也好，团队也好，在这五年，都在不断提升与磨砺，"恩派雅在刚开始的时候，客户与我们的合作可能并不是源于对我们产品的认可，而是冲着集团的声誉，这也意味着客户对品牌的组织与风格不是完全理解，需要我们站在利他的角度，将客户作为自己的直营店来

N.Paia, founded in 2013, became a contemporary designer brand. Zhang Shengqin, design director for N.Paia who has over 20 years of experience in the apparel industry, always kept a low profile but was bold and innovative. She was an admirer of the concept of minimalism and a lover of knitwear; therefore, she proposed the concept of "Simplicity and Sentiment of Knitwear", which combined functionality and modern silhouettes with style, comfort and joy.

"Women always wonder what to wear in the morning. I would say this is a conversation between your heart and your clothes," said Shengqin. Shengqin's designs advocated simplicity on the outside and beauty on the inside, promoting a minimal, comfortable and composed way of life. "We want N.Paia to be easy to wear, effortlessly stylish, and even confidence boosting."

2018 marked the fifth anniversary of N.Paia, and at the brand's anniversary party, Wang Xiang, general manager of N.Paia, pointed out that the character '恩' in its Chinese name means gratitude. "In the beginning, our customers chose us because of the reputation of EP, but we have grown from individuals with dreams into a brand filled with confidence today. And we are grateful to the Group for providing us with the platform and support. At the same time, we must continue to be thankful to our customers and work with them for a successful future."

右页 / 386 - 389 页：
2017 年春夏 N.Paia "型·致" 时尚发布秀于嘉兴龙之梦举行

OPPOSITE / 386-389
N.Paia Spring-Summer 2017 fashion show, Dragon Dream Hotel, Jiaxing

> "
> 极简于外，内在于丰——少是复杂的升华，更加耐人寻味。
> "

左图：
2017 年秋冬 N.Paia 广告大片

LEFT
N.Paia Autumn-Winter 2017 ad campaign

左图／下页：
2017 年秋冬 N.Paia"重·置"时尚
发布秀于北京饭店金色大厅举行

LEFT / NEXT
N.Paia Autumn-Winter 2017 fashion
show, Beijing Hotel

看待，尽可能地达成共赢。"

2016 年 12 月，雅莹又组建了自己的童装团队，并推出了童装产品牌 EP KIDS：传承 EP "平衡·爱·幸福" 的价值主张，以服务当代中国家庭需求为核心，引领国内高品质童装潮流，致力传播自然、精致、优雅的生活方式，提升中国儿童气质之美。

EP KIDS 注重精心剪裁、健康舒适及童趣元素的创意应用，以充满匠心精神的高定系列、优雅童趣的精致系列、活力个性的潮流系列为三大产品线，满足中国儿童不同场合的各种需求。时任总经理邓联东介绍，"做童装其实是很快乐的事情，用爱温暖儿童的身心，绽放中国新时代儿童的精彩童年。把孩子装在心里面，体会他们的需要，了解他们的感受，我们给孩子的就不仅是一件衣服，而是为他们带去美好，带去幸福。我们携手父母，让孩子从小接触品质，接触工匠，接触时尚，让孩子认知美、提升美，不仅要在有形价值上研发

In December 2016, EP also sets up a childrenswear team and launched EP KIDS. EP KIDS was dedicated to serving the needs of contemporary Chinese families through leading high-quality children's fashion. The brand aimed to promote the natural, elegant and refined lifestyle of EP — celebrating the values of Balance, Love, and Happiness in life — while enhancing the style and fashion of China's children.

The childrenswear brand emphasised meticulous tailoring, the use of healthy and comfortable materials, and the creative use of playful elements. Its intricately crafted *Couture* line, its fun and exquisite *Elegant* line, and its lively *Lab* line catered to the different occasional needs of every child. Deng Liandong, general manager of EP KIDS, said, "It's great fun designing childrenswear. It gives us a lot of satisfaction to create something that will warm a child's heart and make his or her childhood more interesting. We collaborate with parents to understand their child's needs and feelings so that we can provide children not just with good clothes, but fun and joy, while also bringing the concept of fashion closer to them. There is a lot of knowledge in fashion, from craftsmanship to aesthetics, from

66

用爱温暖儿童的身心，
绽放中国新时代儿童的精彩童年。
把孩子装在心里面，
体会他们的需要，了解他们的感受，
我们给孩子的就不仅是一件衣服，
而是为他们带去美好，带去幸福。

99

左页：
2017 年秋冬 EP KIDS 广告大片

OPPOSITE
EP KIDS Autumn-Winter 2017 ad campaign

出孩子需求的产品，更要在无形价值上为孩子传递中国文化、艺术审美、工匠品质等熏陶。"

除了在时装上致力美好生活的呈现，2010 年后，实力更强的雅莹也以时装为媒介，向美好生活的更多领域衍生。

2013 年 5 月，雅莹推出 GraceLand（雅斓名店），这是雅莹集团旗下的首家高端精品零售集合店。它以自有品牌为导入，切入时尚时装的更多领域，在服务更多消费者的同时，强化了集团对不同年龄阶段人群的品牌覆盖。

Chinese culture to the arts, and from the tangibles to intangibles, and we want to work with parents to boost the growth and learning of children in this regard."

In 2013, the Group opened its first multi-brand luxury retailer, GraceLand, filling its space with internationally-renowned brands, as well as a number of outstanding independent designer brands, bringing together high-end personalised products. The brands paid great attention to selecting the most beautiful products and conjuring up artistic inspirations for customers who prioritise a high standard of living, have a keenness for experimentation and pursue a beautiful life.

"

雅斓名店以自有品牌为导入，
切入时尚时装的更多领域，在服务更多消费者的同时，
强化了集团对不同年龄阶段人群的品牌覆盖。

"

左页：
2013 年雅斓名店嘉兴旗舰店

OPPOSITE
GraceLand flagship store, Jiaxing, 2013

"

LITTLE SPACE 以美丽中国儿童为己任，
向中国儿童和社会传播美和爱。

"

2017 年，雅莹又在 EP KIDS 的基础上推出了致力于打造精致、潮流、休闲的儿童新时尚的 LITTLE SPACE 小雅童装集合店品牌。让雅莹品牌的女性消费者，在给自己买衣服的同时，也可以给孩子挑选衣服，并通过这样的链接，让雅莹推崇的"平衡、爱、幸福"理念更融入消费场景。LITTLE SPACE 以美丽中国儿童为己任，向中国儿童和社会传播美和爱。它传承雅莹时尚文化基因，整合国际优秀儿童用品资源，与国内外众多知名童装品牌开展深度合作，既是一家儿童品牌集合店，又是一个品牌的孵化平台，一个成就商业伙伴和童装团队的平台。

女性消费者是掌管家庭生活方式与消费的主力，除"衣"之外，家庭生活还包括很多方面。于是，与推出 LITTLE SPACE 的逻辑相似，2016 年，雅莹还通过学习国外先进模式与理念，结合本土市场特征推出了将"衣食住知"产品和空间融于一体的多品类经营新概念集合店——大雅家 DA YA JIA。立足新

Based on the success of EP KIDS, the Group unveiled LITTLE SPACE in 2017, a multi-brand luxury retailer of international childrenswear fashion labels. The retailer provided diverse and high-quality childrenswear collections for a new generation of parents and children aged 0-14, and offered a delightful, loving and imaginative shopping experience. More than just a store, LITTLE SPACE was also a brand incubator that connected the Group's childrenswear team with new brands from home and abroad.

上图：
2018 年 LITTLE SPACE 上海恒隆店

ABOVE
LITTLE SPACE store, Plaza 66, Shanghai, 2018

大雅家
EP YAYING FACTORY STORE

奢生活方式，以自然环保、创意时尚、舒适实用和高性价比为价值特征，致力于满足消费者高品位、精致、健康、平衡的美好生活方式。

大雅家是强调以衣为本，精选趣味生活好物，共创现代都市生活方式的集合店。因此品牌深入研究当下中产阶级的生活方式，打造以自主时装为主体，集鞋服配饰、居家清洁、整理收纳、美妆养护、食材餐饮和文创办公等多品类经营的新集合店模式，提供自然环保、创意时尚、舒适实用、高性价比的多品类优质商品。

中国集合店市场的发展无论对于行业巨头，还是新进入者来说，前方的道路依然充满不确定性，但对于许多品牌，以数字为中心、以社区为主导的方式仍将是未来几年指引航向的北极星。

大雅家通过进一步强化"都市综合店"的升级定位，继续将时尚、艺术的生活方式融为一体，凭借同一区域或城市内多家店铺的形式展开，布局社区销售，提供店内体验及本地化产品组合，借助定位一个"人"的生活品位来拟化品牌个性，真正满足衣、食、住、趣、休、美不同方面的生活需求，持续为消费者的美好生活加分。

通过这些拓展，张华明也推动雅莹从一丝一线出发，持续丰富美好的产品和服务，一步步将"衣食住知"融于一体，提供满足消费者从时尚产品到生活方式的全方位消费体验。

美好生活的指引下，雅莹正不断壮大着自己的事业。

The decision making behind household items and lifestyle goods is largely influenced by women. Lifestyle goods also involve much more than "clothing", which inspired the Group to open DA YA JIA, a new-concept multi-brand lifestyle retailer, in 2016. DA YA JIA combined its factory outlet concept with a specialised product selection covering everything from food & beverages to home essentials and travel solutions.

Inspiring a new style of affordable luxury living, DA YA JIA placed strong emphasis on the comfortable and practical, creative and fashionable, and value-for-money products. It positioned itself as a community-based retailer, creating localised in-store experiences and products for each city, while studying the way of life of the middle-upper class, to create a model of multi-brand retailing that focused on the four basic needs of people in daily lives — food, clothing, shelter, traveling — while offering an exciting range of beauty and lifestyle products for an increasing cosmopolitan way of life.

With the company's new brands and ventures, it continued to broaden its offerings of products and services, growing into a global fashion group that explores a holistic and beautiful way of life.

左页 / 下图上：
2017 年大雅家生活方式集合店嘉兴旗舰店

下图下：
2019 年春夏大雅家广告大片

扬帆出海，走向世界
CHINESE FASHION, GLOBAL STAGE

从 2004 年与外资企业建立合资企业起，张华明和戴雪明就有一个梦想：代表中国时尚走向世界。2010 年，他们朝向这个目标迈出又一关键步伐：当年 8 月，EP 澳门专卖店在威尼斯人大运河购物中心正式开启，两年后，又开出了澳门首家生活馆。

在澳门建立起试水国际市场的窗口后，张华明开始更大力度推动雅莹的国际化。一贯稳中求进的他没有急于拓展更多的海外门店，而是选择了另一条路来学习，也是积累雅莹的国际化经验和资本：通过世界性舞台提升雅莹的国际能见度，探索中国时尚的国际道路。

2015 年，EP 成为意大利米兰世博会中国馆的全球合作伙伴，为中国国家馆设计定制了包括志愿者、场馆工作人员及政府代表的三类馆服，男女装共 11 套，以及配套的鞋、包、丝巾、领带等服饰品。期间，为了更好地诠释出当年世博会"滋养地球，生命之源"的主题，EP 还面向全球举行了馆服设计创意大赛，最终征集到 600 多份设计作品，并邀请获奖设计师加入内部设计团队参与到馆服设计中，历时 9 个月完成了方案。最终方案中，EP 不仅在材料上大量采用了中国传统面料，还将中国民间的很多传统手工艺运用到其中。此外，团队还以天、水、地为灵感设计了主题秀服，并运用编织、针刺，包括泼墨的印花图案等，彰显中国传统文化、江南文化的风采。

在走向世界和展示东方时尚之美的同时，雅莹也努力将世界时尚引入它的植根之地。2016 年 3 月，EP 在刚刚因为世界互联网大会声名鹊起的水乡乌镇的大剧院举办了大型发布会，也

Since the establishment of their international joint venture in 2004, Hwaming and Xueming have had a dream — to take Chinese fashion global.

In 2010, they tested the waters for this venture with a Macau store at the Grand Canal Shoppes. In 2015, EP became a global partner of the China Pavilion at Expo Milano in Italy and was responsible for the custom design and production of the three types of uniforms for volunteers, venue staff and government representatives. It was a different way of going global, as Hwaming chose to first increase the brand's exposure and recognition on the global stage prior to retail expansion.

There were 11 sets of men's and women's wear for the Expo, as well as matching shoes, bags, scarves, neckties and other accessories. Based on the Expo's theme of "Feeding the Planet, Energy for Life," EP organised a design competition to brainstorm ideas and received over 600 design submissions. EP invited the award-winning designers to join its creative team, and they worked together for 9 months to design and produce the uniforms.

The final design not only used traditional Chinese fabrics, but also showcased many examples of traditional Chinese craftsmanship. The team also created a conceptual fashion series inspired by the natural elements of earth, wind and water for the Expo's fashion exhibition, using a variety of techniques such as knitting, needle punching and calligraphy, all of which exuded the charm of Chinese traditional culture and Jiangnan style.

1	2
3	4

右图：

2015 年，由 EP 设计制作的米兰世博会中国馆工作人员服装

1. 志愿者户外服装

2. 场馆内工作人员服装

3. 政府代表服装

4. 志愿者室内服装

RIGHT

Uniform for the China Pavilion at Expo Milano, 2015

1. Outdoor volunteers

2. Government representatives

3. Indoor volunteers

4. Working staff

左页 / 上图 / 右图：
2015 年，EP 世博主题秀服，天韵系列

OPPOSITE / ABOVE / RIGHT
EP Sky-themed designs, Expo Milano
China Pavilion fashion exhibition, 2015

左页 / 上图 / 右图：
2015 年，EP 世博主题秀服，水之锦系列

OPPOSITE / ABOVE / RIGHT
EP Water-themed designs, Expo Milano
China Pavilion fashion exhibition, 2015

上图 / 右图 / 右页：
2015 年，EP 世博主题秀服，丰壤系列

ABOVE / RIGHT / OPPOSITE
EP Earth-themed designs, Expo Milano
China Pavilion fashion exhibition, 2015

上图：
2015 年 1 月，EP 于上海音乐厅举办的 "敬自然·米兰世博跨界艺术音乐会"上，闪亮发布以 "天、水、地" 为灵感设计的世博会主题秀服

ABOVE

"Respecting Nature, Expo Milano Music & Arts Concert", Shanghai Concert Hall, January 2015. EP launches a conceptual series for the Expo's fashion exhibition, inspired by the theme of "Sky, Water and Earth"

上图：
2015 年 9 月，EP 世博主题秀服展
在米兰世博会中国馆揭开帷幕

左图 / 下页：
2015 年 9 月，米兰世博会中国馆志
愿者风采

右页上图：
米兰世博会中国馆志愿者馆服设计
研发团队

右页下图：
2013 年 6 月 25 日，时任中国国际
贸易促进委员会展览部副部长赵振
格与雅莹集团董事长张华明签署 EP
2015 年意大利米兰世博会中国馆合
作事宜

ABOVE

Expo Milano fashion exhibition, EP's "Sky, Water, and Earth" conceptual series, September 2015

LEFT / NEXT

Volunteers representing the China Pavilion at Expo Milano, September 2015

OPPOSITE ABOVE

Design team for the uniforms of the China Pavilion at Expo Milano

OPPOSITE BELOW

Zhao Zhenge, then vice minister of the Exhibition Division of China Council for the Promotion of International Trade, and Zhang Hwaming, chairman of EP YAYING Fashion Group, signs a partnership for the China Pavilion at Expo Milano 2015, 25th June, 2013

从那一年开始，雅莹集团连续多年成为世界互联网大会的服装供应商之一，持续作为本土品牌的代表，向世界展示东方服饰之美。

世界互联网大会，旨在搭建中国与世界互联互通的国际平台和国际互联网共享共治的中国平台，主要邀请国家和地区政要、国际组织负责人、互联网企业领军人物、互联网名人、专家学者出席会议，涉及网络空间各个领域，体现多方参与，是中国举办的规模最大、层次最高的互联网大会，也是世界互联网领域的高峰会议。至今，雅莹已连续多年负责世界互联网大会工作服的设计、生产，在服务大会的同时，也获得品牌的再提升。

不断于世界舞台崭露头角的另一边，充分把握中国经济崛起和消费升级机遇的雅莹，也发展到崭新的高度。截至 2018 年 3 月 1 日，雅莹集团零售网络已覆盖全国 210 个城市，拥有 800 多家优质门店、多种门店类型和渠道组合，为消费者带来非同一般的品牌体验。

在中国服装协会公布的 2017 年中国服装行业产品销售百强企业榜单中，雅莹集团位居第 34 位，而在利润和利润率百强企业榜单上，其排名则更高，分别位居第 17 位和第 8 位，领先于一众已经上市的服装企业。具体到女性时装领域，无论销售，还是利润，雅莹的表现都高居前列，为行业领先者。

In 2016, the same year EP held a large-scale trade fair at the Grand Theatre in Wuzhen, a historic town in east China's Zhejiang Province, in March, the Group returned to Wuzhen in November to become one of the main sponsors of the World Internet Conference, designing and producing the uniforms for the volunteers.

The annual event, attended by national and regional politicians, heads of international organisations, leading Internet companies, celebrities, experts and scholars, discusses various subjects pertaining cyberspace and involves multi-party collaboration. It has become China's largest and highest-level conference in the field, and is known as the world's summit of the Internet. This successful design collaboration would continue for five years and was another key channel by which the Group stepped onto the world stage.

The Group continues to grow in strength. As of March 2018, the Group's retail network covered over 210 cities across China, with over 800 high-quality stores, supplemented by a variety of online channels, creating an extraordinary brand experience for customers. According to the China National Apparel Association's 2017 list of 100 Top Companies, the independent EP YAYING Fashion Group ranked 34th in terms sales, while ranking 17th in profits and 8th in profit margins, ahead of many listed companies in the industry.

上图／右页：
2017 年第四届世界互联网大会，由 EP 设计制作的志愿者礼仪服

ABOVE / OPPOSITE
Volunteers in EP designed uniforms at the 4th World Internet Conference, 2017

下页：
2016 年第三届世界互联网大会，由中国雅莹设计制作的志愿者礼仪服

NEXT
Volunteers in China YAYING designed uniforms at the 3rd World Internet Conference, 2016

第四篇

CHAPTER 4

世界的EP，
中国的雅莹

2018~
WORLD EP, CHINA YAYING

2018年10月，嘉兴乌镇，雅莹举行了自己的30周年励志庆典。张华明在庆典大会的致辞中表示：雅莹会像过去30年在国内各大城市、各大商场成为一道道靓丽风景一样，于未来10年、20年、30年，在世界各大城市、各大商业场合成为一道道靓丽风景！他说，未来30年，将是全世界追捧中国元素、中国服装、中国品牌的30年。"伟大的时代给了我们大好的机会，作为一家时尚集团，雅莹将积极努力、贡献力量，把最好的中国之美带到全世界，不辜负这个时代的重托。"

In October of 2018, EP YAYING Fashion Group held its 30th Anniversary Gala in Wuzhen, Jiaxing. In his opening speech at the gala, Zhang Hwaming said, "Just as the past 30 years have seen us grow EP into beautiful beacons in major shopping malls in major cities across China, the next 10, 20 and even 30 years will see us do the same in major cities around the world." Hwaming added that in the next 30 years, the world will begin to seek Chinese fashion and Chinese brands. "Great times have given us great opportunities. As a fashion group, each and every one of us should work hard and contribute to bringing the best of Chinese beauty to the world and living up to the great responsibility of this era."

三十而立，立的是根本
STEADFAST AT THIRTY

正心奉道、自强不息、厚德载物，是张华明对雅莹人能够经历时代变幻获得今日成就的因果总结，也是他要雅莹人在未来岁月始终坚守的发展信念。

Staying truehearted, constantly improving and upholding virtue were how Zhang Hwaming believed that the people of EP YAYING Fashion Group were able to consistently keep pace with the changing times and reach today's achievement. These beliefs remain at the core of the Group's development and he called for the Group's people to adhere to these principles in the years to come.

此心庄严，优雅而立
DIGNIFIED HEARTS, STEADFAST IN ELEGANCE

时间进入 2018 年，雅莹的第三个 10 年，张华明举行了一系列活动，总结过去，前瞻未来。

2018 年 7 月 9 日，雅莹在嘉兴华云路本部举行了 3C 周年庆启动仪式，邀请 30 年发展的不同见证者，分享与雅莹一路走来、共同成长的点点滴滴，正式拉开 30 周年庆典序幕。

2018 年 10 月 18 日，以"此心庄严，优雅而立"为主题，雅莹在乌镇互联网会议中心举行 30 周年的励志庆典，回顾 30 年的历史，也在新时代的关键节点，展望未来 30 年的发展方向。2500 余名员工、合作伙伴、顾客朋友等嘉宾悉数到场，资深媒体人杨澜也惊喜现身，一起见证雅莹集团新 30 年的优雅启航。

2018 年 11 月 2 日，EP 于北京以"融生"为主题，重磅发布 EP 2019 年春夏系列产品以及首次发布中国雅莹高级定制系列，表达品牌对自然天地的敬畏，对中国文化的尊崇，传递"平衡·爱·幸福"的哲学，分享"好人，好衣，好生活"的理念，在人与自然的和谐融合，艺术与人文的交相辉映，传统美学与当代设计的共生共融中，彰显出雅莹的品牌个性与魅力，以及雅莹作为现代时尚集团的新风尚。

从 30 年前的服装加工生产起步到如今多品牌的现代时尚集团，雅莹一直在变：从产品设计到生产，从渠道到品牌，从人力到管理，从整体发展战略到一针一线……方方面面、点点滴滴，都在与时俱进、求新求变。

求新求变的精神引领雅莹人不断地创新创意，并以此开创了中国服装业的诸多先河。但回顾 30 年一路走来，张华明强调

2018 marked an emotional and momentous year for EP YAYING Fashion Group. It was a year of reflection, tributes and promise.

On the 9th of July 2018, the Group held a kick-off ceremony for its 30th Anniversary celebrations, inviting various former and current employees to share their thoughts and experiences of their journeys with the Group.

On 18 October 2018, the Group officially celebrated its 30th Anniversary, with the theme of *Dignified Hearts, Steadfast in Elegance*, in the town of Wuzhen, Zhejiang Province. More than 2,500 employees, partners and customers, as well as famous media personality Yang Lan, took a trip down memory lane together and launched a bold vision for the future together.

On 2 November 2018, the Group's EP brand held an unforgettable fashion show in Beijing that showcased its 2019 Spring-Summer collection, while also debuting YAYING's haute couture fashion line in Beijing. The twin line-up echoed the show's theme of "Harmony", and passed on the brand's values of "Balance, Love and Happiness" in life. It conveyed the harmony of people with nature, arts with culture, and traditional aesthetics with contemporary designs. This was a show of EP's heritage and how far it had come as an ongoing creator of modern Chinese fashion.

From a small makeshift workshop 30 years ago to EP YAYING Fashion Group today, every step and every change embodied the relentless efforts of each and every Group member — from design to production, from retailing to branding, from human resources to operations management, and from corporate strategy to each stitch of needlework. With its constant pursuit of innovation that opened up the Chinese fashion industry, Hwaming still emphasised the importance of remaining steadfast amidst all the change:

"An unwavering heart and spirit are present in our work. For 30 years, we never wavered in our original aspiration of using high-

OUR 30 YEARS 你我 TA 30 年

EP ELEGANT PROSPER | YAYING | 雅瑩集團 EP YAYING FASHION GROUP

《雅莹人》风尚志从第 1 期到第 72 期，一直在发掘和传递雅莹人温暖的故事，传播雅莹人的真情心声。2018 年，雅莹"你我TA30年"的主题特刊经由戴总提出，便开始了它的孕育之旅。从最初全员范围内的故事征集，到我们确定入册169位人选，并逐步深入每个人的专访、摄影、摄像，沉淀了这份属于雅莹人"你我TA30年"的纪实之作! 在书中，我们不仅翔实记录了雅莹 30 周年的系列庆典，而且有幸与雅莹颇有渊源的贵人、前辈、合作伙伴以及新老员工诚挚相谈。依循雅莹 3 个 10 年不一样的时间段落和背景，这些雅莹人的故事连同泪水、欢笑、激昂与失落，像一颗颗精彩而饱满的句点，注脚着你、我、TA 与雅莹相互交织独特的火凤凰精神、美丽初心、真诚之心和专注创新之心。

EP YAYING Fashion Group's corporate publication *People of YAYING* has been collecting, writing and publishing heartwarming and inspiring stories of the Group's people. In 2018, the Group's vice president, Dai Xueming, kick-started our 72nd issue with a 30th Anniversary special theme, "30 Years of You & I". After a year of interviewing, writing and photographing, this special publication features touching stories of 169 old and new employees, partners and customers that reflect the incredible growth of the company, showcasing the Group's "Fire Phoenix" spirit, beautiful aspiration, sincere hearts, and its focus and innovation across its 30 years. This issue also includes scenes from our exciting 30th Anniversary Gala and the inspiring speeches from our chairman, vice president and invited famous media personality, Yang Lan.

左页：
雅莹集团 30 周年励志庆典盛况

OPPOSITE
Scenes from EP YAYING Fashion Group's 30th Anniversary Gala

扫码可下载雅莹集团 30 周年《雅莹人》主题特刊 "你我TA30年"

Scan QR code to download EP YAYING Fashion Group's special Anniversary publication, themed "30 Years of You & I"

此心庄严，优雅而立
DIGNIFIED HEARTS, STEADFAST IN ELEGANCE

上图：
雅莹集团董事长张华明30周年励志庆典，满怀深情地发表了《此心庄严，优雅而立》的演讲，本文为致辞精选

ABOVE：
Excerpt from Zhang Hwaming's, chairman of EP YAYING Fashion Group, speech — *Dignified Hearts, Steadfast in Elegance* — at the Group's 30th Anniversary Gala

张华明

雅莹集团董事长兼总裁张华明
公元 2018 年 10 月 18 日
农历戊戌九月初十

2018 年，是一个特殊的年份。于国家而言，今年是改革开放 40 周年；于我们而言，今年是雅莹 30 岁的生日。

40 年前，我的父亲张宝荣先生感受到了时代的"春意"，他参与筹建了洛东第一家乡办集体服装企业并担任厂长，父亲这种敢为人先的精神，今日想来，仍然让我们十分佩服！

1988 年，我的父亲凭借 18 台家用缝纫机和 34 号人马，勇敢地走上了个人承包村办集体企业的经营之路。历经磨难，百折不挠。更重要的是，父亲用实际行动教会了我们"想要做好事，先要做好人"，做事先做人的道理，让我一生受益。

回望雅莹的 30 年，今天的一切来之不易！我常问自己，创业 30 年，一路走过来，我们靠的是什么？

一是"火凤凰"精神的引领和支撑。火凤凰精神是坚毅专注、开拓创新、百折不挠、永不放弃的精神，这是雅莹 30 年的创业精神。我父亲当初创业条件是何其艰难，但最终我们都过来了，靠的就是这种精神！

二是对美丽初心的坚守！30 年来，我们一直坚持用好材料做好衣服，为女性顾客带去美，坚持走品牌之路，毫不动摇！

三是真诚之心，这是雅莹真诚的力量！"要做好事、先要做好人"，雅莹一直抱着一颗赤子之心，对事业、对顾客、对合作伙伴、对员工，我们都报以了最大的真诚。我们相信以心换心、以诚换诚，互惠共赢、共同成长、长长久久！

四是专注和创新之心。30 年来，无论外界如何浮躁，别人如何跨界，我们从未离开自己热爱和选择的服装行业。30 年来，雅莹唯一不变的就是不断地创新，一直走在创新变革拥抱变化的路上。

总结一下，一种精神，三心合一，一心一意！

一切过往，皆为序章！未来 30 年，大有可为！

未来的30年，是中华民族伟大复兴的30年。

未来的30年，是中国时尚产业厚积薄发的30年。

未来的30年，是我们立足中国，深耕中国，走向世界的30年！

大好的时代，大好的行业，大好的自身发展潜力，"好人，好衣，好生活"是我们雅堂要秉承的理念，"世界级的品牌，国际化的公司"是我们这代人和这代年轻人共同努力去实现的目标！

"历史从不等待一切犹豫者、观望者、懈怠者、软弱者。"面向伟大的新时代，我们将一如既往秉承"平衡·爱·幸福"的经营哲学，不忘美丽初心，真正把顾客装在心里，为顾客持续创造价值，通过我们小小的平台，助力中华文化在时尚行业的伟大复兴，实现我们每一个人的人生价值，这是多么自豪的选择和担当！

"身之主宰便是心，不能胜寸心，安能胜苍穹？"

新的30年扑面而来，不放手一搏，更待何时？我们每个雅堂人都应该"此心庄严，优雅而立"！

此心，我们应该拥有一颗怎样的心？我们应当建立起一颗为祖国伟大复兴而奋斗的心！一颗为中国时尚品牌崛起而奋斗的雄心！同时要不忘那颗雅堂人一路砥砺前行的初心！

生命的意义不就是能为更多人更好地服务吗？明白了生命的意义，我们应该为自己感到庄严，庄严自己，庄严事业，庄严祖国。这就是此心庄严。

优雅，雅者正也，德行雅正，代表着雅堂集团正心奉道。好人，好衣，好生活，优雅也。

而立，立的是根，立的是本。何为本？志为本、顾客为本、产品为本、文化为本，本立而道生！

志为本。志不立，天下无可成之事！我们选择了创建和发展中国民族品牌为自己的宏伟大志，这是一份君子才能承载的伟大事业。

顾客为本。顾客的痛点我们知道吗？唯有一颗真诚之心，感恩之心，敬畏之心，才能与顾客建立心与心

的链接。

产品为本。如何能够做出好产品？以一颗纯粹的心，永葆创意激情，以卓越的创意及品质去感知顾客的需求，满足顾客对美好生活的向往。

文化为本。文化是一个国家、一个民族的灵魂，也是一个公司的灵魂。5000年的中华文化是我们取之不尽的宝藏。我们不断从中汲取，为产品创意找到源源不断的灵感，传承并发扬传统文化，手工技艺，工匠精神。5000年的中华文化是有道的文化，我们应该不断磨炼自己，建设提升自己的心灵，使自身的仁爱、智慧、胸怀和能量不断地提升，引领我们前行！这就是文化的高度自信！

最终，以人为本，而本在人心，"道心惟微，人心惟危"，我们每个人的心原本就是清澈光明，我们每个人的心原本就拥有无尽的宝藏。一个人的真正成功，不是因为财富有多少，也不是因为创造财富有多少，真正的成功，成就是他帮助多少人建设了心灵品质，帮助多少人开发了心灵宝藏。

过去30年，一路走来我们靠的是火凤凰精神、美丽初心的坚守、真诚之心和专注创新。走向未来，我相信困难问题无时不有，但唯有建设我们心灵，唯有开发了自己的心灵宝藏，心灵强大，心上有力量，才能不断突破工作、事业、人生的天花板。

新的30年，时代、行业、顾客给了我们新的期望，让我们一起努力，共同托起世界的EP、中国的雅堂，建立起文化的高度自信，为中华民族的伟大复兴而奋斗！

最后，祝愿所有的朋友们平衡·爱·幸福！谢谢大家！

2018 is a special year. For the country, this year marks the 40th anniversary of China's reform and opening-up, which is of great historical significance; for us, this year is EP's 30th birthday.

40 years ago, my father, Mr. Zhang Baorong, responded to the call of the times, joined in the setup of Luodong Garment Factory, the first local collectively-owned township garment enterprise and was appointed as director of the factory. To this day, his pioneering spirit still wins our admiration!

In 1988, with 18 household sewing machines and 34 villagers, my father bravely decided to strike out on his own and undertake the management of Luodong Hongzheng Garment Factory, overcoming numerous challenges but he never gave up. More importantly, my father taught me through his actions that "we have to become a virtuous person if we want to succeed in anything", a lesson which I have benefited from throughout my entire life.

Looking back at EP's 30 years, everything today has not been easy to come by! I often ask myself what has kept us going these 30 years?

Firstly, it is the guidance and support of our "Fire Phoenix" spirit. Our "Fire Phoenix" spirit is about tenacity, focus, innovation, perseverance and never giving up. This has been our entrepreneurial spirit for over 30 years. In the early years, my father operated the business in extreme conditions, and even when I took over, I almost lost the company several times, but in the end, we all made it through. That is the power of our entrepreneurial spirit!

Secondly, it is our dedication to our beautiful original aspiration. Over the past 30 years, we have never wavered and always insisted on using high-quality materials to make good clothes and bring about beauty to our female customers. We remain steadfast in our journey to create a high-quality fashion brand.

Thirdly, is a sincere heart, which is also our unique strength. Our previous generation taught us that we must be virtuous if we want to succeed in anything, henceforth, we have continued to maintain a pure heart towards our work, customers, partners and employees. We believe in the power of treating people as how you wished they treated you — with sincerity, growing together and achieving success together.

Fourth, is focus and innovation. Over the past 30 years, no matter how uncertain the outside world is, how other companies have engaged in crossover investment, we have never left the fashion industry we love and chose. Over the past 30 years, we have grown from a brand into today's fashion group. This is only possible because we have embraced the notion that change is the only constant, and we continue to pursue constant change and innovation.

To conclude, our spirit and a united heart have kept us going strong for so long!

Nonetheless, what is past is prologue! The next 30 years will see us strive more and thrive more!

In the next 30 years, China will experience a great national rejuvenation. In the next 30 years, China's fashion industry is poised to develop rapidly after establishing years of strong foundation. In the next 30 years, we will entrench our brand in China and expand globally.

This is a great era, with a great industry, with a great potential, and we shoulder the responsibility to succeed in the next 30 years. "Virtuous people, elegant clothing, beautiful lives" and becoming "a world-class brand and a global company" are the common goals our generation and the younger generation will work hard to achieve.

Time and tide does not wait for the hesitant, the bystander, the idle and the weak. As we face a great new era, we will continue to uphold our business philosophy of "Balance, Love and Happiness", stay true to our beautiful original aspiration, continue to create value for our customers, support Chinese culture's great rejuvenation through the fashion industry, and fulfill each and every one of our dreams. This is a proud choice and responsibility, and I believe that all these are worth striving for together.

"The heart is the master of the body. If one cannot conquer the heart, how can one succeed in life?" In the face of the next 30 years, we must seize the opportunity of the times, it is now or never. All of us in EP YAYING Fashion Group must possess *Dignified Hearts, Steadfast in Elegance.*

Heart, what kind of heart should we possess? Every one of us should keep our hearts united in striving for the great rejuvenation of our nation. Every one of us should keep our hearts united in striving for the rise of Chinese fashion brands! We should not forget our original aspiration that continuously gives us the strength to keep striving forward.

Isn't the meaning of life to help more and more people? Having understood the meaning of life, we should feel dignified, about ourselves, our work and our country. This is what it means to have a Dignified Heart.

Elegance means being virtuous and refined. And stands for EP YAYING Fashion Group's truehearted passion. "Virtuous people, elegant clothing, beautiful lives", this is what Elegance embodies.

Steadfast means having firm roots and strong foundation. What makes up this foundation? Our aspirations, our customers, our products and our culture.

Aspirations are our foundation. Nothing in the world can be achieved without setting aspirations. We have chosen to create and develop a China fashion brand as our grand ambition, which is a noble responsibility to undertake.

Customers are our foundation. Do we understand their pain points? Only with a sincere, grateful and respectful heart, can we establish heart-to-heart connections with our customers.

Products are our foundation. What is a good product? One that is made with a pure heart, with passionate creativity and excellent quality, fulfilling our customers' needs for beautiful lives.

Culture is our foundation. Culture is the soul of a country, a nation and a company. 5000 years of Chinese culture is our infinite treasure trove. We should keep drawing inspiration from our culture for our product creativity, and preserve and promote our traditional culture, artisanal handicraft and craftsmanship spirit, truly building stronger confidence in our culture! 5000 years of Chinese culture has a culture of the *Dao*. We should continue to grow as a person, cultivate our heart-mind, so that our benevolence, wisdom, magnanimity and energy can continue to grow and give us guidance!

Lastly, everything we do should be people-oriented and the seed of achievement lies in every human heart. All of our hearts are pure and bright to begin with, and contain infinite treasures. One's success lies not in how wealthy one is or how much wealth one has attained, real success is how many people you have helped to improve the quality of their inner character, how many people you have helped to tap into the infinite treasures in their heart, this is real success.

Over the past 30 years, our "Fire Phoenix" spirit, our dedication to our beautiful original aspiration, our sincerity, and our focus and innovation have been our driving forces. Going into the future, I believe that difficulties and problems will always be present. Only if our hearts are pure, only when we tap into the infinite treasures in our hearts, only when we improve the quality of our inner character, can we achieve breakthroughs in our work, our career and our lives.

In the next 30 years, the new era, the industry and our customers have new expectations of us. Let us work together as one to bring "World's EP, China's YAYING" to greater heights, bolster greater confidence in our Chinese culture and strive for the great rejuvenation of our Chinese nation!

Let me end of by wishing all friends "Balance, Love and Happiness!" Thank you!

何为真正的美
WHAT IS REAL BEAUTY?

上图：
在雅莹集团 30 周年励志大会庆典上，资深媒体人，阳光媒体集团董事长杨澜女士以《何为真正的美》主题演讲阐述了她作为中国优雅女性代表对"美"的理解与感悟。本文为演讲节选

ABOVE:
Excerpt from Yang Lan's, famous media personality and Chairperson of Sun Media Group, speech on *What is Real Beauty?* at EP YAYING Fashion Group's 30th Anniversary Gala

公元 2018 年 10 月 18 日
农历戊戌九月初十

美到底是什么，它从哪里来？一个小小的婴儿他已经对美有感应，当我们看到自然的时候，我们产生一种敬畏，真美。我们看到大自然会爱它的壮美，看到一个小生命会爱他的柔美，所以美是我们内心的一种强烈的感应。那么到底什么是美呢？

如果用我个人的理解的话，我觉得美是心对道的感悟、感知和一种创造。庄子曾经说过，天地之间有大美的存在，但是我们很难去听到或者说感受到它的存在，除非我们用心体察。

说到心，当然要提到我们古代的王阳明，也留下了这样的话，他说你未看花时，你与花同归寂寞，你看花时，花的颜色一时明白起来。当你的心与道产生呼应的时候，花的颜色都变得鲜艳起来了。所以说心的感悟是多么的微妙，又是多么的富有诗意。我们的心会通过外在的美而深入到灵魂层面的沟通和理解。

我在今年非常有幸还制作了另外一档节目《匠心传奇》，我带着小伙伴们走访了 12 位意匠大师，我感受到中华文明在传承中不断突破和创新艰难的历程，同时也感受到意匠大师的一颗颗的匠心。其实匠心是一个过程，比如说他要有初心，他要有一份专心。同时还要理解一份恒心，就是你能够耐得住寂寞，同时经历时间的考验，回应时间的答卷。同时要有一份欢喜心，如果你不是真正地爱自己的事业，你不能达到自己的真正的水准。

我最后想跟大家分享的是道心，刚才前面说以心悟道，最后落到一个心就是道心。美给生命带来的加持，给生命带来的生生不息的力量，大概是美的更高的境界。所以说美就是生命的成就与圆满，达己者达人，达人者达己，当你能够成就更多人的生命美满的时候，你的生命和事业也将更加的美好。

在今天这个时代，中国在消费升级，从一个制造大国变成了一个消费大国，我相信雅莹的事业有着非常广阔的未来和巨大的想象空间，同时也相信在这条创造美的道路上，我们也在创造着文明本身。

What is beauty indeed? Where does it come from? Even infants respond to beauty. When we are in Nature, we can't help but be awed and utter "How beautiful!". We love the majestic beauty of Nature, we love the tender beauty of a baby. So, beauty is a strong feeling from deep down in our hearts. What is real beauty then?

In my humble understanding, beauty is the heart's understanding, perception and even manifestation of the *Dao*. Zhuangzi once said, "Heaven and earth have their great beauty but do not speak of it." Therefore, if we do not use our hearts to observe, we will not be able to experience its beauty. Speaking of the heart, the name of our ancient philosopher Wang Yangming must be mentioned. He once said, "When you cease regarding these flowers, they become quiet in your mind. But as you come to look at them, their colours at once become clear." This shows us how subtle and poetic the perception of the heart is, when your heart is in tune with the *Dao*, the flowers become full of colour. Through these external objects of beauty, our heart can evoke an internal dialogue of the soul.

I was lucky to be the producer of a programme called *Legend of Ingenuity*, in which my team and I visited 12 world-class and progressive Chinese artisans. It is from this programme that I experienced the arduous journey of these artisans to make breakthroughs and innovations in their craft as they sought to preserve its cultural heritage. I also felt strongly what it is to have the heart of a craftsperson. Indeed, craftsmanship is a process, one that starts from having a pure heart of intent and a focused heart. At the same time, having a determined heart that can overcome loneliness, trials and the test of time. And also, a passionate heart. Those who do not truly love what they do cannot reach their due levels.

Finally, I would like to share with you my understanding of the *Dao* Heart, the last "heart". I mentioned beauty is the heart's perception of the *Dao*. Beauty improves the quality of our lives and provides our lives with endless strength, perhaps this is the highest level of beauty. That is why beauty can make a person feel fulfilled and content. We help

ourselves by helping others, when we help more people find happiness in their lives, our lives and career will become more beautiful.

China's consumption is undergoing an upgrade in this new era. China is transforming from a manufacturing giant to a giant consumer market. I firmly believe EP YAYING Fashion Group has a promising future and immense room for all possibilities. Again, I congratulate your past achievements and I believe when we create beauty, we are shaping civilisation.

感恩雅莹人
THANK YOU FRIENDS

上图：
雅莹集团副总裁戴雪明，细数往日对雅莹有恩的伙伴，字字流露雅莹人之间独有的温情。本文为致辞精选

ABOVE:

Excerpt from Dai Xueming's, Vice President of EP YAYING Fashion Group, speech during the awards presentation for partners and suppliers at the Group's 30th Anniversary Gala

雅莹集团副总裁戴雪明
公元 2018 年 10 月 18 日
农历戊戌九月初十

亲爱的雅莹朋友，30年来，我们一直在一起，一起经历、一起见证，今天回首过往，那一幕幕场景仿佛历历在目，满腔的谢意难以言表；那一段段岁月依然心潮澎湃，如山的众望铭记于心。

时代的风帆，使我们成为行业的弄潮儿，这是我们的幸运；因缘而聚，有了相知、相携、相守的一群人，是我们彼此的幸运；危难时的援助、困苦时的支持、贵人恩人的提携，是雅莹的幸运！怎能不感慨、怎能不感激、又怎敢相忘！请让我们献上最为诚挚的谢意，给予我们无私帮助的好人、贵人们！更要感谢在我们极尽艰难时，给予无私帮助的人。

雅莹的今天除了这些人以外，还有很多很多的人值得我们一一去感恩、感谢。我们会铭记在心，更会将这种精神传承下去。感谢这个好时代，让我们有拼搏的舞台；感谢缘分，在合适的地方遇到了合适的你；感谢贵人、恩人、朋友、伙伴们，我们勤勉、我们忘我、我们无畏；让我们一起经历失败，更收获成功。

我们要如同走在平衡木上，无论过去30年，还是更长远的未来；我相信我们会以从容、优雅的姿态，持续走在绽放中华时尚之美的道路上，我相信世上没有难做的生意，只有难做的人。过去30年，我们只做一件事，就是"做好人，做好衣"；未来30年，我们还只干这一件事，"做好人，做好衣"；我相信因为我们拥有众望所祝的托付，不屈的精神，勇闯的力量；未来，不管我们经历什么样的风雨与危机，我们都能浴火而生，我相信时尚自有温度，世界你我点靓！

My dear friends, we've been working alongside one another for 30 years. Together, we've experienced and witnessed a lot. Looking back, our past seems so very fresh and I cannot find the words to describe how thankful I am for all of you. Our past memories still inspire me and your high expectations of me continue to be my motivation.

It was our stroke of luck that we rode the tides of time to become a hotshot player in our industry. It was fate that led us together and our blessing that we have each other's support and company. It was also truly a blessing that EP had people that reached out their helping hands to us, raised us up from adversities and gave us so many opportunities. How can we forget them, and how can we not thank them and honour them? Here, I would like to take this opportunity to express my heartfelt gratitude to all who have helped us in one way or another, especially in our times of need and distress, your selfless help and support.

Apart from all those aforementioned, there are still so many people we want to thank. We keep you in our hearts and your persevering spirit will continue to inspire us. We need to thank this great era that has set the stage for us to go all out to achieve. And once again, fate that has brought us together at the right time, in the right place. Thank you once again, our benefactors, our partners and our friends. We will continue to work hard, selfless and fearless in our pursuits. Let us experience failures together, but most importantly, reap the sweet rewards of success together.

No matter for the past 30 years or in the far future, I believe we'll keep walking, with elegance and poise, like a gymnast on a balance beam, showcasing Chinese fashion's beauty. It is my firm belief that there is no such thing as a difficult business, only the difficulties we will face in staying true to ourselves. For the past 30 years, we have focused on only one thing, "be virtuous people and make good clothes". In the 30 years to come, we will still focus on this one thing, "be virtuous people and make good clothes." In our possession are the trust from many, the spirit of perseverance and the power of belief. I believe these will tide us over any forms of hardships and crises, and we will be reborn from the ashes. Lastly, I believe in the human touch in fashion, so let us beautify this world together.

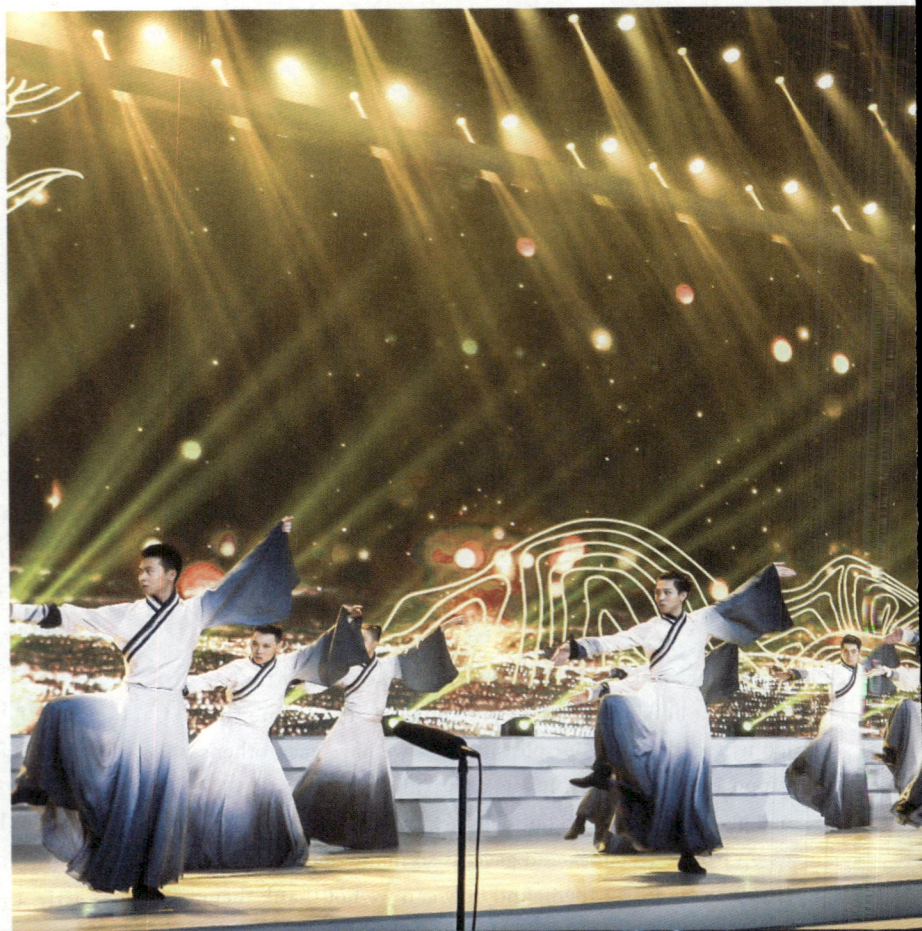

右图：
励志庆典四大主题篇章表演："理解
美""发现美""创造美""展现美"

下页：
励志庆典现场雅莹人合影，现场演出
及花絮集锦

RIGHT

The four themes of the Gala's performance:
"Understanding Beauty" "Discovering
Beauty""Creating Beauty" and "Inspiring
Beauty"

NEXT

Scenes from EP YAYING Fashion Group's
30th Anniversary Gala

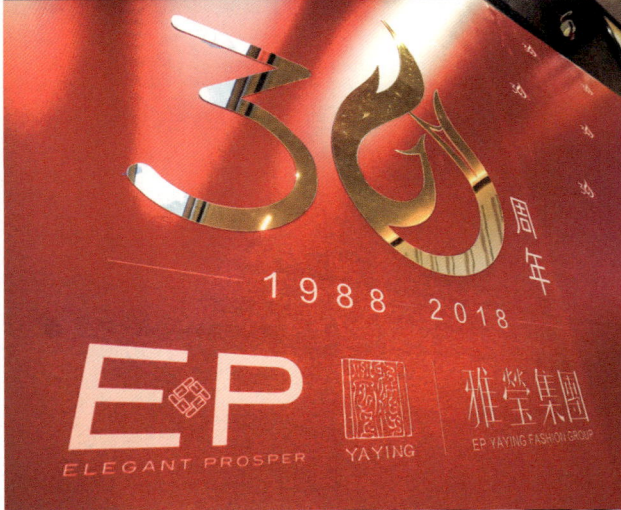

30周年
1988 2018
EP
ELEGANT PROSPER
YAYING
雅莹集团
EP YAYING FASHION GROUP

此心庄严 优雅而立

30 周年
1988 - 2018

精选自雅莹集团 30 周年特刊

Selected articles from EP YAYING Fashion Group's
30th Anniversary Special Publication

最多的不是如何拥抱变化，而是要坚守不变。

首先不变的，是做事业的心态和精神。张华明说，雅莹 30 年一路走到今天，靠的是"一种精神一颗心"的坚守。一颗心是美丽初心，是专注创新之心，也是真诚感恩之心。

30 年来，雅莹一直坚持用好的材料做好的衣服，为女性顾客带去美，坚持走品牌路线，毫不动摇，始终保持初心不变。30 年来，雅莹坚持"想要做好事，先要做好人"，始终抱着赤子之心，对事业、对顾客、对合作伙伴、对员工，以心换心、以诚换诚，互惠共赢、共同成长、长长久久！30 年来，无论外界如何浮躁，别人如何跨界，雅莹都从未离开自己热爱和选择的服装行业，并始终围绕自己的初心不断地创新，一直专注走在创新变革、拥抱变化的路上。

一种精神则是火凤凰精神，也就是坚毅专注、百折不挠、永不放弃、精诚团结的精神，是雅莹 30 年的创业精神。"我父亲当初创业的条件是何其艰难，我自己带领雅莹之后也有好几次差一点满盘皆输，但最终我们都挺过来了，靠的就是这种精神！"张华明说。

靠着"一种精神一颗心"，雅莹以"此心庄严，优雅而立"，三十而立出今天的成就。

而在张华明看来，三十而立，立的仍是根本。"一切变化都是从不变的根本而来。"他认为，雅莹能够经历 30 年变迁获得成功，要得益于对四个"本"的坚持：志为本、顾客为本、产品为本、文化为本。

志为本。志不立，天下无可成之事！雅莹在发展壮大的过程中，树立了创建和发展中国民族品牌的宏伟大志。公司 30 年心无旁骛，专注在服装业发展，首先是因为坚定了这个志向，坚定了这个目标。

顾客为本。顾客是企业的衣食父母。从张宝荣时代，雅莹便十分重视为顾客创造价值，到张华明、戴雪明时代，更进一步提出以顾客为中心，从方方面面关切顾客的需要。这是公司持续创新的初衷，也是赢得顾客信任的关键。

产品为本。张华明一直坚信，企业的失败归根到底都是产品

quality materials to make good clothing and bring beauty to women — all while building a high-quality fashion brand. For 30 years, we never wavered in being virtuous before all else, whether in our work, with customers, with partners or with our employees, treating everyone with respect and sincerity to achieve mutual growth. For 30 years, we never wavered in our focus and love for the fashion industry, no matter how uncertain the outside world and no matter how other fashion companies have pursued different paths."

He added, "In the early years, my father operated the business in extremely volatile conditions and even when I took over, I almost lost the company several times. But in the end, we all made it through. That is the power of our entrepreneurial spirit!" Dubbed the "Fire Phoenix" spirit, the Group's essence was about tenacity, perseverance, never giving up and staying united.

United in heart and spirit, the Group turned 30 with *Dignified Hearts, Steadfast in Elegance*. Steadfast means having firm roots and strong foundation. "All changes come from an unwavering foundation. What makes up this foundation? Our aspirations, our customers, our products and our culture."

Aspirations: When it comes to EP YAYING's aspirations, nothing could be achieved without them. In its 30 years in the garment and fashion industry, the Group has come to understand its responsibility and its mission to develop a Chinese fashion brand and to advance the Chinese fashion industry.

Customers: Zhang Baorong paid a great deal of attention to creating value for his customers, and when Zhang Hwaming and Dai Xueming took over, they pursued a consumer-centric business strategy, caring for all aspects of their customers' needs. For two generations, the Group placed customers at the core of its innovations and built a strong rapport with them.

Products: Hwaming always firmly believed that the failure of a company is ultimately due to the failure of its products — once its products and services are no longer able to satisfy and even delight customers. Since EP's founding, products have always been the top priority of the company, and the foundation that supported the company's innovation in retailing and its business strategies.

Cultural heritage: Culture is the soul of every country, nation and company. The 5000 years of Chinese culture is the source of inspiration for the Group's management and cultural development. It is also the Group and brand's unique competitive advantage in the industry both in the past and in the upcoming new era.

According to a famous Chinese proverb, "The heart is the master of

的失败，是没有真正提供出令顾客满意甚至欢心的产品与服务。从成立至今，产品始终是雅莹的头等大事，也是支撑公司在渠道和商业模式创新的根基。

文化为本。文化是一个国家、一个民族的灵魂，也是一个公司的灵魂。5000年的中华文化不但是张华明推动经营管理和建立雅莹文化的源泉，也被张华明视为建立品牌竞争力与护城河的宝藏。雅莹能以优雅之姿立于行业和时代前沿，脱颖而出，也是靠着对文化的根植。

"身之主宰便是心，不能胜寸心，安能胜苍穹？"张华明强调"心"的重要。他说："志为本、顾客为本、产品为本、文化为本。归根到底都是以人为本，而人又以心为本。"

从创业到今天，雅莹人守护住了自己的一颗"好心"，被张华明视为最关键的地方，也是他和雅莹不断进步的所在。

"人心惟危，道心惟微。人们常常说一个人、一个公司多么有策略和方法，但真正的关键是你安的是什么'心'，用的是什么'心'在做事。"张华明说，从父亲当年强调的"想要做好事，先要做好人"，到自己创立雅莹时提出"要用好的材料做出好的衣服，为女性朋友带来美"，再到戴雪明提出"平衡·爱·幸福"，30年来，雅莹的"安好心""做好事"一直没变。

站在公司30年的里程碑上，张华明以"此心庄严，优雅而立"总结雅莹的过去，也勉励雅莹的未来。他要求雅莹人把握民族复兴伟大机遇，坚守一颗与祖国同频共振、为祖国伟大复兴而奋斗的心；把握中国时尚产业厚积薄发的产业趋势，建立起一颗为中国时尚品牌崛起而奋斗的雄心；始终不忘践行美丽事业，书写生命的意义，一路砥砺前行的初心！

这是雅莹人生命的意义。"明白了生命的意义，我们应该为自己感到庄严，庄严自己、庄严事业、庄严祖国。这就是此心庄严。"

为了继续守住这颗"好心"并让此心更加庄严，张华明还以强化心灵品质为核心，对雅莹展开一系列的文化与心灵提升，这也让雅莹更加优雅、晶莹。

the body. If one cannot conquer the heart, how can one succeed in life?" Hwaming placed absolute importance on the heart, saying, "Our aspirations, our customers, our products and our culture — all of these foundations are rooted in our hearts. Everything we do should be people-oriented and the seed of achievement lies in every human heart."

He added, "The hearts of humankind are unstable and the *Dao* Heart subtle. A company can have its many strategies and plans, but the most critical elements are the people's hearts. What kind of heart do your people have?" From his father's ethos of "being a virtuous person if you want to succeed in life," to his aspiration of "using high-quality materials to make good clothing and bring beauty to women" since the registration of yaying, to Dai Xueming's launch of EP's value proposition of "Balance, Love and Happiness", the Group has always focused on self-cultivation and self-improvement.

Hwaming marked the Group's 30th Anniversary milestone by announcing its new mission — Dignified Hearts, Steadfast in Elegance — dedicated to improving oneself, developing the industry and committing to China's progress.

"We must seize the opportunities of the new era. Every one of us should keep our hearts united in striving for the great rejuvenation of our nation. Every one of us should keep our hearts united in striving for the rise of Chinese fashion brands! We should not forget our original aspiration that continuously gives us the strength to keep striving forward and write a new chapter for both our lives and this beautiful enterprise of ours." Henceforth, the Group would deepen its studies into culture to cultivate stronger character in its people.

www.globaltimes.cn   MONDAY NOVEMBER 5, 2018

GLOBAL TIMES — DISCOVER CHINA, DISCOVER THE WORLD

METRO SHANGHAI

▶**Today's weather**   22° HIGH   18° LOW

▶**Pulse**
Young Chinese Consumers   2

▶**Community**
Showcasing and selling   8

Models attend the EP YAYING Night at the closing ceremony of China Fashion Week Spring Summer 2019 held in Beijing from October 25 to November 2. Photo: Courtesy of EP YAYING Fashion Group

▶ Iconic Chinese brand EP YAYING celebrates 30th anniversary

Culture & fashion

Amid the amazing music, lights and visual effects, old and new friends of EP YAYING Fashion Group recently reunited for the 30th anniversary of the iconic company during China Fashion Week Spring Summer 2019 in Beijing. For the gala event, EP YAYING premiered its new collection from the group's dual-brand development strategy, namely The World's EP, which features a contemporary lifestyle brand inspired by culture, nature and art, and YAYING of China, which highlights regal Oriental craftsmanship and Chinese culture heritage-focused luxury artisanal designs, blending Western and Oriental aesthetics with a modern perspective for the modern Chinese woman. ▶ **4** A 30-year

Address: 18/F, 1576 Nanjing Road West, Shanghai 200040, P.R.China
News Dept (8621)62532530 editor-sh@globaltimes.com.cn   Ads Dept (8621)62532780 ad-sh@globaltimes.com.cn   Subscription Dept (8621)62442667

右图：
2018 年 11 月 5 日，*GLOBAL TIMES*《环球时报》整版报道的 2019 年春夏"EP 雅莹之夜"盛况

430 - 455 页：
2018 年 11 月 2 日，"EP 雅莹之夜"时尚发布秀为庆贺品牌 30 周年，于北京 751D · PARK 首次以双产品线发布 EP 2019 年春夏系列及中国雅莹高级定制系列

RIGHT
GLOBAL TIMES cover page feature of EP Spring-Summer 2019 fashion show, 5 November 2018

430-455
EP Spring-Summer 2019 fashion show celebrates the brand's 30th Anniversary, 751D PARK, Beijing, 2 November 2018

中国雅莹 2019 高级定制系列 YAYING 2019 Haute Couture Collection

455

以人为本，提升心灵品质
DEVELOPING HEARTS AND MIND

"企业的品质来自人的心灵品质，企业的力量来自人的心灵力量。"张华明认为，安一颗好心，守住自己的发展之道，至关重要。

"心是一座宝藏，一切都是从心开始，心灵品质不足，就算再好的策略和方法，也不会产生美好的结果。"为此，张华明将开发心灵宝藏、提升心灵品质作为雅莹的重大战略推动，以此鼓舞每一个雅莹人成就更好的自己，更好地成就他人，最终达成人人充分发挥自我、成就自我、奉献自我的合力，继而汇聚成雅莹的软实力和竞争力。

服装是一个生产美的行业，明心净心尤为重要。"心里如果没有净土，怎么静下心来做创意？衣服的衣料好，设计师的心境好，做出来的衣服穿起来都会是有灵气的，否则他设计的衣服肯定不好。"把公司布置得像花园的戴雪明也强调，"我无法改变公司周围的环境，但可以塑造自己的一片净土。"

张华明求学不断，并努力将雅莹发展成学习型企业。学习的过程中，他注重现代经营管理的知识和理念，注重行业发展的专业与信息，更注重心灵品质和人文观念的培育及提升。目前，雅莹已在张华明的推动下成立了30多个常设性的学习小组，学习内容既有中外服饰和全球经营管理的各种专业典籍，也有从《道德经》到《论语》《活法》等心灵与文化经典，并且对学习过程和成果高标准、严要求。

从中华优秀传统文化汲取营养，带领公司上下读圣贤书、悟圣贤道，是张华明推动心灵品质提升的核心方式。他说，中华优秀传统文化对心灵修炼的关切和探讨，看似与高科技和高

"A company's quality is only as good the character of its people." Zhang Hwaming believes in the importance of a good heart and staying true to one's path.

"Everything starts from the heart. All of our hearts are pure and bright to begin with, and contain infinite treasures. But if we do not cultivate a good heart, even the best strategies and plans will not produce good results." To this end, Hwaming placed the development of the hearts-and-minds of his people as a major strategic priority, to inspire and encourage everyone in the Group to continue to seek improvement to achieve their full potential, which ultimately improved the Group's soft power and competitiveness.

Fashion is an industry that creates beauty, and it is especially essential to have a pure and clear heart. "We all have that place deep down in our hearts, an inner sanctum, that we hold dear. If we do not cherish it, how can we find the quietude to create? Only if the materials are good, and the heart of the designer pure, will the creations be filled with life," Dai Xueming also said. She remains a strong advocate of a beautiful work environment, saying, "I may not be able to change the environment around our headquarters, but I can create an inner sanctum of our own."

Hwaming was always one to lead by example, having spent his time studying not only modern management concepts and industry trends, but also reading many self-improvement books and gradually infusing a new learning culture in the company. At present, the company has established more than 30 regular study groups, with rigorous learning processes set in place and topics ranging from fashion to global management, whilst also including cultural and spiritual classics such as "The Classic of the Dao and Virtue", "The Analects" and "Living Law".

Hwaming emphasised learning the essence of fine traditional Chinese culture and learning from the sages as the best way to

上图：
《清雅颂莹》·书法·2014 年·范曾

竞争时代的企业经营管理没有太直接的联系，却是企业持续发展的根基，圣贤指引则是生命的雨露。

2011 年，张华明便已开始接触中华优秀文化，在一遍又一遍对照过往历程的熟读、深思、体悟中，他与自己对话，与古代先贤对话，在对话中对人生和事业的成败得失有了更深的理解："每次读这些圣贤之道都有新体会，过去很多事情我们虽未总结，但事实就是按照古已有之的大道所行，所以，获得了成功。还有一些事情我们失败了，当时觉得是策略和方法的问题，现在对比检讨下来，还是心的问题、良知的问题。比如，我们可能在那一个时间点急于求成了，违背规律去追求原本就不该追求的东西了……"

人生重大的价值在于不断提升自身心灵品质，也帮助他人提升心灵品质。他说："一个人的真正成功，不仅在于他做了多少有形贡献，创造了多少业绩，做出了多少利润，做出了多少好事，更重要的是他成就了多少人。而在帮助他人之中，最重要的也是帮助了多少人明心、净心，帮助了多少人建设美好的心灵品质，帮助了多少人开发心灵宝藏。"

cultivate and improve oneself. "While it may seem that these traditional Chinese cultural studies on the heart and mind are not directly related to business management in this era of technology and intense competition, I believe they are the foundation for a company's sustainable development. More than that, these teachings by the sages provide nourishment for our lives."

In 2011, Hwaming began learning more about traditional Chinese culture and implemented a self-imposed learning system. He started by understanding the history and development of Chinese teachings and then began to read every classic to broaden his knowledge, before reading them again to deepen his understanding. He would make extensive records of his reflections and learnings, gaining a deeper understanding of both his life and the company. "I would gain a new level of understanding each time I read the teachings of these sages. When I look back on some of the success we achieved, I found that we largely followed in their path of success. And while at that time we may have concluded some our failures to be strategic mistakes or failures of implementation, I understand now that the problem lies in the heart. We were too eager and greedy for success that we meaninglessly chased things that were not meant to be."

上图：
2012 年以来，雅莹积极倡导对中华优秀传统文化的深入学习，长期举办各类培训学习

也是因为倡导对中华优秀传统文化的深入学习，张华明把雅莹 30 年的成就归结为安了一颗"好心"，守住了"做好事、先做好人"这个根本，并且将这颗"心"、这个"根本"作为持续赢得未来的关键去建设和维护。"用阳明先生的良知和心学总结，长久成功的事业都是正心奉道、自强不息、厚德载物的结果。用在我们的经营上，经营的根本是为顾客创造和奉献价值，利润只是副产品，这个根本坚守不住，偏离了，利润也就没有了生长的土壤。"

"一切学问、修养归结到一点，就是要为善去恶，即以良知为标准，按照良知去行动。经营事业也是一样，要按良知去做，自强不息先要守住良知。"透过对传统经典的学习，以及心灵品质建设的持续，雅莹也让自己根植文化建立卓越品牌的理念更加深入人心，成为融入企业血液的本色。

He shared one of his learnings: "A person's real success lies not only in one's tangible contributions, whether it be in revenue, profit or achievements, but more importantly the difference one makes in other people's lives — how many you have helped to uplift their hearts and minds, how many you have inspired to tap into the infinite treasures within their hearts." The meaning of life perhaps lies in self-improvement and the people you have helped to uplift.

With his deep love and knowledge of traditional culture, his commitment to constantly self-improving and being virtuous, Hwaming called for the Group's people to adhere to these principles in the years to come. The culture and these beliefs at the core of the Group's development were how the people of EP YAYING Fashion Group consistently kept up with the changing times. This was also one of his key learnings from the renowned Wang Yangming classics. "To put it in management terms, the root of management is creating value for our customers. Profits are just by-products. If we do not cultivate this root, profits will not be stable, or for that matter, grow," Hwaming said.

66

长久成功的事业都是正心奉道、自强不息、厚德载物的结果。

99

文化是根，也是终极竞争力
ROOTED IN CULTURE

2008年，全球金融海啸爆发，但中国经济依然持续向前，并且以史无前例的奥运盛事令全球瞩目。这带来东西方经济发展和国际影响力的变化，也让张华明看到新的机会。

"北京奥运会以前，国人对真正有自己文化底蕴的大品牌还是比较欠缺信心的，但2008年北京奥运会，再加上美国的次贷危机以来的此消彼涨，民族的自信心得到很大的提振。"

随后，在2012年，"中国梦"——实现中华民族伟大复兴的核心目标正式提出，雅莹也相应提出了"我们的美丽中国梦"的概念，力争将发扬中华优秀文化作为发展新阶段的重要举措。洞见到潮水方向之后，张华明及时对雅莹的品牌文化进行了重新定义。

根植中国文化，彰显中国文化和中国时尚之美，以中国文化自信成就品牌自信，建立品牌优势，由此成为雅莹品牌的核心基因。"作为中国时尚产业人，我们不但要从5000年的文化中汲取精神营养，指引我们的人生观、价值观和世界观，也要从中华服饰和文化元素中汲取创意灵感，将中国服装美学继承创新发扬到世界舞台。"张华明说。

这是雅莹对时代人心的敏感，也是雅莹作为中国服装企业对自己在新时代的使命升级。具体到产品上，就是雅莹开始更加强调以中国文化和东方时尚为创意设计之源。作为这一工程的实践者、时任中国雅莹设计总监陈曦回忆说："用传统的手法直接将中国美学嫁接到服装设计中的方式有些过于直白，用更为内敛、更为简约的方式将东方美学传递出来，才真正能够彰显品牌深厚的文化底蕴。"所以2010年之后雅莹陆续

The global downturn in 2008 did not detract China's growing economy and the monumental Beijing Olympics in the same year became a catalyst for China's growing influence on the world's stage. Hwaming saw new opportunities: "Before the Beijing Olympics, Chinese people still lacked confidence in local brands, even if they had rich cultural heritage. However, the Beijing Olympics, coupled with the subprime mortgage crisis in the United States, greatly instilled in the nation a sense of self-belief and self-confidence."

In 2012, the "Chinese Dream" — the great rejuvenation of the Chinese nation — was formally put forward by the country; in 2013, Hwaming proposed a shared vision of "EP, Our Beautiful Chinese Dream" — making the development of the cultural roots of the Group the top priority in its new phase of development. "As a Chinese fashion brand, we must not only look to the 5000 years' history of Chinese culture to guide us in our views of the world, life and values, but we must also draw creative inspiration from traditional Chinese clothing and cultural elements, to preserve, pass on and innovate. Let us showcase to the world the beauty of Chinese fashion and Chinese aesthetics."

Over the years, EP has developed a strong level of awareness and sensitivity to the changing times, and deeply understood its new mission as a Chinese fashion brand. From 2010, EP began to place more emphasis on Chinese culture and Oriental fashion styles in its product designs. As the designer in charge of this new line at the time, and design director of China YAYING today, Chen Xi said: "The traditional method of directly transferring Chinese cultural elements to clothing was too straightforward. We felt that a more introspective and minimal design style was better suited to expressing the profound cultural heritage of our brand." From 2017, China YAYING dedicated its efforts to studying and passing on the aesthetics of the royal family, which was seen as the pinnacle of Chinese culture.

"

我们的美丽中国梦
——'引领时尚、优雅的生活方式，
传递平衡·爱·幸福的价值理念，
打造代表中国的最美时尚品牌，
为顾客、社会创造美，让所有人
共享人生出彩的机会是我们的梦想和目标。
历经 30 年、两代人的创业发展历程，
始终坚持专注、创新、用心成就未来的创业理念。
引领服装行业转型升级，推动中国时尚产业发展。
向世界展示来自中国的时尚与美丽。
时尚品牌，来自中国！'

"

开始整体调整，基于中国文化这一方向，2016年独立开辟中国雅莹产品线进行创意研发，2017年中国雅莹逐步聚焦东方皇家美学。

这一定位很快赋予雅莹新的个性与魂魄。"首先，在当今商业化的环境中，若想实现这样的设计理念，一方面要求设计师能够潜心了解中国本土文化，把民族的、传统的、有代表性的精粹真正理解和领悟到；另一方面也要求设计师在设计语言上，不是完全应用中国式的语言去诠释，而是将这些取材于中国文化的设计元素进行有效的平衡，呈现既摩登又具有东方美学特点的国际化设计。"陈曦介绍说。

此后，中国雅莹围绕东方皇家美学从内到外进行了一系列的理念培育和行为落实计划。最显著的标志就是，在集团的众多场所，抬眼即见各种皇家文化、艺术的图书、资料和素材，从绘画到书法，及至诗词歌赋等。如今，这样的氛围环境已是雅莹集团本部最鲜明的特征之一。

为将东方美学与产品更完美地相融，雅莹还围绕工艺展开一系列既传承又创新的探索。比如，中国雅莹始终坚持手工艺，融入刺绣、珠绣和编织等技法，把每一件衣服都当成一件艺术品去雕琢。其部分手工刺绣，需绣娘花费几个月，甚至一两年时间才能完成一件。一件简单的白衬衫，会采用古代朝堂礼服中十二章纹的元素设计，让每个纽扣都不一样，让消费者从细节中体会心思。这些独具匠心的工艺，也赋予雅莹独特的气质和魅力。

对中国传统文化的演绎，中国雅莹成就了"极致的美学、极致的面料、极致的工艺、极致的剪裁"四大核心价值，并以这四大核心捍卫着品牌的高端地位。其每季一个主题的东方皇家文化元素演绎，从龙袍到《桂鹤图》，再到《桃源仙境图》等，就更令品牌彰显尊贵。

This positioning soon instilled in China YAYING a new personality and soul. "In today's commercial environment, if you wish to realise such a concept, designers must devote themselves fully to understanding the Chinese local culture, including its history, the different ethnic groups and key iconic elements. Furthermore, designers must not simply use Chinese style, but must find the balance to incorporate these Chinese cultural elements into an international and modern design," Chen Xi added.

Since then, China YAYING has organised many learning sessions to foster a deeper level of Chinese culture within the team. The most visible sign of this culture can be found around the headquarters of the Group, with many Chinese cultural paintings, calligraphy, poems, books and various art works on display. This is one of the most distinctive features of its headquarters to-date.

Increased focus was given to developing the exquisite traditional craftsmanship of the brand's artisans. The team was given the time, space and resources to study, develop and innovate these exquisite traditional handicrafts, from embroidery to beading to weaving, all signature artisanal skills of China YAYING. For example, a piece of embroidery work would take months or even years to complete, because each one was treated like a piece of art. A simple white shirt would incorporate handicrafts of the twelve imperial symbols that were embroidered on the robes of the imperial family or high-ranking officials in ancient China. These symbols represented imperial authority and also symbolise beautiful moral qualities. The details of China YAYING's craftsmanship are priceless and exemplified the Group's rigorous adherence to its artisanal doctrine that aimed to bring out the artistic value of every creation.

China YAYING prides itself on delivering the very finest of traditional Chinese culture with its four codes: quintessential aesthetics, quintessential fabrics, quintessential craftsmanship and quintessential tailoring — all of which have established the luxury status of the brand. Each season was inspired by different themes from the royal family's culture, such as their dragon robes or the renowned *Crane and Osmanthus* and *Immortal Realm of the Peach Spring* artwork, gradually imbuing the brand with an air of royalty as well.

在张华明看来，立足悠久灿烂的文化之根，也是中国企业可以区别于西方企业，建立差异化竞争力的关键所在。这种差异化竞争力，既可体现在企业经营管理的宏观层面，也可以体现在企业产品与品牌价值的微观层面。

于前者，张华明认为，经营管理归根到底也是管理人心。"这方面的很多事情，几千年前的老祖宗就已经替我们解题了。如何从中国博大精深的文化积淀，从中国的圣贤文化寻找营养，形成自己独特的经营之道，这是事关企业根本的核心问题。有根的企业才能走向世界，悠久的文化就是我们夯实企业根基的最大资源和优势！"

于后者，他认为，中华民族的伟大复兴，让中华文化和文明被世界更高度关注与欢迎，而且这一趋势还将持续并且上升，这为品牌以中国文化底蕴服务世界提供了基础，而一旦中国品牌以此底蕴为优势建立起品牌的优势，相对西方企业来说，便是建立了独有的价值壁垒。

"中国文化这张牌打好了，真正做出长项了，外资品牌想要超越你才比较难，这就会成为你的独特优势，因为这是我们中国企业天然的优势，也是外资不具备的优势。"他说。

更世界、更中国，这也是雅莹最近几年最大的发展特色。无论在米兰世博会，还是在乌镇世界互联网大会，甚至是走出去，在马来西亚有别于一般国际流行快消时尚实现开拓国际市场的开门红，致力倡导中国服饰之美，都是雅莹被欢迎的重要保障。

"我们对此底气十足，信心十足。信心既是来自大国崛起的自信，也是来自对自己品牌 30 多年发展的自信，更是来自对悠久灿烂的历史文化的自信。立足中国、融合世界，讲述一个立足中国悠久璀璨历史的品牌，为消费者呈献来自中国时尚品牌的惊喜，这是我们坚定不移的目标。"张华明说。

In Hwaming's view, being rooted in a culture that has such a rich and fascinating history was critical for a Chinese company establishing competitive differentiation from Western brands. This competitive differentiation can be embodied not only on the macro level of business management, but also in the micro level in its products and brand values.

"At the macro level of business management, this goes back to the concept of the heart-and-mind, in which our ancestors from thousands of years ago have given us the answers. How can we then find wisdom in our rich culture and our famous sages, to form our unique method of management? Only with firm roots can a company go global. Now we must turn this culture into our greatest resource and advantage, and lay a strong foundation for the company to take deeper roots."

Hwaming also believed that the great rejuvenation of the Chinese nation has made Chinese culture and civilisation more highly regarded and welcomed by the world, and this trend will continue, providing a foundation for the brand to deliver to the world products and values with a unique Chinese cultural heritage and identity.

"If the Chinese culture is well-conveyed, it becomes more difficult for foreign brands to surpass you. This is our unique advantage, a natural advantage of our Chinese enterprises that foreign brands do not have."

Becoming more global and more Chinese is EP's unique trait in recent years. Whether at the Expo Milano, the World Internet Conference or its inaugural Southeast Asia store, the brand has seen Chinese fashion with strong cultural elements receive the most positive reception. Hwaming further shared, "We are full of confidence in our future development. This confidence comes not only from the great rejuvenation of our country and its vast and deep culture, but also how far we have come as a brand and company these past 30 over years. Rooted in China with a global vision, we tell a story of a brand with strong Chinese cultural heritage; of a Chinese fashion brand with beautiful surprises in store every day for our customers. This is our unwavering commitment."

坚守平衡之道，持续以火凤凰引航
THE BEAUTY OF BALANCE

平衡，是张华明经常强调的一个词。这不单因为雅莹提出的"平衡·爱·幸福"已通过长期的实践成为集团经营哲学的一部分，更因为对各种关系和事物的平衡，一直被他视为可持续发展的成功之道。

张华明成长在京杭大运河边上，身心也深受运河的滋养和影响。他还记得，小时候，每年寒暑假最开心的事就是去外婆家，那是苏州下面一个古镇，坐船差不多要两小时。张华明说，运河的开放、包容与日夜不息地向前奔流，造就了他开放、敢闯和求新求变的精神，而运河上的行船，在水面上的平稳行驶，可算是他对平衡之重要的初认识。

在张华明看来，"平衡"无处不在，且永无止境——人从两条腿走路开始就需要平衡，一呼一吸皆是平衡。漫长的人生如此，做企业也是如此。雅莹以及他本人一路走来的历程中，由平衡二字演化出来的特质，也已成为鲜明而深刻的特征，甚至是其精髓。

产品的平衡。雅莹最初以丝绸为主料的春夏装起家，后来张华明认为必须推出冬装，因为"四季要平衡"，再到后来推出系列——让着装和所在环境匹配，都是平衡。

设计的平衡。太保守会和潮流脱节，太激进又会失去实穿性；东西方文化要平衡——既要从西方设计中汲取养分，又要真正体现东方美学。

管理的平衡。雅莹引进了西方系统化的管理体系，但是，"管理体系化之后的问题是容易僵化，创新不足。"于是同时提倡，以东方哲学和人文主义去中和西方管理体系中的僵化。

Balance is a word often mentioned by Zhang Hwaming. This is not only because it is the value proposition of EP, but also because of how he has lived in a constant balance between the multiple forces and layers around and within the Group. He has come to see this as a key success factor in the Group's sustainable development. The brand's value proposition of *Balance, Love and Happiness* has today become the Group's business philosophy and provides meaningful guidance to its pursuit of a sustainable society.

Hwaming grew up by the Lanxi River, a section of the Beijing-Hangzhou Grand Canal. He still remembers when he was a child, how his happiest time during winter and summer vacations was taking a two hour boat ride down the river to his grandmother's house in an ancient town in Suzhou. Reflecting on his childhood days, he said: "Perhaps the vastness of the river and the constant rush of water, in one way or another, shaped my character — open-minded, fearless and always looking for change. Despite the busy river, each boat maintained its own steady pace, finding a kind of balance." In his view, balance is everywhere and is in perpetual change. People start learning about balance from the moment they learn to walk; every breath in and out is also about balance. Even more, life itself and the management of an enterprise is about balance. Balance has come to be the distinctive trait and essence of both the Group and Hwaming's entrepreneurial journey.

Balance in products: The balance of the four seasons was behind Hwaming's push to launch the winter wear collection. Thereafter, EP began to balance their collections with the diverse lifestyles of its customers.

Balance in design: Too conservative and one loses touch with the trends; too trendy and one loses practicality. By infusing Western styles and asserting Oriental aesthetics, EP designs were always about finding the right harmony between cultures.

各部门之间，也要平衡。"做销售永远觉得我们家产品不行，做产品的永远觉得我们家销售不行。这是服装行业的通病。"多年来，雅莹一直在治这个病。

张华明夫妇对于时尚的定义，还是平衡。"这个人的衣着打扮跟她本身融为一体，能把人的美和能量散发出来，这种感觉就是最舒服的。"美学中的平衡之道，即在于自然、匹配。

张华明对于平衡重要性的认识，上升到人生层面，最终体现在雅莹的价值理念上：平衡、爱和幸福——归根到底，服装是一个生产美的行业。雅莹追求气质优雅、心地晶莹，在此之上实现生活的和谐平衡，释放爱的能量，获得幸福，拥有美丽人生。

即使雅莹已经走过 30 年，他还是不断强调，平衡最重要的仍是打好根基，通过深耕企业根基，加强企业的历史传承、文化建设去不断赋能好、平衡好企业未来的发展。

张华明还将雅莹 30 年的创业比喻成"火凤凰"精神的引领和支撑。企业的发展离不开"天、地、人"赋予的时机与挑战，在时代的江河中，涅槃重生的"火凤凰"精神成为雅莹最核心的精神品质，在雅莹人的手中薪火相传，生生不息，鼓舞着一代又一代的雅莹人昂扬向上，焕彩新生。

2012 年，雅莹确立企业发展的核心文化——"火凤凰"精神。张华明、戴雪明与团队伙伴共同设计了"火凤凰"形象。2013年，"火凤凰"雕塑落成。"火凤凰"融汇两种力量，阴阳相济，能量流动上升，生生不息。凤与凰环抱相合，象征精诚团结，是雅莹人奋发向上、永不言弃的精神力量，有着浴火重生、至美永恒的坚毅不拔。

这份生生不息之力，不仅支持父亲在改革开放伊始打下创业基石；也支持他挺过多次困难和挫折，发展壮大了雅莹。尤其在非典疫情、金融危机中与雅莹员工同舟共济、共克时

Balance in management: In addition to integrating advanced western corporate governance methodologies in its business, the Group also instilled the core values of Chinese culture that develop employees' character and contribute to their overall success and growth.

Balance among departments: This is a concern that plagues almost all enterprises, an example being tension between the sales and product team. Hwaming acknowledged this difficulty in balance but knew it is always a work in progress.

Both Hwaming and Xueming have remained of one mind that fashion is about balance. Both have highlighted that a person must feel at one with her dress, as it is like a skin that brings out her inner beauty and energy. It is the feeling of comfort that they always are focused on. Balance in aesthetics lies not only in styling but also in the concept of the natural being.

Hwaming translated his insights on the role of balance in life to the company's strategy, making EP's value proposition of *Balance, Love, and Happiness* the Group's business philosophy in recent years: "*Balance, Love and Happiness*, at its core, embodies the beauty that the fashion industry creates. EP pursues innate elegance and a pure heart, which is reflected in a balanced lifestyle and a beautiful life that is filled with love and happiness."

Any new era features new challenges, new possibilities and new breakthroughs, followed by new innovations for both individuals and enterprises. Hwaming believed that all achievements are the result of the continuous balance between risk and opportunity — with successful enterprises enduring trying times, renewing and transforming, moving from strength to strength.

In 2012, the "Fire Phoenix" was put forward as the emblem of the company's corporate culture, with Hwaming, Xueming and the team working on the design before completing the associated sculpture the following year. The emblem is a reference to the Phoenix in Chinese mythology and represents the unification of two boundless energies — the male *Feng* (Chinese: 凤) and the female *Huang* (Chinese: 凰), each embracing one another in *yin-yang* harmony. The motif signifies the spirit of the Group and the fire in the peoples' hearts, as they remain united and dedicated to inspiring beauty, never giving up.

上图：
2012 年，雅莹火凤凰设计手稿及近 8 米高雕塑

左图：
2020 年，在雅莹火凤凰雕塑前员工们留下的影像

ABOVE
The Group's "Fire Phoenix" emblem design sketches and 8m-high sculpture, 2012

LEFT
Team photoshoot in front of the Group's Fire Phoenix sculpture, 2020

艰；在转型升级、发展创新中，与行业同伴们，精诚携手、勇往直前。其中就有互为助力的平衡，也有危机转换、持续上升的守恒之道。

以"平衡·爱·幸福"的经营哲学致力持续发展，将"火凤凰"精神视为企业前行的引航之力，构成雅莹 30 多年创业的重要支点。

The Fire Phoenix is a powerful representation of rebirth and renewal, and holds significant meaning for the company, symbolising its rise from its many adversities. It is a symbol of the spirit of camaraderie between Baorong and those who followed him in the company's founding in the early years of 1988. It is a symbol of the unyielding bond and deep love between Hwaming and Xueming, the company's second-generation entrepreneurs who successfully expanded the business into Beijing in 1991 and whose breakthrough silk products showed their belief in continuous innovation. And it is a symbol of a closely-knit community of employees and partners who stuck with each other in crisis through product design faults in 1997 and the SARS pandemic in 2003.

The ups and downs faced by companies are part of a journey of self-discovery, interwoven with challenges and opportunities. The Fire Phoenix spirit, passed from one generation to another, gave strength to the company and fuelled its culture of perseverance, driving every individual and every aspect of the Group forward.

"

火凤凰精神：
凤与凰环抱相合，象征精诚团结，
是雅莹人始终奋发向上、永不言弃的精神力量，
有着凤凰浴火、至美永恒的坚毅。

"

与社会共赢，持续发展的根基
A SUSTAINABLE SOCIETY

火凤凰精神能够持续并结晶出雅莹的不断发展，得益于雅莹坚守了自己的"心"和"根本"。这个"心"和"根本"的坚守，也包括对社会责任的承担，对环境的建设与呵护。

当年，医者仁心的张宝荣在创立服装厂时就秉承朴素的"想要做好事，先要做好人"的原则：发展企业，造福乡邻，带动地方经济发展，张华明接任后也接过这一使命。如今，雅莹不但是嘉兴最具规模实力的服装企业之一，在增加就业、贡献税收、带动地方经济发展方面发挥着重要作用，同时，也通过自己的发展，带动着中国服装产业于文化发展、自然生态、成就他人以及回馈社会方面贡献着榜样力量。

2020年，历时多年，几易设计蓝图的雅莹·时尚艺术中心落幕并逐步向社会开放，这也是雅莹在更高层面为贡献地方和中国服装行业发展的行业创举。

由雅莹的母公司华之毅投资建设的雅莹·时尚艺术中心坐落于浙江省嘉兴市，是一个囊括雅莹美述馆（含企业发展史展厅、服装史展厅）、艺术展览、秀厅、图书馆、学院等多功能区的建筑群，整个雅莹·时尚艺术中心占地37亩，建筑面积2.5万平方米，由著名建筑大师张永和担纲设计，设计融入雅莹"平衡·爱·幸福"的文化特色，极具江南特征，并通过与同济大学建筑设计研究院、浙江恒力建设有限公司、上海艾舍尔设计等百余家单位，历经2170多个日夜，近1000名工人的通力合作，让创意设计完美实现。

时尚艺术中心还创下了多项国内首次应用的技术工艺：在结构上实现了华东区首个混凝土预应力大悬挑（跨度15.4米），

The Group's mission of *Dignified Hearts, Steadfast in Elegance* underlie its commitment to social and environmental responsibility, which serves as an important driving force in the apparel industry — promoting Chinese culture, sustainable fashion, talent development and giving back to society. Hwaming also carried forward his father's love for his hometown and developed EP YAYING Fashion Group into one of the most successful apparel companies supporting Jiaxing's growth, while strengthening its status in the Yangtze Delta region.

In 2020, after more than five years of design and construction, the Group officially opened its *EP YAYING Fashion & Arts Centre,* affirming its commitment to the arts and culture, Chinese heritage and contemporary Chinese fashion. The Centre occupies a total area of 37 acres and a floor area of 25,000 square metres, being comprised of the Group's headquarters and Academy, a museum housing the Group's 30 years of heritage and fashion, EP YAYING flagship store, a library, a Chinese tea house, and many fashion and arts spaces. Designed by famous local architect Zhang Yonghe, and put together by more than 100 outstanding design and construction partners including Tongji Architectural Design (Group), Zhejiang Holdland Construction and A3 Vision, the Centre's bold design concept draws inspiration from the Group's philosophy of *Balance, Love and Happiness*, harmoniously integrating the concept of a Jiangnan courtyard with the functional requirements of a modern fashion brand, whilst emphasising environmental sustainability and efficiency in its design and construction.

The construction of the Centre featured many technological firsts in the country, composing of a one-of-a-kind pitched roof using a concrete prestressed large cantilever spanning 15.4 metres and using BRB anti-buckling support; a large number of high-performance bamboo fibre composite (bamboo steel) louvres were used for the walls between the columns and the ceilings for its environmental factor, and formed a double enclosure together with the screen

上图：
雅莹·时尚艺术中心建筑设计效果图

ABOVE
3D models of EP YAYING Fashion &
Arts Centre

并运用 BRB 防屈曲支撑；整体设计与用料注重生态环保，大量采用高科技的竹纤维复合材料（竹钢／磁化竹），因竹的可再生性更高，从而提高了建筑的整体环保性；双层幕墙围护体系，对建筑整体起到冬暖夏凉的温度调节作用；另外在园区内实行立体水循环系统，通过收集雨水，灌溉植被，清洁净化池塘等。经过了无数次的现场打样以及各种现场测试，真正秉承了一丝不苟、精益求精的工匠精神。

投入使用后的艺术中心将成为雅莹二次创业的里程碑和对外交流、交往的殿堂。艺术中心的建设，是雅莹对过去 30 年在服装行业经营发展的总结，是以文化积淀和创新技术，为未来的设计师提供灵感的重要来源；也是雅莹立足嘉兴、辐射长三角，搭建更大时尚艺术文化资源共享平台的初衷，更是雅莹立志发展成为中国民族时尚品牌的重要基石。

华之毅是雅莹的母公司、大股东，除了资本层面控股雅莹，这些年还陆续发展了集合食、商、艺范畴的项目，包含红庵里生态农场、餐饮、雅莹·时尚艺术中心等，以此协助雅莹的时装发展。

与"雅莹"两个字代表着张华明的品牌追求一样，"华之毅"三个字也蕴藏着他的事业理想、精神和梦想。其中的"华"代表"华裳、华美、中华"；"毅"代表"坚毅、坚持、专注"。 华之毅与时尚联系起来，透露的是张华明期望以坚毅、坚持、专注，打造中国时尚品牌，传扬中国时尚、文化、社会责任的目标。而通过对这些更多元领域的涉猎，雅莹高举文化、艺术、生态时尚的旗帜也愈加鲜明。

wall to help in regulating the temperature of the building; a three-dimensional water circulation system was implemented in its small sunken garden in the middle of the courtyard.

The resulting experience echoed Hwaming's strong affection for traditional Chinese culture and his long-standing belief in a beautiful workspace that encourages creative ideation and cultural exchange. The Centre is both a result of the Group's strategic transformation into a global Chinese fashion group and a representation of yet another milestone in its journey to showcase Chinese fashion brands on the world stage.

The design and construction of EP YAYING Fashion & Arts Centre was also supported by EP YAYING Fashion Group's parent company and major shareholder, HWA Fashion Group. HWA Fashion Group adds range to EP YAYING Fashion Group's focus on sustainable development with investments in food and beverage, retail, arts and community development, such as its Hong'anli farm, restaurants and the building of the fashion and arts centre.

Hwaming never wavered from his singular focus on creating beauty for society, and ensuring that the beautiful business of Chinese fashion provide diverse points of contact and engagement with the community. Improving quality of life and contributing to the construction of beautiful villages in rural regions have also been regarded as important parts of the work of giving back to the society and improving public welfare. The company worked together with the province of Zhejiang when the latter launched the "5 Water Initiatives" plan aimed at improving the water quality in the province's villages and set up a local agricultural company to work more closely with the villagers in Hong'anli to improve local farming methods. Today, the Group's Hong'anli Village offers a year-long collection of fruits and vegetables, and is a representative of ecological farming, combining traditional farming techniques and modern agriculture technology, that promotes the concept of

左图 / 472 – 475 页：
2020 年，中国嘉兴，
雅莹 · 时尚艺术中心

LEFT / 472-475
EP YAYING Fashion & Arts Centre,
Jiaxing, China, 2020

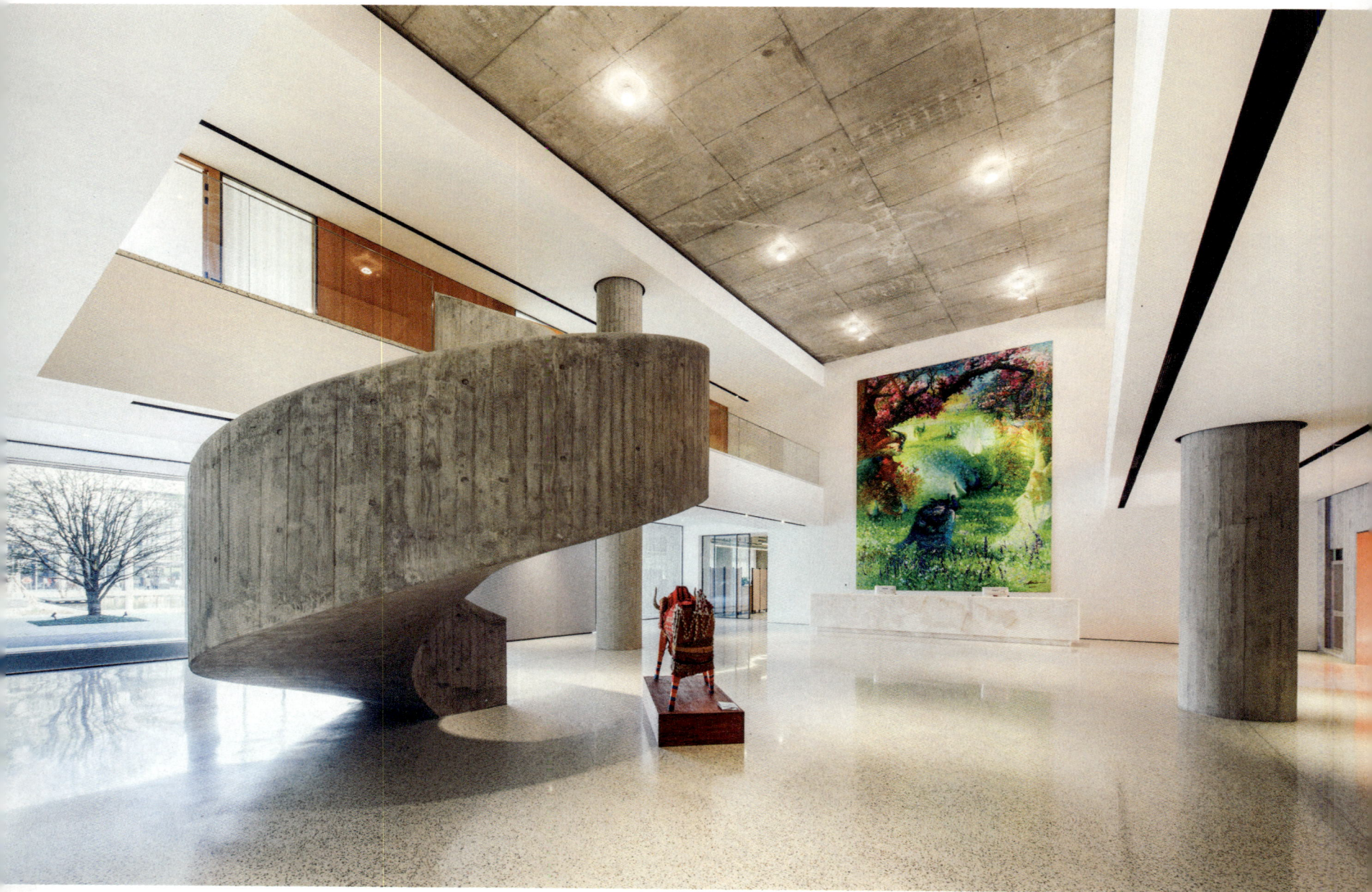

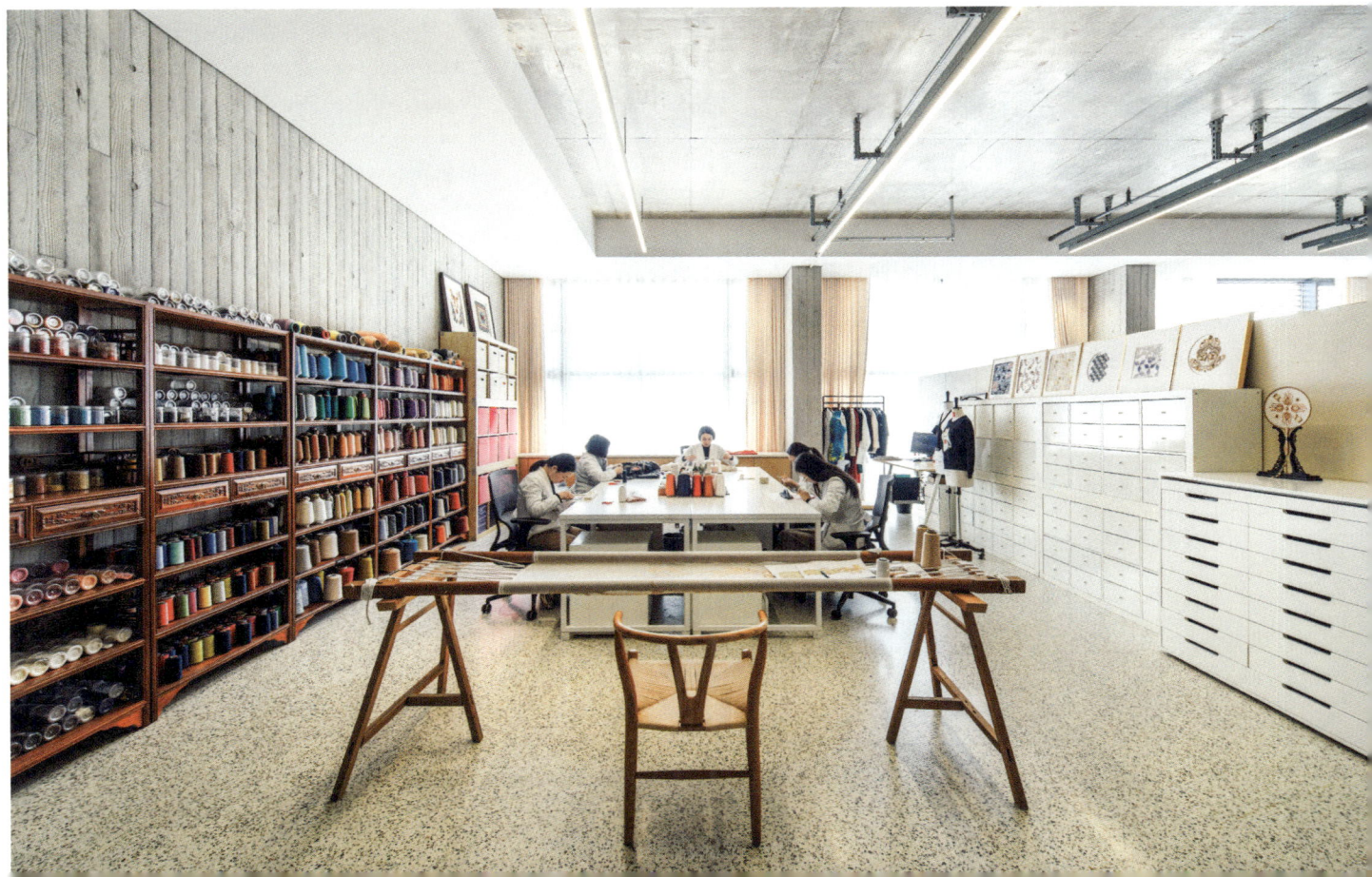

多年以来，公司在发展自身的同时，不断关注产业的生态发展，以可持续发展的全产业链建设作为重点。另外，还将教育和美丽乡村建设作为回馈社会的重要工作，积极参与公益和慈善事业，并将党建与公益慈善结合，持续投入。

浙江省开展"五水共治"期间，张华明积极捐款支持。之后，雅莹成立红庵里农业公司，导入现代经营管理理念，与乡村结队，致力生态发展。在红庵里生态农场，所有的果蔬都遵循应时应季的自然原则，"红农"们日出而作，日落而息，从种子到果实，严格推行"五拒"原则——拒绝化肥、拒绝农药、拒绝除草剂、拒绝激素、拒绝转基因，守护健康。

为探索生态保护与经济发展并举的道路，雅莹还长期通过推动天然材料的应用，在产业链建设上向生态资源良好的西部地区倾斜，比如建立材料基地，推动当地的产业发展，助力低收入地区人民增收致富，助力美丽中国梦。

2018年5月，雅莹供应链带队调研了云南陆良真丝生产基地，对真丝面料的制作发展提出建议及后续协作发展。近十年来，我国东部的桑蚕业受天气、生态等不稳定因素的影响，养蚕的系统化、规模化和工业化发展艰难，蚕桑产业持续萎缩，并且随着全国经济转型，优质的蚕桑基地越来越少。因此"东桑西移"战略项目逐步落地到了天然优势充足的大西南区域。云南陆良和四川宁南都是中国目前桑蚕丝原料质量最好的蚕茧产区。特别是宁南县，地处四川省凉山彝族自治州

"5 NOs", refusing to use chemical fertilizers, pesticides, herbicides, hormones or genetic modification.

In order to achieve a win-win outcome of environmental protection and economic development, the Group never stopped improving its supply chain, including expanding its value chain to the rural regions of Western China and collaborating with local partners to protect the sources of raw materials, developing local industries and improving the quality of life for locals.

In the past ten years, sericulture in Eastern China has suffered and declined due to a number of natural and socioeconomic factors such as the weather, land conditions and lack of investment in quality mulberry plantations. Therefore, more mulberry plantations have gradually shifted to the southwestern region with natural advantages in its ecological environment. In May 2018, the Group's supply chain led a team to one of the production sites of mulberry silk in Luliang County, Yunnan Province, aiming to deepen the Group's study of the raw material, seek long term collaboration right from its source and improve the sustainability of the entire end-to-end process of its value chain.

Both Yunnan's Luliang County and Sichuan's Ningnan County are currently two of the top areas producing the highest quality mulberry raw silk in China. Ningnan County in the southeastern part of Liangshan Yi Autonomous Prefecture, Sichuan Province, is of particular importance. Located on the edge of the Hengduan Mountains and along the Jinsha River, the county has an average elevation of 1,000 metres, annual sunshine of 2,257.7 hours, annual average temperature of 19.3°C and a frost-free period of 321 days per year. Its dry winter, humid summer and sunny days with rainy

东南部、横断山区边缘、金沙江沿岸，全县平均海拔1000米；全年日照时数 2257.7 小时，年平均气温 19.3℃，无霜期 321 天；冬干夏湿、昼晴夜雨、干湿分明、光热充沛——这样的地理环境与气候条件，非常有利于桑叶的光合作用。加之选用上佳的蚕卵品种，给予蚕宝宝充足的喂养，配合一流的缫丝技术，使得此地出产质高品优的蚕茧和生丝。

雅莹团队探访优质的蚕桑基地及生产者，不仅是以追本溯源的方式获得上佳的原材料，也是一次产业链寻根，希望打通整个桑蚕丝产业链，从源头把关，运用绿色可持续发展的方式生产、严选桑蚕丝面料。这是雅莹在而立之年对自我的要求与尝试，也是雅莹对社会、对消费者、对行业从业人员力图去承担的责任。

同年，嘉兴市与四川省阿坝藏族羌族自治州组成了扶贫对接城市。雅莹从自身特点出发，联合产业链上下游的合作伙伴一起，以中国特有纤维牦牛毛绒综合开发利用为突破口来推进产业协作发展。

世界上约 95% 的牦牛生活在我国青藏高原及其毗邻地区，牦牛毛绒几乎是中国藏区独有的高档服装原材料。当下的牦牛绒和牦牛毛产业，拥有着巨大的开发潜力和发展空间。追本溯源之旅，让我们实地直观地看到牦牛的生活环境和牦牛绒产业的源头。

nights, means that the dry, wet, sunny and hot periods are clearly distinct, providing ideal conditions for the growth of mulberry plantations. Coupled with some of the best silkworm breeding techniques and processes, as well as first-class silk reeling skills, the county produces the highest quality cocoons and raw silk.

The team visited these regions and people, not only to obtain the best raw materials, but also trace the roots of the industry. This enabled them to forge a more tightly connected silk industry — from responsible sourcing, to green and sustainable production, to high-quality materials for customers. This is its responsibility towards society, the industry and customers.

As part of its poverty alleviation strategy, China has strengthened collaboration and paired assistance between the eastern and western regions to encourage the flow of talent, capital and technology to poor areas so that they can complement each other and narrow the gaps between them. In 2018, Jiaxing was tasked with helping the Aba Tibetan and Qiang Autonomous Prefectures in Sichuan Province, and EP YAYING Fashion Group joined the team. It leveraged its strengths to connect partners across its supply chain to develop the yak wool industry, a natural and valuable fibre unique to China that remained underdeveloped at the time.

About 95% of the world's yaks live in China's Qinghai-Tibet Plateau and its adjacent areas, and its fur is one of the key raw materials for high-quality clothing. The yaks have a habit of grazing on grass but not pulling out its roots, hence avoiding the desertification of the grassland and being "a natural protector of the environment". Developing a yak wool industry that is unique to China not only

左页：
2020 年 6 月，位于四川省阿坝藏族
羌族自治州若尔盖县，牧民放牧的
情景

牦牛"食草不吃草根"的习性，天然地避免草场沙化，助益环境的可持续发展。开发这种中国珍稀原材的举动，不仅实现了对西部自然生态的保护，又得以扶持当地经济建设，同步带动中国纺织、材料等方面发展，真正深度地推进国内大循环，促成雅莹与合作伙伴一起共建"生态时尚"，对中国可持续时尚创新行动有着深远影响。

为更大范围推动生态文明建设，张华明还提出"生态时尚"的理念——在整个产业链，从设计理念、面辅料选择、相关领域材料和能源的使用入手，甚至带动顾客强化环保意识，提高环境质量，与供应商、合作商一起创建共同的"生态时尚"，追求"敬天地·爱人"之美。具体举措包括：使用环保、天然有机、安全的材料；对边角料和其他剩余材料环保化、艺术化综合利用；积极利用清洁能源，进行光伏发电改造；评估雅莹自身以及供应商的环保状况，形成一致的环境理念并设立监督机制等。

早在 2006 年，雅莹就与嘉兴慈善总会合作，每年资助考取大学的优秀特困生学费，并提供寒暑假勤工俭学机会。2008 年起，雅莹又与嘉兴市教育基金会合作，开展资教、资学活动，并在此后设立了"雅莹奖教金"和"雅莹奖学金"。雅莹每年都会举办一系列的发布会和品牌推广活动，张华明也将救助贫困及残疾儿童、弘扬传统艺术与文化等公益慈善导入其中。比如，推出"聋艺天使"公益项目，帮助有艺术梦想的聋哑人士；与华谊在上海国际电影节进行公益合作，还吸引成龙、张震、宋承宪、杨幂等国内外明星人物参与其中等。

推动公益慈善事业，张华明也是强调用"心"做，而且做好、做长。"我们有时候会要求把某个公益项目当成一项任务去完成，但张总说，把它作为任务是错的，要凭良知去做，要长期地做，真正去改善。"雅莹党委书记仇瑛说。

张华明始终认为，企业最大的社会贡献还是成功创业经营，推动经济社会迈向更美好。比如，贡献税收、创造工作岗位等。近年来，雅莹每年都以数亿的纳税贡献于国家财政，如 2017 年纳税 5.6 亿元，2018 年纳税 5.3 亿元，并直接为 5000 多人提供就业，为社会不断做出积极的贡献。但张华明依然强调：

protects the local ecosystem, but also contributes to the economic growth of the local area, while becoming a new and rising catalyst for the upgrade of China's textile industry. To date, EP YAYING Fashion Group remains the pioneer and strong innovator of this new and highly sought-after material.

Hwaming believed eco-fashion is an ongoing project with all of the Group's suppliers and partners — from the design stage, to production material choice, to, most importantly, uniting the efforts of its customers, so that the combined energy to improve the environment is greater than the sum of its parts. Quoting from traditional Chinese philosophy, Hwaming would always say, "Respecting nature and loving humankind is a form of beauty in itself." Some of the initiatives the Group would carry out included moving to 100% use of environmentally-friendly and natural materials; setting up a creative recycling department that turns waste fabrics and scraps into lifestyle artworks and products; ensuring clean energy use for electricity generation; and working even more closely with strategic suppliers and partners to ensure that they abide by similar responsibility standards. In his view, "The origin of our clothes lies in our land. And this very land and the skies above us, our entire ecosystem in fact, nourishes every living being. Today's fashion enterprises should be the bedrock for sustainable development, a reflection of our respect for the heavens, our earth and our people."

The Group has also been very active in philanthropy to help those in need. As early as 2006, the Group collaborated with Jiaxing Charity Federation to subsidise the school fees of academically deserving and financially needy university students and provide needy students with access to work-study opportunities. Since 2008, the Group also partnered Jiaxing Education Foundation to organise various learning activities and establish different scholarships for students to support their educational dreams. Even during EP's branding and marketing activities, Hwaming would incorporate charitable initiatives to support a range of sectors, that include the disabled children with artistic dreams.

Hwaming has never thought of charity as a one-off campaign. "We sometimes think of charity as a project or even a task that needs to be completed. But Mr. Zhang has always warned us against thinking this way. Charity must come from our conscience, from our hearts and it must be pursued long term to truly create change," said Qiu Ying on EP YAYING Fashion Group's philanthropy. In 2014 and 2015, the Group was awarded outstanding public welfare awards by the government for its efforts and contributions.

"对于社会的责任和可持续发展，我们深知雅莹还做得不够，与国际品牌相比差距还很大。"

在张华明看来，"服装的本源就来自土地，天地水源哺育了万物。今天的服装企业应该是一个平台，通过这个平台来体现对天、地、民族的尊敬和敬畏。"同时，他总结，企业这个平台，不仅是事业的平台，也是服务社会、回馈社会、创造税收的平台，更是帮助员工和合作伙伴建设心灵、助人实现梦想的平台，是一个有大爱精神的平台。

一贯秉承低调作风的张华明不以领袖或公众人物自居，也很少出现在聚光灯下，但除了经营发展好雅莹这个平台，他也投入大量时间和精力到更多平台努力服务于社会。他出任嘉兴市工商联主席，曾是第十二届全国人大代表，持续为经济社会发展建言献策，出智出力。

2014 年、2015 年，公司连续获得第四届、第五届中国公益奖荣誉。

"A company is not only a platform for business, but also a platform for serving and giving back to society. It is also a platform to help employees and partners alike to cultivate their characters and help them to realise their dreams." Hwaming always believed that the biggest social contribution of an enterprise is to help develop the economy and create a better society, by both contributing to tax revenue and creating jobs. In recent years, EP YAYING Fashion Group has contributed hundreds of millions in tax revenue to the national economy every year, with 560 million yuan in 2017 and 530 million yuan in 2018. However, Hwaming acknowledged that the Group still has too much to improve on, saying, "We have not done enough in terms of our social responsibility and sustainable development efforts. Compared to the high standards of international brands, we still lag far behind."

Hwaming, who always adhered to a low-key style, does not regard himself as a public figure and rarely appears in the spotlight. However, in addition to managing the Group, he has also invested a lot of time and energy in various sectors to serve society. Today, he serves as the chairman of Jiaxing Federation of Industry and Commerce and had served as a member of the 12th National People's Congress. Today, he continues to advise and assist the government on many economic and social policies.

"

企业是一个平台，不仅是事业的平台，
也是服务社会、回馈社会、创造税收的平台，
更是帮助员工和合作伙伴建设心灵、助人实现梦想的平台，
是一个有大爱精神的平台。

"

左页：

1. 2014 年 10 月，雅莹集团为支持年轻的新兴设计师积极开展院校合作，冠名赞助东华大学·环东华时尚周

2. 2018 年 5 月，雅莹集团结对嘉兴秀洲区残障儿童，助力提升康复中心儿童伙食计划项目，做到每天为孩子们加餐

3. 2018 年 10 月，EP 联合海尔和卡萨帝共同发起"衣梦想"旧衣回收爱心捐赠，将捐赠衣物经专业洗涤消毒后赠予潍坊蒋峪海尔希望小学

4. 2015 年 6 月，EP 推出限量版公益 T 恤，用以支持华谊 ELLE 之夜的"零钱电影院"公益项目

OPPOSITE

1. The Group collaborated with Donghua University for their fashion week, October 2014

2. The Group works with Xiuzhou District's Rehabilitation Center for Disabled Children in Jiaxing, to improve the nutrition plan for its children, May 2018

3. EP partners with Haier and Casarte to launch a clothing donation program for Haier Hope Primary School in Jiang Yu Town, Weifang, Shandong, October 2018

4. EP designed a series of limited edition T-shirts to support ELLE's charity project, June 2015

左页 / 上图：
旗下生态农场红庵里，丰富的农耕体验活动；自创业以来，雅莹集团持续助力美丽乡村建设

OPPOSITE / ABOVE

The Group continues to support the development of Hong'anli Village since its establishment, by committing to building ecologically sustainable farms

世界级的品牌，国际化的公司
WORLD-CLASS BRAND, GLOBAL COMPANY

未来的30年，是中华民族伟大复兴的30年。张华明看到了中国即将发生比过去40年更巨大、更深刻的变化，也看到了"未来的世界属于中国"的巨大机遇，并在机遇中看到了中国时尚产业将厚积薄发的壮阔前景。

"The next 30 years will witness the national rejuvenation of China." Hwaming saw potential for future changes more significant and profound than those of the past 40 years, which would come with unparalleled opportunities for China's role in the future of the world. In these unprecedented opportunities also lie the prospect for China's fashion boom.

大好的时代，大好的行业
A GREAT ERA, A GREAT INDUSTRY

"一切过往，皆为序章! 未来 30 年，大有可为! "张华明在雅莹 30 周年励志庆典大会上掷地有声。

信心不光来自雅莹过去 30 年的积累，也来自他对未来大势的笃定。"未来的 30 年，是中华民族伟大复兴的 30 年。'张华明从十九大报告的"两个一百年"奋斗目标，看到了中国即将发生比过去 40 年更巨大、更深刻的变化，也看到了"未来的世界属于中国"的巨大机遇，并在机遇中看到了中国时尚产业将厚积薄发的壮阔前景。

"习总书记在十九大报告中指出：'中国特色社会主义进入新时代，我国社会主要矛盾已经转化为人民日益增长的美好生活需要和不平衡不充分的发展之间的矛盾。'今天，时尚产业已经成为各级政府在美丽城市打造以及产业转型中的重要抓手。"张华明说。5000 年的文化底蕴造就中国消费者发自内心对美、对时尚的追求，庞大的内需群体将成为中国时尚产业蓬勃发展的源动力，最终推动中国时尚产业伴随民族的伟大复兴而真正腾飞。

最重要的是，在消费升级的趋势下，"消费者从来没有像今天这样追求品质、追求美丽。"而雅莹过去 30 年已经建立了优势，也为其赢得消费升级新机遇打下了坚实的基础。

由此，雅莹也更看重在更高层面的乃至国际舞台的发展，首先对自身的责任与担当有了更清晰具体的要求。所以雅莹在新 30 年启程之际，首次正式发布《雅莹集团 2018 社会责任报告》，全面呈现了雅莹在社会责任方面取得的进展和遇到的挑战。不仅进一步厘清了雅莹需承担的社会之责，也对与利益

"Our past is our prelude. The next 30 years will see us strive and thrive even more!" Hwaming proudly said at the Group's 30th Anniversary Gala.

The Group's confidence is built not only on thirty years of experience, but also on conviction about the future. With the "two centennial goals" put forward by the 19th National Congress of the Communist Party of China, Hwaming saw the potential for changes more significant and profound than those of the past 40 years, along with unparalleled opportunities for China's role in the future of the world. In these unprecedented opportunities also lie the prospect for China's fashion boom.

"As General Secretary Xi Jinping pointed out in his report at the 19th National Congress of the Communist Party of China, 'As socialism with Chinese characteristics has entered a new era, the principal challenge facing Chinese society has evolved. What we now face is the gap between unbalanced and inadequate development and the ever-growing expectation of the people for a better life.' Today, the fashion industry has become a key instrument for all levels of government to beautify their cities and transform their industries." Hwaming added that the 5,000 years of Chinese culture has directly or indirectly shaped the Chinese consumers' inner desires for beauty and fashion; and the enormous size of China's domestic consumer population has become the driving force of the fashion industry, and ultimately the impetus to the nation's great rejuvenation.

Most importantly, the growth of spending power among Chinese people is making bigger waves than ever, both domestically and globally. "Consumers are pursuing quality and beauty like never before," Hwaming said. The experience and competitive advantages accrued by the Group in the past 30 years have laid a solid foundation for the Group to seize the new opportunities that come with this trend. To mark the beginning of its new 30 years,

30 周年
1988-2018

EP | 雅瑩集團
EP YAYING FASHION GROUP

雅莹集团
2018社会责任报告

EP YAYING FASHION GROUP
2018 SOCIAL RESPONSIBILITY REPORT

雅莹集团股份有限公司

上图：
2019 年，首次正式发布的《雅莹集团 2018 社会责任报告》。扫描二维码阅读报告

相关方所产生的具体影响进行了认真思考与交流，尤其是雅莹在执行与解决社会问题之间，所承载的社会文化、生态影响、人文情感以及时代使命。

此外，雅莹依托上海、巴黎等国际大都市的平台和资源，在商业模式、品牌战略、产品战略、渠道零售、供应链和信息化建设，以及人才机制 7 个领域全面开启一系列的战略创新，励精图治、不断精进，缩短与国际化优秀公司的差距。

商业模式上：坚持主品牌和生活方式集合店品牌两种模式的并行发展。一方面集团在 EP 和中国雅莹双产品线的战略上，持续推进两者清晰化、差异化的深度发展；另一方面拓进大雅家集合店平台模式经营，继续将时尚、艺术的生活方式融为一体，并依托该平台，发展集团"五朵金花"——高端精致雅斓名店，个性特色 DOUBLOVE、N.Paia、LITTLE SPACE和生活方式综合大雅家。

品牌战略上：以中国文化底蕴为根基，将 EP 塑造为代表中国的民族时尚品牌，并强化旗下各子品牌的特色和独立性，将其塑造成体现各自精致生活艺术的品牌大使。

EP YAYING Fashion Group officially published its first social responsibility report in 2019 that shared its long-term commitments in culture, service, environment, people and philanthropy.

Relying on the resources and infrastructure of international cities such as Shanghai and Paris, the Group also introduced a series of strategic innovations in 7 areas: business model, brand strategy, product strategy, retailing, supply chain, information technology and human resources, all to ensure continual renewal and narrow the gap with top global companies.

"In our business model, we will maintain a two-pronged approach — grow our main EP fashion brand and our multi-brand lifestyle retailer."

"In terms of our brand strategy, we will root EP in the rich culture of China and enforce our positioning as a Chinese national fashion brand. At the same time, we will develop our family of sub-brands with unique identities, ensuring they become representatives of different styles of a better life."

"In product strategy, we still regard womenswear as our star product. But we will optimise our accessories and childrenswear. We shall continue to ensure nature, life, culture and art remain key sources of our creative inspiration and develop more attractive products for the progressively youth-oriented and globalised markets."

产品战略上：立足女装，优化配饰，强化童装，让创意源于自然和生活，让创意根植文化和艺术，为逐步年轻化、国际化的消费市场，打造更具有吸引力的产品。

渠道和零售上：持续扎根长三角一体化发展，立足中国，精耕国内市场，积极推进海外市场布局，走向国际化，实现线上线下一体化。

供应链建设上：追本溯源，推进原材料的研究和发展，深化各品类的生产专业化，打造柔性化、高质量的供应链，和西部进行产业对接，用产业扶贫来推动行业的发展。

信息化建设上：实现门店科技化，顾客体验数字化，生产仓储智能化，商品研发数据化等一系列从消费者到消费者的可视化管理。

人才和机制上：从人力资源管理到心力资源开发，以成就他人、建设自己为己任，让每一位雅莹人的心灵品质不断提升，凝心聚力，建立事业使命的共同体。

大好的时代，大好的行业，大好的发展潜力，让张华明发出"放眼新30年舍我其谁？"的激情感概，也让他在"好人，好衣，好生活"之后为雅莹立下更大的目标：成为世界级的品牌，国际化的公司。

"As to our retailing channels, we will strengthen our presence in the Yangtze Delta region, fortify our position in China and actively link up with high-quality resources from around the world, while integrating our online and offline stores."

"To reinforce our supply chain, we will continue to advocate the pursuit of traceability in our key fabrics — researching from downstream to upstream, from the final product to its source, from our supply chain to agriculture — so as to create a greener end-to-end value chain."

"As far as information technology is concerned, we aim to provide enhanced consumer-to-consumer management. This includes digitalising the customer experience, making production and storage more intelligent, and encouraging data-driven product research and development."

"In human resources and our management, we have started shifting from managing people to developing our people's hearts-and-minds, guided by the concepts of altruism and self-improvement, to foster a strong and united culture with a shared mission."

"Virtuous people, elegant clothing, beautiful lives" has been the common goal for the people at the Group since its founding. Now, this great era and great industry with great prospects have lent confidence to Hwaming's passionate words: "The next 30 years is ours to make, together." This has led him to set higher goals for EP — to become a world-class brand and a global company.

以中国优雅，屹立世界
STAND TALL IN THE WORLD BY VIRTUE OF CHINESE ELEGANCE

民族在世界舞台的复兴必定带动民族文化在世界舞台的复兴，文化的复兴需要很多载体，服装就是其中之一。

"把中国的文化、艺术以及哲学思想，以时尚行业为载体传递给世界。"以中国文化彰显中国品牌的魅力，带给世界消费者差异化的价值与贡献，这也是张华明推动雅莹走向世界的核心。

根植于中国传统文化，但要国际化、现代化演绎，是雅莹在设计上对传统与现代、中国与世界的平衡之道。其设计师们致力于把传统元素，通过设计语言转换成当代的、富有时尚感的元素体现在每件产品之上，进而让整个品牌的基调时尚并引领潮流，中国韵味十足又具备国际风范。这也是"世界的EP，中国的雅莹"的内涵体现。

在此之下，雅莹一方面聚焦东方皇家美学，挖掘中国传统文化，倾力将高端产品线中国雅莹，打造得更中国、更东方、更高贵优雅；另一方面也以中国文化去演绎国际流行趋势，让EP更世界、更大众、更亲民。

"EP的市场面更大，更大众化，从设计的角度来讲必须更快速，把国际流行趋势和本国的东西结合，与自己消费群体的取向结合，去做中国化的转化。所以EP总体来说需要更国际化，把国际的流行趋势加入到自己的设计中来。"时任EP设计总监田玲介绍说。

无论是文化复兴还是走向世界，首先都需要"知己"——深刻理解自己的历史和文化；其次也需要"知彼"——学习更多元

The rejuvenation of the Chinese nation is bound to lead to more people from all over the world to integrate Chinese cultures into their lives. One key aspect is in their clothing.

"Our creations embody rich Chinese culture, Chinese art and Chinese philosophy, and we hope to expand and even deepen its experience across the world through the fashion industry." Hwaming hopes the world will come to know EP from its unique and rich expressions of Chinese culture.

EP striked a balance between tradition and modernity as well as between China and the world by rooting its designs in traditional Chinese culture, while keeping them international and contemporary. Every product of EP aimed to breathe new life into traditional elements with contemporary and modern elements, so that each piece was uniquely Chinese yet trendsetting for the world. Hence, its positioning: World EP, China YAYING.

Since 2016, China YAYING's focus on the culture, aesthetics and craftsmanship of the costumes of the royal family have nurtured its quintessential and luxurious modern Chinese style. At the same time, World EP, being the "big sister" product line, continued to bridge the two worlds of Chinese and Western culture with its own contemporary and effortlessly chic style.

"World EP targets a bigger market and reaches many different types of women. This requires us to launch new designs faster and to incorporate global trends with local characteristics, as well as the personalised preferences of our key customers. For this reason, EP, needs to be more open and stay on top of global fashion trends," the design director of EP, Tian Ling said.

From 2015, Hwaming had already thought of creating a bigger and more open platform for the Group and the brand, to not only increase interaction with the global fashion world, but to bring the

的艺术文化。张华明推动建立雅莹·时尚艺术中心首先就是为了"知己知彼"：不仅展现雅莹一路走来的诗篇和经典，也体现整个中国服装的发展轨迹，不仅展现中国，也展现世界。

雅莹·时尚艺术中心的美述馆，正是以人、衣、环境作为表达之要素，构建一个人与物交互对话的空间，借助每一段时期的珍贵影像、历史实物及代表服饰，记录、保存、展示 30 多年的发展成果。这里容纳了实业振兴的精粹，呈现了创业、革新的感人故事，讲述了一个鲜活多彩的中国雅莹。

这是雅莹的故事，也是中国时尚的流变。同时，它展示了中国和世界服饰的发展与趋势，经典与精彩，为雅莹，也为更多服装业同行了解自己、学习他人提供支持，为服装根植于文化的现代演绎催生灵感与创意。

雅莹近年来还持续与国际大公司和世界级设计师深入合作，不断引入国际创意，邀请设计人才加入公司，对标国际大牌展开新一轮国际化和世界级提升。

世界级的国际化创意设计人才选择加入雅莹，不但因为看好雅莹具备成为国际化品牌的基础，更因为张华明对他们的坚定承诺：按照国际大品牌的目标去投入，并给这些国际人才亲手缔造一个东方大牌的机会舞台。

张华明认为，未来 30 年，将是全世界追捧中国元素、中国服装、中国品牌的 30 年。"伟大的时代给了我们大好的机会，作为一家时尚集团，雅莹将积极努力、贡献力量，把最好的中国之美带到全世界，不辜负这个时代的重托。"

world right to its home. And what better way to do so than to build a fashion and arts centre. The EP YAYING Fashion & Arts Centre is not just about EP YAYING, and not just about China, but about the world — its people, its fashion and its culture. At the Centre, fashion and culture, aesthetics and technology, arts and craftsmanship, all fuse in a fascinating way. Its exhibition areas and workspace explore fashion's enduring influence on society across generations, especially the Group's dedicated musuem in its fashion and arts centre, that features hundreds of objects, documents, photos, film materials and fashion collections stored for many years in the brand's archive.

The Centre is a modern, living, breathing space that puts interaction at the core of every facet so that not only the people within the Group, but also people from all sectors and cultures can gather more frequently and comfortably to exchange ideas and experiences, stay relevant, learn from one another and be inspired to create. In recent years, the Group has continued its collaborations with international designers and global companies. Their vast experience and vision also add to the Group's high-level innovations and upgrades. Hwaming believes this is a two-way relationship: "We invest in them because we are confident we are giving them a world-class Chinese brand to showcase."

Hwaming added that in the next 30 years, the world would begin to seek Chinese fashion and Chinese brands. "Great times have given us great opportunities. As a fashion group, each and every one of us should work hard and contribute to bringing the best of Chinese beauty to the world and living up to the great responsibility of this era."

"Throughout the world, there is not a single top-level brand which does not operate globally. The same holds true for Chinese fashion brands." Hwaming asserts that EP YAYING will catch peoples' eyes in all aspects from all corners of the world in the coming future. "Just

上图：
2019 年 3 月 14 日，EP 吉隆坡 KLCC
店盛大开业，马来西亚当地 40 余家知
名媒体、身穿 EP 及中国雅莹时装的众
多明星、名媛和时尚达人齐聚现场

ABOVE
Opening ceremony of EP store in Suria
KLCC shopping mall, Kuala Lumpur,
Malaysia, 14 March 2019

"放眼全球，没有哪个国际一线品牌不是全球化发展的，中国的时尚品牌未来也一样。"张华明坚信，就像雅莹在过去 30 年成为国内各大城市、各大商场的一道道靓丽风景一样，未来 10 年、20 年、30 年，雅莹也会在世界各大城市的商业场合，成为一道道靓丽风景！

雄心壮志之下，雅莹将在持续深耕中国市场的基础上，努力发展亚洲时尚版图，积极推进国际市场发展进程，描绘中国品牌在国际时尚版图的宏伟蓝图，向全球华人及消费者敬献中国的当代时尚。

as the past 30 years have seen us grow EP into beautiful beacons in major shopping malls in major cities across China, the next 10, 20 and even 30 years, will see us do the same in major cities around the world."

World EP, China YAYING. This is the Group's vision today, offering Chinese contemporary fashion right from the heart of China and drawing a magnificent blueprint to put Chinese brands on the map of world fashion, for Chinese people and consumers all over the world.

"

雅莹将持续深耕中国市场，
发展亚洲时尚版图，
积极推进国际市场发展进程，
描绘中国品牌在国际时尚版图的宏伟蓝图，
向全球华人及消费者
敬献中国的当代时尚。

"

看见未来，永续时尚
SEEING THE FUTURE, CARRYING FASHION FORWARD

三十而立的雅莹，立于时尚潮头不断回望来时的路，绵延五千年的华夏文明为她提供了迎面未来，踏浪而行，生生不息的文化土壤。

EP YAYING, now in its early thirties, looks back to its past from the cutting-edge of fashion, and finds that fashion and growth rooted in the cultural strengths of the nation will continue to flourish with booming vitality in the new era.

任重道远, 激发时尚中国心

ENVISIONING CHINESE PURSUITS, ENDOWING CHINESE BEAUTY

2019 年, 正逢新中国成立 70 周年, 70 周年国庆盛典展现出的恢宏气势和大国风范, 让国人发自内心地骄傲与自豪, 看到文化自信的力量和民族复兴的希望。新中国 70 年的文化发展中, 时尚的变迁不仅直观反映了国家的政治、经济、文化和生活水平, 更见证了中国女性对美的永恒追求和国家软实力的不断强大。

从着眼东方的世界浪潮来看, 如今中国的时尚界更热衷于向内探索。新中国经历了"建国创业"和"改革开放", 如今走在"实现伟大复兴"的壮阔道路上 ; 中国时尚产业经历破旧立新, 从追随国际潮流, 到在世界舞台上独立发声 ; 雅莹从 1988 年的嘉兴洛东红政服装厂萌芽, 紧跟国家发展步伐, 时至今日已成为初具规模的现代时尚集团。中国时尚所代表的中国力量, 正在传统文化的赋能下, 日益强大, 蒸蒸日上。

在 2018 年雅莹 30 周年的庆典大秀上, 首次以"世界的 EP, 中国的雅莹"品牌双产品线对外发布, 充分表达品牌对中国文化的尊崇。当时国际新闻报刊 GLOBAL TIMES (《环球时报》) 以 CULTURE & FASHION 为题整版报道大秀, 寓意着海内外人士对中国时尚所蕴藏的深厚文化, 表现出深厚兴趣与关注。

2019 年 11 月, 在新中国 70 周年华诞, 中国雅莹 2020 年高定发布会在毗邻故宫的文华东方酒店成功举办。这是品牌首次独立办秀展示中国雅莹产品线, 不仅从美学到匠心工艺, 深度展现了中国文化魅力, 同时也向外界传递了雅莹发力定制化业务的信息, 收获了业界和顾客的认可与喜爱, 确立了品

The year 2019 saw China celebrate its 70th birthday. People took pride in the magnificence and majesty of the ceremonies because it signified a new era of cultural confidence and national rejuvenation. In the 70 years' cultural history of the People's Republic of China, the evolution of fashion not only mirrored the developmental changes in the politics, economy and culture of the country, but also witnessed the remarkable growth of the country's soft power and Chinese women's steadfast pursuit of beauty.

The People's Republic of China experienced a founding period of construction before embarking on an era of economic reform and opening up, and welcoming a new era of national rejuvenation today. Along with this development, the Chinese fashion industry rose from being a follower of global trends to becoming a trendsetter on the world's stage. During this time, EP followed in the footsteps of the nation and grew from a town's garment processing factory into a budding modern fashion group today. Chinese fashion has become an embodiment of China's influence, whose growth which is rooted in the cultural strengths of the nation will continue to flourish with booming vitality in the new era.

To celebrate the company's 30th anniversary in 2018, the Group also premiered its dual product line-up — World EP, China YAYING — at the China International Fashion Week with a distinct cultural approach, and received unanimous acclaim from the media and public. GLOBAL TIMES, a leading international news agency, published a full cover page report of the show, conveying the keen interest and attention paid by people at home and abroad to Chinese fashion, and its inherent profound culture.

On the first day of November the following year, China YAYING launched its 2020 haute couture collection in Beijing. On the rooftop of the Mandarin Oriental Hotel in the capital's Wangfujing area, set against the backdrop of the city centre and overlooking

LIFE

Plenty of homegrown fashion houses look to China's rich history for design inspiration, but a few, like Yaying, are finding ways to continue a cultural legacy.

Fanning fashion's cultural flame

By XU HAOYU
xuhaoyu@chinadaily.com.cn

On the first day of November, Chinese womenswear fashion brand Yaying launched its 2020 haute couture collection in Beijing.

Set against the backdrop of the city center, on the rooftop of the Mandarin Oriental Hotel in the capital's Wangfujing area and overlooking the Forbidden City exactly one month after National Day celebrations, the show was a testament to the grandeur of the brand's vision and the global relevance of its exquisite Chinese culturally-inspired fashion.

This season, Chen Xi, the creative director of the brand, draws inspiration from the Forbidden City as not just a tribute to the finest Chinese aesthetics and craftsmanship, but also as a celebration of the Forbidden City's 600th anniversary next year, with a focus on the private collection of Chinese fans housed within the palace's museum.

With the theme of "Chinese Fans (*Hua Shan*)", the show and the collection seeks to renew tradition and reshape it for the present.

Fans are the epitome of Chinese culture with a long heritage, and are an excellent witness of time with many symbolic meanings in Chinese culture and tradition, especially among the former royal family as well as within art and culture — as seen in Xu Yang's classical painting *Emperor Qianlong's Southern Inspection Tour*.

From his research on the subject, Chen provides examples of particular fans that stood out among the paintings of both Emperors Kangxi and Qianlong, such as the big round ceremonial fan used for shade when they departed Beijing (once referred to as *Jingshi*); the folding fan that was popular among scholars of the time; and the small round fan the courtesans carried while on excursions to Yanyulou (a landmark building in Jiaxing, Zhejiang province, that Qianlong visited eight times).

"These fans are beautiful, elegant and graceful, and we extracted elements from their outline or pattern and arranged them into a new form to produce a modern visual effect," Chen says.

The selection of the fans was not just a whim, either, according to Chen, who notes that he always wanted to design a collection inspired by the shapes, colors and designs of the artifacts, particularly citing their exquisite craftsmanship and a sense of duty to preserve that.

"We have a responsibility to preserve and develop these skills and traditions," he says, adding: "Yaying has always humbly dedicated ourselves to making good clothes, and we aim to continue passing on and renewing the concept and craftsmanship of Eastern royal aesthetics to our consumers."

In contrast to the impression of traditional Chinese aesthetics in the past, the brand employs light and bright colors as its main tone.

Drawing from the color palette of the Forbidden City, Chinese jade is complemented by the relaxing color of living coral, indigo blue and futuristic silver, a reference to the concept of time and to balancing modernity and Eastern aesthetics to tell a beautiful story of timeless Chinese elegance.

Oriental aesthetics

These oriental aesthetics have long been a subject and the highlight of the designs for many local brands.

Ne Tiger, as the fashion brand that has opened China Fashion Week for 19 consecutive years, brought its collection based on the travels to the west of Ming Dynasty (1368-1644) explorer, Zheng He. The collection displays the exotic charm and culture of countries along the ancient Silk Road, as well as offering modified Chinese traditional costumes, such as *qipao* dresses made with breezy fabric more suited to the hot weather in regions of Southeast Asia.

Meanwhile, Guyan, a brand from Shenzhen, Guangdong province, draws inspiration from plum blossoms, orchid, bamboo and chrysanthemum — four kinds of flowers that are widely used to eulogize noble virtues in China since ancient times. They are embroidered on modern-styled Tang suits and *qipao* while, once again, fans also play a role.

It brings us neatly back to Yaying's latest collection, which portrays Chinese aesthetics and traditional elements in a more abstract form, with motifs taken from Chinese fans appearing throughout the collection.

The geometric tailoring and structures allude to the ceremonial fan used by the royal family that symbolizes their majesty. Dragon, river and cliff patterns add a cultural and poetic elegance, as well representing the independent and self-confident feminine spirit today.

The three-dimensional structure of the folding fan is recreated using a number of precise, hand-pleating techniques, underlining a women's strength underneath her gentle temperament.

The circular court fan is a symbol of refinement and is piece of exquisite art in itself, and is adapted to include iconic Chinese elements such as the *ruyi* cloud, which symbolizes blessings and harmony, and peony flowers that exude energy and elegance.

Exquisite Craftsmanship

With its suits, the brand is looking to accentuate a woman's strength with simple, yet strong, silhouettes, especially that of its three-dimensional curved shoulder

blade design — masterfully made-to-measure and adorned with beaded patterns, once again alluding to *ruyi* clouds, rivers and cliffs. Each pattern is the product of 351 hours of hand-sewn craftsmanship.

Inspired by a Yuan Dynasty (1271-1368) blue glazed plum vase with a white dragon pattern, the brand's artisans spent over 104 hours recreating the pattern with embroidery entirely by hand, emblazoned with iridescent sequins of 15 different colors and sizes. There is even a stunning black gown covered with 1,032 small, hand-pleated fans that required 203 hours of skill and precision to create.

Just a month after the celebration of the 70th anniversary of the founding of the People's Republic of China, Chinese fashion continues to be buoyed by the increasing popularity and attention given to Chinese culture.

And as Zhang Huaming, chairman of EP Yaying Fashion Group, will attest, culture is the soul of a country and its people. It is also something that the brand has remained committed to protecting in its role as both inheritor and innovator.

Founded in Jiaxing city, Zhejiang province, in 1988, Yaying's fortunes have been almost directly tied to the country's reform and opening-up policy of the past 40 years. The fashion group has grown from a small garment factory into a modern business with more than 5,000 employees and an enviable portfolio of luxury fashion brands and retailers, including EP Yaying, Doublelove, N. Paia, Da Ya Jia, GraceLand, and Little Space.

Rooted in arts and culture

To keep pace with the market, in 2016, the group reinvented its main brand EP Yaying, launching a dual-brand development strategy, "The World's EP, China's Yaying".

EP, which focuses on producing ready-to-wear clothing, offers contemporary fashion styles that harmoniously integrate Oriental and Western aesthetics and artistic elements, reflecting both global fashion and contemporary Chinese lifestyle.

Yaying, meanwhile, is the company's haute couture line, tracing its Chinese roots and focusing on the deep exploration of China's traditional culture, aesthetics, fashion and craftsmanship — integrating contemporary aesthetic tastes into its designs for the modern women, but with a clear, exquisite Chinese cultural identity.

Yaying's 2017 Spring/Summer collection saw the debut of its imperial robe-themed series, which met with rave reviews, firmly establishing its "Eastern royal aesthetics" credentials. The brand continues to draw inspiration from Chinese culture, not only for creative inspiration but also in the hope that it can help connect the past with modern fashion, injecting new energy into the industry and enabling a new generation of fashion-conscious women to rediscover that culture.

"In the age when fashion designer is no longer an unusual occupation, Chinese fashion seems to be a concept that is getting confusing and contradictory. However, if I have to define Chinese fashion, Yaying is one of the first brands that

jumps into my mind," says Xu Fengli, a Chinese fashion blogger.

To celebrate the company's 30th anniversary last year, EP Yaying premiered its dual-brand 2019 Spring/Summer collection at the closing ceremony of the China International Fashion Week Spring/Summer 2019. Themed "Convergence & Creation", the two collections displayed the balance between mankind and nature, art and culture, tradition and the contemporary. Both the show and collection received unanimous acclaim from the media and the public alike.

In order to preserve and develop traditional handicrafts, the group set up a workshop in 2012 that gathers many professionals who have been practicing traditional craftsmanship for decades, such as embroidery, beading, weaving and hand painting. It also grooms their successors; young and new talent to inherit and innovate these traditional crafts.

"What makes excellent Chinese haute couture? Only those who know how to both inherit and innovate can witness and create the future," Xu concludes.

It is an area in which another homegrown fashion brand is looking to excel. Like the other Chinese fashion houses mentioned, Jefen — established by Xie Feng — used the recent China Fashion week to present a clothing line that introduced elements of traditional culture in a modern context. In this case, rather than motifs and symbolism, the brand took a rather more practical approach, combining fabrics and materials, such as silk gauze and linen, with western-styled tailoring.

The future direction

Today, EP Yaying is represented in more than 210 cities with over 500 stores across China and Malaysia, including Beijing, Shanghai, Guangzhou, Shenzhen, Macao and Kuala Lumpur.

In 2020, the brand will enter the American and Australian markets, and continue to share its contemporary, elegant fashion aesthetic with the world.

Looking forward to the next 30 years, Zhang notes: "We will continue to cultivate a higher degree of cultural self-confidence, rooted in Eastern culture with a global perspective.

"The Chinese believe in harmony and the world is home to all. We will continue to create more value for our customers and contribute to the great rejuvenation of Chinese culture in the global fashion industry."

Chinese womenswear brand Yaying aims to accentuate a woman's strength with simple, yet strong, silhouettes.

右图：
2019 年 11 月 30 日，*CHINA DAILY*（《中国日报》）整版深度报道中国雅莹 2020 年高定系列发布秀

RIGHT

CHINA DAILY full-page story on China YAYING Haute Couture 2020 fashion show, 30 November 2019

左页 / 上图：
中国雅莹 2020 年高级定制发布秀，历经 7 个月准备，手工耗时 3643 小时，研发出 40 多种工艺小样

OPPOSITE / ABOVE
China YAYING team preparing for the Haute Couture 2020 fashion show. Over 7 months of work was put into the show's collection, including more than 3643 hours and 40 different kinds of artisanal creations

牌在行业中的独特形象。雅莹再度收获了来自 *CHINA DAILY*（《中国日报》）的高度褒奖："大量的本土品牌都会从中国传统文化中探寻灵感，但甚少有像雅莹这样进行文化传承与创新的民族时尚品牌……"

值此，中国雅莹进一步坚定了立足"东方皇家美学"的风格定位，通过云裳、物华、牡丹三种视角深化了中国雅莹产品的文化基因。以极致的手工技艺、剪裁、材质，糅合东方美学与当代艺术，构建起衔接过去与未来、东方与西方的美学对话空间。

这次大秀的灵感源自创意团队在故宫所见的藏品扇。作为文明古国的中国，器物文化源远流长，"扇"即中华文化的缩影，是极好的时代见证者，在中国传统文化中拥有多种含义。在张华明看来，以"华扇"为题，取其风雅古意，又志在突破边界，焕新传统，塑造当下之美。

近年来，雅莹还在全国精选门店开展了高级定制专场活动，品牌派驻了资深的设计师、制版师到现场，悉心服务每位 VIP 客户。活动现场还有手工坊的艺匠展示中国传统刺绣的各个环节，让顾客更近距离、更生动地接触到高级定制以及中国经典技艺之美。

而 2018 年开启的马来西亚吉隆坡双子塔店则是雅莹首家东南亚海外店，通过海外店，国外的媒体、明星、知名商界人士和消费者都对品牌表现出了浓厚的兴趣，也让品牌看到了海

the Forbidden City exactly one month after the National Day celebrations, the show was a testament to the grandeur of the brand's vision and the global relevance of its exquisite Chinese-inspired fashion. From aesthetics to craftwork, the show received recognition and adoration from the industry and customers. Among the praise and honour given the show was an article from *CHINA DAILY* (Global Edition), which reported, "Plenty of homegrown fashion houses look to China's rich history for design inspiration, but a few, like YAYING, are finding ways to continue a cultural legacy."

For the collection, the creative team drew inspiration from the Forbidden City, not just as a tribute to the finest Chinese aesthetics and craftsmanship, but also as a celebration of the Forbidden City's 600th anniversary, with a focus on the private collection of Chinese fans housed within the palace's museum. The Chinese fans are the epitome of Chinese culture with a long heritage, and serve as a witness of time, with many symbolic meanings in Chinese culture and tradition. Hwaming said, "I love the theme of 'Chinese Fans', not just because they are classical icons, but because of their implications went beyond that. The choice was about shaping modern beauty by innovating traditions."

In recent years, EP has also brought China YAYING's haute couture collections closer to its customers, through invite-only events held at selected stores across the country. Designers and tailors interact with and take measurements for customers, while skilled artisans perform exquisite Chinese traditional embroidery in stores, so that more customers can not only learn, but experience first-hand, the beauty of Chinese craftsmanship.

At the brand's first Southeast Asia store, opened in 2018 in Kuala Lumpur's Suria KLCC, local media, stars, renowned businesspeople

上图 / 508 - 513 页：
2019 年 11 月，在新中国 70 周年国庆之际，中国雅莹 2020 年高定发布会"华扇"于毗邻故宫的文华东方酒店举办

ABOVE / 508-513
China YAYING Haute Couture 2020
fashion show, Mandarin Oriental
Wangfujing, Beijing, November 2019

507

右页：
1995 年以来，雅莹历次更新换代的
品牌标识

OPPOSITE
EP YAYING iconic brand labels
since 1995

516 - 519 页：
2020 年春夏 EP YAYING 广告大片

516-519
EP YAYING Spring-Summer 2020
ad campaign

外市场最直接的认可和中国文化自信的姿态。未来，雅莹还将陆续进驻美国市场，以更加年轻、开放、包容的姿态同全球消费者分享来自中国的美学与文化。

在中国雅莹传承古老东方文明，明确皇家美学风格持续深化发展的同时，品牌的另一大产品线 EP 也完成了年轻化的创意转型。2019 年，在艺术总监的创新引导下，EP 融合外部创意力量，与更多全球优质的艺术、文化资源展开合作，通过学习国际化的优秀创意模式，成功确立 EP 全新的产品风格——更年轻、更有趣、无龄感。

随即，品牌还对外输出全新的视觉形象，品牌标志被重新设计定义为"EP YAYING"，以更开放、更当代的简约风格，与逐步年轻化的消费市场高度契合。

如今，迈入 21 世纪第三个 10 年，也是雅莹新 30 年当中的第一个 10 年，国内外无论是消费的理念、消费的环境还是消费的方式都发生了巨大的变化。新时代是大有可为的时代，雅莹看到文化自信、民族复兴带来的巨大机遇。

作为中国传统文化的传承者和创新者，这种与生俱来的使命感与责任感赋予了雅莹更为专注的探索精神，也是雅莹提升中国时尚文化与品牌国际形象，最深厚和可持续的动力源。

"九层之台，起于累土；千里之行，始于足下。"接下来的发展，要实现从"好"到"非常好"的成长，在张华明看来，依然要坚持以人为本，以心为本。"雅莹始终心怀真诚，带领全体雅莹人、合作伙伴在高质量发展的道路上，持续加大在各业务领域的文化艺术创意投入以及科技创新研发，激发时尚的中国心，让雅莹在时尚行业成为文化自信、文化复兴和民族复兴的实践者。"

as well as consumers showed avid interest in the brand, reflecting on the reach and beauty of Chinese culture. In the coming years, the Group plans to expand its Southeast Asia market and to gradually enter the American market, sharing gorgeous Chinese aesthetics and culture with even more customers around the world.

In 2019, under a new artistic director and a new creative approach, EP launched a rebrand targeted at an increasingly younger consumer market. Introducing new creative styles that were more youthful, fun and "ageless", the brand also unveiled a new name and logo — EP YAYING — which adopted a sleek, minimal and contemporary look, that still paid homage to its roots by incorporating the brand's first trademark, "yaying".

Storytelling through fashion for over 30 years is just a small step for the pioneers of New China's fashion. Today, the Group is embarking on its next 30 years and regardless of the ever-changing waves of changes of consumer beliefs, or shopping methods, or spending patterns, the Group is excited for China's further-blooming beauty. Hwaming believed that culture is the soul of a country and its people. It is also something the Group has remained committed to protecting, in its role as both inheritor and innovator of Chinese culture. The evolution of Chinese culture over time has never stopped enriching Chinese aesthetics and fashion, and this is the driving force behind the Group's sustainable development.

According to a traditional Chinese saying: "A nine-storied tower rises from a heap of earth; a thousand-mile journey begins with the first step." Hwaming emphasised, "We must always maintain a sincere heart and work together with our partners, to ensure high-quality growth. And we will continue to increase our investments in our arts and culture, design and creative, innovation and technology. At the heart of Chinese fashion is a beautiful China that is confident, prospering and thriving, and we at EP YAYING Fashion Group are all the key agents of change!"

1995 年

1998 年

2009 年

2001 年

2016 年

2006 年

2020 年

EP YAYING

EP YAYING

至美中国，与爱同行
FASHION WITH LOVE, CHINA IN LOVE

那些热爱的、被热爱的时尚艺术，归根结底都来源于文化，来源于生活。时尚，不仅有关服装，更关乎我们的日常生活，涉及视觉艺术、文化创造、建筑设计、数字制作和科技创新。时尚包罗万象，而时尚的创造者亦与时俱进。今天的全球时尚版图上，中国时尚已成为发展最快、最具创新性的力量。而背后不仅凝聚着消费者的支持与从业者的付出，更是源自女性顾客们不断地追求美、涵养美，实现内外兼修美的要求。

成全对美好生活的追求，这个朴素纯粹的愿望来自1979年的雅莹创始人，张宝荣先生。他秉持"好人，好衣，好生活"的理念，从一名丝厂厂医转型投身实业。就像"二战"之后，百废待兴，象征柔和亲善的女性审美和价值取向，从男性审美的霸道强势中得到释放。彼时，国人的审美也在改革开放后悄然发生了转变。春雷一声醒天地，拥抱世界的多彩时尚终结了"蓝灰绿"的无彩时代，中国时尚的春天"破土而出"。无论生逢何时，人对于美好生活的希望是坚不可摧的，无论身处何境，有不可动摇的热爱，才有不可摧毁的希望。

Fashion, art and love, can all ultimately be found in life and our diverse cultures. Fashion was never just about garments. It is about our everyday lives — encompassing visual arts, cultural creations, architectural designs, digital productions and technological innovations. Fashion is all-inclusive and creators of fashion need to keep pace with the times. The Chinese fashion industry is becoming the fastest growing and most innovative driver of the global fashion market. Underpinning this growth is not only the support of consumers and contributions of the people working in the industry, but generation after generation of women who pursue beauty, both inside and outside.

Zhang Baorong founded the company with the simple wish that he could accommodate people's pursuits of a better life. Adhering to his faith of "virtuous people, elegant clothing, beautiful lives," he responded to the nation's call and transitioned from a working as doctor in the silk factory to running a garment business. It was a time when economic reform and opening-up enabled people to embrace the colours of fashion, putting an end to the dull age of "blue, grey and green." The spring of Chinese fashion arrived. Women's storied beauty began to revel in the myriad seasonal fashion creations that empowered Chinese women with greater self-confidence and freedom in expression. It is this spirit and inner beauty of modern young Chinese women that has shaped EP YAYING's creative output and direction since its establishment. In the never-ending pursuit of freedom and fashion, EP YAYING is there to light up every woman's dreams.

如今，雅莹感恩来自社会方方面面的信任与支持，也承担起了更多的责任，努力为社会、为人民的安全与福祉贡献绵薄之力。

企业和社会是一对紧密的"命运共同体"，在信息高度发达的当今社会，时装企业竞争不断加剧，线下传统零售与互联网结合的商业模式正在中国上演得如火如荼。雅莹更热衷于自查自省，不停地寻找差距："在不远的未来，雅莹将加大与院校的合作，积蓄更多的时尚年轻力量；带动全产业链绿色生产以及协作；扶持供应链合作方面构建起更为强大、健全的支持体系，雅莹愿与所有志同道合的伙伴共同成长，与责任同行，与爱同行。"

这里是世界的 EP，更是中国的雅莹。

雅莹清晰且坚定自己的初心和使命：此心庄严，优雅而立，以至美永恒的内心力量，不懈追求精致、优雅的美好生活。展望未来，张华明相信："雅莹集团将坚定文化自信，根植传统文化，以全球视角，秉承'世界大同，天下一家'的世界观，让文化在中国时尚行业光荣复兴，向世界展示来自中国的东方之美。"

"中国的雅莹，终将优雅于世界。"

Today, EP YAYING is grateful to people from all sectors of society for their trust and support, and remains committed to its responsibility as a Chinese national fashion brand that strives for the well-being of the Chinese people.

Since the company's founding, inspired by the late founder Zhang Baorong's love for his hometown, the Group has understood that businesses and communities have a shared destiny. The Group is committed to social entrepreneurship and its social responsibility strategy is implemented across culture and art, sustainable fashion, investments in people and giving back to the community. "As a long-standing Chinese fashion brand and facing a new golden age of growth, we know we are united and connected by love — a love to tell more beautiful stories of China, a love for the betterment of society and a love for passing on the values of Balance, Love and Happiness in Life that Chinese beauty continues to inspire," Hwaming said.

"We are EP of the World. We are YAYING of China." EP YAYING has never been more resolute in its aspiration and mission. Dignified Hearts, Steadfast in Elegance: EP YAYING believes in the power of a person's inner beauty and remains steadfast in its pursuit of the exquisite and elegant art of living. "We will continue to cultivate a higher degree of cultural self-confidence, rooted in traditional Chinese culture with a global perspective. The Chinese believe in harmony and the world is home to all. We will continue to create more value for our customers and will contribute to the great rejuvenation of Chinese culture in the global fashion industry," Hwaming concluded.

"When all is said and done, EP YAYING's elegance is about Chinese beauty that crosses boundaries and culture."

世界的EP，中国的雅莹

世界的EP，中国的雅莹

"

中国的雅莹，终将优雅于世界。

"

1994

1996

雅莹丝绸系列
嘉兴市永利来时装行限公司
电话：(0573) 3544088

yaying 雅莹

yaying fashion
AUTUMN & WINTER
Charpter
秋冬篇

1997 aw

雅莹丝绸系列
嘉兴市永利来时装有限公司
电话：(0573) 3544088

1999

2000 SS

2000 aw

2001 SS

2001 aw

2002 SS

2002 aw

2003 SS

2003 aw

2004 ss

2004 aw

2005 SS

2005 aw

2006 ss

2006 aw

2007 SS

2007 aw

2008 ss

2008 aw

2009 ss

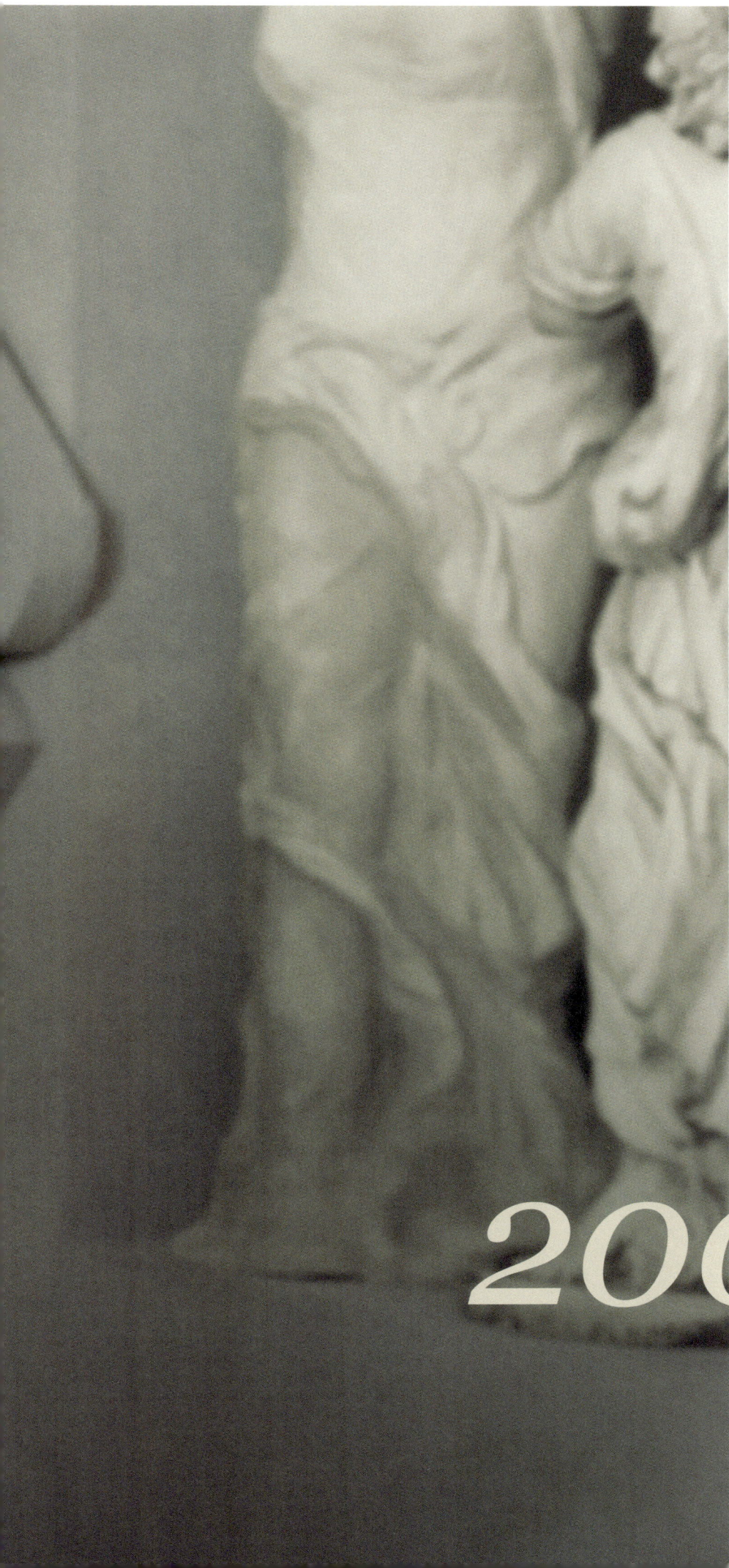

2009 aw

2010 ss

2010 aw

2011 SS

2011 aw

2012 SS

2012 aw

2013 SS

2013 aw

2014 SS

2014 aw

2015 SS

2015 aw

2016 ss

2016 ss

2016 aw

2016 aw

2017 SS

2017 SS

2017 aw

世界的EP，中国的雅莹

2017 aw

世界的EP，中国的雅莹

EP

2018 ss

611

2018 ss

世界的ＥＰ，中国的雅莹

2018 aw

世界的ＥＰ，中国的雅莹

世界的EP，中国的雅莹

2018 aw

世界的EP，中国的雅莹

2019 ss

2019 ss

2019 aw

2019 aw

2020 ss

527

2020 SS

2020 *aw*

2020 aw

30

雅莹集团
EP YAYING FASHION GROUP

雅莹对生活美学的探求，始于1979年，企业创始人张宝荣先生为造福乡里，投身实业，组建了嘉兴洛东第一家乡办集体服装企业——洛东服装厂，从一名丝厂厂医转变为服装厂厂长；1988年，他带领34名工匠，以18台家用缝纫机承包经营洛东红政服装厂，开始制作好衣服，诚心为消费者增添更多美丽。

1990年代，张华明、戴雪明以丝绸服装成功开拓北京市场，受到当地女性的青睐，并在1995年创立"雅莹"品牌，确立了品牌初心——用好的材料做好的衣服，为女性顾客带去美。之后，张华明从父亲手中接过美的使命，雅莹用臻美材质裁剪出东方女性特有的优雅四季，让中国女性开始以精致自信的姿态，释放自由的灵动。

步入千禧，雅莹从最初的手作工坊发展成拥有全球近5000位人才的时尚家族，包含时尚主品牌 EP YAYING 雅莹、多品类生活方式集合店 DAYA+ 大雅家及新兴自主时尚品牌在内的近800家精品门店，遍及中国北京、上海、澳门，马来西亚吉隆坡等210多个城市。多年的专注、创新与用心，使雅莹成功成为集设计研发、生产制造、终端零售为一体的现代时尚集团，并以文化艺术和科技创新作为企业发展的两翼，成为代表中国民族的时尚品牌之一。

对于未来，雅莹集团有着更大的憧憬：立足中国，走向世界，以可持续的长远愿景和稳健的步伐，将 EP YAYING 带到更多地方。"此心庄严，优雅而立"，雅莹将不仅是一件产品、一个品牌，她更代表着一种生活方式，一种艺术精神，一种中国文化。始于江南嘉兴的我们，将不断深化雅莹独特的"平衡·爱·幸福"经营哲学，积极扎根长三角一体化发展，持续深耕中国市场，链接全球优质资源平台。"世界的 EP，中国的雅莹"，我们期待与全球华人及消费者共同分享来自中国的当代优雅时尚美学。

历程 MILESTONES

1979 年

雅莹集团创始人张宝荣先生，在改革开放春风的吹拂下，为带领乡亲们脱贫致富，满怀热情投身服装行业，组建嘉兴洛东第一家乡办集体服装企业——洛东服装厂。从一名厂医转变为服装厂厂长，工厂主营生产男士中山装和女士上衣。1980年4月，他向国家工商行政管理总局申请注册了洛东乡第一个服装商标——洛丰。

Against the backdrop of China's economic reform and opening-up, Zhang Baorong is elected to join in the setup of Luodong Garment Factory, the first local collectively-owned township garment enterprise in the village of Luodong in Jiaxing, and is promoted from the factory's in-house physician to director of the factory in 1981. Luodong Garment Factory's primary business includes the processing and manufacturing of men's tunic suits and women's tops. In April 1980, Baorong successfully registers the village's first trademark — Luofeng.

1988 年

张宝荣在极其艰苦的条件下承包经营洛东红政服装厂。最初的红政服装厂以340平方米的厂房，34名员工，18台家用缝纫机生产男士衬衫和丝绸加工起家。在1980年代末，物资短缺、开放不久的中国，张宝荣率先从集团所有制走向了自主创业经营的先锋路径。

在洛东红政服装厂的厂前，生长着一株百年牡丹，"国色天香"的不凡花容，成为现雅莹集团董事长张华明最重要的记忆片段之一，为其留下了关于"美"的最初记忆。这份记忆后来成为雅莹的品牌基因，在多年来的服饰创作中不断被演绎。

Baorong breaks new ground by deciding to strike out on his own and undertakes the management of Luodong Hongzheng Garment Factory. Starting with 18 household sewing machines and 34 craftspeople in a 340-square-metre workspace, the factory focuses on the production of men's shirts and the processing of silk garments.

Century-old Peonies, dubbed Hong'anli Peonies, grows beside Baorong's factory and leaves a deep mark of beauty and prosperity on the villagers. The Peony, also China's national flower, becomes an important footnote in EP YAYING's signature elegant style many years later.

1991 年

张华明和未来的夫人戴雪明女士携手以享有丝绸之府美誉的杭嘉湖优质真丝服装成功打开北京市场。张华明先生以踏实肯干的性子和敢为人先的态度受到了各个商场经理人的好评，为家中的工厂挣得无限商机和利润。江南高品质的真丝深受当地女性的垂青，并迅速风靡，他们从中积累了服装销售和现代商品经营技巧。

Hwaming ventures north to break into the attractive capital city Beijing together with his future wife, Dai Xueming. They successfully launch renowned silk products from Hangzhou, Jiaxing and Huzhou for the local market, and their chic silk clothing becomes a huge hit among local women who now have more high-quality, comfortable and beautiful fashion choices. Hwaming accumulates valuable retail and merchandising experience.

1994 年

有了资本积累的张宝荣先生实施跨越式的发展宏愿——将当时已经更名为洛东制衣的红政服装厂改为时装有限公司，申请成立嘉兴市永利来时装有限责任公司。自此，工厂正式升级为一个初具现代企业管理模式的民营企业，拥有自行设计、自主生产和自主销售的产供销体系，设计生产男式保暖衬衫和女式真丝服装。短短数载，从投身服装行业到承包办厂，再到成立时装有限公司，张宝荣厂长实现了企业早期发展的关键三步曲。

Baorong upgrades the factory and creates Jiaxing Yonglilai Fashion Co., Ltd, creating a fashion brand with its own end-to-end value-chain, producing men's detachable shirts and women's silk shirts. In a short span of ten or more years, Baorong has grown from trying his hand at setting up a garment factory to becoming a private owner and then to owning a fashion company, his three-part entrepreneurial journey lays a strong foundation in the company's continual transformation towards a modern fashion enterprise.

1995 年

张宝荣电函远在北京开拓市场的张华明回家接班。张华明在北京商标局注册"雅莹"商标，取意"高雅、晶莹、自然、高品质"，并以此确立品牌初心——用好的材料做好的衣服，为女性顾客带去美。

Hwaming registers the "yaying" trademark that symbolises elegance, purity, nature and perfection, representing their original aspiration of "using high-quality materials to make clothing and bring about beauty to women."

1996年

张华明正式接任公司总经理，开始企业转型升级，立志打造高品质的女装品牌。同年，"雅莹"品牌真丝女装在北京、天津、太原、南京、上海等地一炮打响，被市场广泛认可。

In 1996, Zhang Hwaming officially takes over the company as general manager and fully launches the company's womenswear development strategy. With new creations and innovations, yaying's silk collection rises rapidly in popularity, especially across big cities such as Beijing, Shanghai, Tianjin, Taiyuan and Nanjing.

1997年

公司租用嘉兴戴梦得大酒店9楼，设立商业运营中心，并于当年10月18日，正式成立嘉兴雅莹时装有限公司。

同年，公司以重价购入高级面料尝试生产羊绒大衣，拓展秋冬市场，由于缺乏制作经验，产品大批量失误，损失惨重。得贵人相助，公司迅速总结教训，研发改进版型与策略，成功生产出了阿尔巴卡大衣。后来，阿尔巴卡大衣成为这一时期的经典之作。

The company moves its management and operations to one of the most high-end commercial buildings in the heart of Jiaxing. The company changes its name to "Jiaxing Yaying Fashion Co., Ltd."

In the same year, the brand works to debut yaying's first winter collection, but due to a lack of experience in pattern making, the overcoats fail and the company suffers heavy losses. The company secures much-needed capital, resources and skills, selects the popular Peruvian Alpaca wool for the brand's new winter coat launch and recovers to become one of the top brands selling Alpaca coats.

1999年

公司度过金融危机及产品研发失败的重创，改进创新的新款真丝女装及阿尔巴卡大衣销售火爆，针织面料也开始广泛运用于产品中。"雅莹"女装逐步从单季产品向四季延伸。同年，全国首家专卖店——嘉兴专卖店正式开业。

By the turn of the 21st century, yaying's product mix includes silk in the summer, overcoats in the winter, and sweaters in the spring and autumn, successfully extending its product line from a single season to all four seasons. In the same year, yaying opens its first specialty store in Jiaxing.

2001年

1月18日，公司总部由戴梦得大酒店搬迁至嘉兴市华云路。自此，一个集产销研于一体的时尚女装企业初具雏形。雅莹正式推出英文品牌名称"Elegant Prosper"。

The company moves into its new headquarters to bring its design, manufacturing and retail functions together to improve synergies, signifying a new milestone for the modern fashion enterprise. yaying changes its name to "Elegant Prosper".

2003年

非典来袭，服装行业市场环境低迷，雅莹坚持工厂不减人、不降工资。张华明还组织百天内部培训，通过学习悟道明白雅莹的产品由6部分组成，开始了品牌各领域的转型与升级。

SARS strikes and seriously affects retail businesses. The company does not cut workers or wages, and instead organises a 100-day team training, concluding its learnings with a customer-centric business strategy that lays out 6 critical elements of an exceptional product, which becomes a catalyst for the company's transformation.

2004年

8月，雅莹与意大利 Miroglio S.p.A 公司合作，全面引入国际化运营理念，成为国内首家与意大利合资的女装企业。

The company formally signs a joint venture agreement with Italian Fashion Group Miroglio S.p.A — China's first Sino-Italian joint venture for womenswear — marking a new stage of international development for the company.

2005年

雅莹首次参加中国国际时装周举办的大型时装发布会，并连续多年进行专场时装发布。同年，首家购物中心店广州正佳广场店开业，标志着渠道多元化策略的开启。

Elegant Prosper holds its first fashion show at the China International Fashion Week. Riding on the success of its inaugural fashion show, Elegant Prosper continues to debut its collections at the Fashion Week from 2006 to 2008. The brand opens its first shopping mall store in Guangzhou Grandview Mall.

EP YAYING Fashion Group is committed to the beauty of life. The Group's origins can be traced back to the city of Jiaxing in Zhejiang Province, during the country's period of economic reform and opening-up in 1979, when late founder Zhang Baorong pioneered the establishment of the first local collectively-owned township garment enterprise in the village of Luodong — Luodong Garment Factory. In 1988, he undertook the management of Luodong Hongzheng Garment Factory with 34 craftspeople and 18 household sewing machines, and began making fine clothes so that people could have more beautiful choices in life.

In the 1990s, his son, Zhang Hwaming, and Dai Xueming successfully expanded into Beijing with their high-quality silk clothing, which became very popular among the local women, and Hwaming registered the brand's original trademark "yaying" that embodied their original aspiration of "using high-quality materials to make good clothing and bring beauty to women." He took over the business from his father and officially launched a full line-up of four seasons of exquisite womenswear collections, empowering Chinese women with evermore self-confidence and freedom in expression.

Entering a new millennium, the growth of EP YAYING from a small factory into a modern fashion enterprise covering the entire fashion value chain, with nearly 5000 employees across nearly 800 stores in 210 cities that include Beijing, Shanghai, Macau and Kuala Lumpur, is a story of the Group's growing creative energy and inventive craftsmanship. The Group's visionary management and innovative spirit also ensure that its family of brands that include its main fashion brand EP YAYING, multi-brand retailer DAYA+ and self-owned young fashion brands, continue to remain key ambassadors of Chinese fashion.

Committed to its mission "Dignified Hearts, Steadfast in Elegance", EP YAYING is more than just a product or brand, it also represents a sustainable way of life, an artistic spirit and a type of elegant Chinese culture shaped by its signature business philosophy, "Balance, Love and Happiness". "World EP, China YAYING" is rooted in China with a global vision, and a double wing strategy that focuses on both culture and technology for sustainable development. The Group and its brands continue to write more stories right from the heart of Zhejiang Province, strengthen its presence in the Yangtze River Delta region, fortify its position in China and actively link up with high-quality resources from around the world. Looking forward, the Group is proud and excited to share with consumers from around the world contemporary fashion and exquisite culture from China.

2015 年

雅莹时尚艺术中心奠基启动，集团致力于在文化与艺术产业多方投入，通过艺术交流、文化传承等多方面努力，推动时尚文化事业长远发展。设立循环创意部，通过回收生产过程中的零料、废料，进行再创造，回馈予自然。

同年，雅莹成为米兰世博会中国馆全球合作伙伴，为中国国家馆设计并定制馆服。

The Group builds "EP YAYING Fashion & Arts Centre", committing to the development of the arts and culture, traditional Chinese cultural heritage and contemporary Chinese fashion. The Group also sets up a "Creative reDesign" department with the aim of creatively repurposing leftover fabrics into new lifestyle artworks and products.

EP becomes the Global Partner to Expo Milano in Italy, designing and creating the uniforms for the China Pavilion.

2016 年

雅莹开始连续 5 届成为世界互联网大会志愿者服装的独家设计、制造和赞助企业，向世界展示来自中国的东方之美，以时尚连接世界。

旗下新概念集合店品牌大雅家正式创立，品牌以衣为本，精选好物，将"衣食住知"融于一体，满足消费者从时尚产品到生活方式的全方位消费体验。

The Group designs the uniforms for the World Internet Conference, showcasing to the world chic Chinese fashion through crossover partnerships.

The Group launches DA YA JIA, a new-concept multi-brand lifestyle retailer, with a specialised product selection covering everything from food & beverages to home essentials and travel solutions, aiming to offer customers a holistic and beautiful way of life.

2017 年

秉持美丽中国儿童的愿景，旗下雅莹童装 EP KIDS 品牌及 LITTLE SPACE 小雅童装名品集合店品牌创立。

Hoping to bring style and fashion to China's beautiful children, the Group's childrenswear team creates EP KIDS and a multi-brand retailer of childrenswear fashion labels, LITTLE SPACE.

2018 年

10 月 18 日，雅莹集团 30 周年励志庆典在乌镇盛大举行，确立了"此心庄严，优雅而立"的新使命和"志向为本、顾客为本、产品为本、文化为本"的责任战略。

雅莹首家东南亚海外店马来西亚吉隆坡 KLCC 店启幕。

On the 18th of October, EP YAYING Fashion Group celebrates its 30th Anniversary at Wuzhen, Jiaxing. The Group affirms its mission of "Dignified Hearts, Steadfast in Elegance" through unwavering dedication to its aspirations, customers, products and culture.

EP opens its first Southeast Asia store in Kuala Lumpur, the capital city of Malaysia.

2019 年

雅莹新 30 年开局之年，首次正式发布《雅莹集团 2018 社会责任报告》，呈现雅莹作为中国民族时尚品牌，在文化、服务、环境、人文和公益五大方面，矢志不渝践行的社会之责。

集团主品牌以"EP YAYING"的全新形象优雅转型，确立全新产品风格：更年轻，更有趣，无龄感。

EP YAYING Fashion Group officially publishes its first social responsibility report that shares its long-term commitments in culture, service, environment, people and philanthropy.

EP revitalises its brand with a new brand name and visual identity in "EP YAYING", and new product styles that are more youthful, fun and "ageless".

2007 年

公司将工业化与信息化提升到新的战略高度，时尚园现代生产物流中心正式启用。

公司携手美国翰威特树立人力资源战略，建立国内领先的人才开发体系，打造最佳雇主品牌。

The company launches a new dedicated production and logistics centre called "Fashion Park", as it continues to improve its production and operational competencies.

The company collaborates with Aon Hewitt, a leading global provider of human capital and management consulting services, to upgrade its talent management and bolster its employer branding.

2009 年

雅莹新品牌标志"EP"的启用，开启品牌新世纪的优雅升级。

旗下年轻高端时尚品牌 DOUBLOVE（贝爱）创立。

同年，雅莹首次通过"国家高新技术企业"认定，并连续三次通过国家高新技术企业复评；雅莹高度重视两化融合工作，2013 年被认定为首批"国家级两化深度融合示范企业"，2018 年获评"国家两化融合管理体系贯标企业"。

Elegant Prosper refreshes its brand image to reflect more modern times, shortening its name to "EP".

The company launches a new brand in DOUBLOVE, to bring new styles to younger women.

The company is awarded the title of "National High-tech Enterprise" — the first in China's apparel industry; and continues to be recognised at the national level for its innovations and management.

2011 年

雅莹对女性如何成就美好事业、家庭与生活，提出"平衡·爱·幸福"的品牌价值主张，并逐步深化成为集团发展的经营哲学，令品牌别具魅力。

EP launches its new value proposition "Balance, Love and Happiness" to support modern women who have to balance the increasing number of roles in her life — her career, her family and her personal life. The brand's value proposition eventually becomes the Group's business philosophy, synonymous with the concept of Chinese beauty today.

2012 年

雅莹手工坊成立，专注对中国传统工匠技艺的传承与创新。公司逐步展开了中华优秀传统文化学习。2013 年，雅莹提出了"雅莹·美丽中国梦"的概念，并在产品研发、品牌建设、人才建设中积极融合，将环境、艺术、文化建设上升到集团战略层面，致力于建设代表中国的民族时尚品牌。

公司成立人文关怀中心，通过党工妇团联合，搭建了一个服务员工、服务企业发展的平台。人文关怀成为企业的凝聚力之源，也是注重"以人为本"的落脚点之一。

EP establishes an artisanal workshop focused on passing on and innovating traditional craftsmanship. The company begins to deepen its studies into fine traditional Chinese culture, in 2013, the Group proposes a shared vision of "EP, Our Beautiful Chinese Dream" — making the development of the cultural roots of the Group the top priority in its new phase of development, and making it a strategic priority to infuse elements of the environment, arts and culture into the company's ethos, especially in its creative design, branding and team management, as it aims to strengthen EP's positioning as a national fashion brand.

The Group jointly establishes a "Employee Well-Being Centre" together with the organisation's Party Committee, Labour Union, Youth League and Women's Union.

2013 年

雅莹第六代店铺，首家"雅莹之家"北京华贸旗舰店开业。

同年，旗下高端零售集合店品牌 GraceLand（雅斓名店）启幕，致力构建生活艺术的集合领地，给热爱生活的顾客身心愉悦的购物体验。旗下当代设计师品牌 N.Paia（恩派雅）创立，设计以简约、针织情怀为主张，大胆坚韧、时尚廓形为显著风格。

EP upgrades its Beijing Huamao flagship store to its sixth generation store concept, also known as "EP Mansion".

The Group opens multi-brand luxury retailer, GraceLand, paying great attention to selecting beautiful products and conjuring up artistic lifestyle inspirations for customers. The Group creates N.Paia, based on the concept of minimalism and a love of knitwear, combining functionality with bold shapes and distinctive silhouettes.

人物索引
INDEX, PEOPLE OF
EP YAYING FASHION GROUP

张宝荣 P13

1979 年，改革开放春风的吹拂下，张宝荣先生满怀投身实业、造福乡里的热情，组建嘉兴洛东第一家乡办集体服装企业——洛东服装厂。在 1980 年代末期，物资短缺、刚刚起步改革的中国，张宝荣又率先开辟了从集体所有制走向自主创业经营的先锋路径。1988 年，他在极其艰苦的条件下承包经营洛东红政服装厂，仅以 340 平方米的厂房，34 名员工，18 台家用缝纫机生产男士衬衫和丝绸加工起家。张宝荣一生敬业勤恳，务过农，当过会计，且是中国第一代走在田埂上的赤脚医生。作为被时代选中的先行者，张宝荣在他初创企业的年代筚路蓝缕，逐步实现了跨越式的发展，从承包经营红政服装厂到洛东制衣厂，再到成立永利来时装有限公司，他实现了企业早期发展的关键三步曲。将原先的村办企业承包经营发展升级为一个初具现代企业管理模式的民营企业，拥有了自行设计、自主生产和自主销售的初建产供销体系，为雅莹品牌的诞生与发展奠定了良好的根基。

Zhang Baorong

Zhang Baorong both worked on the farm and as an accountant at a production brigade before he joined the rural healthcare team and became part of China's first generation of "barefoot doctors". Against the backdrop of China's economic reform and opening-up in 1979, he was elected to join in the setup of Luodong Garment Factory, the first local collectively-owned township garment enterprise. In 1988, Baorong decided to strike out on his own and undertook the management of Luodong Hongzheng Garment Factory. Starting with 18 household sewing machines and 34 craftspeople in a 340-square-metre workspace, the factory focused on the production of men's shirts and the processing of silk garments. In 1994, Baorong upgraded the factory and formed Jiaxing Yonglilai Fashion Co., Ltd., creating a fashion company with its own design, manufacturing and retail. Baorong was a trailblazer who took the courageous step forward in a new era, driven by his passion to improve the quality of life in his hometown. He remained an enthusiastic learner in a new industry and his three-part entrepreneurial journey laid a strong foundation for the company's continual transformation towards a modern enterprise.

张华明 P64

1990 年，张华明跟随父亲张宝荣先生开始学习办厂与经营。并于 1990 年代早期与未来的夫人戴雪明携手以杭嘉湖优质真丝服装进京立业，因产品深得当地女性青睐，成功打开北京市场。他积累了服装销售和现代商品经营技能，并于 1995 年注册"雅莹"商标，确立初心"用好的材料做好的衣服，为女性顾客带去美"。1996 年，张华明正式接任公司总经理一职，开启了雅莹时尚女装品牌的发展历程。

创业 30 多年，张华明带领全体雅莹人，在各个时期不断革新雅莹发展之路，在商业模式、零售服务、商品经营、品牌发展、供应链建设、人力资源和信息化等各方面赋予企业前瞻的战略布局，全方位建设时尚产业价值链，推动雅莹的集团化发展，使得雅莹成长为拥有近 5000 名员工，零售网络覆盖近 800 家优质门店，210 多个城市，初具规模的国际化现代时尚集团。

如今，雅莹集团拥有时尚品牌 EP YAYING 雅莹、时尚生活方式集合店品牌 DAYA+ 大雅家，及其他自主时尚品牌，并以"此心庄严，优雅而立"为使命，秉承百折不挠的火凤凰精神，坚守美丽初心、真诚和专注创新之心，矢志不渝地践行企业社会责任，坚持可持续发展，致力于共创代表中国的民族时尚品牌，与全球华人及消费者共享来自中国的当代优雅时尚美学。

Zhang Hwaming

Zhang Hwaming officially joined his father's factory in 1990. In the early 1990s, he and his future wife, Dai Xueming, sought for new opportunities in Beijing and broke new ground in the Chinese fashion market with their high-quality silk products from Hangzhou, Jiaxing and Huzhou. Their casual chic silk garments became a huge hit among local women, who had more comfortable and beautiful fashion choices. Hwaming accumulated valuable retail and merchandising experience, and registered the brand's original trademark "yaying" that symbolised their original aspiration of "using high-quality materials to make good clothing and bring beauty to women." In 1996, Hwaming officially took over the company as general manager and fully launched the company's womenswear development strategy.

For over 30 years, Hwaming has led the company on a transformational journey into a global fashion group, through the implementation of modern business models and investing in the entire fashion chain, including retail, service, product management, branding, supply chain, human resources and information technology. Today, EP YAYING Fashion Group is comprised of nearly 5,000 employees across nearly 800 stores in 210 cities, and its family of brands include its main fashion brand EP YAYING, multi-brand retailer DAYA+ and other self-owned fashion brands.

Hwaming launched the Group's new mission "Dignified Hearts, Steadfast in Elegance" at the Group's 30th Anniversary in 2018, passing down the brand's founding aspiration and "Fire Phoenix" spirit, whilst pledging focus and sincerity in its innovations and long-term sustainable commitments. Looking forward, he is excited to share EP YAYING with more consumers from around the world, showcasing contemporary fashion and exquisite culture from China.

戴雪明 P72

1990 年代早期，戴雪明与张华明共赴北京携手开拓市场。她凭借坚毅的品质、敏捷的商业头脑，充分了解商场动态以及顾客需求，为当地的女性朋友带去了美丽的高品质服装。千禧年之际，戴雪明基于对当代女性的洞察与理解，开启雅莹从商品到零售整体运营的深入管理，助力企业的初创与成长，并通过洞悉女性日常生活方式的多元化，提出"平衡·爱·幸福"的品牌价值主张。30 多年来，戴雪明坚持只做一件事，即"做好人、做好衣"，让每一位顾客感受幸福喜悦，为她们引领精致优雅的生活方式。同时，戴雪明主张现代管理模式与人性化相辅相成，令整个公司充满凝聚力；她知人善任，注重为雅莹的未来挑选与培育合适人才，她相信企业如人，品牌亦如人，只有成就员工，才能成就企业。

Dai Xueming

In the early 1990s, Dai Xueming joined Zhang Hwaming on his Beijing venture to expand the company's business. With her persevering spirit and keenness of perception, she quickly gained strong understanding of the local market and the preferences of the local women, and successfully launched many fine and beautiful garments for them. At the turn of the millennium, she began to deepen the brand's product and retail management to reflect the evolving and diverse way modern women interact with the world, and launched EP's new brand proposition "Balance, Love and Happiness" in 2011. For over 30 years, she has been an integral part of the company's entrepreneurial culture of "being virtuous people and making good clothes" — creating fashion with love, and ensuring every customer feels happy in their pursuit of a refined and elegant lifestyle. She loves being around people and is also a strong advocator of modern management that is people-centric. She is always on the lookout for the best talents to take the Group into the future — only in their success, can the Group find future success.

仇瑛 P56

1988 年，仇瑛在嘉兴丝绸服装总厂担任厂长助理兼技术质管科长，她到洛东红政服装厂做质量检验和技术培训时，结识了张宝荣。2003 年，她被张华明和戴雪明的为人处世打动，也为雅莹的企业文化所吸引，开始了与雅莹的携手同行。时任供应链总监的她，带领团队担当起供应链发展与升级的重任。2006 年，公司进入快速发展期，着手信息化建设，开启 ERP 项目，这成为仇瑛繁忙却收获巨大的一年。2007 年雅莹集团党支部成立，2013 年党支部升级为党委，仇瑛被推选为集团党委书记，工作重心逐渐转移至党建。在她和党员骨干的带领、推动下，雅莹党委创建的"五美"党建品牌，成为全心全意服务员工，服务企业发展的重要平台。

Qiu Ying

As early as the 1980s, Qiu Ying had become acquainted with Zhang Baorong. In 1988, she was the chief of Technical Development and Quality at Jiaxing's Silk Mill and would visit his factory to provide technical trainings and conduct quality inspections. In 2003, she was moved by Zhang Hwaming and Dai Xueming's invitation to join the company, and took on the role of director of the company's supply chain, taking on the important task of upgrading its quality, processes and information systems such as implementing an industry's first ERP system. In 2007, the company's CPC branch was formally established and in 2013, Qiu Ying was elected as Party secretary of the Group, focused on fostering social cohesion and leading community work. She continues to set a role model for young people with her more than 40 years of work experience and unyielding passion.

王惠明 P60

1988 年，二十出头的王惠明因为张宝荣老厂长的勤勉踏实，在风头正盛的集体企业和张宝荣刚刚承包经营的洛东红政服装工厂之中，毅然选择了后者，一待就是 30 多年。最初的洛东厂生产环境艰苦，王惠明负责生产环节的第一道裁剪步骤，为了提高效率，她和工友们经常白天裁剪，晚上把剪刀带回家打磨。随着公司发展，2001 年，厂里买了第一台自动裁剪机。当时王惠明与工友们看到机器可以实现电脑排版、直接输入数据，再借由自动脱料机自动脱料，十分兴奋。再后来，这样的欣喜与进步不断发生，助力雅莹的发展，王惠明她们也在变化中不断学习、蜕变、成长，而她们的专注严谨则始终如一。

Wang Huiming

Wang Huiming joined Zhang Baorong's factory in her early twenties in 1988 because of his down-to-earth character and hardworking personality. In the beginning, the factory's production environment was very poor. In order to improve productivity, Huiming and the workers would bring home their scissors to sharpen at night so that they could spend their time cutting more fabrics and patterns in the day. She experienced firsthand the growth of the company, recalling especially how excited she was at seeing new automated sewing machines and more high-technology equipment that aided production. These first-generation workers embraced change throughout the years, with their focus and detailed-oriented attitude setting an example for future generations. Huiming would become EP YAYING's longest-serving employee.

沈林秀 P76

1993 年，当时还是北京复兴商业城服装部经理的沈林秀，对张华明的经营能力和品德留下了深刻印象。从采购面料、生产制作、销售陈列等方面，她看到了张华明和戴雪明认真经营公司当时在北京热销的真丝衬衫，便决定进一步扩大商场对真丝产品的投资。她还对当时的洛东制衣厂进行了深度考察，看到工厂对品质的把控井井有条，便和张华明提出大胆创新的经营思路——两次先后预付 50 万资金，通过合作生产、扩大销售，合力共赢。这一举动，开创了当时国内百货商场预付产品资金的先河，即风险投资的先例。雅莹随后在复兴商场的销售业绩创下新高，短短几年，成为北京各大商场积极合作的对象。

Shen Linxiu

In 1993, Shen Linxiu, who was the manager of the garment department at Beijing Fuxing Department Store at that time, was impressed by the sales of the high-quality silk products that Zhang Hwaming and Dai Xueming had brought from Jiaxing, and proposed to increase its supply. Unfortunately, the supplier did not have enough fabric for them, but this missed opportunity opened the door to a new method of cooperation. Linxiu would visit Hwaming's factory and be won over by their attention to quality. Thereafter, she proposed a bold and innovative business model of co-production between a department store and a counter, by providing a 500,000 CNY advance payment to the factory for its orders and the advance payment could be deducted later from the sales revenue. In a few years, Hwaming set a new sales record in Fuxing Department Store and several of the top department stores in Beijing reached out to him to discuss similar collaborations.

王阿六 P81

王阿六是雅莹创业时期核心奋斗者之一，他亲眼见证了浙系制衣产业的兴起，并在 1992 年与当时还是洛东制衣厂的雅莹结识，成为雅莹历史上的第一位营销总监。他的工作就是跑专柜供销，不断结识人，开拓渠道。他曾在零下 30 摄氏度的天气里骑车送过货，还曾开拓了雅莹自南向北的国内市场。那些年，王阿六与张宝荣老厂长一起，在改革开放中探索前行，在供需架构不完整中择机而动。在为雅莹打造销售渠道方面，"老销售"王阿六事必躬亲，无论是专卖店、百货店，还是后来的购物中心，他陪伴了雅莹成长的诸多关键时刻。

Wang Aliu

Wang Aliu joined Zhang Baorong's factory in 1992 and would later become the company's first sales and marketing director. He played a key role in developing the factory's sales channels across the country in a bid to boost orders and sales, even delivering garments in weather as cold as minus 30 degrees. It was a difficult era but Aliu worked closely with Baorong through the many uncertainties they faced, as they charted a course towards a better life and a better company. Across the years, he successfully established the company's sales channels in south and north China, including opening the company's first specialty store, and new stores in key department stores and shopping malls.

杨和英 P81

1995 年，从业经历丰富的杨和英正式加入当时还名为永利来的雅莹，她以自己审慎进取的个性与真诚开朗的待人方式，不断为雅莹的销售市场开疆扩土。从西安市场瞄准"校园直销"永利来金属棉衬衫，再到陌生的山东市场开辟全新的商业合作。又在公司需要人才的情形下，从销售回到生产，转型当起了"场厂长"。临近退休，杨和英退居二线，投身资产管理岗位，有条不紊地协助雅莹生产运作，成为大家口中和善负责的"杨阿姨"。杨和英同雅莹一起度过了老厂改制、非典来袭以及经济危机等诸多考验。退休之后，她成为雅莹的重要合作伙伴，将这份情谊继续延续下去。

Yang Heying

In 1995, Yang Heying, who had rich experience in the industry, joined the company when it was still known as Yonglilai Fashion. With her enterprising and sincere personality, she was very successful in expanding the company's retail business whether it was selling the company's shirts in Xi'an or opening up new markets in Shandong Province. Zhang Hwaming saw her potential and recalled her back to the headquarters to oversee the company's production and supply chain. She experienced many testing challenges over the years with the company such as the SARS and global economic crises, but would always come out stronger than ever. She was also known for her affable nature and responsible attitude, and was affectionately known to everyone in the company as "Auntie Yang". After her retirement, she still remains an important partner to the Group.

戴雪英、张建明夫妇 P82

是一家人，更是风雨同舟的事业伙伴。1991 年，因发展毛衫业务在北京与 21 岁的张华明结识，戴雪英与丈夫张建明欣赏这位勤奋踏实、聪明诚恳的年轻人，便在 1992 年的春天将妹妹戴雪明介绍予他。1999 年，新生的雅莹遭遇到资金链断裂的危机，戴雪英毫不犹豫地拿出 30 万支持雅莹的事业。后来公司的发展一路向上，在缺乏人才的当口，戴雪英与丈夫放下自己的生意，前往天津帮助雅莹开拓市场。每一次的雪中送炭，每一次的共渡难关，将一家人紧紧牵绊在一起。家人，永远是雅莹前行中最温暖的支持力量。

Dai Xueying and Zhang Jianming

They say family bond is the strongest. Dai Xueming's elder sister, Dai Xueying, has always been there for her sister in every stage of her life. In 1992, she introduced her future husband, Zhang Hwaming, who was a business acquaintance of her sweater business, to her sister, and thereafter the two would make the business trip to Beijing together. In 1999, as the young yaying was facing multiple crises, Xueying and her husband, Zhang Jianming, not only provided strong financial support to the company, they also put aside their own business to help yaying expand their Tianjin market. Each time was like sending coal for warmth during snowy weather, as a saying goes in traditional Chinese culture. Each time the family overcame adversity together, their bond grew stronger. Family remained the strongest support for yaying in her journey forward.

宋世楹 P122

宋世楹是雅莹以心相交、情谊深厚的贵人。1997年，雅莹对产品结构进行调整，正处在从单季产品转型成四季产品的关键时期，得宋世楹老板的喜盈盈公司（前身为湖州第二毛纺厂）鼎力相助，诞生了经典款的"阿尔巴卡大衣"，让雅莹有了冬季产品，帮助雅莹逆境重生。宋世楹曾说过"湖州第二毛纺厂的仓库就是雅莹的仓库"的仗义之言，不仅给予雅莹充足的面料支持，那款奠定了雅莹发展基石的"爆款"阿尔巴卡大衣，更是改变了中国冬季大衣"万里江山一片灰蓝"的单调色彩。因为缘分与信任，宋世楹还在雅莹千禧年新建本部之际，为雅莹在中国银行的贷款作出仗义担保，此后更与雅莹有了长久的相伴和合作。

Song Shiying

Song Shiying is one of the closest friends and trusted partners of EP YAYING to-date. In 1997, when he was in charge of Huzhou No.2 Woolen Mill (known today as Zhejiang Xiyingying Textile), he provided yaying with key fabrics as its was expanding its product mix from a single to four seasons, especially the popular Alpaca wool fabric that helped launch yaying's famous Alpaca coat collection and lifted the company out of adversity. This deep bond shared between both Hwaming and Shiying, and the two companies, was also the reason Shiying volunteered to be the guarantor for yaying's bank loan to build its new headquarters in 2001.

黄龙新 P139

1996年，黄龙新是中国银行的一名职员，当时张华明刚从父亲手中接过帅印，开始发展雅莹品牌。他们因贷款业务往来而结识。在品牌创立初期遭遇危机之际，幸得黄龙新雪中送炭，他用一张6个月百万的承兑汇票为雅莹的名誉、诚信做了最大的担保，解决了雅莹资金的燃眉之急，不仅救彼时的雅莹于水火，更是帮助雅莹这一高端女装品牌真正地走到了大众面前。

Huang Longxin

Huang Longxin met Zhang Hwaming in 1996, when Longxin was still a staff at the Bank of China and Hwaming had just taken over the company. Not long after, the company met with a serious crisis but Longxin vouched for Hwaming's character and capability to recover from the crisis, and patiently assisted the company with a critical loan application that solved their urgent need for funds, which became a key turning point for their recovery.

梁贤安 P139

梁贤安是雅莹的一位亦师亦友、志同道合的朋友。1997年，在中国服装博览会上，梁贤安一眼看中了雅莹，开始了此后长久的合作扶持，他更是和张华明成为患难与共的知交老友。1998年，为了帮助雅莹研究改进秋冬大衣，梁贤安人在重庆，一个月要来四次嘉兴，经常在样衣室工作到凌晨三四点帮助改进大衣板式。梁贤安看重雅莹，看重友情，认为他不做雅莹的现在，要做雅莹的将来。他以踏实的行动，践行着自己的诺言，和雅莹一起站得更高，走得更远。

Liang Xian'an

Liang Xian'an was both mentor and friend to yaying. In 1997, he became the agent of yaying's silk products after discovering the brand at the China Fashion Expo in that year. In 1998, in order to help yaying with researching and correcting their winter coats, he travelled to Jiaxing four times a month, despite being based in Chongqing. He often worked in the workshop together with Zhang Hwaming and the team until three or four in the morning to help improve the coat's pattern. He was a man of action and stood with yaying throughout its entrepreneurial journey.

李成林 P139

1994年，李成林是永利来的合作商，后来又成为张华明的创业伙伴。1999年，为了帮助雅莹突破大衣的技术困难，李成林把自己的工厂关掉，甚至把设备都拉进雅莹，他们一起扛过了创业最艰辛的岁月。没有资金就各方筹集，没有市场就全国一站站地去开拓，需要整改就学习先进的管理经验。而作为制版专家，李成林的帮助让雅莹当时的阿尔巴卡大衣如获新生，在核心市场一炮而红。在研发面料和服装款式上，他提供了大量的技术支持，助推了雅莹的成长与飞跃。

Li Chenglin

Li Chenglin was a supplier for Yonglilai Fashion from 1994 before subsequently joining Zhang Hwaming's new company. When he learnt that the newly established yaying was facing a crisis due to its overcoats, he boldly shut down his factory in 1999, transferred his equipment into yaying and began to work with the team on improving the overcoats. A pattern maker by training, he used and shared his expertise to help yaying achieve breakthrough in the pattern making of its coats, and also supported the development of many new fabrics and styles for the brand.

朱适、朱佩君兄妹 P142

朱适、朱佩君兄妹于1997~1998年间。与雅莹因面料结缘。直至1999年，雅莹对雪纺材料的自主研发尚未成行，当时主做夏季面料的朱适、朱佩君兄妹开始为雅莹提供进口雪纺材料。雅莹一方面着手自行研发雪纺材料，另一方面选用朱氏兄妹提供的进口雪纺生产夏季服装。他们提供的雪纺拥有与丝绸类似的细腻滑爽手感和良好的垂坠性，却突破了真丝的诸多局限，不会起皱、不易褪色，在款式和花型设计上更加灵活，当时这种面料在国内市场还是空白。这份专供的情缘，不仅帮助雅莹生产出了风靡一时的雪纺单品，也让雅莹的春夏装一时成为品质的代名词。

Zhu Shi and Zhu Peijun

Zhu Shi and his sister, Zhu Peijun, were fabric suppliers for yaying from 1997. As yaying was researching on and developing the chiffon fabric in 1999, the sibling pair began supplying yaying with high-quality imported chiffon fabrics that was a boost for the brand's summer collection. The chiffon fabric made up for the shortcomings of the silk fabric, and was well-known for its outstanding texture, colour and breathability, and also its versatility in production. The quick response and exclusive supply provided by the sibling pair ensured yaying's chiffon collections were one of the earliest and most popular in the market.

孙林燕 P162

孙林燕是雅莹成长的见证人。1999年，当时还在中国银行负责贷款业务的孙林燕开始接触雅莹公司。2001年，营业规模尚小的雅莹在为初创的品牌扩张发展寻求出路。要扩大规模，首先要有更大的生产与办公基地，而当时公司新建本部资金困难。为了申请新建厂房的贷款，孙林燕和张华明商量，通过湖州的企业担保和湖州的中国银行成功申请下这笔贷款。资金到位后，雅莹的发展规模得以扩大，企业经营逐步走上快速成长的轨道。孙林燕也用信义成就了雅莹的发展版图。多年的相识了解，2012年从中国银行退休的孙林燕，便受到张华明邀请加入雅莹，并在雅莹的行政后勤事务上发挥了重要作用。

Sun Linyan

Sun Linyan oversaw the company's key growth period at the turn of the millennium. She worked closely with the company from 1999, when she was in charge of the loan business at the Bank of China, to plan and apply for a loan to build their new headquarters. Funding was critical to the success of its new headquarters and Linyan proactively assisted Zhang Hwaming in his communication with his guarantor in Huzhou and the bank's Huzhou branch for the loan application. She was a key player in the company's transformation and was invited to join the company's administrative department by Hwaming after she retired from the bank in 2012.

李炜中 P162

2000年，正值而立之年的李炜中选择转行来到雅莹负责人事行政事务。当年，雅莹正筹备从嘉兴戴梦得大酒店搬迁到本部华云路，为确保新基地建成后能在最短时间内正常生产，他提前招纳了35名班组长前往洛东工厂培训；2007年9月，雅莹党支部成立，李炜中担任起第一任党支部书记；2018年年底，他携带雅莹"六代+"店铺概念于马来西亚吉隆坡亮相，成就雅莹在东南亚的首家海外店。如今，耗时5年多巨制的雅莹时尚艺术中心向世人展示了雅莹时尚、文化相融的大气之美……在美的事业上深耕近20年的李炜中，历经行政、人资、管理服务、空间工程等岗位的锻造，沉浸出一颗匠心、一双慧眼，陪伴雅莹在至美空间的道路上坦荡前行。

Li Weizhong

Li Weizhong joined yaying in 2000, when the company was preparing its move from the Diamond Hotel to its new headquarters at Huayun Road. He began to oversee a variety of positions with the company, including administrative management, human resources, and design and construction, enabling him to hone a sharp eye for detail and quality essential to his work. In 2018, he led the design and construction team to open EP's first Southeast Asian store with a new sixth-plus generation design in Kuala Lumpur, Malaysia. In 2020, after more than 5 years, his team, together with more than 100 local and international partners, officially completed the construction of the Group's fashion and arts centre.

庞家俊 P166

庞家俊和张华明是亦师亦友的忘年交。1983年，同在嘉兴参加企业培训班的庞家俊和老张总相识，半个月的培训让两人建立起长久的友情。张华明接管公司后，在父亲的引荐下，逐渐与其熟识。当年雅莹刚起步，由于企业资产评估不高，公司融资贷款需要担保，少有企业愿冒这个风险，张华明找到庞家俊。深思熟虑后，庞家俊毅然选择为雅莹担保盖了章，由此赋予了企业经营的流动资金，为雅莹的前期发展注入了长久的血液。

Pang Jiajun

Pang Jiajun, the then general manager of Lanxiang Aviation Equipment, who is also a native of Luodong town, met Zhang Baorong at a corporate training course in 1983 and the friendship between the two deepened across the two weeks long training course. In 1997, when he learned of the difficulties that his son, Zhang Hwaming, who had taken over the company, was facing in one of his loan applications for the company, he did not waver in his trust in the Zhang family and their company, and had no hesitation in becoming the guarantor for the company's bank loan, despite its high risk assessment.

田玲 P174

2002 年，田玲和高鹰夫妇一起来到雅莹，她以设计师的一颗炙热初心，为雅莹的产品提供了见解独到的设计理念与产品掌控。在她和团队的共同努力下，雅莹从一开始的单一线转变成了两条产品线，一条女性化的产品线，另一条偏运动感的产品线，并逐步实现了从单品设计转换成系列设计的蜕变。不仅如此，她和设计团队为雅莹的美丽事业创造着更长久的接力砝码，将雅莹甄选的好材料呈现出工艺、版型、创意融合等多方面的可能性，令产品更优雅、时髦，进而一步步地帮助雅莹发展成为现今中国时尚产业中不可忽视的风向标。在她看来"一件好的衣服，能疗愈人心，能平衡人与自然、社会、文化的关系，能激发内在能量，达成自洽、自信、自然。"

Tian Ling

Tian Ling and her husband, Gao Ying, joined Elegant Prosper together in 2002. She brought fresh creative energy to the brand, introducing new lines and new stories to Elegant Prosper, by asserting the brand's dedication to elegance, whilst introducing sporty collections and infusing a freer, contemporary spirit. She was a visionary designer who saw the importance of choosing high-quality fabrics to combine with innovative dressmaking and artistic designs, setting a new standard for the Chinese fashion industry in the new millennium. Over the years, she developed her own vision of fashion, "A good dress is not only therapeutic, but can also balance the relationship between humankind, nature, society and culture. A good dress can stimulate inner energies that help women feel natural, be confident and find harmony."

高鹰 P174

2002 年，高鹰和妻子田玲心怀对时尚事业的梦想，从大连转战上海，最终落脚嘉兴，在雅莹开启了长情而坚定的征程。近 20 年来，高鹰从最初的产品经营管理开始，见证、参与并推动了雅莹品牌日益成熟的发展。他带领团队一步步实现了产品管理的突破与创新，将单一品类向序列化、故事化转变，为雅莹的产品注入了当代创意，将生活场景化概念融入产品经营理念中，每一步革新都凝聚了他和团队热忱创新的愿望，一直致力于更好地满足女性更多元的生活需求。

Gao Ying

Gao Ying and his wife, Tian Ling, moved from Dalian to Shanghai and finally Jiaxing in 2002, continuing his passion for fashion with Elegant Prosper for over 20 years now. In these 20 over years, he led the team to achieve breakthroughs and innovations in product management, successfully enriching Elegant Prosper's product line with more creative styles, collections and categories. Not only so, he was given the responsibility to lead multiple revamps of the brand, providing fashion that continuously satisfied modern women's increasingly diverse lifestyle needs.

顾海明 P198

顾海明是雅莹培养的第一代英才之一。1996 年，刚刚毕业的顾海明来到永利来，跟着老一辈营销人学习，在零售经营方面受益匪浅。从非典悟道到雅莹大店航母渠道战略，再到百货大店，一路行来，他与团队劈波斩浪，不断超越，成功实现一个又一个的业绩目标，并一步步提升了团队的整体实力与业务水平。这位倾注半生精力的初代英才，如今作为身担雅莹零售重任的副总裁，始终在这份美丽事业上孜孜不倦，为伙伴们提供更广阔的发展平台和空间。在顾海明看来，关注顾客需求，背后需要的是拼搏奉献与成就他人的决心与能力。"正是顾客的优雅美丽使我们所有雅莹人不断前进，这是我们为之奋斗的最大动力，很感谢顾客给我们服务的机会，这是我们最好的成长机会。"

Gu Haiming

Gu Haiming was one of the company's earliest management trainees. In 1996, Haiming, who had just graduated, came to Yonglilai Fashion and began learning the ropes of retail from the company's first generation of sales team. Strategy after strategy, he has seen many successes together with the team, from the implementation of the company's SARS learnings across its stores, to opening new experiential retail stores and flagship stores, and establishing the excellent service standards that the brand is known for today. The brand's strength grew exponentially and he took on the responsibility of the head of retail and subsequently, the Group's deputy CEO. He is a believer of pure hard work and has always emphasised that in order to meet the needs of customers, everyone has to always embrace change and improve oneself. "It is the elegance and beauty of our customers that keeps all of us at EP YAYING inspired, growing and moving forward."

倪美华 P203

1999 年，已经从事纺织行业 17 年的倪美华，入职了当时还租住于戴梦得大酒店的雅莹，负责管理面辅料仓库。那时候一年的夏、冬两季是最忙碌的时间，她和同事们几乎每天都要工作到半夜 12 点。当时大家心里想的就是要珍惜工作，把任务完成好，确保要发货的成衣准时送达下一个环节。这份淳朴的责任心跟着她一路行来，历久弥珍。至此，她不仅历经了品质管理、采购管理、生产计划等多项重任与挑战，也见证了公司规范化、信息化等现代化管理技术日益提升的作业水平。如今作为负责生产供应链的集团副总裁，倪美华依然心怀热忱，在应对生产供应链的智能制造、绿色工厂建设、供应链"三个八大"战略等内外部挑战中，她与团队始终勤恳真切，专注创新。

Ni Meihua

Ni Meihua, who had been in the textile industry for 17 years, joined yaying in 1999 to manage the fabrics at its warehouse. At that time, the summer and winter seasons were the busiest times. She and her colleagues worked until midnight almost every day. Everything was simple at that time and everyone cherished their work — complete the task at hand and ensure that delivery was on time. This unsophisticated sense of responsibility followed her from 1999 and she took on many important tasks across the company's supply chain, including quality management, procurement, production planning and digitalisation. As the Group's deputy CEO in charge of its supply chain today, she continues to lead passionately the team's R&D and implementation of its triple "8 Cores" sustainable strategies — sourcing premium raw materials, establishing high-quality manufacturing processes and developing exquisite artisanal workshops.

吕虹 P211

吕虹与雅莹的结缘，更像是一场与美的邂逅。从年少时，吕虹便对美的事物怀有一腔热情，2005 年来到雅莹后，她感受到了雅莹创造的美能为女性朋友们的日常生活带来神奇的改变，这种致力于创造美的雅莹情怀让吕虹一见如故。从接手人力资源规范化发展到逐步打造雅莹花园式办公环境，从沉浸于人的发展到关注公司的艺术文化氛围营造，在吕虹看来，美不仅具有生命力，更是一种生产力。她和团队一起学习，努力为公司呈现美的多种可能，让员工们在充满细节美的工作环境中更能体验到"家"的氛围。她认为，"最好的文化是在所有员工感到幸福的基础上，让他们可以从内心露出最真实的笑容。"

Lv Hong

The bond between Lv Hong and EP YAYING is a thing of beauty. From a young age, Lv Hong had always been attracted to beautiful things. When she joined in 2005, she had a strong feeling for the brand's founding aspiration of bringing beauty to women. From taking charge of human resources to the revamp of the workplace environment, and the development of the Group's arts and culture, Lv Hong and the different teams she has led across the years had continued to deepen their understanding of the concept of beauty and how it can become a strong catalyst for change. She wanted the Group's people to feel at home when they come to work, and shared the company's belief that the best corporate culture is built on the well-being of all employees and the smiles that come from the bottom of their hearts.

陈伟健 P334

2006 年毕业至今，雅莹就是陈伟健迄今全部的职场生涯。2010 年，全国奥特莱斯渠道刚刚兴起，雅莹致力成为中国奥特莱斯女装领跑者，他是首批进军奥特莱斯市场的团队成员。紧随其后互联网红利期到来，在陈伟健及其电商团队的努力下，雅莹天猫旗舰店上线并于 2018 年逐步实现"正价化品牌化经营"的战略转型。2016 年，在奥特莱斯亲民、便捷的基础上，为消费者提供更多精选好物的多品类现代都市生活方式集合店品牌大雅家应运而生。在他和团队的共同努力下，大雅家正立足"优质生活 +"的理念，塑造以融"衣食住知"为一体的新型零售空间，为消费者带去全新时尚生活方式。

Chen Weijian

Chen Weijian joined Elegant Prosper since graduating in 2006. With the advent of outlet malls in 2010, he joined in the setup of the brand's outlet business that became a pioneer in the industry, and with the gradual rise of the Internet, he began to also oversee the brand's first foray into e-commerce. In 2016, he launched the Group's multi-brand factory outlet store in DA YA JIA, before leading its revamp into a new-concept multi-brand lifestyle retailer covering everything from fashion and food & beverages, to home essentials and travel solutions for a modern way of life. Together with a young team, they continue to create a new retail space based on the concept of "Quality Living+".

曹青 P370

时任 DOUBLOVE 的设计总监曹青，自 2009 年品牌成立以来，她便和团队致力于找寻更多的东方、浪漫、俏皮、精致的元素，服务于更多元的年轻女性，以更专业的时尚语言共塑有故事、有梦想的品牌。在她看来，"当今女性既有少女般柔美、浪漫的一面，又兼具大女人率性、干练的一面。这些特质共同存在于现代女性身上，令女性散发出前所未有的多重魅力。"这和她 1999 年初入雅莹时，研习从制衣的工艺、流程、细节到最终大货的要求一样，既要领悟其中的匠心精神，又需懂得无论在怎样的环境中，解读消费者的需求，诠释好浪漫美学的每一环节至关重要。

Cao Qing

Cao Qing, design director of DOUBLOVE today, is committed to designing for a young girl's hopes and dreams. She mixes romance with playfulness, and oriental charm with classy styles for her collections. "Today's young women are both little girls with romantic dreams and big girls with vision and professionalism. They bring a new charisma to this generation," she said. Just like when she first joined the yaying brand in early 1999, she had been fascinated with the innate desires of a young women and the romantic aesthetics of their fashion styles.

张声琴 P384

2004 年，张声琴和丈夫王翔先后加入了雅莹。雅莹的文化氛围，让她产生了一种久别重逢的熟悉与亲切，也让她选择在这里长久地驻足，踏实地实现梦想。2013 年，已参与雅莹创意设计多年的张声琴，共同创建了集团旗下全新的设计师品牌 N.Paia 。"女人每天都在愁自己今天应该穿什么，其实这就是内心与服装之间的对话。"因循于此，张声琴要求自己的设计，极简于外，内在于丰。由此她将自身的设计风格，与 N.Paia "简约主张·针织情怀"的初心相融合，用简约明快的线条、立体挺阔的廓形，呈现出现代精英女性独立优雅的独特气质。

Zhang Shengqin

Zhang Shengqin joined Elegant Prosper in 2004, attracted by the company's culture and its forward-looking vision. In 2013, Shengqin, who had been involved in the creative design for Elegant Prosper for many years, cofounded the Group's new designer brand N.Paia with her husband, Wang Xiang, who had joined her at Elegant Prosper shortly after she arrived."Women always wonder what to wear in the morning. I would say this is a conversation between your heart and your clothes," she said. She hence advocated the concept of "Simplicity and Sentiment of Knitwear", designs that were simple on the outside but provided women with confidence and warmth from their hearts. Her styles also combined functionality and modern silhouettes to exude a kind of sophisticated elegance.

王翔 P384

2006 年，王翔加入雅莹，与妻子张声琴并肩作战，共同为雅莹事业奋斗。其间，王翔与团队开辟了雅莹加盟市场的繁荣局面。2013 年年底，雅莹集团旗下当代设计师品牌 N.Paia 诞生，这让王翔的事业翻开了全新的篇章。一个品牌从无到有茁壮成长，倾注了他巨大的心力，从团队到品牌塑造，从产品经营到渠道建设，在他的带领下，N.Paia 不断提升与打磨。"如何把自己的商品做好、把自己的客户做好、把品牌价值做好，服务做到位，成为日臻完善的重要工作。"如今，N.Paia 已成为女装设计师品牌中富有个性特点的佼佼者。深耕零售事业 10 余年，王翔与团队用敬业和热爱为公司的发展注入了无限能量。10 多年的风雨同行，王翔也怀着这颗真诚的利他之心，与雅莹始终相知相惜。

Wang Xiang

Wang Xiang joined his wife, Zhang Shengqin, at Elegant Prosper in 2006, and scaled the company's franchise business to new heights. In 2013, he created the designer brand N.Paia under the Group. From building a new team to developing the brand's own product mix and retail channels, Wang Xiang and his team dedicated years of hard work and passion to establishing a new identity for N.Paia. He shared, "In the beginning, our customers chose us because of the reputation of EP, but we have grown from individuals with dreams into a brand filled with confidence today. And we are grateful to the Group for providing us with the platform and support. At the same time, we must continue to be thankful to our customers and work with them for a successful future."

邓联东 P396

2001 年，邓联东与雅莹初识，并在雅莹一线的零售市场深化零售运营与管理。至此，他致力于传播美的步履从未停歇，在渠道、服务及营销等层层维度不断突破，一年年、一步步发展。2016 年年底，他开始了在小雅童装的新征程，而那份对美的初心从未更改。作为两个孩子的父亲，邓联东对童装事业有着特殊的感情，他所带领的童装团队以美丽中国儿童为己任，立志向中国儿童和社会传播美和爱。他与伙伴们的目标就是俯下身去了解孩子，懂孩子的生活方式，懂孩子的思维方式，懂他们每个阶段成长的真实需求。在他看来，"用爱温暖儿童的身心，绽放中国新时代儿童的精彩童年，意义深远。我们给孩子的不仅是一件衣服，而是为他们带去美好和幸福。"

Deng Liandong

Deng Liandong joined Elegant Prosper in 2001, and step-by-step, he immersed himself into the retail business of the brand, taking charge of its marketing, service and market expansion. In 2016, he started a new journey with the brand's childrenswear team. Liandong always has a special affection for children, and as a father of two children, is inspired by the mission of enhancing the style and fashion of China's children, "It's great fun designing childrenswear. It gives us a lot of satisfaction to create something that will warm a child's heart and make his or her childhood more interesting. We collaborate with parents to understand their child's needs and feelings so that we can provide children not just with good clothes, but fun and joy, while also bringing the concept of fashion closer to them."

陈曦 P460

2010 年，陈曦来到雅莹，热爱东方文化的他，在这里进一步激发灵感，在传统文化与现代时尚的碰撞中，诠释美的灵性。2016 年，集团提出"世界 EP，中国雅莹"的新品牌发展方向，作为中国雅莹的设计总监，他与团队开始深度挖掘东方皇家美学，采撷云裳、物华、国色等元素，呈现出当代中国式优雅，不仅收获了创作之外的学识与机遇，也为雅莹注入了东方大美的设计灵魂。对他来说，"过去用传统手法直接将中国美学嫁接到服装设计中的方式常常过于直白，更为内敛、更为简约地将东方美学传递出来，才真正能够彰显品牌深厚的文化底蕴。"大道至简，中国雅莹团队设计的东方审美、国风神韵，正不断通过中国雅莹的服饰语言，把悠久的中华文化润物无声地分享给全世界。

Chen Xi

Chen Xi's strong passion and respect for Chinese culture have nurtured his designs and collections ever since he joined EP in 2010. In 2016, when the Group introduced a new positioning — World EP, China YAYING — for the brand's new stage of development, Chen Xi became appointed as the design director for the China YAYING line. He and his team would devote their time to studying Chinese classics and aesthetics from the royal family which they viewed as the pinnacle of Chinese fashion. He believed strongly that culture is the soul of fashion and sharing this cultural knowledge with rich history through contemporary Chinese elegant styles can invoke a strong emotional resonance with the world. He said, "The traditional method of directly transferring Chinese cultural elements to clothing was too straightforward. We felt that a more introspective and minimal design style was better suited to expressing the profound cultural heritage of our brand." Great truths are always simple, this is the guiding philosophy of China YAYING's aesthetics and codes, and through which the team continues to share Chinese culture with the world.

摄影作品
PHOTO CREDITS

P16-17：视觉中国 Visual China Group

P19：视觉中国 Visual China Group

P20：雅莹档案 EP YAYING Archives

P23：徐海峰 Xu Haifeng

P24：《中国日报》CHINA DAILY

P25：盖蒂图片社 Getty Images

P26-27：雅莹档案 EP YAYING Archives

P30-31：雅莹档案 EP YAYING Archives

P32-33：徐海峰 Xu Haifeng

P34-35：王钊 Johnny Wang

P37：雅莹档案 EP YAYING Archives

P39：雅莹档案 EP YAYING Archives

P41：沈峰 Shen Feng

P43：雅莹档案 EP YAYING Archives
《张宝荣生平》连环画插页 Zhang
Baorong, A Comic Strip Memoir Insert：
戴奔鸿 Dai Benhong

P50-51：雅莹档案 EP YAYING Archives

P53：雅莹档案 EP YAYING Archives

P55：吴钰超 Haro Wu

P56：雅莹档案 EP YAYING Archives

P58：徐海峰 Xu Haifeng

P59：王钊 Johnny Wang

P65：孙景刚 Sun Jinggang

P68：（上 Top）雅莹档案 EP YAYING Archives,
（下 Bottom）徐海峰 Xu Haifeng

P71-72：雅莹档案 EP YAYING Archives

P74：（左 Left）百度地图 Baidu Map
（右 Right）吴文彬 Wu Wenbin

P77：雅莹档案 EP YAYING Archives

P79：雅莹档案 EP YAYING Archives

P81：雅莹档案 EP YAYING Archives

P83：雅莹档案 EP YAYING Archives

P87：雅莹档案 EP YAYING Archives

P90-91：雅莹档案 EP YAYING Archives

P92：吴文彬 Wu Wenbin

P93：徐海峰 Xu Haifeng

P94-95：雅莹档案 EP YAYING Archives

P97：雅莹档案 EP YAYING Archives

P98：徐海峰 Xu Haifeng
《雅莹丝绸系列》插页 yaying Silk Collection
Insert：雅莹档案 EP YAYING Archives

P101：徐海峰 Xu Haifeng

P102-103：王钊 Johnny Wang

P104：吴文彬 Wu Wenbin

P105：雅莹档案 EP YAYING Archives

P106-107：《北京晚报》Beijing Evening News

P108-110：雅莹档案 EP YAYING Archives

P118：雅莹档案 EP YAYING Archives

P120-121：吴钰超 Haro Wu

P123：徐海峰 Xu Haifeng

P125-131：徐海峰 Xu Haifeng

P133-138：雅莹档案 EP YAYING Archives

P140-141：雅莹档案 EP YAYING Archives

P145：徐海峰 Xu Haifeng

P147-149：雅莹档案 EP YAYING Archives

P151：徐海峰 Xu Haifeng

P152-153：雅莹档案 EP YAYING Archives

P155-161：雅莹档案 EP YAYING Archives

P163-165：雅莹档案 EP YAYING Archives

P167：雅莹档案 EP YAYING Archives

P171-172：雅莹档案 EP YAYING Archives

P174：徐海峰 Xu Haifeng

P175：沙浩 Sha Hao

P176：雅莹档案 EP YAYING Archives

P180-189：雅莹档案 EP YAYING Archives

P191：雅莹档案 EP YAYING Archives

P194-195：雅莹档案 EP YAYING Archives

P197：雅莹档案 EP YAYING Archives

P201-202：雅莹档案 EP YAYING Archives

P205：雅莹档案 EP YAYING Archives

P207-208：雅莹档案 EP YAYING Archives

P211-213：雅莹档案 EP YAYING Archives

P223：雅莹档案 EP YAYING Archives

P224-225：何映廷 He Yingting

P226：雅莹档案 EP YAYING Archives

P228：雅莹档案 EP YAYING Archives

P229：张翩 Zhang Pian

P230-231：Paul Alexander Thornton

P232-233：雅莹档案 EP YAYING Archives

P234-235：梅远贵 Mei Yuangui

P236-237：蒋懿 Jiang Yi

P241：蒋懿 Jiang Yi

P242：雅莹档案 EP YAYING Archives

P243：沙浩 Sha Hao

P244-245：梅远贵 Mei Yuangui
《品质，心造之境》插页 Quality from the
HEART Insert：李凯 Li Kai

P248：雅莹档案 EP YAYING Archives

P251：吴文彬 Wu Wenbin

P252-253：孙郡 Sun Jun

P254-257：尹超 Yin Chao

P258-265：雅莹档案 EP YAYING Archives

P268-269：Michael Lau

P270-271：尹超 Yin Chao

P272-273：Stefano Galuzzi

P274-275：雅莹档案 EP YAYING Archives

P276-295：徐峰立工作室 Peter Xu Studio

P297-309：徐峰立工作室 Peter Xu Studio,
PRphoto

P311：雅莹档案 EP YAYING Archives

P312-313：徐峰立工作室 Peter Xu Studio,
PRphoto

P318-333：雅莹档案 EP YAYING Archives

P337：雅莹档案 EP YAYING Archives

P340-341：罗兵 Luo Bing

P342：邱超 Qiu Chao

P343：（左 Left）罗兵 Luo Bing，
　　　（右 Right）徐海峰 Xu Haifeng

P346-349：徐海峰 Xu Haifeng

P350-351：吴文彬 Wu Wenbin

P352-353：徐海峰 Xu Haifeng

P355-356：雅莹档案 EP YAYING Archives

P360：吴文彬 Wu Wenbin

P361：王晓恩 Wang Xiaoen

P362：Charles Belle

P363：吴文彬 Wu Wenbin

P364-365：吴钰超 Haro Wu

P366-367：何艳 He Yan

P372-373：Shxpir

P374-383：徐峰立工作室 Peter Xu Studio

P385-389：雅莹档案 EP YAYING Archives

P390-391：HART+LESHKINA

P392-396：雅莹档案 EP YAYING Archives

P398：雅莹档案 EP YAYING Archives

P341-403：雅莹档案 EP YAYING Archives

P405-417：雅莹档案 EP YAYING Archives

P418-419：徐海峰 Xu Haifeng

P420：浙江省教育厅 Department of
　　　Education of Zhejiang
　　　《雅莹集团 30 周年励志庆典》插页
　　　EP YAYING Fashion Group 30th Anniversary
　　　Gala Insert：何艳 He Yan, 沈默 Shen Mo

P429：《环球时报》 GLOBAL TIMES

P430-455：徐峰立工作室 Peter Xu Studio,
　　　PRphoto

P457：范曾 Fan Zeng

P458：雅莹档案 EP YAYING Archives

P466：雅莹档案 EP YAYING Archives

P469：非常建筑 Atelier FCJZ

P470-475：金静仪 JJYPHOTO

P476：吴文彬 Wu Wenbin

P477-479：雅莹档案 EP YAYING Archives

P480-481：赵丹 Zhao Dan

P482-484：吴文彬 Wu Wenbin

P486：雅莹档案 EP YAYING Archives

P488-489：雅莹档案 EP YAYING Archives

P493-495：雅莹档案 EP YAYING Archives

P498：雅莹档案 EP YAYING Archives

P503：《中国日报》 CHINA DAILY

P504-505：小宇 Xiao Yu

P506-513：徐峰立工作室 Peter Xu Studio

P515：吴文彬 Wu Wenbin

P516-519：Oliver Pearch

P524-528：雅莹档案 EP YAYING Archives

P530：雅莹档案 EP YAYING Archives

P533-534：雅莹档案 EP YAYING Archives

P537-538：雅莹档案 EP YAYING Archives

P541-542：雅莹档案 EP YAYING Archives

P544-545：潘杰 Pan Jie

P547-548：雅莹档案 EP YAYING Archives

P551：冯海 Feng Hai

P552：雅莹档案 EP YAYING Archives

P554-555：雅莹档案 EP YAYING Archives

P557：王化人 Wang Huaren

P559：王化人 Wang Huaren

P561：王化人 Wang Huaren

P562：屠树礼 Tu Shuli

P565：屠树礼 Tu Shuli

P566-567：雅莹档案 EP YAYING Archives

P568-569：陈权秀 Chen Quanxiu

P570-571：雅莹档案 EP YAYING Archives

P572-575：陈权秀 Chen Quanxiu

P576-577：Michael Lau

P578-579：何映廷 He Yingting

P580-581：梅远贵 Mei Yuangui

P582-583：何映廷 He Yingting

P584-586：梅远贵 Mei Yuangui

P588-589：陈漫 Chen Man

P590-591：雅莹档案 EP YAYING Archives

P592-596：Michael Lau

P598-599：尹超 Yin Chao

P601：Michael Lau

P602：Kt Auleta

P604：孙郡 Sun Jun

P606-607：Stefano Galuzzi

P609：尹超 Yin Chao

P610-611：Stefano Galuzzi

P612：尹超 Yin Chao

P615：Alasdair Mclellan

P617：孙郡 Sun Jun

P618-619：冯志凯 Feng Zhikai

P621：孙郡 Sun Jun

P622-623：寇 KO

P624-625：尹超 Yin Chao

P626-627：Oliver Pearch

P628：王子千 Wang Ziqian

P630-631：许闯 Xu Chuang

P632：王子千 Wang Ziqian

鸣谢
ACKNOWLEDGEMENTS

感谢诸位的鼎力相助，使得《雅莹·美述史》得以圆满出刊。我们谨致谢忱。

感谢所有为此书资料收集、整理付出努力，并提出宝贵意见的朋友、雅莹人；感谢所有参与筹备和访谈工作的雅莹新老员工、合作伙伴们；感谢所有为全书提供内容策划与创意设计指导的老师、前辈。

我们尽可能对参与本书编撰的伙伴一一致谢，但仍有部分未能确认来源的作品，以及对部分图片的所有者无法一一取得联系，未尽之处，敬请海涵。如您在阅读中有任何问题与建议，欢迎通过"雅莹集团"官方公众号联系我们。

We are extremely grateful to the many people who provided generous support and contributed greatly to the successful launch of this beautiful book *EP YAYING: Fashion & Culture*.

We would like to specially to thank all the friends and people at EP YAYING Fashion Group who made efforts to help collect and organize the materials for this huge project. We are also sincerely grateful to all the new and old employees, and partners, of EP YAYING who took the time out for our multiple interviews and questions. We must also specially acknowledge our seniors and mentors whose guidance and encouragement have provided us with invaluable inspiration in our content and creative process.

Finally, we would like to extend our heartfelt appreciation to any individual or contributor who we might not have properly acknowledged, and will be glad to correct any inadvertent errors or omissions in future editions. If you have any questions or suggestions, please feel free to contact us through our official WeChat account at EP YAYING Fashion Group by scanning the QR code below.

本书主体用纸采用来自瑞典的蒙肯纸厂，全球最环保的纸厂之一，出产的高松厚度、柔软轻盈非涂布环保纸张印制。插页用纸采用通过 FSC 和 SFI 环保标准认证的巴川纸。

This book is printed on high-quality uncoated fine Munken paper produced by one of the world's most environmentally friendly paper mills in Sweden. The inserts are printed on Tomoe River paper certified by FSC and SFI environmental standards.

图书在版编目（CIP）数据

雅莹·美述史：汉英对照 / 雅莹集团编委会编著
. -- 北京：中国纺织出版社有限公司，2022.11
ISBN 978-7-5229-0085-8

Ⅰ.①雅… Ⅱ.①雅… Ⅲ.①服装工业 — 企业集团 —
概况 — 浙江 — 汉、英 Ⅳ.① F426.86

中国版本图书馆 CIP 数据核字（2022）第 219786 号

雅莹·美述史：汉英对照
雅莹集团编委会编著
2022 年 11 月 第 1 版第 1 次印刷
雅莹集团股份有限公司
中国浙江省嘉兴市昌盛中路 2029 号

出 品 人：张华明
顾　　问：戴雪明、谢立昕、张雪冰、王菊、沈国勤、罗拥华
编　　者：蔡锦汉、何雅萍
中文著者：华商韬略 毕亚军
别册著者：《品质，心造之境》沈蓉蓉
英文著者：蔡锦汉、尹谢晶
英文校对：凯旋先驱 闵诗卉
书籍设计：Generation 大量、朱倩倩、吴凡、蔡锦辉
图片后期：关科科
人物访谈：冷芸时尚 冷芸，华商韬略 毕亚军
资料支持：雅莹集团档案馆 耳琳
统筹支持：华商韬略 周怡，陈华
出版支持：北京润商文化传播有限公司

出版发行：中国纺织出版社有限公司
责任编辑：林启
技术编辑：施华熙
印　　刷：上海艾登印刷有限公司
纸　　张：上海美升纸业，上海金顿印务
开　　本：255 毫米 × 325 毫米 1/8
印　　张：88
字　　数：501 千字中文，263 千字英文
ＩＳＢＮ：978-7-5229-0085-8

EP YAYING: FASHION & CULTURE (Bilingual Edition, English and Chinese)
EP YAYING Fashion Group Editorial Team
November 2022 First Edition First Printing
EP YAYING Fashion Group
Chang Sheng Zhong Lu 2029, Jiaxing City, Zhejiang Province, China

EXECUTIVE DIRECTOR : Zhang Hwaming
CONSULTANTS : Dai Xueming, Xie Lixin, Zhang Xuebing, Wang Ju,
Shen Guoqin, Luo Yonghua
EDITORS IN CHIEF : Terence Chua, He Yaping
AUTHOR : HSTL Beijing Cultural Communication (Bi Yajun)
AUTHOR (*QUALITY FROM THE HEART INSERT*) : Shen Rongrong
ENGLISH : Terence Chua, Christine Yin
ENGLISH PROOFREADING : Ketchum Greater China (Acy Min)
CREATIVE & DESIGN : Generation (Leah Chen, Zhu Qianqian,
Wu Fan, Cai Jinhui)
PHOTO EDITING : Guan Keke
INTERVIEW : LengYun Fashion (Christine Tsui),
HSTL Beijing Cultural Communication (Bi Yajun)
EP YAYING FASHION GROUP ARCHIVES : Er Lin
COORDINATION : HSTL Beijing Cultural Communication (Zhou Yi), Chen Hua
LITERARY AGENT : Beijing RunShang Culture Communication Co., Ltd.

PUBLISHER : China Textile & Apparel Press Co., Ltd.
EDITOR : Lin Qi
PRINTING ASSISTANCE : Shi Huaxi
PRINTING : Shanghai ADD Print Co., Ltd.
PAPER : Shanghai Amazing Team, Shanghai KingDon Printing
DIMENSIONS : 255 mm × 325 mm 1/8
SHEETS : 88
WORD COUNT : 501,000 Chinese, 263,000 English
ISBN : 978-7-5229-0085-8